GENDER & CRIME

The **Key Approaches to Criminology** series celebrates the removal of traditional barriers between disciplines and, specifically, reflects criminology's interdisciplinary nature and focus. It brings together some of the leading scholars working at the intersections of criminology and related subjects. Each book in the series helps readers to make intellectual connections between criminology and other discourses, and to understand the importance of studying crime and criminal justice within the context of broader debates.

The series is intended to have appeal across the entire range of undergraduate and postgraduate studies and beyond, comprising books which offer introductions to the fields as well as advancing ideas and knowledge in their subject areas.

Other books in the series ...

Yvonne Jewkes, *Media and Crime*, 3rd Edition (2015)

Katja Franko Aas, *Globalization and Crime*, 2nd Edition (2013)

Michael Rowe, *Race & Crime* (2012)

Roy Coleman and Mike McCahill, *Surveillance & Crime* (2011)

Gerry Johnstone and Tony Ward, *Law and Crime* (2010)

Craig Webber, *Psychology and Crime* (2010)

Barry Godfrey, Paul Lawrence and Chris Williams, *History and Crime* (2008)

GENDER & CRIME

2ND EDITION   **A Human Rights Approach**

MARISA SILVESTRI
CHRIS CROWTHER-DOWEY

Los Angeles | London | New Delhi
Singapore | Washington DC | Melbourne

Los Angeles | London | New Delhi
Singapore | Washington DC | Melbourne

SAGE Publications Ltd
1 Oliver's Yard
55 City Road
London EC1Y 1SP

SAGE Publications Inc.
2455 Teller Road
Thousand Oaks, California 91320

SAGE Publications India Pvt Ltd
B 1/I 1 Mohan Cooperative Industrial Area
Mathura Road
New Delhi 110 044

SAGE Publications Asia-Pacific Pte Ltd
3 Church Street
#10-04 Samsung Hub
Singapore 049483

Editor: Amy Jarrold
Assistant editor: George Knowles
Production editor: Katie Forsythe
Copyeditor: Christine Bitten
Indexer: Silvia Benvenuto
Marketing manager: Sally Ransom
Cover design: Wendy Scott
Typeset by: C&M Digitals (P) Ltd, Chennai, India
Printed and bound by CPI Group (UK) Ltd,
Croydon, CR0 4YY

© Marisa Silvestri and Chris Crowther-Dowey 2016

First edition published 2008. Reprinted 2014

This edition first published 2016

Library of Congress Control Number: 2015951591

British Library Cataloguing in Publication data

A catalogue record for this book is available from
the British Library

ISBN 978-1-4739-0218-3
ISBN 978-1-4739-0219-0 (pbk)

At SAGE we take sustainability seriously. Most of our products are printed in the UK using FSC papers and boards.
When we print overseas we ensure sustainable papers are used as measured by the PREPS grading system.
We undertake an annual audit to monitor our sustainability.

For Helen

For my mother Viola – an unlikely feminist

Contents

About the Authors   xii
Acknowledgements   xiii
Discover the Key Approaches to Criminology Website   xv

1 Introduction   1

   The state of criminology   3
   New directions: Human rights   5
   Overview of the book and its contents   7

PART I GENDER AND CRIME IN CONTEXT   15

2 Theorizing Gender and Crime   17

   Introduction   17
   The emergence of feminist perspectives in criminology   19
       A project in feminist empiricism and theorization   21
   The critique of feminist criminology   24
       A lack of complexity   24
       The co-optation of feminist ideals and backlash   25
       Challenging mainstream criminology   26
   The development and growing importance of
   human rights discourse   28
       Bringing rights home: Cleaning up our 'own back yards'   31
   Human rights meet criminology   33
       The offender   36
       The victim   37
       The criminal justice professional   38
   Concluding thoughts   39
   Summary   40
   Study questions   40
   Further reading   41

3 Gender, Crime and History   43

   Introduction   43
   A note on historical sources   45

Exploring the gender gap over time   47
    Women offenders as non-violent   48
    Mad not bad   50
    Women as liars/deceivers   52
    Dangerous and risky bodies   53
    Risky and in need of regulation   54
    Feeblemindedness and in need of rescue   55
The problem of girls   55
Civilizing and criminalizing men   56
Gender and victimization   59
Concluding thoughts   61
Summary   62
Study questions   63
Further reading   63

4 Contemporary Issues in Gender and Crime in a
   Globalized World   65

Introduction   66
What is globalization?   67
    Comparative criminology   72
Globalization, gender and human rights   75
Globalization and crime   76
    Drug trafficking   77
    Human trafficking   80
Gender, crime and human rights: Global drivers of crime   82
    New Public Management and modernization   82
    Victim-centred justice   83
    Public protection and penal populism   84
    Decline of the rehabilitative ideal   87
    Risk assessment and management   88
    Commercialization of crime control   91
Concluding thoughts   92
Summary   93
Study questions   94
Further reading   94

PART II OUT OF CONTROL   95

5 Women as Offenders   97

Introduction   98
Who is the female offender?   99
    The problem of 'mean girls'   100
    Women who sexually offend   103
    Women and terrorism   104
Acknowledging women's agency in offending   106

Processing and punishing the female offender   109
What can human rights do for women in prison?   111
   Suicide and self-harm   112
   Imprisoning mothers   114
   The incarceration of girls   116
Concluding thoughts   119
Summary   120
Study questions   121
Further reading   121

6 Men as Offenders   123

Introduction   123
Key themes in the study of men, masculinities and crime   124
Male offending and criminality – the evidence base   125
   General offending   125
   Self-report studies   126
   The criminalization of men   127
   Remand and mode of trial   129
   Sentencing and penal policy   130
Men's offending and the international crime drop   133
Theorizations of men, masculinities and crime   134
   Connell – 'gender relations'   135
   Psychosocial and other approaches to thinking about crime
   and masculinities   138
Men, masculinities and crime – towards a human rights
perspective   141
   Male offenders and human rights discourse: Threats and
   opportunities   143
   Men as beneficiaries of human rights discourse   145
   Men as inhibitors of human rights discourse   149
Concluding thoughts   150
Summary   152
Study questions   153
Further reading   153

PART III IN NEED OF CARE   155

7 Women as Victims   157

Introduction   158
(Re)conceptualizing violence against women   159
Violence against women and girls   161
   Women involved in prostitution/sex work   163
   Forced marriage   164
   'Honour'-based violence (HBV)   165

Female genital mutilation (FGM)   166
Responding to violence against women   **167**
The problem of attrition   168
Constructing the 'ideal' victim   169
**A 'specialist' and 'coordinated' approach to violence
against women**   **172**
Global concerns and responses   **174**
Reconceptualizing domestic violence as torture   **176**
Making the state accountable for violence against women   **178**
Concluding thoughts   **181**
Summary   **182**
Study questions   **183**
Further reading   **183**

8 **Men as Victims**   **185**

Introduction   **185**
Key debates   186
Men as victims of crime – the knowledge base   **187**
The criminal justice response to male victims   197
**Explaining patterns of male victimization: Masculinities
and the fluidity of victim–offender statuses**   **199**
Male victims and their human rights: A critical framework   **201**
'Responsibilizing' male victims   202
Anti-social behaviour (ASB) and masculinities   202
The origins and definitions of ASB   203
ASB, youth and crime policy under New Labour:
Enforcement strategies to tackle ASB   205
Compromising the human rights of children: Victimizing boys   208
Concluding thoughts   **209**
Summary   **210**
Study questions   **211**
Further reading   **211**

PART IV IN CONTROL   **213**

9 **Gender and Criminal Justice Workers**   **215**

Introduction   **216**
A gender audit – men and women working in criminal justice   **218**
The police service   219
The Crown Prosecution Service (CPS)   221
The Ministry of Justice   222
National Offender Management Service (NOMS)   222
The prison service   222
The probation service   223

Other criminal justice agencies   225
Para-professionals   228
Policing: The gendered nature of the police and private security   229
The limitations of statistical information   **232**
Addressing human rights: The gendered working of power   **232**
Restating the importance of power   239
Concluding thoughts   **239**
Summary   **240**
Study questions   **241**
Further reading   **241**

10 The Criminal Justice System: A Gendered Site   **243**

Introduction   **244**
The rationale for gender representation   **245**
The business case   245
Making a difference   246
Social justice   247
The call for more women in policing   **247**
The call for more women in law   **250**
The gendered organization   **254**
Gendered policing   **255**
Gendered judiciary   **259**
Concluding thoughts   **263**
Summary   **265**
Study questions   **265**
Further reading   **266**

11 Conclusions   **267**

An overview of key debates   **268**
Historical and theoretical debates on gender and crime   **269**
Out of Control   **270**
The female offender   270
The male offender   271
In Need of Care   **272**
The female victim   272
The male victim   273
In Control   **274**
The criminal justice practitioner: A gendered perspective   274
Future debates about gender and crime   **275**

Glossary   278
References   293
Index   339

About the Authors

Marisa Silvestri is an Associate Professor in Criminology at Kingston University. Her main research interests lie at the intersections of policing, gender and criminal justice. More specifically her work centres on exploring the position and role of women in police leadership and the gendered nature of the criminal justice system in relation to its impact on women offenders and victims. As a strong advocate of participatory action research with an emphasis on practitioner involvement, her work not only advances theoretical understandings of these issues but aims to inform policy and practice. She has published extensively in the field, including *Women in Charge: Policing, Gender and Leadership* (2003, Willan) and 'Gender and crime' in the *Oxford Handbook of Criminology* (co-authored with Frances Heidensohn; 2012, Oxford University Press). She is also an editorial board member for *Policing & Society* and is currently working on exploring the gendered impacts of the current police reform agenda on the selection of its chief officers, together with an analysis of the gendered nature of language within policing.

Chris Crowther-Dowey teaches Criminology at Nottingham Trent University and has considerable experience of teaching criminology and criminal justice at all levels of study. He currently teaches *Gender, Crime and Criminal Justice* and *Policing*. His research interests include policing and policy interventions targeting gendered violence and abuse. Crowther-Dowey's criminology teaching is interdisciplinary and attempts to synthesize material from a range of academic disciplines in the social sciences, political sciences and the humanities. His recent publications include: *Researching Crime: Approaches, Methods and Application* (co-authored with Pete Fussey; 2013, Palgrave); *Understanding Modernisation in Criminal Justice* (co-authored with Paul Senior and Matt Long; 2007, Open University Press); *An Introduction to Criminology and Criminal Justice* (2007, Palgrave).

Acknowledgements

We owe a great many thanks to a number of people during the undertaking of this book. The original concept of the book owes much to existing works on gender, crime and social justice. A great number of feminist writers have worked relentlessly to expose the ongoing gendered and discriminatory nature of social justice. These works have had an important impact on our motivations to write this book, encouraging us to be ever vigilant of claims that 'things are equal now'. We hope that this book balances realism with optimism on the issues explored.

As a joint project, we would firstly like to salute each other. Borne out of a friendship developed some years ago, working together on this second edition has been an effortless project, which we have enjoyed enormously.

We are grateful to Yvonne Jewkes (Series Editor) for commissioning us to write the first edition of this book and for inviting us to undertake this second edition. We also thank everyone at Sage with whom we have worked, but especially to Natalie Aguilera, Amy Jarrold and George Knowles for their patience and support in seeing this book to fruition. Thanks also to the anonymous reviewers of the book proposal who provided challenging yet constructive comments and we hope that we have responded as much as possible to their recommendations. Needless to say we are both responsible for any errors or omissions.

We are both indebted to a wide range of academic colleagues, friends and the many students we have taught. In particular, Marisa would like to thank Frances Heidensohn for being a truly inspirational pioneer in the field – providing intellectual support and guidance, sharing ideas, networks and contacts freely and for her friendship over the years. Especial thanks also to dear friend Cait Beaumont for after-work drinks full of straight talking, no-nonsense advice in all things that matter and a salute to long-standing and loyal colleagues and friends, Steve Tong, Roger Matthews, Richard Wild, Carol Williams, Brian Clark, Chris Gifford and Robert Cook, who have provided support, friendship, humour and distraction over the years.

Chris is grateful to Paul Senior and Matt Long for some of the ideas the three of them developed in another project, which have proved to be useful here. At work he has enjoyed working with, and appreciates the friendship and support provided by, Azrini Wahidin and Terry Gillespie. Many thanks to his old friends, whom he sees less often than he would like to. He apologizes for missing too many football and cricket matches and gigs. Also, he appreciates the distraction provided by newer friends, especially Sandy Partridge and Paul Wynne (and all of Derby Soul) as well as John Poole and Steve Hay who have both taught him a lot about music. Apologies to Rosie, but more time and attention will come your way now this project is out of the way.

Last but not least, many thanks to our families. Chris, as always, would like to thank Helen for putting up with him and her continuing love and patience.

Marisa thanks Braddie and Sophie for 'keeping it real' at home doing all the things that teenagers do and Stef, for his enduring patience, love and support in mitigating her capacity to 'do it all'.

Discover the Key Approaches to Criminology website

Visit the Key Approaches to Criminology website at: https://study.sagepub.com/keyapproachestocriminology to find a range of resources for this book, and other criminology titles in the series, including:

- **Key Terms and Glossaries** which help you get to grips with jargon and terminology
- **Summaries** which recap key topics to help with revision
- **Study Questions** to help you check you understand key concepts
- **Further Reading** with annotations directs you to carefully selected additional reading, an ideal supplement for assignments, essays, and literature reviews
- **Overviews** of suggested learning objectives

1

Introduction

With early feminist work in British **criminology** focused on understanding the **female offender** (Heidensohn, 1985; Smart, 1977), the past 40 years or so has seen the stock of knowledge on **gender** and criminal justice grow exponentially. Criminologists interested in gender have taken on the challenge of making women, and more recently men, visible within the criminological enterprise. Criminology is now abundant with works considering the issue of gender, from general textbooks on gender and **crime** (Barberet, 2014; Heidensohn, 2006; Mallicoat, 2011; Muraskin, 2012; Naffine, 1997; Renzetti, 2013; Renzetti et al., 2006; Walklate, 2004) to more specific texts on women in the penal system (Carlen, 2002; Carlen and Worrall, 2004; Wahidin, 2016), women's and men's **victimization** (Dobash and Dobash, 2001; Newburn and Stanko, 1994) and the gendered nature of criminal justice organizations and those who inhabit them (J. Brown, 1998; Brown and Heidensohn, 2000; Heidensohn, 1992, 2003; Kenney, 2013; Martin and Jurik, 2007; Silvestri, 2003). With such a good range of work available, might readers be right to question our motives for writing yet another text on gender and crime?

We are guided by three main motivations in writing this book. Firstly, we believe contributing a second edition to this major series by Sage offers us an opportunity to restate the continuing significance of gender in criminology, not least because some of the issues raised in the 1960s still have resonance today, albeit in a modified form. Secondly, despite the mass of literature available, part of the impetus for this book stems from a desire to challenge the idea that the appetite for knowledge of gender and crime has been satiated. We feel that no other book currently synthesizes the material in the way that this book does. We outline both women's and men's experiences as victims, offenders and criminal justice professionals. In doing this we are calling for students of criminology to avoid empirical and conceptual complacency and for them to be aware of the evolving and ever-changing nature of the field. Lastly, we attempt to breathe new life into existing and well-rehearsed debates about gender and crime. We do so by considering the usefulness of drawing on a **human rights** discourse for making sense of gender, crime and criminal justice. These motivations are all underpinned by a desire to combat the growing mantra in criminal justice and broader circles that 'all things are equal now'. Indeed one of the main purposes of the book is to draw attention to the highly differentiated and complex patterns of equality and inequality. In short, for those unfamiliar with debates on gender and crime, this book will offer a comprehensive guide into some of the major debates that have influenced and shaped the study of this topic. For those already familiar with the industry of texts on gender and crime, this book will act as an *aide-memoire* to existing debates but at the same time will make an innovative contribution to debates in this field of inquiry. Since the publication of the first edition the connections between all aspects of gender and crime remained topical issues in academic criminology and crime and public policy, and the book needs updating to take into account new research and the emergence of new issues and debates (e.g. 'honour'-based violence (HBV) and **female genital mutilation** (FGM), sex trafficking, the wide range of professionals working across the whole of the criminal justice sector). Also, there has been talk of a 'crime drop' across the world, which suggests that the **crime reduction** industry has got to grips with crime, disorder and anti-social behaviour; yet this book tells a different story where existing as well as new crime types still have an adverse effect on individuals and communities and in gendered ways.

The first part of the introduction sets out the main aims and objectives of the book and provides an overview of its overall structure. The first section will consider the relationship between gender and crime from a historical perspective. This is followed by a discussion of criminological theory and maps out the logic behind searching for new directions within the study of gender and crime. In doing so it will allow a greater appreciation of what has been, what currently is, and what is possible for studies on gender and crime. We put forward here our case for a human rights perspective for the study of gender and crime, which has been acknowledged as a line of inquiry, 'which holds real promise for achieving justice for women' (Silvestri, 2006 cited in Heidensohn, 2012: 131); and to that we might add men. Thus our book departs from most traditional texts on gender and crime (see Barberet, 2014, for an exception to this rule). The reluctance of many criminologists to take account of the significance of a human rights agenda will be outlined and its importance emphasized. We argue that academic communities have for too long clung to a very narrow conception of human rights. The decision to focus on the human rights agenda is timely for several reasons. Debates on gender and crime have rightly considered the themes of **diversity**, difference, **discrimination** and division, sometimes showing in stark terms that women's and men's lived experiences of criminal justice are highly differentiated. This conceptual point has been demonstrated through different theoretical perspectives and an expanding body of empirical work drawing on qualitative and quantitative methodologies, underpinned by competing epistemologies. Academics, policy-makers and practitioners have started to come to terms with the gendered divisions created through complex processes of differentiation. There is a mixed bag of responses and although there is some evidence that men and women today are more equal in the domain of criminal justice than their historical counterparts several decades ago, this complex equality is muddied further by increasingly complicated forms of inequality.

The human rights agenda, at least in principle, strives towards eradicating gender differences through an emphasis on the universal characteristics of a genderless human subject. However, closer investigation of human rights discourse shows further diversification, division and differentiation of men's and women's respective experiences of criminal justice. This book suggests that when class and race are added to the equation not only are there novel configurations in terms of relationships between men and women, but divisions among men and women are in some instances much sharper and more pronounced. In providing a comprehensive overview of women and men, we do outline some of the dominant explanations for women's and men's behaviours, but we should state here that the book is much more concerned with exploring how their experiences of the **criminal justice system** might relate to a human rights agenda. Our position is a simple one: we argue that rethinking the experiences of women and men as offenders, victims and those in control of the criminal justice system within a human rights framework will encourage a transgression of traditional debates about gender and crime.

The state of criminology

As criminology progresses into the twenty-first century, those discussions about its state of health registered in 2008 in the first edition of this book still have resonance today. The diagnosis is mixed and readings of the past, present and future states of criminology vary enormously depending on your perspective. South (1998: 222) sums these debates up well when he states that criminology 'is either in deep crisis, close to being dead and buried, or else has come through a period of conflict, resolution and consolidation, to reach a point of renewed vitality'. He concludes that criminology seems to be in a rather vigorous state of good health, producing new directions and some reflexive debate. Before giving criminology a clean bill of health, however, it might be prudent not to overstate its vigour. If we look at the indices being used to map its condition, Walters (2003) reminds us that the traditional markers, normally associated with health – in this case, the growth of criminological centres, journals, programmes and student numbers – are not necessarily evidence of a discipline in a healthy or productive state. Indeed in many cases, he argues, it may indicate the converse. From different perspectives there are criminologists who have questioned the narrow and restrictive research agendas that have been set by central government and welcomed by administrative criminologists (Hall and Winlow, 2015; Matthews, 2014). Matthews (2009) has even questioned the social relevance of the discipline with an allusion to '"So what?" criminology' despite much talk of research having 'impact'. Some commentators, again from very different vantage points, have bemoaned the lack of theoretical innovation within criminology (Hall and Winlow, 2015; Rock, 1994) and others have pointed to the 'perverse' and 'deeply disturbing trends in the *content* of criminology' (Hillyard et al., 2004, original emphasis). Hillyard et al. offer an insightful discussion on the state of the criminological research agenda in the 2000s, but their observations are still germane. They argue that 'alongside the noise of criminology – the ceaseless chatter advocating the extension of criminal justice practices and "solutions" – there stands a series of telling, sustained silences' (Hillyard et al., 2004: 371). In particular, they note the absence of questions about **power** within criminological research agendas and detail the lack of attention dedicated to investigating state criminality and liability. On a more optimistic note, such characterizations fail to appreciate some of the innovative and interesting work being conducted today by newer generations in criminology. It may be that as predicted by Heidensohn (2000) change is afoot as the fortunate generations begin to retire and new generations assume their positions.

When thinking more specifically about the issues of gender and criminology, we can see that the relationship between women, femininity and crime – and increasingly men, **masculinity** and crime – continues to assume an increased visibility and political significance within both criminology and the public arena. The impact of feminist perspectives is clearly observable on criminological research, policy and practice agendas. Not only have such works assumed a greater visibility, but they have also matured within criminology. As the disciplinary boundaries become increasingly blurred in most fields, criminological works have become much more interdisciplinary in nature. If you scan the criminological literature that has emerged over recent years, it becomes fairly evident that authors of some of the more interesting work have spent considerable time searching for new vocabularies, new terms and concepts outside the discipline. In support of this position, Heidensohn (2000: 3) notes that 'criminology has to be renewed every so often from external sources or outside visitors'.

With the impact of feminism so clearly visible there is much to be proud of. Yet, not all is as good as it could be – there is no doubt that feminism and those with a gender agenda remain very much on the margins of the discipline. We concur with Heidensohn (2000) above and argue that the ability to be interdisciplinary is a key strength that provides us with new and exciting sources for the future renewal of criminology. In comparing findings from research studies over nearly three decades on various groups of women involved with the criminal justice system, Heidensohn (1994: 27) concluded that the impact of modern feminism had affected the consciousness of women. In this work, she characterizes a shift from 'being to knowing', in which women now know they are interesting, to themselves, each other and to men. She also notes other important transitions in which women were more likely to 'resist' than 'accept' their ascribed status and to be more ready to 'voice' dissent than to maintain 'silence'. With masculinity studies still in their infancy its effects on men are harder to quantify. There is no doubt, however, that the need to understand men through an appreciation of masculinities has secured a place within criminological circles. The significant transformations that have occurred through feminist work, which will unfold in this book, are unquestionable but the extent to which mainstream criminology has acknowledged their significance is best described as tokenistic.

New directions: Human rights

The first edition of *Gender and Crime* published in 2008 was influenced by two events: firstly, the publication of the *Commission on Women and the Criminal Justice System* (Fawcett Society, 2004) following concern about the impact of current laws and practices on women in England and Wales; and secondly, the New Labour government's announcement of its intention to create a single **Commission for Equality and Human Rights (CEHR)** in 2007. These were important developments that gave greater prominence to the issues of gender and crime, placing them within an alternative discursive framework. Since the publication of the first edition, there has been a significant change in government with two general elections – May 2010 and May 2015. Coming to power in May 2010, the Conservative–Liberal Democrat Coalition government embarked on a fundamental reform of public services calling for a less centralized **state** and more **discretion** for local authorities, with deep and sustained cuts in public expenditure (Crowther-Dowey and Long, 2011). At the same time, we can see a diminishing commitment to a human rights agenda. Some of the choices taken by the Coalition, though conditioned by political economy, are also consequences of political and ethical agency. For example, in the run up to the 2010 election campaign the Liberal Democrats were broadly supportive of the Human Rights Act (1998) whereas the Conservatives were more distrustful, with some prominent figures calling for it to be scrapped and replaced with a Bill of Rights. This scepticism was displayed when the **Home Secretary**, Theresa May, refused to sign a Council of Europe Convention on Domestic Violence (CETS no. 210), calling for full commitment to prevent violence against women and treat it as **torture** (Shackle, 2011). The Coalition government made many ambitious and progressive statements but the refusal to add a signature to this convention and the proposed cuts suggests their commitment to eliminating human rights violations, like violence against women, is partial. We wait to see the direction taken by the Conservative government elected in May 2015.

In this second edition we restate our commitment to developing our analysis within a framework of human rights. We feel that the discourse of human rights is uniquely placed to take on board a number of current issues in criminology. It also has the capacity to render the concerns of criminologists through a discourse of power. In doing so it seeks to make the state much more central in the quest for accountability. We think at this time it is both criminologically and politically relevant to do so. In this book the existence of power and the state are taken as a given although it is necessary to recognize that for the purposes of this book there are different state forms involved in the regulation of crime. These forms have a bearing on gendered relations in criminal justice and they are affected by the human rights agenda and/or discourses on human rights.

Alongside this, the social and economic insecurities generated by rapid global change pose a range of challenges for criminology and human rights. The study of gender, and crime more particularly, has gone global with a deluge of international and transnational research mapping a broad array of gendered global crime and **social harms** (Cain and Howe, 2008). In developing a global conversation about gender and crime, we draw on human rights as a unifying framework within which to consider the connections between the local and the global, enabling a more constructive appreciation of the possibilities and limits of national and international human rights.

The bulk of this book focuses on developments in criminal justice in England and Wales and to some extent the UK. Before providing a summary of the book we outline the main features of the Human Rights Act 1998, which informs the analysis of the book that follows.

The Human Rights Act is based on the European Convention on Human Rights, which was drawn up following World War II. It is the main piece of legislation in place, which is there to protect the human rights of UK citizens. A core aim was 'bringing rights home' by making it possible for people to access home rights at home instead of having to go to the European Court of Human Rights. This was reinforced by a 'culture of human rights' which attempts to ensure that basic human rights principles are an element of government policy and practice at central and local levels. The Act places a legal duty on public authorities (such as central and local government, and **criminal justice agencies**) to protect, respect and fulfil citizens' human rights when delivering services. Thus public authorities are legally accountable for any decisions they take in their everyday activities.

Table 1.1 A summary of the main articles of the Human Rights Act 1998

Article 2 – Right to life	Article 8 – Right to private life and family
Article 3 – Right not to be tortured or treated in an inhuman or degrading way	Article 9 – Right to freedom of belief
Article 4 – Freedom from slavery or forced labour	Article 10 – Right to freedom of expression
Article 5 – Personal freedom or the right to liberty	Article 11 – Right to freedom of assembly and association
Article 6 – Right to a fair trial	Article 12 – Right to marry and found a family
Article 7 – No punishment without law	Article 14 – Right not to be discriminated against in relation to individual differences such as sex and race

There are 16 rights or articles, yet for our purposes we refer to 12, and there are many different ways these rights are protected (see Table 1.1).

Some of the above rights are 'absolute', which have no limits (Articles 3, 4 and 7) whereas others are 'limited' (for example, Article 5) when it is legitimate to deprive someone of their liberty under certain circumstances, such as the **arrest** and/or detention of a **suspect**. There are also 'qualified' rights, which can be interfered with under certain circumstances (Articles 8, 9, 10 and 11) (see Newburn, 2013: 938). Not all of these rights are relevant to our concerns, but we will draw attention to those that are throughout the book.

Overview of the book and its contents

An understanding of both *femininities* and *masculinities* is a central part of this book. The book will be divided into four main parts consisting of ten chapters. The first part, *Gender and Crime in Context*, provides a historical overview of the study of gender and crime, which is informed by a chapter introducing key issues and debates relating to theorizing gender and crime. Following that we appraise contemporary issues in gender and crime in a globalized world.

Beyond this, a key and overarching theme of the book is the issue of care and control. Here we consider the ongoing tensions and problematic nature of women and men's interactions with the criminal justice system as offenders, victims and criminal justice professionals. Our concern with the issue of 'care' is an addition to the first edition and is reflective of contemporary discourses in relation to debates about gender and crime. Thus the second part, *Out of Control*, offers an insight into the differential patterns of female and male offending behaviour, their interactions with the **police**, the prosecution process, the courts and the wider penal system.

The third part, *In Need of Care*, explores conceptions of risk, fear and victimization through an insight into women's and men's experiences of being victims of crime. The fourth part, *In Control*, considers the discriminatory nature of social control through an appreciation of the ways in which both the law itself and criminal justice organizations and its agents are gendered. A more detailed account of the chapters follows below.

Firstly, we outline the contents of Part I, which focuses on gender and crime in context. Chapter 2 has two general aims. Firstly, it will survey the theoretical landscape and outline the broad theoretical shifts that have occurred within the study of gender, deviance, crime and harm. More specifically, it will chart the major conceptual and methodological developments that have shaped **feminist criminology**. We explore the origins of the discipline of criminology and consider how gender gradually became an issue for researchers and policy-makers. In particular, we emphasize the contribution of feminism to the study of crime from a historical perspective. Although the origins of feminist thought can be traced back at least to the nineteenth century, it did not have any bearing on criminology until the latter half of the twentieth century. We consider the emergence of several feminist critiques of so-called 'malestream' criminology in relation to the different levels and types of offending, the conceptualizations of male and female offenders, as well as epistemological and ontological assumptions (Heidensohn, 1968; Smart, 1977). There has also been somewhat of a renaissance of historical work within contemporary criminology, with studies of women offenders forming part of this broader narrative (Heidensohn and Silvestri, 2012). Also acknowledged is the theme of **intersectionality** and how gender relates to other **social divisions** (e.g. **race**, **ethnicity**, class, age, etc.). It will provide an introductory overview of issues past and present, ranging from gender blindness to backlash politics. It is here that the interdisciplinary nature of the way in which gender studies has matured within criminology will be emphasized. Secondly, readers will be introduced to the theoretical importance of a human rights perspective for the study of gender and crime. Criminology's failure to take account of the significance of a human rights agenda will be outlined and its importance will be stressed. It will be argued that academic communities have for too long clung to a very narrow conception of human rights. It will be argued that thinking about the experiences of women and men as offenders, victims and those in control of the criminal justice system within a human rights framework will encourage a transgression of traditional debates about gender and crime.

Chapter 3 explores how criminology has benefitted from the contribution of historians, which adds to the strong interdisciplinary nature of the subject. Chapter 2 looked at historical developments in the discipline beginning in the 1960s but this chapter goes much further back to explore how gender, crime, victimization and social control have changed over the centuries. The overarching purpose of the chapter is to consider the issue of the 'gender gap' in offending behaviour and to make the experiences of women more visible. This is achieved by scrutinizing five cultural myths that have emerged as an enduring feature of accounts of female offending – specifically that she is not violent; mad rather than bad; a liar and deceiver; dangerous and risky; and in need of both care and control. Historical work is essential for identifying the relevance of the past for coming to terms with contemporary issues such as the fear and anxiety caused by the crime and anti-social behaviour of young women. We focus more on women but also acknowledge male criminality, particularly violence and how this is influenced by class and power in the context of broad social changes such as the 'civilizing' process. The final part of the chapter concentrates on victimization and how historical narratives on male violence against women include continuities with the present, especially **victim** blaming and the failure to prosecute and convict **defendants** accused of sexual and intimate forms of violence. Thus, a core argument of the chapter is that while gendered historical accounts of crime and the criminal justice system are important in their own right, exploring 'new' historical insights into women offenders have much salience in relation to contemporary discourses about gender and crime.

In Chapter 4 we reflect on contemporary issues in gender and crime in a globalized world. Since the twentieth century criminologists have become increasingly concerned about globalization and the various opportunities and threats this presents to both the individual and society. A key idea is that through technological, cultural, political, social and economic changes the world is becoming a smaller place in which individuals are more closely connected to each other. Although time and place are still important, the internet and cheap travel means people and commodities are physically and virtually closer than ever before. In terms of crime we can see how globalization has created new forms of criminal and deviant behaviour, such as trafficking, drugs, criminalization of (im)migration, honour killings, online pornography, online stalking/harassment, social media, etc. This chapter would foreground the global drivers of crime (i.e. **New Public Management** (NPM), penal populism) which appeared in the conclusion of the first edition, so these can be embedded, where appropriate. Criminological research and policy tend to be concerned with what is happening in a particular nation state, which is confirmed by the content of Parts II–IV. However, the purpose of this chapter is to show how **globalization** has impacted on the complex relationship between gender, criminality and the control of crime. Despite people becoming physically and virtually closer, we also know that in a globalized world gender-based inequalities are becoming more evident in all societies. Another purpose of the chapter is to outline the growing importance of international and global responses to crime and disorder, focusing on the uneven impacts of gender-blind approaches to social control.

The second part of the book, called *Out of Control* begins with Chapter 5 which concentrates on women as offenders. Although criminologists have shown an interest in female offending, this chapter considers the conflicting views about the cause of, and appropriate responses to, a diversity of girls and women who commit acquisitive and violent crimes, including theft, domestic and sexual abuse and 'girl gangs'. In the first part we consider the female offender and her presence in the criminal justice system and argue that despite claims that women, compared to men, are becoming more crime prone, insufficient attention is paid to the context of victimization in which women offend (i.e. sex workers, drug mules). The second part outlines informal social control of deviant females at risk of engaging in offending behaviour and the treatment experienced by women as they pass through the criminal justice system, especially when women are incarcerated. In doing this we demonstrate that the human rights agenda is relevant and has the potential to make a difference. In the third and final part of the chapter we use a case study exploring the difficulties faced by the female prisoner: the over-representation of women in **suicide and self-harm** statistics; contact with children and families; and the experience of girls in prison. In doing so we consider in more detail the relevance of Article 2 (The right to life) and Article 8 (The right to private and **family life**) and the United Nations' Convention on the Rights of the Child. This considers previously neglected issues such as women's involvement in sexual offences and terrorism. We will critically reflect on the broader shift brought about by the **Corston Report** (Corston, 2007) in developing alternatives to **custody** in the form of community sentences and interventions.

Chapter 6 complements the previous one with an overview of men as offenders. As in the first edition, the main aim of this chapter is to consider the response of criminologists who have responded to feminist critiques of academic criminology. The chapter provides an updated review of some of the complex debates about men, masculinities and offending that have been conducted since the 1980s to the present day. It does this by reviewing research that explores the involvement of men and boys in crime, disorder and **anti-social behaviour** and criminal justice responses to this group. The main point is that there is an ongoing discussion, specifically between structural and **psychosocial approaches**, where there are a number of unresolved theoretical, methodological and conceptual issues and debates, especially around intersectionality. Despite the lack of consensus in existing narratives focusing on masculinities and crime, more and more criminologists are accepting that most crimes are mainly committed by males and that for whatever reason male criminality is an indication that masculinity is problematic. In common with the previous chapter this one also considers the relevance of a human rights agenda. For instance, the HRA (1998) is a clear attempt to universalize rights, but many of the structural inequalities pre-dating the Act remain. Above all, certain groups of men continue to be marginalized, disadvantaged and excluded despite interventions in the name of human rights. Wider developments in the political economy may undermine the progressive and liberalizing tendencies of the human rights agenda through perpetuating gendered patterns of inequality. In common with Chapter 5 more attention is directed towards youth justice, the courts and men's experiences of the penal system (i.e. offender-based interventions through prison and **probation**, which are oriented towards desistance).

In Part III of the book our attention shifts towards those in need of care, such as women as victims and this group is examined in Chapter 7. In the first edition this chapter explored the influence of early victimological studies, in particular the growing prominence of the female victim and accounts of the ways in which girls and women are victimized. It included a critical review of existing responses to **domestic abuse** and sexual violence, especially legislative changes and reforms to the **policing** of these issues. The new edition will focus on the victimization of women and girls with reference to HBV and female genital mutilation (FGM), forced marriage, human trafficking, prostitution and sex work. The chapter is divided into three main parts. The first part updates the earlier review of the increased visibility of the female victim, which documented the nature and extent of violence against women. While gender-based violence incorporates a wide range of behaviours, a core theme is domestic abuse against women and girls perpetrated by men and boys. The chapter aims to broaden horizons by considering the global picture and what goes on beyond national boundaries. Despite considerable attempts by government and criminal justice agencies to take violence against women 'seriously', critics have observed that many complainants continue to experience '**secondary victimization**'. The second part of the chapter critically assesses the official responses to domestic abuse, especially by the police, but also by the expanding voluntary and community sectors. The third and final part of this chapter transgresses existing debates within criminology concerning violence against women and situates the issue of violence against women within a human rights framework.

The issue of victim rights is still a contentious area of debate and though there is a more robust statutory response to victims, many female victims are under-protected. In this chapter we consider the possibility of conceiving domestic violence as a form of **coercive control** and torture – a clear and obvious human rights violation. Violence against women by an intimate male partner is now recognized throughout most of the world as a significant social problem and has been identified by many countries as a human rights issue (United Nations, 1995). Through developing this argument we will consider the role of the state and its responsibility with respect to violence against women.

Chapter 8 takes the male victim as its focus. In order that we can develop an understanding of men as victims the chapter consists of three main strands. The opening and longest section considers the knowledge base relating to the phenomenon of male victimization, focusing in particular on **interpersonal violence**. This audit is updated to take into account more recent research. In line with the previous chapter it is suggested that this type of offending behaviour illustrates most starkly the gendered nature of victimization and that gender is less obviously relevant for other types of crime, principally property offences. Because this book is about gender and crime the focus is mainly on men although it is necessary to avoid reifying masculinities above other social divisions because it is intertwined in myriad ways with ethnicity, age, sexuality and **social class**. The salience of masculinities in relation to the services victims receive is then rehearsed, showing how the criminal justice system in England and Wales has been oriented towards victims' needs despite the word 'rights' being in circulation. Secondly, there is a brief review of prevailing explanations of male victimization in light of victimological and masculinities research. A key point emerging from this section is that the distinction between victims and offenders is not hard and fast. Therefore, when we consider boys and men there is a clear need to recognize the intricate linkages between complex patterns of exclusion that marginalize men both as victims and offenders, although spelling out the significance of the former at more length. Thirdly, we utilize human rights discourse to provide an alternative way of conceptualizing the victimization of men. We argue very briefly that given men are culpable for most victimization, male victims can assume greater personal responsibility for their victimization by recognizing the risks they face. Another way of deepening our appreciation of the potential application of human rights discourse is by focusing on how the state has on some occasions unfairly and unjustly criminalized – and victimized – the anti-social behaviour of boys and young men.

The fourth part of our book concentrates on the experiences of criminal justice professionals. Chapter 9, the first of two dedicated to examining the experiences of criminal justice professionals and employees, will build on the chapter in the first edition by outlining the differential employment of men and women working in the sector and how this is shaped by gender-based discrimination. In the first edition we concentrated mainly on police officers and private security workers but this chapter will widen its focus to include youth offending teams, the legal professions and the National Offender Management Service (NOMS). However, the pattern of inequality is far from straightforward and it is necessary to look behind the numbers to show how organizational cultures produce and sustain sexist attitudes, beliefs, processes and practices. The aims of the chapter are achieved in three sections with the first section 'auditing' or quantifying the numbers of men and women working in core and ancillary professions, in addition to para-professionals and an increasingly pluralized sector such as the burgeoning voluntary and community sector and private sector (e.g. women as bouncers). The second section provides a more qualitative take on gendered inequalities throughout the crime control industry showing how masculinist and **heterosexist ideologies** permeate all of these organizations, which bolster male dominance in terms of the power and influence of men, especially though not exclusively, over women. The third part is an updated exploration of the apparent failure of **equal opportunities** policies, despite the production of various statements of good intent and seemingly positive anti-sexist initiatives. We consider the influence of power, which can produce gendered inequalities where the interests of men are privileged, thus cancelling out more progressive human rights based values such as equality, opportunity, diversity, fairness, dignity and balance.

Chapter 10, as with the first edition, focuses on the theme of gendered organizations and career progression, especially the constraints faced by women, to show how discriminatory ideas and practices obstruct the mobility of female professionals and how this tendency is out of kilter with an equal rights-based approach. The main focus is on the police and legal profession. There is also an overview of the broad movement towards developing diversity in society and the legislation in place to govern and tackle discrimination. The chapter is divided into two main parts. The first part contextualizes the debate by providing an account of the broader call for developing diversity within organizations. It is within this context that we situate the debate within a rights-based framework. Unlawful discrimination and the harassment of workers is an important human rights issue and the canon of human rights law now provides a comprehensive framework for challenging the various forces that have created and sustained discrimination based upon sex. The extent to which criminal justice organizations have drawn upon this framework to improve the position of women will become clear as we explore some of the initiatives taking place within criminal justice organizations to encourage a more representative workforce. We also consider the potential benefits of a more gender-balanced and gender-aware criminal justice system on those professionals working in criminal justice and for those who come into contact with criminal justice agents, be they offenders and/or victims. The discrimination that women working in criminal justice organizations now face is far more insidious than that faced by their historical counterparts. With discriminatory behaviour less blatant and visible, its identification requires us to adopt a much more complex approach. The second part of this chapter draws on the theory of gendered organizations to outline the way in which criminal justice agencies and the career trajectories within them are deeply gendered at structural, cultural and individual levels.

PART I
GENDER AND CRIME IN CONTEXT

2

Theorizing Gender and Crime

OVERVIEW

Chapter 2 provides:

- An overview of the emergence of feminist perspectives in criminology from the late 1960s.
- An introduction into the key concerns of early pioneering feminist criminologists.
- An analysis of some of the tensions, conflicts, limitations and challenges that have shaped the development of the study of gender and crime.
- A critique of feminist criminology.
- An overview of the development of a human rights agenda.
- Insight into the importance and value of a human rights agenda in relation to the study of criminology.

KEY TERMS

- feminist backlash
- feminist criminology
- feminist empiricism
- feminist theorization
- human rights
- mainstream criminology

Introduction

The addition of this chapter, together with a new chapter on *Gender, Crime and History* in this second edition, is indicative of a growing interest and appreciation of the gains to be made by adopting historical perspectives to the broad study of gender and crime. Given the transformation of the criminological landscape, with an abundance of research and researchers now interested in gender, it is all too easy to lose sight of a time in which things were different – a time when the academe did not recognize, theorize or debate the significance of gender. With the history of criminology itself dating back over at least two centuries, the arrival of feminist perspectives to the field is relatively new. This chapter takes the academe as its focus and explores the emergence of feminist perspectives within criminology from the late 1960s and early 1970s. We remind readers at the outset that although we begin our analysis with the advent of second-wave feminism,[1] an interest in women as offenders, as victims of violence and as criminal justice professionals has a much longer history and can be found throughout the centuries – we explore this more fully in Chapter 3. In this chapter, we focus more specifically on the emergence and impact of feminist perspectives within criminological academic discourses. Up until the 1970s, the gender blind orientation of the majority of criminologists led to a particular masculinist framework that has assumed 'man' as the normal subject of criminological inquiry (Naffine, 1997). Readers should not confuse this with the idea that such studies developed our understanding of men *as men*; they didn't – simply that women were excluded from such inquiries. Indeed the study of masculinities within criminology, as a topic in its own right, did not get underway until the 1990s with Newburn and Stanko (1994) urging criminologists to take 'masculinities seriously'. Since that time, we have witnessed a growth in research on masculinities, crime and social control (Collier, 1998; Gadd, 2006b; Hall, 2002; Lander et al., 2014; McFarlane, 2013; Messerschmidt, 1993, 2005a; Whitehead, 2002; Winlow, 2001; Winlow and Hall, 2006, 2009). We expand our analysis of the study of men in subsequent chapters but focus more specifically on women in this chapter.

With women accounting for a relatively small proportion of all known offenders over time, early theorizations of deviance and criminality focused on men. When women offenders were considered, they were often done so in relation to men and so were subject to distorted representation, **marginalization** and trivialization (Heidensohn, 1996; Hughes, 2005). It was against such a backdrop that the emergence of a concerted interest by scholars to locate and debate the place of women within criminological debates took place. While contemporary criminological landscapes are rich in studies on women as offenders, victims and criminal justice workers, it was the female offender who took centre stage and preoccupied the inquiries of the early pioneers. A surge of interest in women as victims was to follow in the late 1970s and early 1980s, where she has since then assumed an ascendancy over her offending counterpart as an object of concern on criminological and policy agendas. Indeed, an interest in women's victimization has gone on to shape much of the more contemporary debates about women's offending too (Heidensohn and Silvestri, 2012). In locating women, a focus on women as criminal justice workers was the final strand to join the narrative of feminist criminology. This ordering should come as no surprise given that feminist concerns have long been taken up with 'researching down' rather than 'researching up' (Puwar, 1997). As Heidensohn (1992: 109) explains:

> The study of women as social control agents does not fit as easily into the various feminist paradigms which have informed much modern research on women and from women's perspectives ... women who are, in some way 'part of the problem', who share, however meagerly, in the system of oppression are not, therefore, easily assimilated into feminist politics or happily explained in that framework.

In tracing the origins of feminist criminology to the 1960s, this chapter provides an overview of some of the concerns that dominated early pioneering scholars. It reflects on some of the key contributions made over the past 50 years to the study of gender and crime. At the same time, we provide an insight into some of the tensions, conflicts, limitations and challenges that have shaped the development and narratives of those interested in gender. We argue that in making sense of the past, present and the future, the adoption of a historical gaze offers us a critical lens within which to explore both change and continuity over time. It also provides us with a useful platform from which to stop and reflect on the achievements and challenges encountered by feminist criminology. We end by posturing on the possible future(s) of feminist perspectives in criminology and lay out our arguments in relation to the possibilities of adopting a human rights lens to the study of gender and crime. We chart the development and growing importance of human rights in Britain and more widely in the EU context and provide an insight into some of the ways in which a human rights framework has helped to shape the arguments developed in this book.

The emergence of feminist perspectives in criminology

Reflecting on the history of feminist criminology, Heidensohn (2012) notes two major stages in its development: *the pioneering* stage from the 1970s to 1999 and a stage of *expansion and consolidation* at the turn of the millennium. Most striking here perhaps is the sheer length of time given over to the pioneering stage – that said, a period of 30 years may not seem so long if we consider that the history of criminology is one that spans over 200 years. Absent from broader narratives of crime, one of the key tasks of second-wave feminism from the late 1960s onwards was to develop a comprehensive critique of the discipline. We begin here by observing an often overlooked paper written by

Frances Heidensohn in 1968 on 'The deviance of women: A critique and enquiry'. Noting the lack of empirical data and analysis on women, Heidensohn makes a number of critical and important calls for researchers to drive forward the sociological study of gender and deviance. In surveying the landscape, she called for a 'crash programme of research, which telescopes decades of comparable studies of males' (Heidensohn, 1968: 122). Moreover, she emphasized that explanations for women's deviance must be sought – not in stereotyped assumptions about either their nature or place in the social structure – but in the empirical realities of women's lives and patterns of offending. While this might seem like an obvious task for contemporary scholars, we encourage readers to reflect upon the progressive nature of this call. Written at a time when the concept of feminist criminology remained unimagined or developed, Heidensohn's call was truly extraordinary (Eaton, 2000; Mooney, 2009). Indeed in a recent paper reflecting on the achievements of feminist criminology, Heidensohn herself emphasizes a personal lack of awareness of just how significant that paper was, when she notes that:

> While anticipating much of what was to become the feminist agenda, [the paper] was not written in language or using terms we would recognize as feminist; in short, I was not myself aware of how significant this step was to become. (Heidensohn, 2012: 124)

Women were not completely absent within academic inquiry. Indeed a number of prominent studies on women and deviance can be found throughout the decades before the advent of feminist criminology in the early 1970s. Rafter and Gibson (2004) point out that throughout the early and mid-twentieth century, there has been one substantial publication per decade on the topic, most notably the Gluecks' (1934) *Five Hundred Delinquent Women*, Pollack's (1950) *The Criminality of Women*, and Konopka's (1966) *The Adolescent Girl in Conflict*. Despite foregrounding women's deviancy in name, these works did not form part of the gendered analysis called upon by Heidensohn, but for the most part reinforced distorted views and assumptions about women offenders forged earlier in Lombroso and Ferrero's study on *The Female Offender* (1895). Working within a **positivist paradigm**, early criminological theories looked for an explanation of offending behaviour in an individual's genetic characteristics and psychology. For Lombroso and Ferrero, the criminal woman was genetically disadvantaged; both 'physically and anthropologically' differentiated from her non-criminal counterpart and was best represented as an atavistic, amoral throwback. While the broader study of men's offending took on an altogether different direction during the twentieth century, incorporating theorizations on the importance of the urban space, class structure and state control, explanations of women's offending behaviour remained firmly rooted in notions of biological **determinism** and were framed within dominant sexual stereotypes of women as passive, domestic and maternal (Rafter and Gibson, 2004; Smart, 1977). Tierney (1996: 125) detects the stubborn adherence to biological determinism when he notes that the study of female crime post-war had been 'cast adrift from the main body of criminology'.

A project in feminist empiricism and theorization

The exposure of criminology as the criminology of men marked the starting point of feminists' attempts to find alternative modes of conceptualizing the social worlds of deviance and conformity, punishment and control (Heidensohn and Silvestri, 2012). In advance of that, though, early pioneers embarked upon a project of 'adding' women to the 'criminological knowledge bank' (Carrington and Death, 2014). Best described as a project of **feminist empiricism**, early feminist work set about developing wide-ranging criminological research on women, crime, control and justice to counterbalance the absence of women from conventional work. It was in this early 'pioneering' stage that 'territory was being claimed, mapped out and explored' (Heidensohn, 2012: 124). New theoretical and methodological approaches were advanced during this time which sought to respond to two key problems identified by Heidensohn (1968) and described by Daly and Chesney-Lind (1988) as the 'gender ratio problem' (also known as the 'gender gap') and the 'generalizability problem'. Here questions of research centred on examining why women commit less crime than men and whether theories generated to describe men's or boys' offending could be applied to women and girls. Significant contributions within this endeavour over the past 40 years provide a stock of accounts that have made women offenders visible and by the end of the millennium research has confirmed the presence, range and diversity of women's offending (Gartner and McCarthy, 2014).

There has also been a considerable shift in the way in which women's offending behaviour has been conceived. In Chapter 3 we outline a range of persistent cultural myths that have shaped our understanding of the female offender over time. Pioneering feminists were faced with a discourse that constructed women as 'non-violent', as 'mad not bad', as 'liars and deceivers' and as the possessors of 'dangerous and risky' bodies in need of both care and control. Above all else, the female offender lacked **agency**. The publication of Adler's study on *Sisters in Crime* in 1975 therefore provided a controversial account of the emancipatory elements of women's offending. Written at a time of increased formal equalities legalisation, she argued that an increase in women's offending (particularly for fraud and white-collar crimes) was inevitable given the increased freedoms and access to the workplace following improved gender equality laws. Though Adler's (1975) work has now been widely discredited by the academic community (given the lack of increase in criminal activity by women and the continued marginalization of women in the workplace), her work remains an important contribution to counter the biological and psychological theorizations and characterizations that have so dominated the accounts of women offenders. Subsequent studies have gone on to draw attention to women's economic marginalization as a key factor in their offending behaviour (Carlen, 1983; Carlen and Cook, 1989). More recently, studies have placed a greater emphasis on evidencing women playing more 'active' and meaningful roles as offenders within gang activity, sexual violence, drug use, organized crime and terrorism (Brunson and Stewart, 2006; Cobbina et al., 2010; Fleetwood, 2014; Fleetwood and Haas, 2011; Lopez et al., 2009; Maher, 1997; Miller, 2001; Miller and Mullins, 2006; Young, 2009).

The project of feminist empiricism continued to be developed through a more critical consideration of gender through an emphasis on **feminist standpointism**. The goal of standpoint feminism within criminology is neatly summed up by Moore (2008: 53) when she states that it served to 'free feminist accounts of women's experiences in the criminal justice system from the need to be consistently positioned in relation to male knowledges and understanding'. As a result, accounts that followed in this vein have located women's experience at the centre of knowledge. This is particularly characteristic of feminist scholarship that has emphasized the gendered nature of the criminal justice system more broadly. Documenting women offenders' experiences of the police, courts and of prison have done much to combat the chivalry thesis that has dominated much of the discourse on women and criminal justice. Key to this body of work has been an emphasis on drawing out the complex and multiple forms of victimization that underpin much of women's offending together with an awareness of the ruinous impacts for women of being shoehorned into a 'male-centric' system of justice (Carlen, 1983, 1988b; Chesney-Lind, 2006; Corston, 2007; DeHart and Lynch, 2013; Eaton, 1986, 1993; Fawcett Society, 2004, 2009; Heidensohn, 1985). An appreciation of this has been a central feature of significant policy changes in our thinking and policy directed at women offenders in recent years (Corston, 2007; House of Commons Justice Committee, 2013). We return to a more critical reading of such developments later in the chapter.

Following work on the female offender, feminist criminology has gone on to enjoy an explosion of research on women as victims. Early pioneering work on women's victimization has followed the same pattern as that for offenders, with the primary task firstly focused on making women's victimization visible, and secondly on correcting distorted characterizations of them. There is now a large and impressive body of empirical work dedicated to documenting the experiences of women as victims of crime and their engagements of seeking support and redress within a gendered criminal justice system. Reconceptualizing violence against women from a 'private to a public' matter is perhaps one of feminist criminology's greatest achievements and can be found in a number of influential early works (Brownmiller, 1975; Dobash and Dobash, 1979; Russell, 1975). Early feminist criminologists also worked hard to debunk the popularly held assumption that most sexual assaults were committed by strangers. The pervasiveness of violence within intimate and familial relationships was brought to the fore by Stanko, who detailed the everyday nature of violence experienced by women (Radford and Stanko, 1996; Stanko, 1985, 1989, 1990). Such work has had a tremendous impact, not only within criminology, but also on changing policy, law and criminal justice practice for victims. Walklate describes the contribution of feminist research to understanding the link between gender and victimization as 'without question widening the criminological gaze to problematise what counts as crime and where it occurs' (cited in Carrington and Death, 2014: 106). In expanding and shifting the locations of our gaze, recent years have witnessed an interest in documenting the rise of the international global victim through studies on sex trafficking, 'honour' killings, female genital mutilation and violence against women in conflict settings (Barberet, 2014; Cain and Howe, 2008; Pickering and Lambert, 2004; Rafter and Heidensohn, 1995; Renzetti, 2013; Sudbury, 2004). We return to some of these debates in Chapter 5.

Spurred on by such research, analyses of the experience of women as criminal justice workers followed suit. Albeit a smaller enterprise than that concerned with women as offenders and victims, empirical work has raised awareness of the conditions of women criminal justice professionals. Research has also emphasized the masculine subcultures within criminal justice organizations and the gendered nature of management and leadership (Dick et al., 2013; Kenney, 2013; Malleson and Russell, 2006; Martin and Jurik, 2007; Natarajan, 2008; Rabe-Hemp, 2009; Rackley, 2007; Silvestri, 2003, 2006, 2007). The recent attention on the horrific gendered harms perpetrated against women worldwide, together with an increased emphasis by nation states on improving the level of diversity within its workforces, has resulted in a greater commitment to the increased recruitment of women to criminal justice work. The brutal rape and murder of Jyoti Singh, a 23-year-old university student in Delhi in 2012 is one notable example. In response to this murder and the shocking levels of sexual violence against women, the Indian government has approved a rule that one-third of all police posts in Delhi be reserved for women (*The Guardian*, 2015b).

Though Evans and Jamieson (2008: 251) are right to claim that 'criminology was a much weaker discipline before it was shamed and coerced to pay due regard to issues of gender', the development of feminist perspectives within criminology has not been without difficulty or criticism. Often directed from within the ranks of feminism itself, the critique centres on three key areas: firstly, its failure to develop a complex picture of the differences that exist within and between women; secondly, the potential co-optation of feminist ideals as they are translated into criminological practice; and lastly, its failure to challenge and impact on mainstream criminology more broadly.

The critique of feminist criminology

A lack of complexity

While groundbreaking in its project of feminist empiricism – of 'adding' women into criminological debates – feminist criminology has been subject to much criticism for its attempt to develop a unified approach to the study of gender and crime despite the difference and complexity that exists between and within women's experiences of criminal justice. While much had been achieved through the project of feminist standpointism in making women visible and at the heart of investigations, the main problem with standpoint feminism, as Naffine (1997: 5) points out, is 'constituency' or the 'question of which population is meant to be represented by which voice'. With much of the work being a product of 'white, middle-class, Western women and heavily contingent on Western values of individualism and individual rights' (Barberet, 2014: 16), a theory based solely on sex or gender, it was argued, was insufficient to explain the lived realities of women, including a lack of feminist inquiry into the ways in which sex and gender intersect with dimensions of race, ethnicity, class and sexuality. As a result, more sophisticated analyses of gender have been developed by poststructuralist and deconstructionist frameworks that do not insist on a singular set of relationships among gender, sex, deviance or crime but that theorize women's experiences through an understanding of intersecting identities (Barak et al., 2010; Burgess-Proctor, 2006; Collins, 2000; Creek and Dunn, 2014; Daly and Maher, 1998; Henne and Troshynski, 2013; Potter, 2015; Ritchie, 1995; Simpson and Gibbs, 2006; Sudbury, 2004). This is neatly summed up by Wonders when she states the need for research to be mindful that:

> [I]dentities intersect in complex ways and the salience of particular identity categories may change over time. As a result, feminists emphasise the need to consider gender AND race AND ethnicity AND social class AND nationality AND sexual orientation – and to be open to new and emerging identities and forces that shape gendered realities. (cited in Carrington and Death, 2014: 194)

Bernard (2013) urges future analyses to go beyond the concept of 'doing gender' (Messerschmidt, 1993) and to develop a framework of 'doing identity' within which to understand how individuals:

> navigate through multiple oppressions to achieve his or her desired goals and ultimately find space and place for self in contemporary capitalist society ... [in which] an individual's sex, age, gender, sexual identity, race, nationality, class, level of education, and a host of other factors are significant components. (Bernard, 2013: 8)

We concur with these positions and propose that it is only through an appreciation of such interconnections, together with an acknowledgment of the multiplicity of feminist perspectives within criminology, that we can begin to understand the complexity and reality of lived experiences.

The co-optation of feminist ideals and backlash

There has been considerable criticism from some quarters of the failure of feminist criminologists to acknowledge the often unintended and ruinous consequences of their own investigations and theorizations of women (Balfour, 2006; Hannah-Moffat, 2004, 2006; Moore, 2008; Snider, 2003). Snider (2003), for example, has argued that in making the female offender 'resistant' and 'knowing', feminist knowledge has contributed to the '**incarceration** spiral', that is, an increasing number of women being punished harshly. In this way feminist criminologists are complicit in the surge of punitiveness that characterizes the modern industrialized state. She argues that to understand how criminal women are constituted through criminal law today, one must look beyond the academe and ask not what discourses are produced, but what discourses are heard, by politicians, the public and criminal justice professionals. At the same time, the recent trend to reconceptualize the female offender as a woman with underlying, complex and multiple needs is also being subject to increased scrutiny. Motivated and underpinned by 'good intention' with the express aim of improving the lives of women, the past decade or so has witnessed considerable progress in the development of gender responsive and sensitive interventions for women offenders (Gelsthorpe, 2013; Hedderman, 2010a, 2010b; Hedderman et al., 2011; Heidensohn and Silvestri, 2012). While there is much to gain in changing the ways in which we think about women offenders, there is now a considerable body of international work that points to the co-optation of feminist ideals as they are translated into criminological practice (Carlen and Worrall, 2004; Hannah-Moffat, 2001, 2002; Hayman, 2006; Pollack and Kendall, 2005; Shaw and Hannah-Moffat, 2000). In short, this work exposes the ways in which well-intentioned, radical proposals see women offenders with high treatment needs reclassified as 'high risk'. Moreover, through a treatment discourse heavily characterized by notions of 'empowerment', women offenders become increasingly 'responsibilized'. Through such discourses, there is also evidence of net-widening and uptariffing resulting in a greater number of girls and women coming under the guise and control of the criminal justice system (Blakeborough et al., 2007; J. Brown, 1998; Easton et al., 2010; Hucklesby, 2001). Alongside evidence of cooption, there is an increasing emphasis on the 'backlash' experienced by feminism more broadly, with studies confirming a punitive turn – a state of 'vengeful equity' (Chesney-Lind, 2006) in the way in which criminal justice is experienced by women, particularly girls (Burman and Batchelor, 2009; Chesney-Lind and Irwin, 2008; Sharpe, 2011). We return to these debates more fully in Chapter 5.

Miller (2010) urges feminist researchers to be mindful of the sometimes unwitting collaboration with political agendas harmful to women. Recounting the potential for this in her own research on the commercial sex industry in Sri Lanka, she argues that the recent attention and resources devoted to the trafficking in women serve alternative purposes and actually result in intervention against immigrants and the deflection of attention away from the harmful impact of policies. Most importantly, they support the idea that 'woman equals victim' (Miller, 2010: 134).

Indeed, the impact of acknowledging women offenders' own victimization has been challenged by some in relation to denying women's agency. This strand of critique can be found forcefully in debates about women involved in prostitution/who sell sex. Here there is significant tension between those who argue that women involved in 'prostitution' would rather not do so, are coerced in some way or have little choice, and those who argue that the selling of sex is best understood as 'sex work', which is undertaken voluntarily in some way by the worker and not by force (Barberet, 2014). We return to this debate in Chapter 7.

Challenging mainstream criminology

In comparing findings from research studies over nearly three decades on various groups of women involved with the criminal justice system, Heidensohn (1994: 27) concluded that the impact of modern feminism had affected the consciousness of women. In this work, she characterizes a shift from 'being to knowing', in which women now know they are interesting, to themselves, each other and to other men. She also notes other important transitions in which women are more likely to 'resist' than 'accept' their ascribed status and to be more ready to 'voice' dissent than to maintain 'silence'. With masculinity studies in the context of criminology still in their infancy, its effects on men are harder to quantify. There is no doubt, however, that the need to understand men through an appreciation of masculinities has secured a place within criminological circles.

Almost 50 years since the publication of Heidensohn's (1968) paper, there has been a maturation of feminism within criminology and sociology with scholars working in a transformed environment (Carrington and Death, 2014). Evidence of gender awareness and activism can be located across a number of permanent fixtures, with specialist conferences, panels, divisions, societies and journals all now well established within the field, for example, 2014 saw the Division on Women and Crime (American Society of Criminology) celebrate its 30th anniversary. There are also resounding positive impacts visible in relation to the public agenda, policy, policing priorities and overarching legal frameworks. That said and notwithstanding such contributions, there is some concern among commentators that such achievements remain in a 'cul de sac' (Carrington and Death, 2014) separated off as a niche and specialist area and not yet fully immersed within mainstream criminology. The significant transformations that have occurred through feminist work, which will unfold in this book, are unquestionable but the extent to which mainstream criminology has acknowledged their significance is best described as providing a 'token genuflexion, rather than true respect and consideration' of gender issues (Heidensohn, 2000: 4). Reviewing the contributions from major writers in the field, including David Garland (2001) and Loïc Wacquant (2009), commentators have emphasized the continued marginalization and failure to give little more than a perfunctory acknowledgment to gender in their work (Gelsthorpe, 2010; Heidensohn, 2012).

There is also criticism directed at the lack of theoretical development within theorizations of gender and crime (Heidensohn, 2012; Moore, 2008). In an article about the state of feminism and criminology, Comack (1999) offers an insightful perspective of both the problems with feminist criminology and with the solution to it. She maintains that a large part of the reason for feminists' marginalization from the mainstream discipline rests on the dualistic construction of 'women as victims' and 'men as offenders'. More specifically, she claims that feminist work continues to be sidelined through its reliance on the construction of women as victims of male violence. The consequences of thinking in such dualistic terms are far-reaching and one of its main effects is to encourage us to approach complex issues in overly simplistic ways. For feminism to move from the margins (closer) to the centre of the criminological enterprise, Comack (1999: 162) suggests a 'reconsideration and rethinking of the dualisms on which much feminist and criminological work has been premised'. At first glance, a reading of our work might suggest that we too are engaged in perpetuating the idea of women as victims, not only of male violence but also of a male-dominated criminal justice system. Indeed we do argue that this is sometimes the case, but we also emphasize the need to conceptualize men, as victims of a system that denies their voice and existence as men. In doing so, we are not suggesting that women and men are passive in their existence as offenders, victims or criminal justice professionals, but that they are simultaneously active and resistant. We agree with Comack's (1999) basic position but go one step further in rethinking and reconsidering the dualism that has come to characterize both women and men through their various statuses in the criminal justice system. We are proposing that all individuals regardless of their status can be perceived as potential victims and offenders at the same time. Depending on whose interpretation you are reading, women offenders, for example, can easily be perceived as epitomizing both the victim and offender. Similarly, the female victim is also criminalized by official discourse when she does not employ sufficient **crime prevention** strategies to protect herself. For men too, the male offender who experiences discriminatory treatment at the hands of criminal justice agents is both offender and victim simultaneously. Broadening the focus and blurring the distinctions between such dualisms as 'women as victims' and 'men as offenders' makes it possible to stand outside traditional criminal justice models and offer new insights into pressing criminological issues.

With the impact of feminist perspectives clearly observable on criminological research, policy and practice agendas, there is much to be proud about as we progress into the twenty-first century. Yet, the reality for those working within a feminist tradition is that they remain at the margins of criminology. As the disciplinary boundaries become blurred in most fields, criminological works have become increasingly interdisciplinary in nature, drawing on new vocabularies, new terms and new concepts. Such transformation affords feminist criminolog(ies) important opportunities to be renewed from 'external sources or outside visitors' (Heidensohn, 2000: 3). In the quest for new directions, new vocabularies and new concepts, this book is underpinned by an interest in human rights.

The development and growing importance of human rights discourse

The language of human rights is becoming increasingly common currency in contemporary society with a range of individual and collective actors drawing on this body of law in a variety of ways (O'Byrne, 2012; Weber et al., 2014). The concept of human rights, however, is not new. While the language of rights has a long history, the 'human rights project' should not be confused with the historical concept of natural rights because to do so would be to over-look the crucial fact that so-called 'natural rights' were not rights held solely by virtue of one's humanity. As Kallen (2004: 13) reminds us, 'natural rights, in reality, were rights of dominant Westerners: white European men. Some 80 per cent of all human beings were excluded'. Contemporary references to human rights are those which refer to the rights that belong to every human being solely by virtue of his or her membership of human kind. In this sense human rights are frequently held to be 'universal'.

The various international principles of human rights were developed in response to the world's outrage when the full account of Nazi atrocities became public knowledge. On 9 December 1948, The UN General Assembly approved the Convention on the Prevention and Punishment of the Crime of Genocide. On the very next day, 10 December 1948, the UN General Assembly adopted and proclaimed the Universal Declaration of Human Rights (UDHR). The Declaration itself goes far beyond any mere attempt to reassert all individuals' possession of the right to life as a fundamental and inalienable human right. It is a declaration that represents a statement of principles or moral guidelines for the recognition and protection of funda-mental human rights across the globe (Kallen, 2004). Articles 1 and 2 of the UDHR set out the three cardinal principles of human rights – freedom, equal-ity and dignity – as rights and freedoms to which everyone is entitled without distinction of any kind. The range of articles that follow identify particular rights and freedoms exemplifying the three central principles (see Appendix A of the UDHR). The original aspirations of human rights have been perpetu-ated by, most importantly, the European Convention on Human Rights 1954 and the International Covenant on Civil and Political Rights 1966, which in turn have themselves been reinforced by innumerable other declarations and conventions (see Weber et al., 2014 for an excellent review). Taken together these various declarations, conventions and covenants comprise the contem-porary human rights doctrine and embody both the belief in the existence of a universally valid moral order and a belief in all human beings' possession of fundamental and equal moral status, enshrined within the concept of human rights. They form the centrepiece of a moral doctrine that many con-sider to be capable of providing the contemporary political order with what amounts to an international bill of rights (Nickel, 1992). Woodiwiss (2005) suggests that the presence of a human rights agenda is regarded by many of us in the West as symbolic in confirming our civilized condition. All in all, human rights provide an 'overarching paradigm for social equality and social justice for all of humanity, rooted in the twin foundations of human unity and cultural diversity' (Kallen, 2004: 30).

While symbolic of a 'civilized condition', the idea that human rights are universal or that they are universally enjoyed has come under increasing scrutiny. With the Universal Declaration of Human Rights asserting that 'all human beings are born free and equal in dignity and rights', feminist groups have been vociferous in their attack on the failure of international human rights law to recognize and redress the disadvantages and injustices experienced by women. Whereas the 'rights of man', as originally conceived by the great liberal thinkers, were not intended to include women, today's 'universal human rights' still overlook them as a matter of fact (Cook, 1994). Modern human rights law owes much to the legacy of national pressure for civil and political rights at the end of the eighteenth and start of the nineteenth centuries. As women struggled for access to the public world during this time, men's voices were in the vanguard for political rights. The emphasis on civil and political rights reflected man's desire to regulate his relationship to the state and to set boundaries of permissible state interference in his life. Male hegemony over public life and institutions meant that rights came to be defined by men. The present hierarchy within human rights law, which gives greater attention to civil and political rights as opposed to economic, social and cultural rights, can be perceived as a manifestation of the continuing dominance men have over the process of defining the content of rights; human rights are framed in the language, needs and aspirations of men (Kallen, 2004). The exclusion of women's voices from defining the content of human rights discourse has in turn meant that human rights law has evolved along a gendered 'fault line' that distinguishes between the public and private spheres for the purpose of legal regulation (Cook, 1994). As a result, there has been a lack of understanding of the systemic nature of the subordination of women, a failure to recognize the need to characterize the subordination of women as a human rights violation, and a lack of state practice to condemn discrimination against women (Charlesworth, 1994; Cook, 1994; Fitzpatrick, 1994). Similarly, minority ethnic groups, and to some extent the working- and under-classes, are subordinated. In this sense the respect for human rights has failed to be universal. It is only through women's and other oppressed groups' activism at a global level that the visibility of women and other minority groups on the human rights platform has increased.

Despite what we know about the extent and nature of violence against women, it was only formally recognized by the international community as a human rights issue after unprecedented lobbying by women's groups at the Vienna World Conference in 1993. The formal expression of this commitment can be found in the 1993 UN Declaration on the Elimination of Violence Against Women (DEVAW). This instrument has been widely welcomed as an indicator of the shift within the human rights community towards recognition of the need to address those issues that deny women their human rights. The Vienna Conference not only marked an acceptance of the importance of asserting the human rights of women, but also of strengthening the enforcement mechanisms for protecting women's human rights. A number of more recent developments of the Committee on the Elimination of All Forms of Discrimination Against Women (CEDAW) are designed to enhance the effectiveness of the Women's Convention. What constitutes discrimination against women is not a point on which states readily agree. This observation is equally applicable to nation states and supranational bodies like the EU and UN. Nonetheless, the legal obligation to eliminate all forms of discrimination against women is a fundamental tenet of international human rights law. This Convention moves from a sex neutral norm that requires equal treatment, to one that recognizes the fact that the particular nature of discrimination against women is worthy of a legal response. The Women's Convention progresses beyond the earlier human rights conventions by addressing the pervasive and systemic nature of discrimination against women and identifies the need to confront the social causes of women's inequality by addressing 'all forms' of discrimination that women suffer. More recently, a historic agreement on preventing violence against women and girls was reached at the 57th Session of the UN Commission on the Status of Women which included the recognition that 'custom, tradition or religious consideration should play no part in denying women equal rights or justifying violence against them' (AHRC, 2013). We outline the significance of these developments in more detail in Chapter 7 when we consider the female victim.

Bringing rights home: Cleaning up our 'own back yards'

With human rights firmly established on the statute books since 1948, some important changes have taken place over the past 15 years that have forced the issue of human rights firmly back onto the national and international agenda. During this time, there has been a clear shift in the way in which we think about human rights and our ability to access them. In recent years there has been a clear attempt to acknowledge citizens' human rights at a national level. The Human Rights Act (HRA) 1998 came fully into force on 2 October 2000, enabling the European Convention on Human Rights (ECHR) to be relied on directly in our domestic courts. At the beginning of the twenty-first century the discourse of human rights is no longer the preserve of those suffering international abuses. Rather, the ability to claim one's human rights is now taking place at a national and domestic level. In other words, it is becoming increasingly acceptable to draw upon a human rights agenda to highlight issues within our own nation states. Not surprisingly, given the rampant and atrocious nature of some ongoing international human rights abuses throughout the world, there may be some commentators who question the need to engage with human rights on a domestic level. British citizens do after all enjoy all the benefits that come with living in a democratic state. Kallen (2004: xiv) makes a strong case for focusing on democratic states when she argues that 'If all human rights scholars shifted their attention away from democratic societies, what could well happen is that we neglect to "clean up our own back yards"'. She also makes the case that it is easier to understand human rights abuses when they occur in politically repressive regimes, but harder to explain violations of human rights in democratic societies whose laws are based on principles of human rights and equity for all citizens (2004: xiv).

Making sense of human rights then becomes much more about understanding how justice and equality are defined and enacted in society. In his sociological reading of human rights, Woodiwiss (2005: xiii) argues that they not only tell us about who is protected against what, but also the sort of people and the aspects of social relations that are especially valued (or not) by the governmental body.

If having access to one's human rights is about confirming our civilized condition then focusing on the human rights of *all* citizens is an important project, offenders included. The power of a human rights approach might lie in its capacity to provide redress for those experiencing **social exclusion** and who lack the power or necessary agency to change their disadvantaged status. The extent to which human rights legislation is capable of improving the lives of those who experience social exclusion – in this case of those who come into contact with the criminal justice system – remains to be seen, but the sales pitch that accompanied the Human Rights Act 1998 in the UK was impressive. Clements and Young (1999) described it as having the potential for being one of the most fundamental constitutional enactments since the Bill of Rights over 300 years ago. In December 1996, Jack Straw, the then Shadow Home Secretary, and Paul Boateng MP produced a consultation paper, *Bringing Rights Home* (Straw and Boateng, 1996), which set out the Labour Party's proposals to incorporate the Convention rights into United Kingdom law. The paper is infused with optimism, claiming that the Human Rights Act would 'nurture a culture of understanding of rights and responsibilities at all levels in our society' and 'result in a human rights culture developing across all countries'. In the opinion of the Joint Committee on Human Rights (2002), the government's case was that the Act would 'help to inaugurate a gradual transformation of civil society', create a 'more humane society' and would work to 'deepen and widen democracy by increasing the sense amongst individual men and women that they have a stake in the way in which they are governed'. Others have been even more ardent in their support. Helena Kennedy declared: 'something is happening: a different Zeitgeist, a shift in the legal tectonic plates' and Professor Wade stated that the Act was a 'quantum leap into a new legal culture' (cited in Costigan and Thomas, 2005: 51).

Alongside this sense of anticipation, there has also been much concern over the development of human rights in Britain. Chakrabarti (2005) notes that one of the greatest disappointments of the infancy of the Human Rights Act lies in the way in which its values have failed sufficiently to take root in wider society. Unlike the development of a Human Rights Commission in 1998 in Northern Ireland,[2] Britain's adoption of a rights agenda lacked the provision of a Commission to advise and assist alleged victims in bringing proceedings. Without such a Commission, Lester and Clapinska (2005) have argued that it has been difficult to raise awareness and to promote a culture of respect for human rights. That said, changes in equalities law with the creation of the Equality and Human Rights Commission (EHRC) in 2007 have firmly placed debates about equality and justice within a human rights framework. Set up as a non-departmental public body, EHRC replaced the existing Equal Opportunities Commission (EOC) as well as the Commission for Racial Equality (CRE) and the Disability Rights Commission (DRC) as well as taking on the role of a human rights commission for the UK where previously there had been none. Subsequently, the Equality Act 2010 has brought together all previous anti-discrimination legislation and added to legal protections against discrimination on the grounds of age, disability, gender reassignment, pregnancy and maternity, race, religion or belief, sex and sexual orientation. While such changes have served to build the equalities architecture within Britain, the election of a Conservative–Liberal Democrat Coalition government in 2010 and a Conservative government in 2015 with its oppositional views about the place of human rights within civil society, has further hindered the establishment of a rights-based culture. And this is where criminology enters the debate. For achieving one's human rights is inextricably bound up with achieving justice, an obvious and central concern for criminologists.

Human rights meet criminology

Despite an increased awareness among academics, Murphy and Whitty (2013) claim that very little is known about the role human rights have played within criminology over time. Before we join the chorus of appreciation in adopting a human rights approach to the study of gender, we are mindful of Carol Smart's (1989: 160) powerful critique and warning to feminists to avoid the 'silent call of the law', claiming that the feminist movement was 'too easily "seduced" by law and even when it is critical of law it too often attempts to use law pragmatically in the hope that new law or more law might be better

than old law'. For Smart, and other criminologists working within a poststructuralist, Foucauldian or Marxist perspective, human rights represent an
abstract and limited discursive practice. As Weber et al. (2014: 78) note:

> Scholars working from radical perspectives often advocate fundamental struc-
> tural change that goes beyond the enforcement of the minimum standards set
> out in human rights instruments, reject the abstraction and assertions of univer-
> salism of orthodox conceptions of human rights, and consider that existing
> human rights institutions are incapable of delivering on social justice goals in
> the face of state imperialism and growing corporate power.

Here, human rights are perceived to be 'rhetorical' and 'abstract' (Brown,
2002: 96) and as 'mere **ideology**' (Murphy and Whitty, 2013: 574). As a result,
any appeal to a human rights framework is presented as irredeemably inadequate. Grounded within critical protest criminology, Hogg (2002: 211) has
emphasized the limitations of formal human rights machinery, noting that
injustice can only be addressed 'through political solutions that are centrally
concerned with a redistribution of resources'.

Despite such critiques, we can locate a number of writers in these respective traditions that have gone on to readily incorporate the language of rights
into their work. In her influential book *Justice in the Risk Society*, Barbara
Hudson (2003) gives her qualified support to the concept of human rights,
suggesting that human rights can be reconciled with **postmodern** positions
as long as sweeping claims of universalisms are abandoned. In fact, she
asserts that critical criminologists have a moral obligation to incorporate
social justice and human rights into their theorizing and research methodologies (Hudson, 2003: 369). This stance is echoed by a number of commentators
who, while acknowledging the limitations of human rights, urge that a rights-
based approach be drawn upon to expand and drive forward wider objectives
of social justice and legitimacy (Brown, 2002; Scott, 2013; Scraton, 2002;
Welch, 2012).

Alongside this conditional acceptance, we can observe a growing appreciation of the importance of human rights to the study of criminology in recent
years. An emerging literature on the broad principles of human rights and the
specific legal obligations can be found in relation to policing (Bullock and
Johnson, 2012; Crawshaw et al., 2007; McGarry et al., 2012; Neyroud and
Beckley, 2001); courts and sentencing (Burnard, 2008; Naughton, 2005); probation (Canton, 2013; Hudson, 2001, 2003; Zinger, 2012); and prisons (Coyle,
2003; Liebling, 2011; Moore, 2011; Murphy and Whitty, 2007; Zinger, 2006).
And as crime and harm take on a more transnational and global dimension,
Weber et al. (2014: 82) point to an increased connection, suggesting that
'globalization is reinforcing the alignment between criminology and human
rights'. One of criminology's key proponents of human rights has been Stan
Cohen, who has argued that 'human rights are the last grand narrative' to be

explored within criminology (cited by Halliday, 2007). The centrality of human suffering has underpinned much of Cohen's contribution to the study of deviance and control. For an excellent review of his formidable body of work, see the collection of essays in honour of him by Downes et al. (2007). Through the concept of human suffering Cohen has attempted to offer a unified analytical framework for criminological inquiry.

So what can a human rights discourse offer the study of gender and crime? We argue that one of the key strengths of adopting a human rights framework in criminology is its ability to unify the experiences of vulnerable groups. In doing so, we hope to provoke greater discussion about the location and enactment of power. To emphasize that women, for example, whether they be victims, offenders or criminal justice professionals, can be unified in their experiences renders their **vulnerability** and lack of power visible in a male-dominated legal and criminal justice system. It may also serve to balance up the uneven landscape of criminological knowledge in which we have seen the female victim reign over her other criminologically interesting counterparts. Those women who work as social control agents, for example, remain relatively under-researched and under-explored within criminology. Given the level of power that these women have achieved, there are those who may argue that they are undeserving to be drawn together under the banner of 'powerlessness' in the same way as their victimized and offending counterparts are; for in many ways, it is these women who are part of the problem, part of the repressive regimes that women experience. But, to recap, our argument is a simple one – to unify women in this way serves to expose the unequal relations that exist between women and men and emphasize the gendered nature of the criminal justice system. We are ever conscious, however, that trying to unify groups in this way may strike many as a flawed if not somewhat regressive step, particularly when theorizing about gender. For women particularly, the idea of trying to unify through a singular identity of 'womanhood' can easily be described as risking and undoing much of the feminist work that has already been done. To propose recourse through a human rights discourse runs counter to the main direction of feminist thinking, which is moving away from such universalizing strategies. Similarly, to present men as a unitary and oppressive body is not always helpful. Some writers on masculinities are also keen on emphasizing the multiple manifestations of 'manhood'.

We are also keenly aware of the complex ways that race, gender and class intersect to affect the individual experience. And, given the progressive steps that have been made in the celebration of diversity, difference and the plurality of femininities and masculinities, such a route can easily be described as a dangerous and unwarranted direction for criminology to go in. We believe that embracing a human rights perspective offers us the opportunity to attain a degree of solidarity in an existing context of diversity and difference. Recapturing a common language may provide us with a vocabulary through which to sustain pressure on governments, agencies and citizens in working towards change. As Weber et al. (2014: 1) argue, human rights provide a set of standards by which the performance of governments can be measured. They provide a framework that allows us to talk and ask questions about the harms, benefits and limits of state actions and inactions.

How then can we begin to draw on these developments to improve women's and men's experiences of criminal justice as offenders, victims and criminal justice professionals?

The offender

The belief that individuals lose or forfeit their human rights when they commit crime is often expressed within popular discourse. This view of detainees more particularly as 'civilly dead' has become even more pronounced in a post 9/11 world and in the context of contemporary 'punitive political environments' (Naylor, 2013). This view is compatible with the emphasis placed on individual responsibility within contemporary neo-liberal governance, such that rights are commonly perceived as being 'earned' (Weber et al., 2014). At the outset, we remind readers of the doctrine of *inalienability* that asserts human rights as inherent to the human person (offenders and prisoners included) and therefore cannot be lost or taken away.

In claiming the authority to imprison one of its citizens, Mathiesen (2000) reminds us that the state is undertaking a responsibility for the prisoner's health, safety and physical well-being, which is qualitatively greater than that owed to free citizens. Questions thus arise concerning the scope of prisoners' rights and entitlements and of the mechanisms of legal accountability. And while prisoners may lose much when they enter prison, all persons deprived of their liberty continue to be protected by foundational human rights instruments that are universal and indivisible. Moreover, the UNHRC has made it clear that prisoners are to enjoy all of the rights set out in the International Covenant on Civil and Political Rights (see Weber et al., 2014 for a fuller account). We extend this state responsibility to include those suspects detained by the police.

In making our case, we also want to remind readers of the closed nature of the penal system, which in itself makes all those held in detention, be they women or men, particularly vulnerable to breaches of their human rights. Furthermore, prisoners often share backgrounds and characteristics that heighten their vulnerability. The Chief Inspector of Prisons, Anne Owers (2004: 110), expanded on this when reminding us it is the marginalized who most need the protection of human rights and most of those in our prisons were on the margins (i.e. illiteracy, mental disorder, substance and other abuse) long before they arrived and this may be even more so afterwards.

A more holistic understanding and appreciation of offenders' backgrounds prior to detention makes their vulnerability an obvious concern for criminologists. Factors such as mental health problems, educational difficulties, drug- and alcohol-related issues all pose serious concerns for those working with both female and male offenders. For those who are incarcerated, research has overwhelmingly revealed high levels of mental disorder and drug misuse, and general poor health among prisoners (Corston, 2007; Liebling, 1995; Prison Reform Trust, 2015). The prevalence of suicide and self-harm among young inmates and women more particularly is an ongoing and growing concern within our prisons (Hawton et al., 2014). It was specifically because of the special vulnerability of people in detention that the Northern Ireland Human Rights Commission decided to make the human rights of prisoners one of its strategic priorities. Its work highlighted an alarming number of breaches of human rights, particularly with regard to Articles 2 and 3 of the European Convention, i.e. the right to life (Article 2) and the right to freedom from torture and inhuman and degrading treatment (Article 3) (Scraton and Moore, 2004). Drawing on the accounts of women imprisoned (and tortured), Wahidin's (2016) work provides much evidence of the repressive role of the criminal justice system during the troubles in Northern Ireland.

As we have already argued, the closed nature of the penal system in itself makes those held in detention particularly vulnerable to breaches of their human rights. And, as the delivery of punishment increasingly moves to private hands, the need to be ever vigilant about what goes on behind closed doors becomes more pressing (Easton, 2013; Frawley and Naylor, 2014; Mason, 2012; Naylor, 2014, 2015). It is through the reframing of prisoners as people, with rights rather than privileges conditional upon good behaviour, that the human rights agenda may herald a challenge to custodial thinking, custom and practice.

The victim

We think our ability to convince readers of the usefulness of adopting a human rights approach when dealing with victims will be a less daunting task. Victims, unlike their offending counterparts, are at the outset conceived of as 'powerless' and as 'deserving' of attention. Over the past 30 years or so, the female victim in particular has slowly come to occupy centre stage in terms of visibility. One of the key issues on which this visibility has rested has been the victimization of women at the hands of men. This issue has variously informed feminist-inspired research agendas, analyses of criminal justice policy and practice, and feminist theorizing. Our knowledge of male victimization is also slowly gathering pace. Despite being 'deserving' of attention through their status as victims, there is still much to gain from incorporating a human rights framework when thinking about victims. For example, victimologists have for a long time drawn attention to the fact that victims do not enjoy formal rights like suspects and offenders and that the response to victims has been couched mainly in terms of needs and expectations. By conceptualizing victims' experiences of violence through a human rights lens, the issue of **state accountability** is forced firmly onto the agenda. With regard to women, work in this area is already well underway on an international stage. Leading the feminist critique against mainstream human rights discourse for its gender blindness, rights activists have made notable progress on several fronts, including critiquing the distinction between the public/private divide with respect to women's legal rights. In so doing they have held governments accountable for failing to protect women from domestic violence; led governments to condemn sexual violence against women in armed conflict; and forced governments to treat trafficking as a human rights crisis (Cain and Howe, 2008; Cook, 1994; Coomaraswamy, 1999; Coomaraswamy and Kois, 1999; UNICEF, 2014, 2015).

Situating the issue of violence against a backdrop of human rights violations and an international human rights agenda has also resulted in the development of a global appreciation of women's victimization, allowing differently positioned groups to unite across national boundaries. Such an appreciation enables us to venture into **comparative criminology** in a much more sophisticated way, exposing 'new' criminological problems. This is especially important given the increased opportunities for violence against women and girls brought about by the processes of globalization (Cain and Howe, 2008; Pickering and Lambert, 2004; Segrave et al., 2009).

The criminal justice professional

For those who work in the criminal justice system, we argue our position from a point of social justice. It remains undemocratic to have a criminal justice system that is dominated by men, both in numerical terms and in relation to values. We believe that a modern, democratic society requires a diverse workforce in all areas of life. It is a long time since the implementation of the Equal Pay Act 1970 and Sex Discrimination Act 1975 outlawed discrimination in the workplace on the grounds of sex. Research continues to show that, although theoretically integrated, women still experience social closure when working in criminal justice organizations (Dick et al., 2013; Kenney, 2013; Martin and Jurik, 2007; Silvestri, 2015). They are subject to a broad range of discriminatory cultures and practices which can be seen in a number of areas, including: pay differentials; under-representation in senior positions; ghettoization in certain areas or professions; sexual issues around maternity leave and pay; and inflexible work arrangements for those with caring responsibilities. Individuals who work within the broad range of criminal justice agencies operate within gendered environments in which organizational logics are imbued with notions of heterosexist masculinity. This has serious implications not only for those women (and some men) who exercise power, but also for those service users at the receiving end of criminal justice, either as offenders or victims. We are not suggesting that women are necessarily more competent in carrying out the functions of administering justice (although there are some studies that indicate women's transformative potential here); rather, we believe that a criminal justice machinery drawn from a more diverse background will improve its overall quality by bringing a broader range of views and experiences to criminal justice and to the culture which underpins it.

Concluding thoughts

The theorization of gender and crime has undergone significant transformation since the publication of Heidensohn's (1968) paper and there have been some ground-breaking achievements in the field and an increased awareness of the gendered nature of offending, victimization and social control. The field has also confirmed the need to acknowledge different and at times conflicting feminist criminologies (Gelsthorpe and Morris, 1990; Heidensohn and Gelsthorpe, 2007). Despite the ongoing tensions, contradictions and challenges emphasized within the field, Moore (2008: 58) has argued that in its current state, feminist criminology remains a 'fertile intellectual ground'. Firmly embedded within the discipline and beyond, the study of gender within criminology has become a permanent fixture and one with global reach. As we progress through the book, we hope that readers will find this chapter a useful starting point to refer back to when thinking about the nature and extent of change within the field. We also anticipate its usefulness as a source for identifying considerable continuities in contemporary concerns about gender and crime.

In thinking about the future directions, we have made a case for adopting a human rights lens. We think this even more pressing given the contemporary challenges brought about by the processes of globalization. Such processes have brought with them unimagined landscapes, requiring us to adopt 'well founded knowledge and sophisticated understandings of gender issues' (Connell, 2009: 52) and 'new and powerful ways to continue paying attention to the powerful and the oppressors' (Chesney-Lind and Morash, 2013: 295). As feminist criminology enters this new era, so too, it must embrace the challenges ahead. Before we embark on our analysis of twenty-first-century offenders, victims and professionals, we take readers further back in time to map out our knowledge of gender, crime, victimization and social control over time. In so doing, we provide a more critical reading of the present.

Summary

- This chapter explored the emergence of feminist perspectives within criminology from the late 1960s and early 1970s. The concern of early pioneering feminist criminologists began with making visible and correcting the distorted construc-tions of the female offender; we then see a considerable shift in making visible the female victim with a focus on exposing the hidden nature of violence(s) against women; and lastly, an appreciation of the gendered nature and experiences of women working within the criminal justice system.
- We have also emphasized the considerable tensions, conflicts, limitations and chal-lenges that lie within feminist criminology. Feminist criminologists have been criticized for failing to acknowledge the often unintended and ruinous consequences of their own investigations and theorizations of women – sometimes leading to increased control and repression of women. Feminist criminology has also been critiqued for its failure to acknowledge the intersectionalities that exist between women.
- Despite such critiques, we argue that the theorization of gender within criminology has undergone significant transformations since the 1960s – feminist criminology has matured over time and there have been some ground-breaking achievements in the field, with an increased awareness of the gendered nature of offending, victimization and social control over the past 50 years.
- In mapping out new directions for feminist criminology, we argue that the adop-tion of a human rights lens to the study of gender and crime is a constructive way forward in making sense of the experiences of vulnerable groups; it also offers us opportunities to link the 'local' to the 'global' and increases the opportunity to hold the state more accountable in ensuring fairness, justice and equality.

STUDY QUESTIONS

1. How and in what ways is Heidensohn's (1968) paper 'The deviance of women: A critique and enquiry' significant to the development of feminist criminology?

2. Outline the contributions made by early pioneering feminist scholars in criminology.

3. Why did early feminist scholars set about a project of feminist empiricism and what were the limitations of such a venture?

4. In what ways did theorizations of women's offending lag behind that of men?

5. Feminist criminology has been subject to much critique – outline the key arguments.

6. Discuss the idea that feminist criminology(ists) remain on the margins of the inquiry within the academe.

7. Outline the development and growing importance of human rights in the UK.

8. How might a human rights approach be useful to the study of crime, victimization and social control?

FURTHER READING

All readers interested in the study of gender and crime should begin by reading F. Heidensohn (1968) 'The deviance of women: A critique and an enquiry' (*British Journal of Sociology*, 19: 160–75), followed by a review by J. Miller, (2010) 'Commentary on Frances Heidensohn's "The deviance of women"' (*British Journal of Sociology*, 61: 133–39).

For general reviews of the emergence of feminist criminology and the study of women and criminal justice, see R. Barberet (2014) *Women, Crime and Criminal Justice: A Global Enquiry* (Routledge); K. Carrington and R. Hogg (eds) (2002) *Critical Criminology: Issues, Debates, Challenges* (Willan); C. Renzetti (2013) *Feminist Criminology* (Routledge); and an extensive range of chapters in R. Gartner and B. McCarthy (eds) (2014) *The Oxford Handbook of Gender, Sex and Crime* (Oxford University Press).

For critical insights into feminist criminology, read D. Moore (2008) 'Feminist criminology: Gain, loss and backlash' (*Sociology Compass*, 2(1): 48–61) and L. Snider (2003) 'Constituting the punishable woman: Atavistic man incarcerates postmodern woman' (*British Journal of Criminology*, 43(2): 354–78).

For an insight into the growing importance of human rights to the study of criminology, see S. Cohen (2001) *States of Denial: Knowing about Atrocities and Suffering* (Polity Press) and L. Weber, E. Fishwick and M. Marmo (eds) (2014) *Crime, Justice and Human Rights* (Palgrave Macmillan).

Notes

1. Feminism is characterized by three 'waves' or historical movements. The first wave refers to the late nineteenth and early twentieth centuries and is most notably marked by women's suffrage or securing the right to vote (among other legislative changes designed to promote women's formal equality). The second wave is located in the 1960s and 1970s and is generally framed by women's bids for formal

and substantive equality. Feminism entered a third wave in the mid-1990s – a diverse movement informed by postcolonial and postmodern thinking in which many constructs have been destabilized, including the notions of universal womanhood, body, gender, sexuality and heteronormativity.

2. The Northern Ireland Human Rights Commission was set up as a result of the Belfast (Good Friday) Agreement in April 1998. It is a strictly non-party political body which strives to promote and protect the rights of all people in Northern Ireland.

3

Gender, Crime and History

OVERVIEW

Chapter 3 provides:

- A historical review of gender, crime and victimization, emphasizing both continuities and change over time.
- An outline of the enduring and persistent cultural myths about deviant/offending women.
- An outline of the societal anxiety about the criminality and deviancy of girls.
- An insight into the construction of 'respectable' and 'unrespectable' masculinities.
- An overview of the gendered nature of victimization over time.

KEY TERMS

- civilization and criminalization of men
- dangerous bodies
- gender gap
- historical review
- rescue and regulation
- wayward girls

Introduction

The study of criminology has been reinvigorated, renewed and enriched by the study of history and the presence of historians in the field. The engagement of historians, historical criminologists and feminist historians of crime has contributed significantly to the increased number of publications, dedicated history panels and conferences in the past decade. Moreover, the recently established interdisciplinary research network *Our Criminal Past: Caring for the Future,* with participants from a variety of backgrounds, including experts in the disciplines of history, criminology, education and law, is indicative of an increased appetite to develop a more interdisciplinary and complex reading of the past. Taking the late 1960s as its starting point, the preceding chapter outlined the emergence and conceptual impact of feminist criminology within the academe. In this chapter, we take readers further back to map out our knowledge of gender, crime, victimization and social control over time. The selection of a specific time frame for analysis is often a key starting point for those adopting a historical approach. In their analysis of women, crime and justice in England, D'Cruze and Jackson (2009) take 1660 as their starting point. For them, this date signifies the growth of the modern nation state and the emergence of key regulatory mechanisms and institutions that we recognize today. Walker (2003) takes the early modern period 1500–1800 as her focus of investigation, while Cox's (2003) analysis of *Bad Girls in Britain* provides a snapshot of 50 years from 1900 to 1950. We declare at the outset that we are not historians, and as such, we are aware of the resulting limitations and gaps that may follow in our analysis. In our endeavour to make sense of the present, we have not selected a specific time frame to explore, nor have we adopted a chronological approach. Rather, we have reviewed the literature on gender and crime and have opted to draw out as much as we can from the historical evidence that we feel resonates with contemporary debates within criminology about gender and crime. This does not mean that we have selectively chosen works to 'fit' our arguments, simply that we have focused on issues that enable us to illustrate both the considerable changes and continuities that have shaped our understandings thus far. For more comprehensive and in-depth historical accounts, we encourage readers to consult our list of further reading at the end of the chapter.

Given our focus on the offender and victim in this chapter, we have opted to reserve historical reflection on the gendered nature of the criminal justice workforce for Chapters 9 and 10. We draw upon historical work in those chapters to develop our analysis of the gendered nature of criminal justice work – we argue that contemporary debates about women and criminal justice work have much resonance with earlier debates. Drawing on a historical perspective in those chapters also enables us to better assess the extent and nature of change over time.

Our intentions in this chapter, in many ways, mirror those of early pioneering feminist criminologists. We too, through historical reflection, are looking to make women visible and in the same vein as these pioneers, we give greater attention to documenting women's transgressions and deviancy. While historians have considered the gendered dimensions of victimization and the position of men over time, their focus has predominantly been on women as offenders.

Guided by this, we begin by addressing debates about the 'gender gap' in offending behaviour and go on to map out the extent, location and nature of women's participation in criminal activity over time. Here, we give prominence to tracking and questioning five persistent cultural myths that have shaped the female offender over time. Firstly, that she is *not violent*; secondly, that she is more likely to be *mad than bad*; thirdly, that she is a *liar and deceiver*; fourthly, that through her sexuality she is both *dangerous and risky*; and lastly, that she is in need of both *care and control*. We argue that such characterizations are not expressed in chronological terms but, rather, that they co-exist simultaneously – emerging, receding and re-emerging over time.

In drawing out further connections with the past, we stress the importance of historical work in making sense of the contemporary obsession with identifying a rise in criminality among young women. More particularly, we point to the enduring societal anxiety about the criminality and deviancy of girls and their transgression of the legal, social and moral order. Though we place a greater emphasis on women's offending in this chapter, we do acknowledge the association of men and violence throughout the ages. Underpinned heavily by notions of class and power, we locate the broader societal and changing narratives of acceptable behaviour for men. In doing so, we chart the construction of 'respectable' and 'unrespectable' masculinities and with it, the attendant civilization and **criminalization** of (some) men. In the final part of the chapter, we shed light on the study of women's victimization over time. By utilizing a historical lens, we track the normalcy and everyday nature of violence against women. We emphasize the striking continuities with the present with regard to victim blaming and to the lack of prosecution and **conviction** of defendants accused of **rape** and interpersonal partner violence.

We begin with a brief note on the use of historical sources, and of the opportunities and challenges faced by those looking to adopt such approaches.

A note on historical sources

Given the variety of data sets available and the opportunities to conduct primary research by contemporary scholars, it is all too easy to overlook the complexity of accessing data for historians. Partly to do with the absence of inquiry about gender in the study of criminology, together with a lack of available evidence and consistency in historical sources, D'Cruze and Jackson (2009: 1) have noted that the 'the process of "counting" is riddled with difficulties'. Rather ironically, the smaller number of trials preceding the twentieth century has meant that the archives of the twentieth century are less well studied than earlier periods (Godfrey, 2014). The collation of criminal justice statistics from the early nineteenth century has necessarily meant that historians have been forced to draw upon a wide range of source types to develop their analyses, including literary fiction, film, newspaper and pamphlets. Though problematic in nature, such unofficial sources nonetheless provide terrifically rich insights into gendered ideals, behaviour and regulation over time.

The task of documenting long-term trends in criminality is further complicated by definitional issues. Smith (2014: 140) draws attention to the incompatibility of legal definitions over time, noting that 'crime is historically contingent, [and] what was deemed criminal activity in 1400 may have disappeared from the law books by the eighteenth century'. The disappearance of scolding and witchcraft (both specific crimes to women) from legal codes, for example, was to result in a decline in women's offending rate. The incompatibility of definitions also has important consequences over place, making it highly problematic for researchers looking to make cross-national comparisons (von Hoffer, 2011). The importance of definitional issues has been further emphasized by Conley (2014: 207) in her historical work on rape and victimization, where she notes that 'issues of gender, **patriarchy**, race and sin and respectability' have all influenced definitions of rape.

Further problems can be located in the possible distortions that arise from the general exclusion of women from official records. Studies by Walker (2003), Kilday (2007) and Stevens (2012) point to the principle of the *femme covert*, whereby women were less likely to be charged with or convicted of crimes they committed with their husbands because of their legal subordination to men. Walker (2003) further emphasizes the possible impacts of economic factors underpinning court decisions, suggesting that given the considerable expense involved in charging several people, courts would only charge the male head of the household – in this way, women may be indirectly excluded from appearing within official records of crime.

The tendency of crime historians to focus on serious violent crime also poses considerable limitations to the inclusion of women in their analyses. From contemporary studies on women and crime, we know that women are most likely to be located in minor, less serious **offence** categories, such as acquisitive crimes. It follows, then, that historical analyses may risk overlooking a significant indicator of female criminality (Hurl-Eammon, 2005; Stretton, 1998; Walker, 2003). As Amussen (1994: 75) has argued, 'since women in early modern society rarely carried weapons that caused death, their brawls, though frequent, were rarely recorded'.

In accepting the possible limitations of historical research outlined above, we provide readers with an insight into the importance of historical perspectives for the study of gender and crime.

Exploring the gender gap over time

Chapter 2 highlighted the importance and emphasis placed on documenting the 'gender gap' in criminal activity by early feminist scholars in the late 1960s and throughout subsequent decades. Culminating in a rich body of research, this work maintains that despite women's participation in criminality across a range of offending categories, crime remains an overwhelmingly male activity. Exploring the 'gender gap' in female and male offending has also been a preoccupation of historians working in the field, and here too, the consensus among historians is one in which men and boys dominate in criminal activity. Where opinion is divided rests on the substantial disagreement among scholars on whether and how women's and men's relative and absolute involvement in overall crime changed over the centuries. This difference rests on two key positions: those that propose 'continuity' in women's participation and those that purport a 'decline' in women's participation (also known as the **'vanishing female' thesis**).

The continuity thesis has been emphasized by Heidensohn (1989: 87), who has argued that the ratio of male to female offenders has been relatively stable in nearly all jurisdictions, revealing a 'stubbornly stable' gender gap over time. In contrast to this, Feeley and Little (1991) have advanced the idea that women virtually 'vanished' from criminal records in Britain over the period 1687–1912. Their analysis of a sample of trials at London's Old Bailey court indicates a significant decline from roughly 45 per cent to 12 per cent in the proportion of prosecutions of female defendants, presenting this as evidence of a real decline in the criminality of women and a widening of the gender gap in crime. Since that claim was made, commentators have identified regional variations and methodological issues that challenge this idea of the 'vanishing female' criminal (D'Cruze and Jackson, 2009; Heidensohn and Silvestri, 2012; King, 2006; Zedner, 1991). Zedner (1991: 20), for example, notes that over the period 1860–90 there was a decline in those designated as the 'criminal classes', and the number of women fell at roughly the same rate as men, remaining at around a fifth of the total figures.

She concludes that this relatively low rate was due to the exclusion of prostitutes and vagrants. In terms of convictions, Zedner notes that 'overall, women's crimes made up a steady 17 per cent of all summary convictions' (1991: 34), with drunkenness, assault and larceny the commonest types of offence. Zedner's detailed work on nineteenth-century data confirms on the whole the 'modest share' view of female crime as compared with male. King (2006) also shows significant fluctuations in recorded female criminality over time. Examining a broader range of court records and looking at shorter but still substantial periods within Feeley and Little's (1991) survey, King (2006) argues that rather than vanishing, the proportion of female offenders tried for less serious offences outside London between 1750 and 1850 either remained fairly constant or actually increased in some periods. Historical studies of women and crime have further emphasized the importance of going beyond the traditional boundaries of the criminal justice system, with women's deviancy over time located in a range of sites, including the home and family, the workplace in domestic servitude and, from the eighteenth century onwards, in semi-penal institutions such as lock hospitals, Magdalen asylums, psychiatric hospitals, rescue homes and inebriates' reformatories (D'Cruze and Jackson, 2009: 1–2). So, far from disappearing, the female offender can be found in a range of alternative spaces. In what follows, we track her presence in such spaces and give greater context to the way in which she has been characterized.

Women offenders as non-violent

Chapter 4 draws out the contemporary concern over a rise in the use of violence by women and girls, positing their participation in violence as something 'new' and at odds with the past. Characterized for the most part through a lens of conformity, the capacity of women to be involved in violence has often been minimized, trivialized or recast as something rooted in biology and/or psychology and therefore beyond their control or intention. We challenge such a reading through providing ample historical evidence of women's engagement with a range of violent behaviours, including homicide, infanticide, highway robbery, gang activities and violent political protest.

Historical accounts of patterns of violent crime stretching back to the medieval period in England, and other parts of Europe, have tended to rely on homicide prosecutions (Smith, 2014). Based on comprehensive reviews of multiple European jurisdictions, studies have concluded that while men are responsible for the majority of such crime, committing 85–95 per cent of homicide and other serious violence over the past seven centuries, women are present (Beattie, 2001; Eisner, 2003; Gurr, 1981; Smith, 2014). Eisner's (2003) study suggests women's representation (excluding infanticide) as ranging between 5 and 12 per cent. More localized studies both confirm these general patterns and reveal important temporal variations in the sex distribution. Kilday's (2007) analysis of late eighteenth-century and early nineteenth-century Scotland, for example, reveals that 21 per cent of homicide charges were brought against women and Conley (2007) found that between 20 and 25 per cent of those tried for murder in the late nineteenth century were women. The extent to which such studies provide an authentic account of women's increased presence in homicide rates requires some caution. Smith (2014) acknowledges the possible impacts brought about by an unbalanced population when he notes that, during times of war, the proportion of homicide by women could rise simply because females made up a greater proportion of the population when large numbers of men left their homes to fight. Whether or not such external environments provide a more accurate context within which to make sense of the increased number of women charged with homicide, there is no doubt of women's very real presence in homicide over time.

The one crime of lethal violence for which women are consistently over-represented as offenders is infanticide. In an attempt to curb premarital sexuality and pregnancy in early modern England, a statute made concealing the birth of a child by the mother a capital offence. The result was an increase in the number of females charged with the offence (Smith, 2014). That said, the eighteenth century was to see a pattern of considerable decline in indictments for infanticide. We argue below that much of women's criminal activity has often been recast as evidence of considerable psychological impairment rather than actual intent. Nowhere is this more resonant than in the study of women as perpetrators of infanticide. Shaped by a 'culture of sensibility' where the explanation of a defendant's troubled emotional or mental state began to outweigh physical, bodily evidence in the courtroom, women's agency in the act of infanticide has slowly diminished over time. Believed to strike certain women around the moment of childbirth, this perceived maternal mental instability, defined as **puerperal insanity**, was to emerge as a key feature of nineteenth-century Victorian medical discourse to explain women's actions (Kilday, 2013; Scott, 2014).

Attempting to capture a larger set of possible crimes, Hurl-Eammon's (2005: 127) study goes beyond traditional court reports by scrutinizing the records of recognizances for petty violence. She concludes that early modern femininity appears 'surprisingly assertive and aggressive ... [with] accounts making it clear that both sexes were inclined to deploy violence in early modern London'. While Davies' (1999, 2008, 2014) work on nineteenth-century gangs has suggested a focus on violent male youth, his sample of Manchester cases between 1870 and 1900 indicate that girls in 'scuttling gangs' were present, constituting 6.3 per cent of those charged with gang-related crime – female 'scuttlers' tended to fight with clogs and boots rather than with knives and belts favoured by male gang members.

D'Cruze and Jackson (2009) also offer considerable accounts of women's participation in violent crime, particularly through their involvement in highway robbery and piracy. Designated as 'male' crimes, the highwayman and the pirate assumed a highly masculine cultural identity. Exploring a series of Old Bailey Sessions Papers, they document that women formed around 10 per cent of those tried for highway robbery[1] between the late seventeenth century and early nineteenth century. They also point to data by Stanley (1995) to emphasize women's successful role as pirates in the golden age of West Atlantic piracy between 1710 and 1729. Drawing on case studies of two notorious female pirates, Anne Bonny and Mary Read, D'Cruze and Jackson (2009: 56) describe them as clear examples of women with a 'capacity and capability for violence' and for whom piracy had offered and enabled a 'successful criminal career'. As such, they argue such women '"*did*" violence in masculine ways, rather than the kinds of criminalized violence more closely associated with femininity and its debilities and disorders'.

Often absent from traditional criminological accounts of women's criminality, there is further evidence to indicate women's participation in social protest and violence over the past 300 years. Evidence of women's active and leading roles in early modern subsistence protests and labour disputes in the nineteenth century are indicative of women's willingness to participate in political action (Bohstedt, 1992; Custer, 2007; Robertson, 1997). Women's increased participation in political activism was to result in significant and repressive state responses. The high visibility of and participation of women at the Peterloo Massacre in 1819, for example, saw a markedly higher proportion of women singled out for criminal charges as well as subject to greater injury by the military and the police, leading Bush (2004) to conclude that overall 'the retribution exacted by the police and the military fell more heavily upon women than on men'. Women's ongoing participation in the suffrage movement in the late nineteenth century and early twentieth century also requires some mention here. With over a thousand suffragettes serving prison sentences over the course of the militant campaign and much commentary about their violent behaviour explained in reaction to their imprisonment and force-feeding, D'Cruze and Jackson (2009) remind us that their actions *could* and *should* be recognized for their capacity, ability and willingness to engage with violence to achieve their political ends.

Mad not bad

Perhaps one of the strongest parallels over time has been women's participation in non-violent, low-level offending criminality. Historical commentary has confirmed a large proportion of women's criminal activity in this sphere across a range of offence types, including: shoplifting; pickpocketing; passing counterfeit money; workplace theft and appropriation; burglary; housebreaking; and the stealing of livestock (Beattie, 1975; D'Cruz and Jackson, 2009; Durston, 2007; Johnson, 1995; Morgan and Rushton, 1998; Palk, 2006; Walker, 2003; Zedner, 1991). Indeed at times, male offenders have been outnumbered by their female counterparts in certain categories of property or economic crimes (Beattie, 2001; Eisner, 2003). Women's participation in shoplifting more particularly provides us with an excellent opportunity from which to appreciate the power and enduring characterization of women offenders as 'mad not bad'. The appeal of exploring shoplifting also lies in its capacity to figure strongly as a gender-related offence across time and well into the twentieth century. Judicial statistics show female convictions for larceny from shops and stalls equalling and overtaking male convictions – 46 per cent in 1950, 48 per cent in 1960, and 54 per cent in 1970 (Smart, 1977).

While poverty and economic hardship have often been cited as an incentive for women's shoplifting (Carlen, 1988a; Carlen and Worrall, 1987), the first half of the nineteenth century saw an altogether alternative explanation for women's participation in shoplifting and theft – one that was grounded in issues of mental instability. The early nineteenth century saw the emergence of the middle-class 'shoplifter' (white-lace-collar crime). Though small in number, the involvement of such 'genteel' and 'respectable' women, for whom economic hardship was not a motivation, caused much popular anxiety and debate about women in the public sphere (O'Brien, 1983; Whitlock, 2005). Whitlock (2005) documents the case of Miss Lydia Dixon arrested in April 1849 for shoplifting a number of items from a London draper's shop. A music teacher and solicitor's daughter, the court claimed that she was suffering from 'brain fever' and was imprisoned for one month. By the end of the century, such characterizations of women involved in shoplifting were commonplace and the 'distinctive, irresolvable tendency to steal', more formally defined through a medical diagnosis of **kleptomania**, was to become routinely drawn upon to explain women's shoplifting. Described as a 'female malady', kleptomania was defined as a 'product of women's biological propensity to mania and hysteria, which was sexually charged' (D'Cruze and Jackson, 2009: 39). In denying women's agency in such acts, Whitlock (2005: 39) has argued that the kleptomania diagnosis served as an 'effective solution to the paradox of the lady thief'. It was during the nineteenth century that middle-class identity became strongly constructed around gendered notions of virtue and purity, and as such, acts of theft and dishonesty were clearly out of keeping with idealized notions of womanhood. Alongside this construction of 'virtuousness', women were increasingly positioned as passive innocents, requiring the protection of chivalrous males. Indeed women's victimhood and suffering had become campaign issues from both evangelicals and feminists by the 1880s (D'Cruze and Jackson, 2009).

With scholars keen to locate women's possible agency in their participation in shoplifting, more recent studies of the history of theft have located such crimes within cultures of production and consumption (Mansvelt, 2005; Zweiniger-Barielowska, 2014). Such an approach has done much to shift and reposition accounts within a context of changing economic structures together with a greater appreciation of the arrival of a new form of consumerism. Across the seventeenth and eighteenth centuries, McKendrick et al. (1982) argue that availability and desire led to the wider circulation of goods through more licit circuits of exchange. Following mass industrialization, cheap mass-produced goods, particularly clothing and accessories, were being made available to the mass population within new public spaces, including shopping emporiums and department stores. As a result D'Cruze and Jackson (2009: 31) argue that 'new consumerism – and the spaces it created – provided a crucial context for acts of theft'.

Women as liars/deceivers

Alongside the characterization of women offenders as 'mad', there is a strong narrative that co-exists of them as liars and deceivers. Otto Pollack's (1950) study on *The Criminality of Women* and his claim that women's crime was vastly underestimated, has underpinned much of the mid to late twentieth-century discourse on women offenders. For Pollack, women were inherently deceitful and cunning and were therefore able to conceal their crimes. As evidence he points to the large **dark figure** of crime in abortion, theft and prostitution. Exploiting their status as helpless victims, Pollack suggests that women are aided by men's besotted chivalry and so are able to 'mask' and conceal their crimes. Taking a longer historical overview, there is considerable evidence of the ways in which femininity has been stereotyped in terms of fraudulence and deception. The trickery of women can be located in the crimes of witchcraft attributed to women in sixteenth- and seventeenth-century Europe (Barry and Davies, 2007; Gaskill, 2007; Jones, 2006; Oldridge, 2002; Osterberg, 1996; Sharpe, 1999). The witchcraft trials that took place in England and Wales saw formal accusations against women, who were usually poor and elderly, reach its peak in the late sixteenth century, particularly in south-east England, where 513 witches were put on trial and 112 were executed between 1560 and 1700. The last known execution took place in Devon in 1685 and the last trials were held in Leicester in 1717 (Smith, 2014: 148).

Subsequent studies of women's deception can be found in narratives of female thieves throughout the centuries. The importance of 'clothing' has been central to explanations of women's particular mode of duplicity. Up until the seventeenth century, sumptuary laws had restricted the wearing of luxury fabrics to elite groups within the social order. As a result, such regulation had helped to maintain clear boundaries and indicators of rank within society and between women more particularly. With the repeal of the law in 1604, the capacity to distinguish between societal hierarchies had become more difficult (Dabhoiwala, 1996) and it was within this sphere that women's duplicities flourished. Here we can find accounts of the seventeenth-century 'counterfeit ladies' who used gentility as a cover to defraud (Todd and Spearing, 1993). At the same time, we can locate popular narratives of female thieves and rogues where fictionalized depictions of women came to reflect such a reality. Daniel Defoe's (1922) depiction of *Moll Flanders*, the most famous female thief in English literature, for example, not only passes herself off as a woman of fortune to contract a bigamous marriage, but also uses dress as a pickpocketing trick to escape suspicion. A recurring panic about women's deception can be located in the 1920s, where concern about the female fraudster began to resurface once again; this time, anxiety was located in the context of uncertainty about gender relations that followed World War I. D'Cruze and Jackson (2009: 42) detail the concerns of the popular press on the rise of 'idle gold-diggers' and 'flappers "on the make"' as a consequence of the 'shortage of marrying manhood caused by the war'. They go on to explain such anxiety as evidence of a **feminist backlash** that followed the war and the women's suffrage movement more broadly. They cite the former Scotland Yard detective Cecil Bishop in his condemnation of women's skills of trickery and deception as a result of the 'equality' fought for by 'misguided extremists'. Writing in 1931, he blamed women entirely for an apparent hike in criminal statistics, claiming that 'many efficient gangs, both in London and the Provinces, are led by women, who exploit their sex to maintain control of the men they have gathered around them' (cited in D'Cruze and Jackson, 2009: 45–46).

Dangerous and risky bodies

An obsession with women's sexuality through a focus on their bodies as 'dangerous' and 'risky' is another discernible narrative about deviant women over time. Women's involvement in prostitution provides us with an important site from which to explore such constructions. Perhaps one of the most obvious parallels between the present and the past is the complexity and confusion regarding the law in relation to prostitution – see McCarthy et al. (2015) for an excellent review and debate of the law and interventions over time. Though technically prostitution has never been against the law, women have been disproportionally charged with prostitution and related charges throughout the centuries (Allen, 1990; Casburn, 2010; Laite, 2011, 2013; Rivera-Garza, 2001). Simultaneously vilified, repressed, rescued and celebrated over time, the female prostitute has been subject to both 'offender' and 'victim' labels. Though there is disagreement among historians about the shifting perceptions over women's sexuality, there is some consensus that suggest that the early modern period (1500–1800) saw female sexuality more often understood as *dangerous* because it was 'active and even predatory'. By the mid-Victorian period, while this remained true of lower-class women, the dominant model of 'respectable' female sexuality was to be enshrined as one of passivity and submission (D'Cruze and Jackson, 2009: 65).

In direct contrast to such virtuous qualities, women engaged in prostitution were deemed to be 'unrespectable', albeit inevitable and distasteful elements of the social order (Henderson, 1999; Mazo Karras, 1996; McCarthy et al., 2015). At the same time, we can observe a growth of the 'seduction narrative', which matched a predatory male with an increasingly subservient female response (Hitchcock, 2005). In this way, the 'unrespectable' woman was simultaneously cast as both *deviant* and *victim* and, as such, in need of both *regulation* and *rescue*. Such contrasting positions of women involved in prostitution have endured well into the twenty-first century and she continues to remain at the forefront of contemporary debates about women, crime and victimization – we pursue this further in Chapters 5 and 6.

Risky and in need of regulation

The story of prostitution is also indicative of a broader narrative on the changing disciplinary regimes that women and girls have been subjected to over time. By the mid-nineteenth century, the idea of the 'fallen woman' and the 'wayward girl' as in need of rescue through moral reform was quite forcibly replaced with a more punitive approach aimed at eradicating the dangers that she posed to wider public health (Mort, 2000). In her work on *Prostitution and Victorian Society*, Walkowitz (1980) has emphasized the centrality of the young female prostitute as a symbolic figure in the construction of the city as a risky space, awash with moral and health dangers. The growing codification of criminal law from the early nineteenth century and the development of modern policing in the form of the Metropolitan Police by Sir Robert Peel in 1829 produced greater powers to control prostitutes alongside other 'vagrants' under The Vagrancy Act 1822. As the century progressed, there is an observable growing punitiveness in relation to the regulation of prostitution and in the identification of women's bodies as sites of danger. Fisher (1997) outlines the stringent regulation of prostitutes on public health grounds following the dismal sexual health of the armed forces sent to fight the Crimean war. Parliament reacted swiftly and passed the Contagious Disease Act 1864; two later Acts in 1866 and 1869 went on to extend the geographical range beyond military towns. The Act enabled an 'arbitrary' curtailment of the civil rights of working-class women, who could be arrested on simple suspicion and forcibly detained without having been found directly guilty of any criminal offence. It also empowered local police to arrest any woman *thought* to be a prostitute and submit her to a compulsory internal medical examination. By the end of the nineteenth century, such punitive interventions had attracted much organized public criticism and by 1883 there was a suspension of the working of the Acts (Walkowitz, 1980).

Feeblemindedness and in need of rescue

From here on in, we see a further shift in the narrative on prostitution through a reconceptualization of the prostitute as a woman suffering from 'feeblemindedness' and without agency. In the same way that the female perpetrator of infanticide and the middle-class shoplifter were reconstructed, so too we can observe the erasure of women's agency in her participation in sexual deviancy – acting without reason or autonomy. D'Cruze and Jackson (2009: 75) suggest that 'feeblemindedness' became a plausible explanation of prostitution to those who policed it. With an increased tendency to be marginalized through such characterizations, women engaged in prostitution were increasingly likely to be detained in an array of semi-penal institutions that had emerged over the centuries (Bartley, 2000; Zedner, 1991). The first was the Magdalen Hospital in Whitechapel in London in 1758 and a number of others were founded in the nineteenth century. By 1885, the Church of England ran over 50 penitentiaries and numerous other organizations from the Salvation Army to the Jewish Ladies Association operated such establishments in that decade. Aimed at the penitent prostitute, the intention here was to redeem 'fallen' women through 'religious instruction and moral uplift' (D'Cruze and Jackson, 2009: 74).

The problem of girls

While the recurring problem of male youth has been a central feature of general concern over the ages (Pearson, 1983), the increasing involvement of girls in deviancy has been the focus of a number of moral panics over time. More particularly, the working-class deviant girl has been consistently stereotyped across the modern period as sexually predatory and dangerous. Shore (1994) identifies concern over the decades with the 'flash girl' in the 1830s, the 'vicious girl'/'minx' in the 1880s and the 'good time girl' in the 1940s. By the first half of the twentieth century, the sexualized figure of the predatory adolescent girl had become a central figure of moral panic, seen to constitute a threat to national strength, particularly with regard to worries about the spread of venereal disease and illegitimate pregnancy. Both World War I and II saw increased anxiety related to the high number of young women drawn to military bases with the intent of seducing soldiers in exchange for drinks and entertainment.

The association with transgressive sexuality has meant that there has been a tendency to police girls through welfare mechanisms rather than criminal justice ones and from the 1880s onwards, legal and institutional mechanisms were introduced to 'save' girls deemed to be sexually delinquent or in danger of moral corruption (Cox, 2003, 2012). Changes to the 1933 Children and Young Persons Act, for example, broadened the category of those who could be defined as 'in need of care or protection' to include those under 17 with an 'unfit' parent or guardian and who were in 'moral danger'. Those found in need of intervention could be sent to an approved school. Although technically such an option could be drawn upon for boys, Cox (2003: 55) demonstrates a far greater proportion of girls than boys brought before the courts or referred to such institutions were deemed 'in need of care or protection'. In 1936, just over 50 per cent of girls were sent to approved schools for these reasons compared to 10 per cent of boys and in 1964 only 5 per cent of boys compared to 62 per cent of girls. While subsequent discourse about girls and sexuality is less concerned about the spread of venereal disease, a concern about girls' sexuality and wider transgressions continue to have much resonance in more contemporary narratives about gender and crime. Chesney-Lind (1973) suggests that female delinquency is sexualized and, as a consequence, girls are processed by the courts for 'moral danger' rather than criminal activity. This idea is echoed by a number of studies emphasizing the transgression of girls from stereotypical notions of appropriate gendered behaviour (Casburn, 1979; Datesman and Scarpitti, 1980; Dobash et al., 1986; Farrington and Morris, 1983; Hudson, 1987; Lees, 1989, 1993). By the early twenty-first century, there is an observable shift in the way in which girls' behaviour is now being interpreted. The arrival of the **'ladette'** and the **'mean girl'** has resulted in an increasing number of young women coming under the scrutiny of the criminal justice system (Burman and Batchelor, 2009; Chesney-Lind and Pasko, 2013; Sharpe, 2011, 2015). We extend our discussions of this in Chapter 5.

Civilizing and criminalizing men

Despite the call by Newburn and Stanko (1994) to 'take masculinities seriously', the study of men and masculinities within contemporary criminology remains a niche area of inquiry and rests exclusively with those scholars interested in gender. As we have already argued in Chapter 2, studies on men's offending through a gendered lens has not yet secured as formal a place within discourse or policy agendas in the same way as their female counterparts. Such an absence is remarkable given the presence and availability of men within official categorizations of crime over time. Criminology is not alone here; in the same way that criminology has ignored the study of men and masculinity, so too have historians. Whitlock (2014: 193) notes that despite some ground-breaking work that revolutionized approaches to gender, as a historical category, 'masculinity is implied but has not figured explicitly and prominently in analyses'. Walker (2003: 4) neatly sums up when she states that:

The extent to which criminality is related to masculinity has scarcely been addressed. Historians tend to accept criminality in general to be a masculine category without conceptualising or contextualising it in terms of gender. Male criminality is thus normalised, while female criminality is seen in terms of dysfunction.

That said, recent years have seen an increasing number of historians interested in the study of men and criminality. Work by Spierenburg (1998), Wiener (1998), Shoemaker (2001), Emsley (2005), Houlbrook (2013), Broomhall and Van Gent (2011) among others, have all enriched perspectives on gender, reintegrating men and the study of masculinity into a complex history of crime, honour, trickery and violence. In this section we review, albeit briefly, the association of men and violence, together with an insight into the emergence of respectable and unrespectable masculinities over time. In doing so, we emphasize the importance of class in relation to both the civilization and criminalization of men.

The association between men and the use of physical violence, both in the public and private spheres, can be tracked across the centuries. Indeed Whitlock (2014: 191) suggests that it has been men's participation in violence, especially in relation to crimes of rape and murder, that has prompted much of the work on the medieval and early modern periods. Violent crime committed by men during the early modern period was inextricably bound up with defending honour and was enacted through participation in the *duel*. Emerging among elites, the act of *duelling* quickly spread to men across the social strata as an appropriate response to maintain a masculine honour code (McAleer, 1994; Peltonen, 2003; Smith, 2014). Duels among men from various walks of life were relatively common and unremarkable but by the nineteenth century, ritualized duelling was outlawed. England saw a rapid decline in duelling after the 1840s and was followed more slowly by other European states where it largely died out by the beginning of the twentieth century, although in France and Germany duels with pistols and swords continued until World War I and in Italy until World War II (Emsley, 2005).

The work of Elias (1994) on the 'civilizing' process is central to making sense of the historiography of violence and of men's place within it. For Elias, there was a long-term 'civilizing process' evident in the conduct of elites by the late eighteenth century and to other social sectors thereafter. Commentators have pointed to the steady decline in the acceptability of such public displays of violence by men, and rather than being a sign of masculine honour and social positioning, such violence between men was increasingly perceived as a mark of class difference (Simpson, 1988; Spierenburg, 1998; Whitlock, 2014). Emsley's (2005) analysis of violence in England since 1750 details the societal separation between the ideal of respectable manhood and the 'roughs' who transgressed those boundaries with law-breaking behaviour characterized by physical violence. It is here that we can begin to observe the emergence of a variety of masculinities, with those men from the upper elite classes distancing themselves from such activity and inevitably building difference and distance with their working-class male counterparts. It was within such a narrative that Whitlock (2014: 196) argues that 'knives, fists, gangs and blood seemed to be the antithesis of the honour-based "duel" and denoted the working-class origins of its participants'. Labelled as animalistic and violent, such working-class masculinity was constructed as a threat to 'civilized' masculinity. According to this narrative, 'civilized' behaviour as a social practice became internalized by ever-wider social groups as the centuries progressed and was achieved through complex interactions between social, cultural and psychological processes affecting both violence in the public and private interpersonal spheres (Eisner, 2003; Gurr, 1981).

Although a useful organizing framework for understanding changing perceptions of behaviour over time, we should state here that the idea of the 'civilizing process' is not without its critics and has been subject to much critical debate. In brief, D'Cruze and Jackson (2009) point to a considerable body of research showing the Western state to have been a far less unitary and coordinated entity than this model implies. The decline of violent and disorderly conduct, more particularly, has also been subject to alternative explanations that locate such change within a narrative of changing conditions of social life in the fast-growing eighteenth-century cities (Shoemaker, 2001). There is also considerable evidence to suggest that respectable masculinities continued to be associated with legitimate uses of violence, including violence in warfare, the punishment of offenders, honour-based and interpersonal violence. Moreover, the administering of 'correction' to women and children remained prevalent, as D'Cruze and Jackson (2009: 10) argue: 'although working men were eventually forced into new and more peaceable definitions of masculinity, there was a surprisingly high level of tolerance for the killing of working-class wives for most of the nineteenth century'.

Accompanying the so-called 'civilizing process', research has pointed to the growing criminalization of men in the Victorian period (Wiener, 1998). Focusing predominantly on sentencing decisions and outcomes, research has emphasized the idea that men were subject to far harsher treatment than women. Drawing on quantitative courtroom data between 1880 and 1920, Godfrey et al. (2005: 718) point out that men were more likely to receive custodial sentences (and indeed, longer ones) for involvement in the same crimes as women, leading them to conclude that the courts 'directed their efforts toward "civilizing" dangerous masculinities'. Unlike their male counterparts, evidence suggests that women were dealt with more 'leniently' than men across the modern period; that is, they were less likely to be convicted than men and they tended to receive lesser **sentences** (D'Cruze and Jackson, 2009: 22).

In the early modern period, men were more likely to hang than women, while women were more likely to receive the lesser sentence of whipping (Hall, 1992).

Violence against the person became an increased target of criminal justice during the Victorian period. With violence more likely to involve men as per-petrators than women, together with the recasting of middle-class men as restrained and chivalrous and women (and children) as vulnerable innocents, this period has been hailed as one of considerable criminalization for working-class men (Walker, 2003; Wiener, 1998). Davies' work on gang culture in late Victorian Manchester and Salford adds further support here. Constructed as a challenge to police authority in the public sphere, Davies argues that police constables deliberately targeted young male gang members in order to enhance their own reputation for toughness. He goes on to note that by the late nine-teenth century, records indicate that women were less likely than men to receive custodial sentences and were more likely to be fined or **discharged** and, over the course of the twentieth century, women were less likely than men to be sent to prison and more likely to be made the subject of conditional discharges or binding orders. They were also more likely to be reprieved from the death pen-alty than men (only 9 per cent of women receiving the capital sentence were executed in the period 1900–51 compared to 58 per cent of men). The *Murder* (Abolition of Death Penalty) Act 1965 – made permanent in 1969 – suspended the death penalty in England, Wales and Scotland; the death penalty for mur-der survived in Northern Ireland until 1973.

Gender and victimization

The study of women's victimization over time has been less well researched by historians, although, as we have already noted, the erasure of women's agency in their offending behaviour often had the effect of reducing their status to that of victims. In this section we are more concerned with bringing to light historical evidence on more contemporary understandings of women's victimization – namely, the broad **continuum of violence** experienced by women. In so doing, we draw out the remarkable parallels and continuities across three key areas: firstly, the everyday nature of violence; secondly, the prevalence of victim blaming; and lastly, the lack of prosecution for such crimes over time.

While comparative historic research on intimate-partner violence is in its infancy, findings of a forensic archaeological study of human remains from Europe, Asia and North America presents considerable evidence of violence against women from pre-historic times to the early twentieth century, with the highest rate occurring in late Roman Britain, nineteenth-century England and early twentieth-century America (Walker, 1997). Roth (2014) further emphasizes the common occurrence and severity of violence between husbands and wives in medieval and early modern times, reminding us that the law itself sanctioned the use of violence by husbands, who were given the power to 'correct' their wives with a stick or rope no broader than their thumbs. While the murder of unrelated adults was common at this time, the murder of a spouse remained low in number. It is precisely this 'corrective' purpose that drives Roth's explanation for the lack of spousal murder before the nineteenth century. He argues that violence by husbands stopped short of murder, not only for fear of the consequences if their violence became obvious but more probably because at some level men were aware of the need to maintain a spouse, particularly if they were to survive in a struggling economy. It is worth reminding readers here that marriages in the medieval and early modern Anglo-American world were very much constructed as economic partnerships (Gowing, 1996). In turn, Roth (2014) suggests that the increase in the rate of marital homicide observable in the late 1820s and 1830s may be linked to the shifting balance of power between men and women and the changing ideas associated with marriage. With new ideals of sobriety, companionate marriage, respectability and domesticity raising both emotional and material expectations, women were afforded the opportunity to be more selective in their suitor and to leave unhappy marriages (Goldwin, 1990; Larkin, 1988; Roth, 1987; Ryan, 1981). It is with such changes as a backdrop, that we can begin to track a willingness of husbands to kill spouses as they tried to leave abusive relationships or even after they had left (Anderson, 1987; Roth, 2009, 2014).

In his study on the evolution of the English law, Bellamy (1998) suggests that at least from the time of Alfred the Great in the late ninth century, there is evidence that English law took sexual violence against women seriously. Brundage (1982) argues convincingly that many of the elements of modern law can be traced to the legal scholars of the medieval church, who not only viewed rape as a crime against the person, but also as more serious than other types of violent crime because of its sexual component. Indeed the religious turmoil of the sixteenth and seventeenth centuries heightened concerns about immorality, making the sexual component of rape the primary consideration. Perhaps one of the most striking continuities between historic and contemporary accounts of such victimization is the emphasis placed on *blaming victims*. Since all sex outside marriage was treated as a criminal offence, victims of sexual violence were often deemed guilty as well (Conley, 2014: 210). As Walker (2003: 56) writes: 'rape ceased to count as a crime when it looked like sex ... the language of sexual practice evoked discourse of sin and culpability in which women were responsible'. Though contemporary narratives are less concerned with religious aspects and sin, there is a now a broad base of literature that is underpinned by the concept of victim blaming – we revisit this issue in Chapter 7.

Low rates of prosecution and conviction for such crimes are further evidence of continuity over time. In her analysis of sexual violence, Conley (2014: 211) provides much evidence to suggest that despite being grounded in law from the thirteenth century, rates of prosecution and conviction for sexual violence against women remained low over the centuries. Further support of this can be found in Dean's (2001) study of medieval Europe, in which he suggests that 'of all of the crimes perpetrated against women, rape stands out for the apparent ineffectiveness of the law'. Though convictions remained rare, the mid-nineteenth century did see the number of reported cases and prosecutions for rape in Britain rise rapidly. Against a backdrop of considerable cultural change, commentators have pointed to the increased emphasis on masculine chivalry and feminine delicacy, together with a focus on individual rights and a substantial increase in the state's machinery for policing (Beattie, 1986; Clark, 1987; Conley, 2014; Ruff, 2001; Vigarello, 1998; Wiener, 2004). Prosecutions were later to fall after World War I and did not increase again until the ascendancy of the feminist movement in 1970s. The gendered nature of the law, the dominance of men working in the criminal justice system and the unwillingness of victims to relive the experience of victimization have all been proposed as possible explanations for the lack of convictions over time (Conley, 2014). Indeed, such explanations remain key concerns for contemporary scholars in the field looking to make sense of the ongoing lack of convictions for such crimes.

Concluding thoughts

Through locating the presence of women and men within discourses of crime, harm and victimization, we hope to have convinced readers of the importance of a gendered analysis over time. As readers progress through the chapters in this book, we hope that the value of historical perspectives will speak for themselves. History has demonstrated quite clearly that crime was an activity perpetrated overwhelmingly by men. It has also confirmed women's presence in all categories of crime (both violent and non-violent forms), albeit to a lesser extent. Despite the expectation that some women would claim their share of criminal activity as their roles in public life increased and barriers to gender equality were removed, the historical evidence has not borne this out (Smith, 2014). This remains a persistent gendered reality in the twenty-first century.

Given the growing importance attached to documenting the evidence base within contemporary criminal justice, we have drawn upon historical perspectives as a way of critically reading the present. In doing so, we can see that today's anxiety about women's and girl's offending behaviour is not new. Rather, we have demonstrated that the female offender is an enduring character in public discourse over the centuries. Present in an array of offence groups, she has repeatedly been constructed as symbolically transgressive of both social and gender norms. Indeed historical perspectives tell us much about the social milieu of the time and of the ways in which criminality by both women and men is coloured by the constraints and opportunities available to them within a historically specific gendered order.

We have also drawn upon historical evidence to emphasize the construction of offenders and victims. Here we have pointed to specific moments in time in which the capacity and willingness of women to commit crime has been reconfigured. The recasting of women who commit lethal violence, shoplift and are engaged in prostitution, as feebleminded, mentally unstable and passive, holds much resonance for contemporary debates about women and criminal justice. At the same time, the co-existing narratives that have sought to reform, rescue and regulate women's bodies over time also hold much meaning in the twenty-first century. We explore these issues in forthcoming chapters.

Summary

- Historical perspectives within criminology are undergoing a renaissance, particularly in relation to the study of gender and crime. With the development of digital archives, the future looks set to develop our understanding further.
- Contemporary scholars need to be aware and tread carefully in the interpretation of historical sources, which are dogged by a series of methodological flaws.
- History has demonstrated quite clearly that crime was an activity perpetrated overwhelmingly by men. It has also confirmed women's presence in all categories of crime (both violent and non-violent forms), albeit to a lesser extent. Despite the expectation that some women would claim their share of criminal activity as their roles in public life increased and barriers to gender equality were removed, the historical evidence has not borne this out. This remains a persistent gendered reality in the twenty-first century.
- Adopting a historical perspective enables us to provide a more critical reading of the present, identifying both change and continuities in the past and present in the study of gender and crime.
- We have argued that considerable continuities can be identified, particularly in relation to contemporary concerns about the rise of the 'new' female offender – history

demonstrates an enduring societal anxiety about the criminality and deviancy of women and girls and their transgression of the legal, social and moral order.

- In relation to the female offender we have identified a range of persistent cultural myths over time, i.e. that she is *not violent*; she is more likely to be *mad than bad*; that she is a *liar and deceiver*; that through her sexuality she is both *dangerous and risky*; and lastly, that she is in need of both *care and control*.
- A historical perspective has also afforded us an insight into the construction of 'respectable' and 'unrespectable' masculinities over time.

STUDY QUESTIONS

1. How useful are historical perspectives to the study of gender, crime and victimization?

2. To what extent are contemporary concerns about women offenders grounded in the past?

3. Outline the key themes that have underpinned the construction of women offenders over time – give examples.

4. Critically discuss the problem of using historical data sources.

5. In what ways were women's bodies defined as 'risky' and in need of regulation?

6. In what ways is Elias's work on the 'civilizing process' useful in making sense of the changing characterization of men and criminality?

FURTHER READING

For a good overview of the gender differences in female and male offending and victimization, chapters by Godfrey, Conley, Whitlock and Roth can be found in R. Gartner and B. McCarthy (eds) (2014) *The Oxford Handbook of Gender Sex and Crime* (Oxford University Press).

For work on women, crime and punishment, see L. Zedner (1991) *Women, Crime and Custody in Victorian England* (Clarendon Press); C. Walker (2003) *Crime, Gender and Social Order in Early Modern England* (Cambridge University Press); S. D'Cruze and L. Jackson (2009) *Women, Crime and Justice in England since 1660* (Palgrave Macmillan); and P. Cox (2003) *Gender, Justice and Welfare: Bad Girls in Britain, 1900–1950* (Palgrave Macmillan). For a compelling online dialogue on the history of prostitution, see H. McCarthy, S. Caslin and J. Laite (2015) *Prostitution and the Law in Historical Perspective: A Dialogue* (available at: www.historyandpolicy.org/dialogues/discussions/prostitution-and-the-law-in-historical-perspective-a-dialogue).

For those interested in masculinities and history, see S. Broomhall and J. Van Gent (2011) *Governing Masculinities in the Early Modern Period: Regulating Selves and Others* (Ashgate); A. Davies (2008) *The Gangs of Manchester* (Milo Books); C. Emsley (2005) *Hard Men: Violence in England since 1750* (Hamledon); P. Spierenburg (1998) *Men and Violence: Gender, Honour, and Rituals in Modern Europe and America* (Ohio State University Press); and M. Wiener (2004) *Men of Blood: Contesting Violence in Victorian England* (Cambridge University Press).

Note

1. These tended to be mundane London robberies – at this time London streets had been designated highway.

4

Contemporary Issues in Gender and Crime in a Globalized World

OVERVIEW

Chapter 4 provides:

- An overview of the notion of globalization.
- An exploration of the relationship between globalization and existing forms of criminal behaviour.
- A demonstration of how globalization and its impact on offending and victimization are gendered.
- A consideration of the growing interest in comparative criminology.
- An assessment of the issue of globalization and the challenges and opportunities it poses for coming to terms with the gendering of crime in global and local contexts.

KEY TERMS

- comparative criminology
- globalization
- human rights

- risk
- trafficking

Introduction

Throughout the twentieth century criminologists became increasingly concerned about globalization and the various opportunities and threats it presented to both the individual and society. A key idea is that through technological, cultural, political, social and economic changes the world becomes a smaller place in which individuals are more closely connected to each other. Although time and place are still important, the internet and cheap travel means people and commodities are physically and virtually closer than ever before. In terms of crime we can see how globalization has created new forms of criminal and deviant behaviour. Criminological research and policy tend to be concerned with what is happening in a particular nation state, which is confirmed throughout the following chapters in this book where most of the research outlined refers to developments in England and Wales. The purpose of this chapter is to show how globalization has impacted on the complex relationship between gender, criminality, victimization and the control of crime. Despite people being physically and virtually in closer proximity we also know that in a globalized world there are social divisions (such as gender, race and social class) which separate people, and gender-based inequalities are an enduring feature in all societies.

Another purpose of the chapter is to outline the growing importance of international and global forms of crime and disorder, focusing on the uneven impacts of gender-blind approaches to social control. Accordingly, we introduce six global drivers of crime, which are referred to where appropriate in later chapters. Here we comment on the relationship between globalization and human rights principles. As Nelken observes (2013), as far as criminal justice is concerned, globalization involves an uneasy tension between the inequalities associated with neo-liberalism, which promotes individualism and competition, and universal human rights based on shared values and cooperation.

The chapter has four main parts. Firstly, the notion of globalization is outlined in general terms. We acknowledge that although the notion of globalization is not new (and can be traced back to the founders of social science), interest in the linkages between globalization, gender and crime is relatively recent (Aas, 2013; Findlay, 1999). Globalization is an issue in its own right but here we draw attention to its relationship with **comparative criminology**, which involves criminologists in one country looking at what happens in another country or other countries (Nelken, 2010; Pakes, 2010).

Secondly, we very briefly pay attention to the existence of human rights principles as a safeguard against unfair and inequitable treatment in a global environment (Barberet, 2014; Hearn, 2015).

The third part then explains the significance of globalization in relation to certain types of criminal behaviour where we consider the complex ways in which globalized forms of crime and victimization shape gender relations. We also consider something called **transnational crime** or criminal behaviour that has an impact across national geographical territories that calls into question the ability of individual states to address these problems alone, hence the emergence of transnational forms of policing (Bowling and Sheptycki, 2012). Although global forces are important and have a profound influence on the nature of social life, equally relevant are conditions at a local level where there will be more nuanced and sometimes contradictory developments. Indeed when considering crime, the global and local interact and mutually influence one another. The connection between the local and global is something we do throughout the book.

In the fourth part we acknowledge that although globalization implies late-modern industrial societies – especially in the West – are all affected by similar forces and processes, it impacts unevenly in different parts of the world. Here there is an analysis of the key global drivers of crime, which are: **New Public Management** (NPM) and modernization; victim-centred justice; public protection and penal populism; decline of the rehabilitative ideal; risk assessment and management; and commercialization of crime control (Senior et al., 2007). These drivers are important for interpreting the work of crime control agencies and how their activities have a bearing on the human rights of men and women. Here we use England and Wales as a case study.

What is globalization?

Globalization is a nebulous concept that has proven difficult to define, and to this day its meaning and status are contested. In very general terms, it refers to two separate but inter-related processes. It includes the opening up of the world for trade and economic exchange (of goods as well as people), as well as informationalization, communication and travel. At the same time there is a gradual disappearance of social, political and cultural differences across the world. For example, ideas about globalization have been applied to refer to social developments such as colonialism and slavery, where rich societies invaded and exploited poorer nations and territories on the other side of the world. It features in Karl Marx's thinking about economic development, especially the expansion of capitalist economies, a factor that is of contemporary relevance (Eagleton, 2011). The most discernible trend is that over the last few centuries, either through trade or war, human societies from each corner of the globe have become closer, resulting in more contact and collective experiences, both in material and cybernetic worlds.

As an academic concept globalization has a relatively shorter history and it has only been in currency since the mid-1980s (Giddens, 1990, 2007). Held (2000) provides an often-cited definition that captures the main points that will frame our discussion. Globalization is 'the growing interconnectedness of states and societies' and 'the progressive enmeshment of human communities with one another' (Held, 2000, cited in Aas, 2013: 4). What this means is that individual nation states (e.g. UK) and supranational bodies (e.g. the European Union (EU)) have more porous geographical boundaries, making them – and especially politicians – less able to exercise control over the forces and processes existing beyond their own jurisdiction. While this chapter shows there is much more to the idea than this, there is broad agreement about the increased *interconnectedness* of societies. It is also necessary to consider conflicting views about whether or not globalization can be described as a *progressive* movement. As Nederveen Pieterse (2015: 4) stresses, the 'visions of human unity harboured in the past have been diminished by steep and growing inequality ... and evidence suggesting that [g]lobalization is a long-term, uneven, and paradoxical process in which widening social cooperation and deepening inequality go together'. The opportunities globalization has yielded to some sections of society, such as white, wealthy males, is undeniable and, as Connell (2000: 3) argues, there is a 'transnational business masculinity, institutionally based in multinational corporations and global finance markets [which] is arguably the emerging dominant form on a world scale'. For others, arguably a significant proportion of people across the globe – especially women and children – it has led to experiences of social harms, injustice and inequality, an issue that is revisited in Chapter 7 (Barberet, 2014; Cain and Howe, 2008; Pickering and Lambert, 2004; Rafter and Heidensohn, 1995; True, 2012). As we will show later, globalization has created innumerable opportunities of an illicit and illegal nature for motivated criminals whose actions have led to direct collateral damage for their victims.

There are signs of a reversal in the fortunes of some nations and power blocs, and the evidence cited in arguments about globalization that surfaced in the academe in the 1980s, specifically the contention that the Northern part of the globe (the US and Western Europe) was the dominant force, no longer holds. In the last decade or so the Southern sphere has acquired more weight and influence through economic growth and increased political representation, demonstrated by what has happened most notably in China, which at least until early 2016 (Guardian, 2016) experienced economic growth on a major scale. This shift conceals huge differentials in terms of the distribution of wealth in those Southern countries where many remain poor.

We can see that the types of issues that are prominent in most discussions surrounding globalization refer to economic and technological innovation and changes, especially those brought about as a result of capitalism. As capitalist societies tended to be controlled less and less by nation states, the large, powerful multinational organizations have taken their place. An often-cited book in the globalization literature is Ritzer (1993), particularly the notion of 'McDonaldization', which in some ways updates Weber's (1946) notion of rationalization. Rather than looking at how rationality is embodied in bureaucratic organizations, rationalization refers to the doctrines of scientific management. Ritzer shows how the operational principles of this fast-food chain came to be dominant features of all aspects of society in four main ways.

Firstly, there is 'predictability' or the fact that all McDonalds across the world look and feel the same. Secondly, there is calculability, revealed by the greater emphasis placed on the quantity or size of the product in relation to cost (its relative cheapness). The speed, efficiency and round-the-clock availability of services are also selling points, which is the third principle. The fourth principle is control and the standardization of services, leading when possible to human labour being replaced by technology. To this Ritzer added the notion of 'McJobs', alluding to the low pay and casual nature of this type of employment. While Ritzer's work is not altogether unproblematic it offers a persuasive account of many of the developments associated with globalization.

This concern with speed and efficiency can be found in the criminal justice system where 'crime control' values prioritize these goals above justice and fairness, which are core safeguards against gender-based discrimination by police and the courts (Packer, 1968). There are other structural and macro-level factors.

Since the 1970s political economic arrangements have changed in capitalist societies. This can be seen by the ascendancy of neo-liberalism and what is called structural adjustment policies, which led to a redefined relationship between the state, citizens and commerce (Schrecker and Bambra, 2015). This signalled the arrival of financialization and marketization, evidenced by the preference for free market policies and the privatization and shrinkage of the state and public sectors. The individual citizen was supposed to reduce their reliance on the state for welfare services by remaining economically productive in the workplace in order to provide for their own material needs and to be responsible for the health and well-being of their dependents. These assumptions are encapsulated by the Conservative Chancellor of the Exchequer, George Osborne, who announced in the July 2015 Budget that society should be organized in such a way that there is 'low tax, low welfare, high pay' (*The Guardian*, 2015c). Individuals have also been recast as consumers of the products and services produced by businesses. The size of the state, especially regarding the welfare services it provides, has been curtailed as far as possible. This is sometimes called the 'hollowing out' of the nation state and at one time it was anticipated by some that the state would not only wither away, but be replaced by a 'global empire', a place where state sovereignty was ineffectual when facing an autonomous global economy. This narrative fails to appreciate that states continue to impose their sovereign control internally via legislation, **surveillance** technologies, the legitimate use of force (including the right to kill) and, most tellingly, by the swollen prison estate in some countries (Cavadino et al., 2013).

The recent austerity measures and cuts to the welfare state in Britain following the credit crunch and most recent economic recession commencing in 2008 have a much longer history than we might think. The economic deregulation set in motion during the 1980s lifted barriers to trade at regional and national levels, hence 24/7 global markets. Large corporations and businesses, especially those in the financial services sector, now tend to have a strong influence on government policy, which is increasingly oriented towards economic growth and increasing wealth and profit. Governments are often timid in the face of global capital and are reluctant to regulate large companies, especially when the latter have the flexibility to relocate to other parts of the world where conditions are more business-friendly. Another development is deindustrialization, which since the late 1970s has occurred in the USA and across Western Europe. The staple, manufacturing industries, including mining, shipbuilding and steelworks, have now more or less disappeared, resulting in high unemployment in some regions of individual countries (Hothi, 2005). Although the service sector expanded, especially for financial products such as cheap credit and low-interest mortgages, these jobs were relatively low paid with insecure employment conditions. The literature on globalization refers to flexibility in labour markets and the means of production, which is often shorthand for zero-hour contracts and pay either below or just meeting minimum wage benchmarks (see Ritzer's (1993) notion of 'McJobs' mentioned above). In the words of S. Hall (2012: 120), in the 2000s there was a scenario with a

> Finance-service economy that was boosted by encouraging the advertising industry to intensify demand, using a rising housing market as a guarantor to extend unprecedented amounts of credit to everyday people in difficult circumstances and turning Britain's City of London and the USA's State of Delaware into two of the world's premier tax havens to attract the global finance capital for increased lending.

Another consequence of these changes is that big business can now manufacture and/or distribute their goods and services from other parts of the world. For example, clothes and cars produced by American and European companies are 'made in China' and call centres operate in India where the costs are cheaper to ensure their enterprise can be more competitive and thus increase their profits (Aas, 2013). Consequently, there is a decline in available jobs in some communities across Europe and America, which in a far from straightforward way can lead to increased criminality and margin-alization in some communities (Crowther, 2004; see Chapter 6).

Global organizations such as the Organization for Economic Cooperation and Development (OECD), International Monetary Fund (IMF) and World Bank are there to regulate the economy and flow of capital, but regardless of the effort of the latter to 'end extreme poverty within a generation and boost shared prosperity' (World Bank, 2014), material resources and wealth are not being distributed evenly and equitably and tend to be concentrated among an increasingly smaller group of people (Gamble, 2009), which might be characterized as a 'power elite' (Wright Mills, 1956).

A leading authority on globalization is Giddens (1990), who argues that it is an integral part of **modernity** (since the 1800s) and capitalism (since the 1500s). As well as drawing attention to its economic dimensions, he also raised questions about how, as a cultural process, globalization fosters a 'global consciousness' where we share similar subjectivities and tastes as well as a common fate. The global interconnections that have been created for the most part are based on the interests of the most powerful countries in the world, which until recent times (as noted above) was the United States, resulting in the Americanization of culture (with reference to media, cuisine, fashion, and so on), a trend better encapsulated in the idea of the 'homogenization of cultures' (Nederveen Pieterse, 2015), epitomized by the popularity of Hollywood and Bollywood films.

Giddens (1990) elaborated the concept of globalization by describing its temporal and spatial dimensions. In terms of space, societies and social actors are 'disembedded' and time is increasingly 'stretched'. According to Findlay (1999: xiii):

> Globalization is the collapsing of time and space – the process whereby, through mass communication, multinational commerce, international politics and transnational regulation, we seem to be moving inexorably towards a single culture.

Thus the connection between national economies, commercial activity, politics and cultures is much closer and, more than this, human relationships are intensified because people are influenced by things that are spatially far away from their own day-to-day lives. Due to technological innovation, in comparison to the past, there is more immediacy and greater speed, demonstrated by the various forms of communication and exchange that happen via the internet and media in a matter of seconds. The movement of cultural images, information and ideas make it possible for us to visit – in person or online – distant places in the world. Globalization has induced profound changes to society as well as to individuals and how they form their identity. Individuals may be closer, both temporally and spatially, and there is some homogenization of experience and culture; yet we also know human rights are not enjoyed by all and we show throughout this book how this inequality is gendered.

So far our narrative on globalization might create the impression that it has a powerful, almost unstoppable momentum but this fails to consider the local and the extent to which social actors accept or resist global pressures. The connections – and disconnections – between the global and local occur at different levels and there is a distinction between the flow of global ideas and images and how they are translated in practice.

Comparative criminology

This should not be mistaken as being the same thing as globalization. It is a closely related topic, however, because comparative criminology refers to a branch of the discipline that looks at what is happening in the world of crime and public policy in other societies beyond the society in which a criminological researcher resides. Furthermore, some of the tendencies connected with globalization mentioned in the previous section also make comparative criminology both necessary and feasible: necessary because of transnational crime and the need to find solutions at both national and transnational levels; and feasible because of the ease of communicating in an environment where time and space are compressed.

In simple terms comparative criminology is often described as an approach that is 'outward looking' and, as well as being an academic pursuit, it has the pragmatic aim of learning lessons regarding the formulation and implementation of policy (Bochel and Duncan, 2007). Perhaps its main function is to explore in more than one geographical location the nature of crime (including the extent and prevalence of offending and victimization), different modes of thinking about it and how these ideas inform practice such as social control and punishment. The core elements of comparative criminology are captured in Nelken's (2010: 1) definition:

> Comparative criminal justice is the study of what people and institutions in different agencies do – and should do – about crime problems. More broadly, it looks for links between crime, social order and punishment, and explores the role played by police, prosecutors, courts, prisons and other actors and institutions in the wider context of various forms of social control.

Nelken (2010) continues to show how comparative work is applied to highlight the contextually specific nature of criminal behaviour and crime control, and how these change and vary not only historically and culturally but also spatially. This enables criminologists to explore different explanations of the causes of and solutions to crime. There is evidence of some convergence and harmonization between jurisdictions, and on some occasions there is the transfer of a particular policy intervention from one place to another, such as the 'War on Drugs' or 'zero tolerance policing'. 'Policy transfer' denotes trying out an approach to crime reduction that worked in one place, in another (Rose, 2005), although a closer inspection of what actually happens often reveals that ideas and practices are in fact applied selectively not universally.

Our common-sense experience, based on travelling abroad, tells us that although crime is an issue more or less everywhere, it is not identical to our own society, and although nearly all societies have a criminal justice system, the institutional arrangements and value frameworks underpinning them vary. Even at a more basic level there are difficulties comparing the number of crimes recorded, due to the types of crime statistics that are collated in different jurisdictions. As Crowther-Dowey and Fussey (2013: 99) observe:

> Types of crime are often coded and classified differently in different places. In Malta, for example, an offence committed by more than one person is counted as multiple offences, whereas in most European countries, it is recorded as a single offence. Thus comparative research is difficult unless the same standards are applied across areas, issues and variables. In essence, steps need to be taken to ensure the same thing is measured in each place.

Recently there has been talk of an 'international crime drop', or the view that crime rates are falling across the world (Van Dijk et al., 2012). If scrutinized more closely, this has not happened in parts of the globe, attested to by conflicting evidence published by the World Health Organization (WHO) and the United Nations Office on Drugs and Crime (UNODC) that demonstrate that homicide rates have not fallen everywhere and in Central America and Africa, for instance, they have risen (Aebi and Linde, 2015: 382). Notwithstanding these shortcomings, comparative material of this kind can give an insight into gender-based victimization. There have been attempts to use data comparatively, such as the large-scale International Crime Victimization Survey (ICVS), which has been conducted six times between 1989 and 2010 (see van Kesteren et al., 2014). It compares rates of victimization across 78 countries, surveying to date 320,000 respondents, and among the questions asked are ones focusing on sexual violence. In the late 2000s an International Violence Against Women Survey (IVAWS) was carried out in 11 countries, mainly from the developing world (Johnson et al., 2008, cited in Barberet, 2014). The quantitative data gathered via this survey showed that 35–60 per cent of women had experienced a physically or sexually violent assault after turning age 16. Qualitative data showed that in some countries (Australia, Hong Kong and the Czech Republic) such violence was perceived to be 'something that just happens' (ibid.: 94).

As well as quantifying variations in crime, comparative criminologists aspire to look beneath surface appearances by conducting scientific research to classify different arrangements in the sphere of criminal justice (ibid.). Each society and system will have their own rules, ideals and cultural and legal traditions, which will shape criminal justice and practice in any given jurisdiction. The actors and the roles they perform will not be the same everywhere (e.g. Are police officers routinely armed? Can defendants cross-examine **witnesses** at a trial in the courts?). Thinking about the subject in this way makes it possible to avoid 'ethnocentrism', or leading us to think that our way of doing things is not only the best but the only way of doing this (Nelken, 2009). For instance, the system in England and Wales is based on common law and is characterized as adversarial, which contrasts with inquisitorial systems such as those found in continental Europe and those systems existing in socialist countries before the collapse of the Berlin Wall in 1989. There has been a growing interest in Islamic systems too (Pakes, 2010).

To take an example of the latter, we showed in Chapter 2 that the UK government has taken violence against women seriously for several decades yet in Saudi Arabia domestic violence was not criminalized until 2013 when it passed a draft of the Protection from Abuse Law to make this behaviour a criminal offence. This piece of law defined domestic abuse as

> ... all forms of exploitation, or bodily, psychological, or sexual abuse, or threat of it, committed by one person against another, including if [that person] has authority, power, or responsibility, or [if there is] a family, support, sponsorship, guardianship, or living dependency relationship between the two [individuals]. (Human Rights Watch, 2013)

In Saudi Arabia the guardianship system and gender segregation has curtailed women, who have limited freedom due to the high levels of control and coercion exercised by males. Before the Protection from Abuse Law was adopted judgements about whether or not to treat this behaviour as a criminal offence were based on Sharia law, which were not codified, leaving judges with the latitude to exercise considerable discretion. Even after the legislation banning this behaviour was implemented detail about how the specific agencies and mechanisms would enforce the law was lacking (ibid.).

Thus comparative criminologists are preoccupied with looking for what different societies share in common (the globalizing tendencies of crime and public policy) and the diversity and variability of behaviour locally. Globalization might be a powerful force, but it does not determine every aspect of social life and local social conditions and actions are still relevant and can resist or reshape global forces. The relationship between the general and particular is also important when contemplating human rights.

Globalization, gender and human rights

We demonstrated earlier on in this book that there are many conventions and laws that codify human rights in numerous legal regimes. Humans rights principles, articulated in 1948 – and augmented in 1954 and 1966 – were intended to have international or global appeal and reach, and almost form, as noted in Chapter 2, an 'international bill of rights' (Nickel, 1992). As Matthews (2014: 47) puts it, 'there is something deeply attractive in the idea that every person, anywhere in the world, irrespective of citizenship or territorial legislation, has some basic rights that others should respect'. In other words, human rights discourse is appealing in the context of globalization because of its universality. Feminists have questioned this in the past in the name of difference and diversity, although a global perspective on human rights has more resonance because, in the words of Walby (2011: 132), 'the ability to claim access to a universal standard of justice has been used in an increasing number of political projects as a form of legitimation'. Women in different parts of the world have transcended national boundaries and responded collectively to the global inequalities and injustices arising from the transnational working of corporate and political elites that sustain patriarchal and oppressive practices.

In the view of Walby (2011), feminism has global reach for four reasons. Firstly, the compression of time and space that Giddens discussed has changed the nature of communication so images of injustice can be seen more quickly by a global audience. The Delhi (India) gang rape case occurring in December 2012, already mentioned in Chapter 2, is an example. Jyoti Singh died as a result of the injuries she sustained. The global media exposed the flawed reaction of the authorities and a claim made by the perpetrator at a later date that the victim should not have fought back, eliciting universal condemnation (BBC, 2015). Secondly, the internet and cheap travel makes interpersonal communication easier. Thirdly, debate and action is facilitated though global institutions (e.g. the World Bank, IMF), networks and events. Fourthly, the UN is more globally active, in no small part due to the first three reasons.

The potential advantages of human rights are clear but there are issues. An inherent problem is that it concentrates too much on individual claims made against injustices, which are made at the expense of collective claims and interests that could be mobilized to tackle structural and institutionalized forms of disadvantage. There might be some truth in this argument, although in response to it in recent years women have campaigned successfully to make violence against women a human rights issue, as is manifest in the UN Declaration on the Elimination of Violence against Women (DEVAW) (see Chapter 7).

This optimistic reading is not shared by all and Žižek is dismissive of universalism, suggesting that this 'masks' the 'false ideological universality' of human rights and the ways in which they 'legitimise the concrete politics of domination' and *exploitation* of women (Žižek, 2009: 126). In other words, human rights discourse is synonymous with the idea that 'all things are equal now' between the genders but working against this there are the elements of diversity, difference and discrimination, including gendered divisions, enacted through often paradoxical processes of differentiation. Thus the adoption of human rights principles might be perceived as a regressive pathway and that use of a singular identity (i.e. 'womanhood') may cancel out the labours of feminists past and present to critique and dismantle any universalizing strategies that create artificial unity (Žižek, 2009). Also, at a cultural level, the perception that globalization, at least to a certain extent, concerns the move towards a 'single culture' was considered, but as Findlay (1999: xiii) wryly observes, 'modern, universal cultural iconography .... is more likely to represent Coca Cola than universal human rights protections'. To go some way towards assessing the two sides of this argument the next section explores globalization and crime.

Globalization and crime

To say that each crime event occurs at a particular time and in a specific place is arguably stating what is obvious to us all yet this common-sense view has been called into question, partly as a result of globalization, especially the collapsing of time and space (Findlay, 1999: xiii). Crime in the twenty-first century is very different compared to the nineteenth century, as well as a significant proportion of the twentieth century. The actual offences that are committed both against property and the person might be the same, and traditional forms of crime are still with us, yet these traditional as well as newly emergent types of crime can feel and look different in a globalized world. Offences such as drugs and human trafficking, the criminalization of (im)migration, 'honour' killings (Barberet, 2014), and high-tech or cybercrimes (such as online pornography, cyber-terrorism and cyber-harassment – Gillespie, 2016) and terrorism are all relevant. If we take a brief look at global terrorism post 9/11 and 7/7, specifically Al-Qaeda and IS, the significance of gender may not be immediately apparent. Research shows that most suspected and convicted terrorists are male even though women are starting to play more of an active role (Sjoberg and Gentry, 2011). This existence of groups such as ISIS can be situated in the context of globalization, or what Kaldor (2003) has called 'regressive globalization', involving groups like Al-Qaeda, which react to the insecurities produced by globalization as well as disenchantment with state-sanctioned secular ideologies. They also utilize the opportunities created by globalization – especially to raise income and disseminate their ideas.

The issue of terrorism and gender is revisited in Chapter 6 and we concentrate instead on trafficking as a more detailed case study. Before that we have a few general observations about the intersections between crime and globalization.

Globalization has created the *conditions* and *opportunities* for the adaptation of existing types of crime (and different modus operandi for committing them) as well as innovation leading to new types of crime. Taking the *conditions* first, political and economic globalization is arguably criminogenic because those market economies found in capitalist societies have elevated and justified the pursuit of self-interest at the expense of collective and communal behaviour. Alongside economic deregulation individuals and groups have a greater motivation to engage in illegal and illicit behaviour, and in some countries, such as in the former Soviet Union, where organized crime and corruption are deeply entrenched, this can actually pose a threat to the credibility and capacity of the criminal justice system to impartially uphold the rule of law. The *opportunities* include the relative ease with which people and objects can move and be moved, and especially the increased speed of communication resulting from technological innovations such as the internet. More recently, biometrics or the 'digitisation of psychological and physical attributes' has been deployed to control borders (Muller, 2013: 130).

The tendencies outlined above include transnational crime – or criminal activity which is sometimes organized – that transcend borders and the jurisdiction of state police forces. It has been defined by the UN as an act:

Committed in one State but includes an organized criminal group that engages in illegal activities in multiple States;

Committed in several States;

If substantial planning, preparation, control or direction happens in one State but the actual offence occurs in another;

It transpired in one State but had substantial repercussions in another State. (UN, 2000, cited in Stanislawski, 2004)

Two examples of such crime are drugs and human trafficking.

Drug trafficking

The use and supply of drugs – both licit and illicit – is a feature of all societies and this has been the case since human societies came into existence. On the surface, the issue of drugs might appear to be a gender-neutral topic or at least it is until the patterns of use and distribution of illicit substances are subjected to closer scrutiny, especially when looking through a global and comparative lens. Regarding the use of drugs, prior to the 1990s there was relatively little interest in gender differences (Broom, 1994) and although more research has been done since then, the findings of these studies are of limited generalizability. Despite this there are gender differences if initiation into use, drug users' careers, the nature of addiction and treatment outcomes are explored (Bennett and Holloway, 2007; Measham, 2002). More recent research in England and Wales shows that 11.8 per cent of men and 5.8 per cent of women had taken an illicit drug in the previous year, with men being two times as likely to use cannabis, powder cocaine and ecstasy (Home Office, 2014a). Other factors are influential too, such as age, region, country and the socio-economic status and ethnicity, but a similar pattern to that found in England and Wales is identified by the United Nations (UNODC, 2013a), though with the caveat that women are more likely to use tranquilizers, sedatives and pharmaceutical drugs than their male counterparts. The UN stresses that the factors influencing women to use drugs are also different, in particular their experiences of psychological problems, physical and sexual abuse, and parental drug and alcohol misuse. According to the UNODC (2013b: 79):

> Women using drugs are likely to be more stigmatized than their male counterparts because their activities are regarded by society as 'double deviance', violating social codes of behaviour and affecting the traditional expectations of the female as wife, mother and nurturer. This lower social acceptance of drug abuse by women might restrict their access to drugs, resulting in statistically greater use by males than females.

Women might use illegal drugs less frequently than men, which might come as a surprise because in 2005 in England and Wales 35 per cent of the female prison population – compared to 7 per cent in 1995 – had committed drug-related offences. This figure is significantly higher compared to men (Joseph, 2006: 7). In the USA the proportion of women contained in federal prisons for non-violent drug-related offences is two-thirds and between 2006 and 2011 the female prison population in Latin America doubled largely as a result of drug-related offending (Youngers, 2014).

    The use of drugs is clearly dependent on their availability, hence the relevance of markets.

Markets and supply

Since the 1970s the trends connected with globalization rehearsed above have created the conditions needed for the materialization of a transnational global 'black market' where prohibited substances and illegal drugs are manufactured and/or cultivated, distributed and sold in places far away from where drugs are consumed (UNODC, 2013a). In 1971, President Nixon (USA) launched a 'War on Drugs', comprising enforcement-led strategies targeting drug use and supply not only in the USA but globally. With the notable exception of the UK, there is a consensus in some international policy circles, such as the Global Commission on Drugs Policy (www.globalcommissionondrugs.org/), that this war has not only failed to reduce the size of drug markets but it has also unintentionally – though not unexpectedly – led to huge casualties and social harm in some provider countries, such as Mexico and Columbia (Clegg and Branson, 2015; Jensen et al., 2004). There is not the space to explore this debate here, but it is clear that due to the illegality of drugs their availability is problematic.

Trading in this market is hidden and therefore difficult to measure. The worldwide trade of drugs generates a large amount of wealth (estimated to be $36 trillion) with HM Government (2013) stating that it is worth as much as the gas, oil and tourism industries. In the UK it was estimated that in 2012 drugs were worth in the region of £3.7 million (Mills et al., 2013). The UK is a so-called destination country, which means it receives imported drugs. Many of the drugs consumed in the UK tend to be produced abroad in countries with weak states, which are in political turmoil and have economies that are performing badly (Caulkins et al., 2010). Afghanistan, part of the so-called Golden Crescent, is such an example and this country produces nearly three-quarters of the opiates found in the world with nine-tenths of them ending up on the streets of Europe (Riechel, 2005). Another major route is from Latin America, including countries such as Bolivia, Columbia and Peru, which historically were renowned for their contribution to the market for cocaine in Europe. More recently, the drug market has diversified due to the increased availability of 'new psychoactive substances (NPS)' such as mephedrone, which tend to be imported from India and China (HM Government, 2013). These drugs, widely available across the EU – with the UK accounting for 23 per cent of the total in that territory – are not controlled by existing drug conventions (UNODC, 2013a). Technology has played an important role in the distribution of NPSs and the internet is being used as a new modus operandi, though this has not replaced traditional methods of distribution. There are various modus operandi utilized to export and import or traffick drugs, which has been made easier due to increased mobility and more porous geopolitical borders.

Drugs trafficking is therefore an umbrella term referring to a number of activities including the production (i.e. growth), transportation, sale, possession and use of substances. Most traffickers, at least according to arrest data, are men, and according to the Crown Prosecution Service (CPS) in England and Wales 74.3 per cent of defendants, where their gender was recorded, were men (CPS, 2015). Despite this, globally 20 per cent of arrestees are female. An issue relating to the latter population is that of drug mules or people (invariably women) who carry drugs for someone else both within and across national boundaries (Fleetwood, 2014: 8). For some it is not appropriate to refer to these women as perpetrators;

instead they need to be treated as victims (Barberet, 2014: 139), not least because some of them are coerced into becoming involved. Women all over the world have become involved in this type of transnational crime due to the commodification of women and feminization of poverty, two factors that are pushing economically marginalized and desperate individuals into this illegal economy. It is also an unintended and perverse effect of the 'War on Drugs' (Sudbury, 2004). Fleetwood (2014) has undertaken ethnographic research to investigate the lived experiences of imprisoned female drug mules in Ecuador. These women participated in the movement of cocaine across international borders. It considers the complex social relationships between women and men participating in trafficking, showing that although women can exercise choice, they also experience compulsion and constraints. This study appreciates how these women are both victims and agents in global drug markets and, instead of seeing women as simply being exploited victims, like men they can behave rationally and intentionally. In Fleetwood's own words (2014: 15): 'Most women's narrative about becoming involved revealed a mixture of compulsion, obligation, and willing.'

Drug mules are also a domestic problem and in the mid-2000s Joseph (2006) found that not only one in five women in prison were foreign nationals but 80 per cent of this population were doing time for a drug-related offence. This needs to be seen in the context of the fact that

> the majority of the women's prison population is held for drug offences – women are proportionally imprisoned in much greater numbers for drug-related offences than for any other offence. (HM Inspectorate of Prisons, 2009: 7)

In Chapter 5 we revisit the issue of female imprisonment as a human rights issue, but it has been argued by UN Women (2014) that contemporary global drugs policy also compromises human rights because it is a key cause of gender-based violence. Migrant Mexican women who encountered drug smugglers were susceptible to sexual violence and the military were also criticized for human rights violations during the 'War on Drugs' (ibid.: 3).

Human trafficking

In policy and legislative discourse human trafficking is frequently described as a modern form of slavery (e.g. the Modern Slavery Act 2015), can occur nationally and internationally and is, to a certain extent, organized (Aronowitz, 2009). According to the Palermo Convention, agreed at the United Nations Convention Against Transnational Organized Crime in 2011, trafficking in persons refers to

> the recruitment, transportation, transfer, harbouring or receipt of persons, by means of threat or use of force or other forms of coercion, of abduction, of

fraud, of deception, of the abuse of power or of a position of vulnerability or of the giving or receiving of payments or benefits to achieve the consent of a person having control over another person, for the purpose of exploitation. Exploitation shall include, at a minimum, the exploitation or the prostitution of others or other forms of sexual exploitation, forced labour or services, slavery or practices similar to slavery, servitude or the removal of organs.

The International Labour Organization (ILO) calculated that globally some 20.9 million people were victims of trafficking in 2012 (Occhipinti, 2014). It has been made possible due to globalization and the opening of national borders for the movement of capital and goods and people through migration, which is sometimes illegal. In the less developed world, particularly those places where scarcity, famine and conflict are endemic, migration may be a route to escape from these problems in order to survive. The former Soviet Union in the aftermath of the collapse of the Berlin Wall and natural disasters, such as the 2004 Indian Ocean tsunami and the 2010 Haiti earthquake, have proven to increase the vulnerability of people to traffickers (Caldwell and Williams, 2011; Shelley, 2010). The internet and mobile technologies present opportunities that have made trafficking more efficient and profitable and some traffickers have engaged in cybercrime as a sideline by uploading pornographic images onto the internet for their clients to consume (Hughes, 2002; Narasaiah, 2005).

As noted above, human trafficking includes forced labour and sexual exploitation, as well as bonded labour, domestic work, child slavery and organ trafficking (Anti-Slavery Day, 2014). Trafficking comprises a range of illegitimate activities that entail controlling people for the purpose of exploitation and financial gain. The inclusion of children in the definition has made the case for viewing those who are trafficked to be victims of crime compelling. There is no settled agreement on what trafficking refers to, reflected by the contentious nature of definitions and measurements of the phenomenon, especially surrounding the issues of consent and the extent to which people need to be transported or physically moved from one geographical place to another (Bakirci, 2009; Lee, 2011). Not all aspects of trafficking receive the same degree of attention and sexual exploitation has tended to be the most widely covered issue, perhaps because this accounts for 58 per cent of confirmed cases (Chuang, 2010; UNODC, 2012).

There are fluctuating estimates of the number of people globally who are trafficked and experiencing forced labour (including sexual exploitation) but an emergent trend is that it is a social problem that is gendered, with ILO data showing that women and girls account for 55 per cent of human trafficking victims (11.4 million) compared to men and boys, for whom the equivalent figure is 45 per cent (9.5 million) (International Labour Organization, 2012). Conversely, other estimates for different kinds of trafficking suggest men are more vulnerable. In the UK a charitable organization, the Salvation Army (cited in BBC News, 2014), gathered evidence to show that 42 per cent of cases involved forced labour compared to 38 per cent for sexual exploitation and 10 per cent for domestic servitude. Eighty per cent of the forced labour cases involved men.

Gender, crime and human rights: Global drivers of crime

The socio-economic and political processes underlying globalization described in the previous section also shape crime policy. We argue that there are six key global drivers in crime policy, which impact, albeit unevenly, on all European, American and Australasian societies. Also, the relationship between these drivers and crime and public policy has a complex relationship with human rights values and principles. For example, there might be talk, as well as legislation, driving forward human rights and a respect for gender equality, but other politically determined choices and courses of action in the sphere of crime reduction frequently overshadow this. It is to these drivers that we now turn. Although trends described are global in their significance, the focus is on the British context to aid explanation.

New Public Management and modernization

The principles of New Public Management (NPM), especially that of performance management, have impacted unevenly across the public sector in general and the criminal justice system in particular. NPM is a set of principles and practices which have influenced the general direction of criminal justice policy since they were set in train in British society by successive Conservative governments from the 1980s onwards (Matthews, 2014).

According to Rhodes (Newburn, 2002; Raine, 2002), the main features include: a shift to disaggregating of units, including the creation of Next Steps agencies and the growth of regulatory bodies; de-professionalization and de-privileging staff groups seeking to reduce the control over policy and practice by 'experts'; hands-on professional management, often creating responsibility without authority; explicit standards, procedures and measures of performance management; greater emphasis on output controls and managing by results; a shift to greater competition; and a stress on private sector styles of management practice (Travers, 2007). The principles of the NPM developed throughout the 1980s and 1990s were adopted and reshaped by New

Labour modernizers in the 2000s, although the underlying logic of the 3Es – or the quest for economy, effectiveness and efficiency in service delivery – is still germane. There is scant evidence to suggest that there will be any diminution of its significance and authoritarian austerity is central to modes of governance across the world. All agencies nowadays are expected to achieve what they did in the past – and possibly more – by using existing funding regimes more prudently. It is likely that more will have to be done with less through working 'smarter' in an increasingly competitive environment. All criminal justice agencies are likely to be subjected to this disciplinary mechanism, although it is feasible that this will become second nature as policy-makers and practitioners comply with and commit themselves towards these goals. Other goals, such as gender equality and human rights, are there, and there is compliance, even commitment, to these values, but they are way down a list of increasingly economic and technocratic priorities. This set of politically motivated tactics is principally concerned with the maximization of economic competitiveness, and social considerations such as human rights – equality, dignity, justice, etc. – are marginalized. Performance management is an exemplar of NPM principles (Diamond, 2007).

Performance management

Performance management has been utilized as a mechanism for assessing and auditing the performance of public sector agencies, including the criminal justice system. In real terms this has resulted in the setting of targets, attempts to control outputs and the development of minimum standards. The measurement of performance is oriented towards activities that can be quantified and more abstract beliefs and values, such as gendered equality and human rights, are neglected. It is seen as a politically neutral exercise, although this is disingenuous because the choices made reflect a narrow range of interests (Matthews, 2014).

Victim-centred justice

During the last two decades of the twentieth century the criminal justice system in England and Wales experienced an increased workload due to a focus on victims and witnesses, culminating in victim-centred justice (Goodey, 2005; Spalek, 2006). As noted in Part III, in the victim chapters, since the early 1990s successive British governments have introduced so-called Victims' Charters in 1990 and 1996 (Home Office, 2001), followed by the Victims' Code of Practice, coming into effect in 2004 with the passing into law of the Domestic Violence, Crime and Victims Act 2004 (Spalek, 2006). Although the

Conservatives did launch the first Victim's Charter (Home Office, 1990), it was New Labour that invested many more resources into this area (Williams, 2003). We now look at the status of the gendered victim in the context of certain criminal justice agencies.

In Chapters 7 and 8 on victims, we make the point that there is regrettably a tension in crime and public policy between the respective needs of offenders and victims. In the mid-2000s New Labour showed more even-handedness in its rebalancing act, but as Williams and Canton (2005) rightly point out, the rights of victims are often portrayed as if they are irreconcilable with those of offenders. Thus an apparently benevolent and politically neutral move to look after victims of crime can deepen forms of exclusion experienced by defendants and offenders. Williams and Canton (2005: 2) also argue that one might suspect this to be part of a deliberate strategy so that opponents can be accused of sentimental support for the civil liberties of criminals.

In a relatively short time period victim-centred justice may not have come to dominate crime policy but it has a much higher profile and this seems set to continue. An appreciation of the experiences of victims underpins how society reacts to offenders and the extent to which offenders should be controlled or cared for. Western European criminal justice systems still have safeguards to protect suspects and offenders and they enjoy formal human rights not enjoyed by victims; however, the victim has a new status. It seems impossible that at any time a government will give up on victims. The continued functioning of criminal justice partly depends on the effective valorization and inclusion of victims as a justification of its other more punitive and exclusionary policies. There is, of course, restorative justice, although its future is likely to be limited because of growing public intolerance with nuisance offenders (i.e. the criminalization of anti-social behaviour) and because it is of little utility in the case of mainly male serious and violent offenders. Also, it is necessary to reiterate an observation aired later on in the book where we venture the view that it is not always possible to see victims and offenders as occupying different camps because some young men and women are victims and offenders at the same time (see Chapter 8).

Public protection and penal populism

Public protection has been a fundamentally important consideration, as society becomes ever more fearful of various hazards and potential harms. Significantly, it is men who cause most concern in this regard. Our homes, workplaces and public space all feel less safe, as people do become more knowledgeable about the everyday significance of crime and anti-social behaviour. Sex offending once confined to families is now a computer-generated as well as an actual phenomenon and the rowdy behaviour of young people is increasingly criminalized as anti-social behaviour. High-profile cases of seriously dangerous predatory violent criminals haunt not only the public but probation, **parole** and prison personnel too, who sometimes make flawed life and death decisions about the releasability of these offenders. Anthony Rice, a man with a history of violent offending behaviour, was released from prison prematurely on the grounds that his human rights were being violated. Tragically, on being released he went on to kill again because there were not adequate provisions in place to manage the risks he posed.

Human rights discourse is increasingly making the citizenry aware that governments should assume responsibility for looking after their safety and security. If this book were written less than 10 to 15 years ago it is unlikely that few scholars would have anticipated the long-term consequences of 9/11 in the USA and 7/7 in the UK. While this is not explicitly a crime issue, it has placed a burden on the criminal justice system, augmenting the work of the police, courts and security services. What these events effectively did was to transform the human rights agenda in two ways. Firstly, a preoccupation with human rights at an international level has meant that the focus is not exclusively on domestic problems. An example of this is a law lords ruling that the activities of British troops abroad are regulated by the Human Rights Act 1998, in particular the prohibition of torture (*New Law Journal*, 22 June 2006). Secondly, recent events of terrorism have further strengthened a more punitive approach. The increased use of stop and search/stop and question by the police and the ongoing debate about extending the period terrorist suspects can be held, all indicate a less sympathetic climate for civil liberties and human rights (Parmar, 2013, 2014). It is arguable too that the discourse of 'ordinary' crime has changed as a direct consequence of a focus on terrorism. In describing anti-social behaviour, for instance, some commentators make a subliminal connection to this global agenda in the way in which the terms of the debate are being conducted. References appear in the print media which conflate the nuisance behaviour of 11-year-olds as exerting terror on local communities (Senior, 2005).

Government policies designed to protect the public are closely allied with penal populism and evidence that the public hold punitive attitudes towards criminals. It is necessary to treat notions of punitiveness with caution, though, because the so-called 'myth of punitiveness' downplays the existence of contradictory interventions such as **rehabilitation** and **restorative justice** that are not intentionally punitive (Matthews, 2014). We should not ignore the perilously overcrowded prison estate in Britain, for example, which is one of the highest in Western Europe (Liebling and Maruna, 2005; Padfield and Maruna, 2006; Pratt, 2007). Prison overcrowding has produced further paradoxes in the sense that in the summer of 2007 over 1000 prisoners (out of a total of almost

10,000), who were serving **indeterminate sentences** for public protection, were not being released on time. This population includes some lifers, but mainly individuals who are at risk of harming themselves or others. They are mainly men. This group of inmates were nearing the end of their sentences but could not be considered for release by the **parole board** because they had not attended compulsory programmes that are a condition of their release. Some prisoners in this position claim that they are being detained arbitrarily, which is a breach of the Human Rights Act 1998 (Dyer, 2007a). Ironically, given the government's orientation towards economy and efficiency, it was estimated that the Sentences of Imprisonment for Public Protection (IPP) could lead to a £10 million 'jail backlog' (Dyer, 2007b).

Although crime went down by 30 per cent between 1997 and the mid-2000s, alongside lower risks of victimization, the prison population continues to expand (Garside, 2006). John Reid, the New Labour Home Secretary until the spring of 2007 stated that more prisons would be built to respond to public demand and the decisions of sentencers. It is worth noting that the rate of increase started to slow in the summer of 2007, although it is too early to tell if this is a blip in the context of a much broader punitive trend. It is notable that the Chancellor of the Exchequer until June 2007, Gordon Brown, remarked that there were no resources to honour this pledge, a clear illustration of the influence of NPM.

Overall, it would appear that penal **punitiveness** is becoming more and more irrational and contradictory by the day. When John Reid was Home Secretary large sections of the public expressed their fears about dangerous male offenders in the community who posed risks that had not been assessed or managed appropriately. The actual risk of becoming a victim of one of these offenders or being a witness of their crimes is negligible, although public fears do need to be addressed. Anxiety about the adequacy of public protection – including the vulnerable as well as the respectable majority – mirror not only government priorities but also the deep-seated concerns of both 'middle England' as well as socially excluded communities (Hughes, 2007; Respect Task Force, 2006).

Popular punitiveness is most clearly demonstrated by the intolerance of 'loutish' and anti-social behaviour, especially that of boys, but also, as shown in Chapter 5, in response to the rise of 'mean girls', which is resulting in the criminalization of non-criminal activities (France, 2007). It was Rod Morgan, on his resignation as head of the Youth Justice Board (YJB) in 2007, who questioned such an openly punitive approach to young people. In the current climate there is not much evidence to show a curbing of this desire to punish not just serious and organized crime, such as human trafficking, but also relatively petty incivilities. The targeting of suspected terrorists can conceivably be vindicated, although there needs to be a balance to make sure legally innocent citizens are not subjected to unwarranted attention. Crucially, human rights may not be routinely violated and are rarely mentioned, although civil liberties advocates voice their worries. In their clamour to satisfy public demands to punish, the gender-specific issues faced by those bearing the brunt of this punitiveness is rarely mentioned outside academia and the conference circuit attended by researchers and those campaigning for the human rights of prisoners. The deleterious impact of this climate on women in particular and the blighted futures of male prisoners are not high on the government's agenda.

Decline of the rehabilitative ideal

The decline of the rehabilitative ideal belongs to the past and Martinson's (1974) 'nothing works' pessimism was effectively challenged in the 1990s by the 'what works' agenda and the burgeoning of 'evidence-based' research, suggesting, on the contrary, that future offending behaviour may be reduced (Davies et al., 2000; Hough, 2004; Wiles, 1999). This is underpinned by a belief in progressive change based on scientific evidence. It is all about making sure interventions are targeted at the right people, at the right time, and in the right place (Tilley, 2005). Initiatives designed to reduce crime need to be refashioned to meet individual requirements.

This emphasis has influenced **probation** policy and practice in the past, although offender management and corrections now predominate. Other agencies in criminal justice are also sceptical about **rehabilitation**. In contrast to probation officers, police opinion is more likely to refer to **retribution** and incapacitation of offenders, offering some support to a view that the rehabilitative ideal is perceived to be in crisis because of the ascendancy of penal populism (see above) and, as shown in the next section, techniques of risk assessment and management. Declining faith in the efficacy of rehabilitation is a trend that has resulted in the justification for a policy of mass imprisonment where criminals are warehoused or contained. There is a lack of trust in community-based punishments, leading, for example, to an increase in the female prison population. Due to the overall increase of female offenders coming into contact with the criminal justice system, however, there has been a higher rate of community-based sentences for women (Ministry of Justice, 2014b). This logic is applied to all criminals and has resulted in the imprisonment of individuals who have committed relatively minor offences. Many prisoners serving short sentences do not benefit from interventions intended to tackle offending behaviour and they re-enter society more damaged (in terms of mental and physical health) than when they entered the prison estate. A failure to reintegrate rehabilitated offenders into society leaves prisoners, especially women, in a vulnerable position with regard to human rights.

Risk assessment and management

The idea of risk has influenced debates in the social sciences, most notably the work of the late Ulrich Beck (2015), who in some of his more radical moments argued that consciousness of risk displaced many of the traditional concerns of social theory, not least those of social class, poverty and inequality (Mythen, 2014). Given the prominence of risk in theory and its centrality in crime policy, we consider its pervasiveness in crime control. Ideas about risk are right at the heart of the criminal justice system and are there to predict and classify offenders on the grounds of their dangerousness. Risk can be assessed in various ways, including the use of clinical assessments designed for individual offenders to work out dynamic and static risk factors. Some models of risk examine psychological variables whereas others look at sociological factors. An important aspect of risk is that it is regarded as a scientific crime reduction tool. For our purposes, its deployment of predictive profiling means its commitment to human rights principles is weak and its imprecision means it overstates the protection it can provide to victims of serious violent, often sexually motivated, crimes. The section below suggests that risk assessment and management in relation to probation, youth justice, the courts and the police is heavily influenced by penal populism and a waning belief in the capacity of offenders to commit themselves to change.

Correctional agencies and the management of risk

The probation service has relied on risk management for its work with violent men and prolific male offenders, and there is the expectation that its measurements will be accurate (Kemshall, 2008). While risk assessment is a permanent feature of probation work, there are more novel features in current practice, especially the usage of actual accounting, which is supposedly based on scientific procedures. This helps to predict both the risk of reoffending and the more complex and potentially sensitive risk of harm to self or others (Senior et al., 2007).

Actuarial justice can, in Feeley and Simon's (1994) view, be contrasted with liberal ideas about justice that were created to determine the culpability and **guilt** of individual suspects and offenders as part of an overarching reformist and reintegrative strategy. These assumptions were characterized as untenable in the late twentieth century, especially the focus on individualized justice. Actuarial justice more or less abandons any pretensions that rehabilitation or punishment are effective and that instead policy-makers must devise 'techniques for identifying, classifying and managing groups assorted by levels of dangerousness' (Feeley and Simon, 1994: 173). Accordingly, justice is no longer individualized but is oriented towards assessing and managing the dangers presented by 'groups' and 'aggregates' such as 'permanent-marginal' underclass-type populations. Thus, actuarial justice can maintain the marginalized masculinities described in Chapter 6, though more often than not this logic is applied more routinely to individual violent men.

The careful assessments associated with high-risk male offenders such as represented by the Multi-Agency Public Protection Arrangements (MAPPA), demonstrate progress towards public protection, agency coordination and targeted interventions. However, whether that satisfies the public appetite for risk surveillance of whole populations, particularly an overwhelming male group of sex offenders, is less easy to assess. Sex offenders have been subjected to increased levels of scrutiny, demonstrated by the use of registers and panels (Senior et al., 2007). Still, senior policy-makers in government seem reluctant to face the fact that their expectations about the degree of risk protection that can be provided are essentially unrealistic and unobtainable in practice. Moreover, the human rights of those subject to this type of risk assessment may be denied. Increasing public protection is feasible and there are interventions that can yield positive results, yet for these strategies to be successful it would be necessary to use intrusive surveillance technologies that are out of touch with the values of a civilized society.

Furthermore, such strategies do not guarantee the prevention of reoffending. It is by its very nature impossible to prevent new offenders offending because they have not formally been measured and therefore do not exist. In spite of this, there are occasional demands for so-called 'pre-delinquents' to be identified and tagged as a precaution against future unspecified offending. Again, this process is gendered, with boys most commonly being identified as dangerous. Indeed, anti-social behaviour orders convert *nuisance* youngsters into *criminals* simply through a breach process. In Chapter 7, however, we show that girls and women, and their needs, are identified as risky.

The issue of unrealistic expectations is a factor that the probation service has faced when dealing with the fall out of the Monckton Inquiry in 2006 (Her Majesty's Inspectorate of Probation, 2006). In this case, probation staff committed several errors, and the inquiry shows the contradictions impacting on probation policy and practice. It examined the issue of whether or not the procedures followed and the decisions taken in this case were correct. The problem is that practitioners are urged to give their full attention to agency protocols, although in doing this they are prompted to gloss over those issues usually dealt with as a matter of professional judgement (Senior et al., 2007). This proclivity to devote more time and attention to protocols also ignores a finding taken from the desistance literature, namely that change in individual offenders is often highly individual (Kazemian and Maruna, 2009). As Bottoms has pointed out, an outcome of this is that risk assessment procedures will result in the calculation of false negatives and false positives (Bottoms, 1977).

Subsequently, it is possible that a potential risk of offending is therefore not detected, which means that a victim is not adequately protected.

Conversely, in contradistinction to Articles 5, 6 and 7 of the HRA 1998, it is possible that certain categories of male offenders are going to be wrongly assumed to be guilty. It has been shown that from time to time risk and penal populism co-exist and any effective method of offender management, especially of serious offenders, will include an element of public protection. Risk management is therefore an essential part of the system. It must be noted, though, that defining a situation or a person as a risk and in need of a policy response is a political decision.

Research evidence shows that it is violent men who are most likely to be labelled as a risk and in need of higher levels of surveillance and incapacitation, but we argue later on in the book that girls are increasingly joining the ranks here. Given that over a 10-year period commencing in the mid-1990s crime rates have fallen, it could be argued that risk of crime victimization in general has reduced. Yet the tone of debate both in the popular press and in government circles is one of increasing concern about the risks to individuals and this is fed by occasional high-profile cases which genuinely do challenge our protective capacities, such as the Soham murders. The Soham murders refers to a widely reported double murder of two 10-year-old girls, Holly Marie Wells and Jessica Aimee Chapman, committed by Ian Huntley on 4 August 2002 in Cambridgeshire, England.

Risk assessment and management of risk are also central to crime analysis and offender profiling, which are increasingly important tools for the police service (Ainsworth, 2001). Gender is not an explicit component of risk assessment tools used by the police, yet men are targeted most and it is their human rights that are most susceptible to infringement. This focus on risk cannot be separated from the wider belief that we live in a 'risk society' where social agencies cannot resolve social problems but rather limit the most negative effects they cause (Beck, 1992). Ericson and Haggerty (1997) have drawn on this reasoning in their analysis of 'policing the risk society', an environment in which the police play an increased role in the production and dissemination of crime-related knowledge to a range of agencies beyond the police.

Thus, to sum up this section, risk assessment and management are explicitly underpinned by the logic of actuarial justice. Rather than individualized justice, offenders are assorted into groups whose members share characteristics in common. Such an approach to risk assessment and management provides a useful profiling tool, sometimes to predict who is going to offend. Such reasoning is evidenced by attempts to bring into the criminal justice system individuals who are potentially dangerous before they have committed an offence. This pressure has been resisted thus far, though we anticipate further calls to be made for predicting patterns of offending behaviour. Professionals will continue to call for rehabilitation but the punitiveness referred to in an earlier section could lead to calls for the segregation and exclusion of offenders rather than their rehabilitation.

Commercialization of crime control

The private sector is nowadays a major provider of crime reduction and security services, ranging from the regulation of the night-time economy (Hadfield, 2006; Winlow, 2001) to private policing (Maggio, 2008) and private prisons (Matthews, 2009). Each of the above activities focuses mainly on men and/or masculine behaviour.

In more concrete terms we can see the commercialization of crime control in a number of areas, especially the installation and monitoring of security equipment such as CCTV (Fussey, 2005; Goold, 2004). In 2001 the Private Security Industry Act passed into law a new regulatory framework, including the creation of the licensing body known as the British Security Industry Authority (BSIA). This new framework has made it possible for the private security sector to give off an impression that it is professional and accountable in its operations. Data published in 2001 by the BSIA estimated that there were 8000 security companies and 350,000 employees in this sector in the UK (BSIA, 2001). This unprecedented expansion of private security must be situated in the context of structural changes in post-industrial societies, most crucially the privatization of what was at one time exclusively public space (Shearing and Stenning, 1981).

The police service in England and Wales is not in a position to actively resist such changes and there are potential benefits. However, such developments reinforce earlier patterns of policing inasmuch as interpersonal relationships between men and women, however violent they may be, are not a preoccupation of private, for-profit enterprises.

Another feature of this process is the primacy of the private sector in delivering protective services – electronic surveillance, prison escorting, satellite tracking, lie detectors, etc. Their desire to develop their business, and in a market in which contestability seems somewhat absent, can lead to an unregulated desire to extend control. As will be shown a little later on, the private sector is under no particular pressure to monitor the gender impact of its activities (i.e. there is no section 95 requirement) nor are HR considerations pre-eminent. It has been argued elsewhere that unless there is a balance between the aims of protection, rehabilitation and restoration (Raikes, 2002), then the system ceases to be fit for purpose. The danger with risk is that it becomes a form of both proactive and retrospective profiling, potentially leading to a diminution of the human rights of some male offenders and suspects.

The future looks like being a lucrative place for the private sector, as the commercialization of crime control seems set to continue (Jones, 2012). The correctional services have already been exposed to privatization in various jurisdictions and policing functions are increasingly being performed by private security agencies. In the United States, for example, gated communities exist in many urban areas, existing as a testament to the limitations of federal and state-funded law enforcement. Surveillance systems such as CCTV and **electronic tagging** were once the stuff of science fiction novels and new technological innovations are materializing all the time. Similar develop- ments are occurring throughout Western European cities but not on the scale found across the Atlantic. A hazard with this approach is that socio-economic priorities are of paramount importance. The protection of private property is the priority unless that rare population of predatory strangers is acknowl- edged. Caution must be exercised because technological fixes such as digital technologies, CCTV, forensic science (i.e. DNA) and biometrics are not able to address the underlying causes of crime and disorder. It can also be dis- criminatory (Lyon, 2003). We do not anticipate any reversal of this trend and suggest that it may expand at an unprecedented rate. This is controversial, however, as it is likely to lead to a reawakening of debates about accountabil- ity and further undermine any of the remaining significance attached to the principle of both criminal and social justice. More than that, the commercial- ization of control will see mechanisms of control reflecting the interests of those paying for it without any wider reference to democratic values, gender equality and human rights.

Concluding thoughts

We have attempted to show that debates about globalization have had a far- reaching impact on social scientific analyses of myriad political, economic and cultural processes and developments, so much so that the twenty-first-century world is radically different from societies in the nineteenth and first half of the twentieth centuries. The defining characteristics of the transformations that have taken place include the dominance of capitalism, which has restructured labour markets, and the relationship between the state, society and individual citizen, resulting in the increased concentration of wealth and power in the hands of a global power elite. Meanwhile the poor and minority groups have not enjoyed the benefits of globalization, hence the widening inequalities between the Northern and Southern hemispheres and spatial apartheid within nation states. More rapid methods of communication and increased physical mobility have made the world a smaller place, but the circumstances under which people move and migrate involve different degrees of choice or coercion. From the late 1990s onwards there has been recognition of the criminological salience of globalization for coming to terms with the causes of and solutions to crime with reference to gender. Globalization has produced conditions that have led to the evolution of existing crime problems and the emergence of new ones. Transnational crime has become a major issue and nation states both individually and in collaboration with each other face new threats, such as terrorism and organized crime. What this chapter intended to achieve was to acknowledge these trends but alert the reader to the enduring relevance of the local in the sense that each nation state will have a different experience of crime both domestically and transnationally. The remainder of the book examines in detail the gendered nature of the criminal justice system in England and Wales, illustrating how globalization might shape what happens there, but it never fully determines what happens because local conditions can alter its course. The theme of human rights principles, which emphasize universal values that can be mobilized to tackle gendered forms of inequality, has also been discussed and this will be used to inform our analysis of gender and crime.

Summary

- We have provided an overview of the notion of globalization and some of the controversies generated by this idea. It refers to a number of inter-related socio-economic, political, cultural and technological changes that have opened up the world, but also made it a smaller place. Social relationships have been intensified. Globalization has created many opportunities but it has also created profound gender-based inequalities with a transnational business masculinity being dominant at the expense of women and marginalized men.
- Globalization also has a complex relationship with criminal behaviour. There are opportunities that once did not exist due to criminals having greater mobility and a new modus operandi, such as information technology. Globalization has also opened up more markets for criminals to exploit and made committing crime easier. Also, some of the inequalities engendered by globalization are criminogenic and where the conventional means of making a living are no longer possible, for example, in deindustrialized areas, then crime is an alternative method of survival.
- We demonstrated that globalization and its impact on offending and victimization is uneven, as well as being gendered. We used the examples of drug and human trafficking to delineate gender-based inequalities and exclusion, especially the ways in which the human rights of men and women might be differentially compromised.
- We spent some time outlining the field of comparative criminology to show how our knowledge and understanding of crime issues can be enhanced by looking at what other countries do. We can also see that globalization has not resulted in uniformity across the globe, with the nature of crime, victimization and control still having unique characteristics in individual nation states.
- Finally, we introduced six global drivers of crime, which are at work in many societies, and showed how they have influenced crime and public policy in England and Wales. The key point is that there are global and universal processes, but their effects vary from country to country. They also interact with human rights principles and values.

STUDY QUESTIONS

1. Outline what is meant by globalization and list its main features.
2. Why is globalization relevant for understanding criminal behaviour?
3. What can comparative criminology tell us about the relationship between gender and crime?
4. What is the relationship between globalization, crime and gender?
5. What are the potential uses of the six global drivers of crime for making sense of gender and crime?
6. What is the relationship between the global and local when considering the human rights of men and women and their involvement in crime?

FURTHER READING

A useful starting point to gain a general understanding of the concept of globalization is the work of Anthony Giddens (1990) *The Consequences of Modernity* (Polity Press), although he has not published much material on the topic in recent years. However, below is a link to a lecture he gave on globalization. As you listen to this, think about the relevance of what he says to the core concerns of this chapter and the book as a whole: www.youtube.com/watch?v=n-9rDFN2zPU.

For an up-to-date account of the globalization thesis we recommend you look at J. Nederveen Pieterse (2015) *Globalization and Culture: Global Melange*, 3rd edn (Rowman & Littlefield). Comparative approaches to crime are attracting more interest from criminologists and F. Pakes (2010) *Comparative Criminal Justice*, 2nd edn (Willan) is essential reading. He also touches on the issue of globalization, but it is also necessary to be familiar with the globalization and crime literature to make sense of a complex area. We recommend two books: K.F. Aas (2013) *Globalization and Crime*, 2nd edn (Sage) and M. Findlay (1999) *The Globalization of Crime* (Cambridge University Press). In these books there is some coverage of gender-related issues, but for a book that covers all of the issues that we are interested in – crime, gender and human rights – see R. Barberet (2014) *Women, Crime and Criminal Justice: A Global Inquiry* (Routledge).

PART II
OUT OF CONTROL

5

Women as Offenders

OVERVIEW

Chapter 5 provides:

- An insight into the nature and extent of female offending.

- An analysis of the current trend to 'search for equivalence' in criminality between women and men.

- An overview of the arrival of the 'new female offender' in the form of the 'mean girl', the female sex offender and the female terrorist.

- The impact of the 'mean girl' discourse on the punishment of girls and women.

- An exploration of women in prison and the concept of vulnerability.

- An analysis of what human rights can do for women in prison with a focus on the three main issues that face the female prisoner: the over-representation of women in suicide and self-harm statistics; contact with children and families; and the experience of girls in prison. In doing so we consider in more detail the relevance of human rights legislation.

KEY TERMS

- agency
- Bangkok Rules
- Corston Report
- family life
- female offender
- feminist criminology
- human rights
- mean girl

- punitiveness
- search for equivalence
- sex offender
- suicide and self-harm
- terrorist
- vulnerability
- women in prison

Introduction

Interest in the female offender has ebbed and flowed over the past 100 years. For much of this time, she has been neglected and those representations in existence are distorted in discussions on criminality. When she has appeared, successive generations have done much to erase both her capacity and willingness to participate in criminality, portraying her as peculiarly *evil, unstable* and *irrational*. In this early part of the twenty-first century, the female offender is back in the limelight, occupying a central place on government and criminological agendas. And, in what has been an increasingly punitive climate, she has not been exempted from the 'incarceration binge' characteristic of contemporary Western states (Snider, 2003). The number of **women in prison** nearly trebled between 1993 and 2005 and though there are signs that this trend is slowly reversing, there are still over 2000 more women in prison today than there were 20 years ago (Prison Reform Trust, 2015). Moreover, a more critical reading of the official statistics point to a much more complex picture of the number of women in prison. Findings from the Howard League (2015a) indicate that as the vast majority of the women sentenced to prison serve very short sentences, the female prison population on any one day masks the high level of use of imprisonment for women in England and Wales. In the 12 months ending June 2014, 9204 women entered custody either on **remand** or under sentence – of those serving a sentence, 77 per cent were sentenced to less than twelve months, 71 per cent less than six months and 52 per cent less than three months (Howard League, 2015a).

We are also being confronted with a range of 'new' female criminal characters. The emergence of the 'mean girl' (who is both able and willing to participate in a culture of violence and drinking), the **female sex offender** and the female terrorist are all indicative that the female offender is back, only this time she is back with a vengeance – or so it seems.

This chapter is divided into three main parts. The first part is dedicated to detailing who the female offender is, her participation in crime and her presence in the criminal justice system. While we acknowledge women's involvement across a range of offending categories, we explore more specifically the growing public unease about girls and young women, the female sex offender and the women's increased participation in terrorism. The second part spends considerably more time outlining the treatment that women who offend receive as they progress through the criminal justice system. Since the first edition of this book there have been a number of significant changes to the way women offenders are processed in the criminal justice system. We outline and consider these changes in relation to debates about equity, justice and fairness. In the third and final part we focus more specifically on women's experiences of incarceration. Our rationale for this stems from our belief that it is within this arena that the human rights agenda is relevant and has the greatest chance of making a difference. We focus on three main issues that face women in prison: their over-representation in suicide and self-harm statistics; their contact with children and families; and the experience of girls in prison. In doing so we consider in more detail the relevance of Article 2: The right to life, Article 8: The right to private and family life, and the United Nations Convention on the Rights of the Child.

Who is the female offender?

We have already emphasized in Chapters 2 and 3 the overriding consensus within criminology that women's pattern of offending is different from men's. The reality remains that while women do commit a broad range of offences they commit less crime than men and are less dangerous and violent than their male counterparts (Carlen and Worrall, 1987; Heidensohn, 1996; Heidensohn and Silvestri, 2012). This is also representative when mapping out women's participation in crime on a global stage. Women are consistently arrested less than men, and self-report delinquency studies also find that girls report less offending than boys (Barberet, 2014; Junger-Tas, 2012; Killias et al., 2010). Closer to home, figures for England and Wales in 2013/14 indicate that men continue to make up the majority of offenders and prisoners in the criminal justice system, with women accounting for 23 per cent of those given out-of-court disposals, 18 per cent of arrests, 25 per cent of convictions and 5 per cent of the prison population (Ministry of Justice, 2014f). While the main indictable offence group that female convictions tend to fall into is theft (nearly a quarter of female indictable convictions in 2013), violence against the person and theft and handling were consistently the two offence groups with the highest number of arrests for both males and females, together making up around half of male arrests and two-thirds of female arrests. As of 31 March 2015, the total prison population (including those on remand) stood at 85,664, of which 3866 are women (of which 673 are on remand). Of those receiving an immediate custodial sentence, 887 women are in prison for 'violence against the person'; 98 for 'sexual offences'; 313 for 'robbery'; 170 for 'fraud and forgery'; 418 for 'drug offences'; 24 for 'motoring offences'; 521 for other offences; and 34 women have no offence recorded (see www.gov.uk/government/.../prison-population-q1-2015.xlsx).

Despite the relatively low number of women officially engaged in criminal behaviour, recent years have observed a renewed attempt to identify increased gender neutrality in offending behaviour. Termed the 'search for equivalence' (Worrall, 2002), the idea that women are becoming equal partners in the field of crime is once again gaining ground within media and policy circles. Reminiscent of earlier works, such as that by Pollack (1950) and Adler (1975), contemporary constructions of female offenders suggest that they are breaking into 'new' (traditionally male) criminal territory. We explore the growing public unease and concern about the changing nature of female offending.

The problem of 'mean girls'

We begin by reminding readers of our discussion in Chapter 3 in which we documented anxiety over young women's behaviour throughout the centuries. With an identification of the 'ladette' (Clout, 2008) and the growth of girls' participation in violence and 'gang' activity, such concern remains at the fore-front of public discourse in the twenty-first century. Although the 'ladette' and the 'gang girl' refer to two distinct forms of deviance, we draw on Ringrose's (2006) concept of the 'mean girl' as an overarching term to describe and indicate women's participation in these behaviours. Characterized by binge drinking, smoking and aggressive behaviour, stories about the growing problem of girls have been an enduring feature of the media in recent decades (see Jewkes, 2015 for an excellent overview of the media construction of criminal women). Writing in *The Observer* newspaper, Hill and Helmore (2002) document the 'insidious and sophisticated' cruelty groups of 'mean girls' are exacting on one another. In 2006, *The Guardian* newspaper reported that British girls were among the most violent in the world, with nearly one in three Scottish and English adolescents admitting to having been involved in a fight in the past year. In a survey of young people in 35 countries, child health experts found that Scottish and English girls ranked fifth and sixth in violence (*The Guardian*, 24 January 2006). In 2008, the *Daily Mail* reported on the 'Feral sex: the terrifying rise of violent girl gang' (16 May) and in 2011 went on to highlight the growing concern and 'escalating thuggery perpetrated by girls' (11 February). More recently in 2015, *The Daily Telegraph* emphasized the 'terrifying rise of the all-girl gang' (*The Daily Telegraph*, 2015a). Indeed, such concern over violence among girls and young women has been cited as a growing problem within youth justice systems around the globe, including Scotland (Burman, 2009; Burman and Batchelor, 2009), the United States (Chesney-Lind and Irwin, 2008; Putallaz and Bierman, 2004), the Netherlands (Beijerse and Swaaningen, 2006), and Australia (Carrington, 2006). In line with Ringrose's (2006) analysis, such characterizations of the 'mean girl' are rarely explicitly raced or classed but rather provide a more universalized discourse in which *all* girls are now increasingly conceptualized as mean and aggressive. Such characterizations also sit firmly within a broader narrative of changing societal gender relations. Conceived as 'sexually liberated "post-feminist" criminals' (Batchelor, 2009: 399), their behaviour is cited as evidence of the 'dark side of girl power' (Prentice, 2000) and an unfortunate by-product of young women seeking equality with young men (Chesney-Lind and Irwin, 2008; McRobbie, 2004, 2012; Taft, 2004). Paradoxically, despite the increased concern about girls, relatively little is known about them, leaving Sharpe and Gelsthorpe (2009: 203) to note that:

> The ubiquity of such popular representations of 'ladettes', violent girls and girl gang members has not been matched by either empirical research or policy attention.

In assessing official statistics on crime, we can see that the number of girls coming into conflict with the criminal justice system has increased. More particularly, Heidensohn and Silvestri (2012) locate the concern about girls within police-recorded arrests, with data showing an increase in the number of girls being arrested for 'violence against the person'. We are mindful of the problematic nature of studying changes in female participation in crime, given their small number. Indeed, the low number of women engaged in criminal behaviour has very significant impacts on those seeking to study them and it is now a well-established fact that small numerical increases or decreases can make a great deal of difference in terms of reported rises and reductions (Heidensohn and Silvestri, 2012). The extent to which official figures indicate an increase in the criminality of girls remains a contested issue, with a number of scholars suggesting that the apparent increase may be largely due to the different approaches to reporting and responding to crime perpetrated by girls and young women rather than as a result of their increased offending (Batchelor, 2009; Burman and Batchelor, 2009; Steffensmeier et al., 2005). Before documenting this position more fully, we acknowledge some of the criminological work that has contributed to providing a more complex and nuanced reading and understanding of the behaviour of girls, particularly in relation to their involvement in gang activity.

Traditionally described as playing 'minor', 'support' and 'girlfriend' roles, there is a growing body of research indicating a more 'active' role for girls. Exploring the motivations and activities of girls, this research emphasizes girls as more than just auxiliaries or sex objects. Rather, gang membership and engagement with street violence is claimed to offer young women a means through which to resist dominant gender stereotypes, establish identity, maintain respect and build status and reputation; it also serves as a place of solace from abusive families fostering an increased sense of belonging and empowerment (Brunson and Stewart, 2006; Cobbina et al., 2010; Maher, 1997; Miller, 2001, 2008; Miller and Mullins, 2006; Ness, 2007; Young, 2009; Young et al., 2007). Despite being active, many of the girls interviewed by Young et al. (2007) did not see their violence as gang-related in the same ways as their male counterparts. Examining the rise of the so-called 'shem-ale' gangster in the UK between 2000 and 2007, Young (2009: 234) concurs, suggesting that girls' involvement is largely confined to criminal damage and shoplifting offences, with their use of violence as 'peer related and the result of perceived provocation, and not gang related'. These findings are further echoed by Burman and colleagues in their study of teenage girls in Scotland. Though citing evidence of physical violence by girls, they dispute the idea of a rise in girl gangs (Batchelor et al., 2001; Burman, 2004; Burman and Batchelor, 2009). Again, violence by girls was acknowledged as present but was more readily contextualized against a backdrop of violent family histories, often at the hands of men. Here the use of violence by girls was often perceived as a form of 'self-defence ... an attempt to pre-empt [further] bullying or victimization through the display of an aggressive or violent disposition' (Batchelor, 2005: 369). In this way, research acknowledges that both 'subordination and agency are simultaneously realised in young women's lives' (Batchelor, 2009: 407–8).

In thinking more critically about the official recorded increase in the number of young women coming into conflict with the criminal justice system, others have pointed more specifically to the impacts brought about by changes in the law and policy and the actions of professionals in responding to crimes perpetrated by girls and young women. Sharpe and Gelsthorpe (2009: 198), for example, argue that violent acts constitute a high proportion of girls' recorded offences principally because of their non-participation in other crimes. As a result:

> changes within the criminal justice system that result in a statistical inflation of violent crimes by drawing on low-level assaults and physical altercations – including playground fights and domestic disputes – into the criminal justice system, will affect girls disproportionately.

The reported increase in girls' violence, then, is more attributable to changes in the labelling and criminalization of girls' bad behaviour than to changes in their actual behaviour. This is neatly encapsulated by Worrall (2004: 49) when she talks of 'soft policing' having given way to 'criminalization' of that same behaviour, with increasing numbers of young women being incarcerated.

This position is restated by Burman and Batchelor (2009), who identify the readiness and ease with which young women in Scotland have become problematized as a new source of the 'youth problem'. Research has also pointed to the discernible effect of media commentaries on practitioners' perceptions of women and girls who offend. Steffensmeier et al. (2005) have suggested that sentencers, as members of the public, are inevitably affected by such **moral panics** about girls. Sharpe (2009: 65) concurs, noting that the idea that 'today's girls are rapidly getting "worse" has made inroads into professional youth justice discourse'.

Women who sexually offend

Typically regarded as a male phenomenon and classified as too small in number to warrant any attention, the academic literature on sex offending has almost exclusively focused on men as offenders (Finkelhor, 1984; Grayston and De Luca, 1999). Indeed, Landor (2009) argues that the vast majority of research on the sex offender fails to even contemplate the existence of the female sex offender. Yet, we know that the female sex offender does exist and, like her male counterparts, she does commit a range of serious sexual offences (Adshead et al., 1994; L. Bunting, 2007; Denov, 2004; Gannon and Rose, 2008; Oliver, 2007; Peter, 2009; Vandiver and Walker, 2002; Wijkman et al., 2010). When female sex offenders are acknowledged, their actions have for the most part been conceived in one of three ways. Firstly, they are constructed as being 'beyond evil' and 'monstrous', transgressing all gender expectations and norms; secondly, their behaviour is explained through a narrative of past and ongoing victimization (Hickey et al., 2008; Lewis and Stanley, 2000; Oliver, 2007); and lastly, women who engage in sex offences are perceived through a lens of coercion and 'gender entrapment', undertaking their role as the unwilling accomplices of men (Elliott et al., 2010; Jones, 2008; Matravers, 1997, 2001, 2008; Wijkman et al., 2010).

Though small in number, those women who have been convicted of sexual offences have received a high-profile status within the media as particularly evil and depraved. Myra Hindley was to become the female icon of evil as a result of her involvement in the Moors Murders, which took place between 1963 and 1965. Together with Ian Brady, Hindley was involved in the kidnap, sexual assault, torture and murder of five children (Gavin, 2009; Murphy and Whitty, 2006).

Alongside Myra Hindley, Rosemary West was to become the second woman to have received a whole life sentence for her involvement in the sexual assault and murder of 10 young women along with her husband Fred West. Like Hindley, West became the embodiment of evil for her failure as a woman through her 'inadequacy as a mother and perversion as a wife' (Storrs, 2004: 18).

More recently, the high-profile case of Vanessa George, a childcare worker who was found guilty of sexually abusing the young children in her care at a

Plymouth Nursery School in 2009, has done much to reassert the possibility and capacity of women as sex offenders as well as to engender an increased 'moral panic' over a rise in the number of female sex offenders (Davidson, 2008; Harris and Salkeld, 2009). In 2009, *The Observer* newspaper reported that 'up to 64,000 women in the UK are child sex offenders' (Townsend and Syal, 2009) and in drawing on research by the Lucy Faithful Foundation, it noted that women make 'up to 20 per cent of a reported 320,000 paedophiles' in the UK. Though notoriously difficult to evidence with accurate information, there has been some attempt to document the prevalence rates of sex offences committed by women. Studies from the USA, for example, indicate that female sex offenders comprise around 5 per cent of all sex offenders (Cortoni, 2010). The number increases considerably if we examine victim-based surveys. Green (1999), for example, shows that 14–24 per cent of sexually abused males and between 6 and 14 per cent of sexually abused females report having been abused by a female perpetrator. The official statistics for England and Wales reveal low numbers of women in the criminal justice system, and the National Offender Management Service (NOMS) reports only 32 female sex offender prisoners (NOMS, 2007, cited in Beech et al., 2009). Again, the numbers increase considerably when we consider alternative non-statutory data sources. ChildLine figures for 2005–06, for example, reveal that 5 per cent of girls and 44 per cent of boys report abuse by women (NSPCC, 2007, cited by Gannon and Rose, 2008: 443). Despite an academic emphasis on understanding female sex offenders' past and ongoing trauma, vulnerability and victimization, media characterizations demonstrate an undeniably more pronounced construction of such women as sexual predators. Such a construction fits well with the contemporary search for equivalence in women's and men's offending and with the narrative that portrays women offenders as more 'dangerous' and 'active' than ever before. We concur with Gannon and Rose (2008) in acknowledging that there are still significant gaps in our knowledge surrounding female sex offenders and with Prins (2010: 316) that there remain a range of 'unaskable', 'unthinkable' and 'uncomfortable' questions to be addressed.

Women and terrorism

Alongside the 'moral panic' about girls and female sex offenders, the past decade has witnessed an increased anxiety over women's role and participation in violent extremism. Traditionally conceived as victims of terrorism, there is a marked shift in the way in which women's roles are being perceived. The recent identification in the UK of a number of teenage girls fleeing their homes in Western countries to join Islamic fighters in the Middle East has further fuelled the media panic about the presence of ever more 'active' and 'dangerous' women.

Media reports indicate that women and girls appear to make up about 10 per cent of those leaving Europe, North America and Australia to link up with jihadi groups, including Islamic State. France has the highest number of female jihadi recruits, with 63 in the region – about 25 per cent of the total – and at least another 60 believed to be considering the move (*The Guardian*, 29 September 2014). In January 2015, *The Daily Telegraph* reported on 'the female face of terror', describing the emergence of an online 'Jihadi girl power subculture' (2015b) – reminiscent again of the 'dark side' of liberation noted above.

Since Cunningham's (2003) comprehensive study on cross-regional trends in women's participation in terrorist networks across the world, a number of scholars have gone on to document women's involvement in global terrorism and extremist violence (Berko, 2012; Bloom, 2007, 2011; Dalton and Asal, 2011; Gonzalez-Perez, 2008; Hasso, 2005; Pratt, 2012). At the heart of much of this literature is an observable yet familiar tension that often accompanies the 'discovery' of women in new criminal terrains, that is, the extent to which women involved are 'pawns, victims or agents' (Jackson et al., 2011). Not surprisingly, the findings are mixed, demonstrating that female terrorists can be both victim and aggressor, often at the same time – though as with female sex offenders, there is a noticeable trend in recent years to portray women as willing, active and aggressive. Fink's (2010) study of terrorism, political violence and governance in Bangladesh, for example, emphasizes the active role played by Bangladeshi women in supporting or encouraging jihad. In exploring Al-Qaeda, Von Knop (2007) suggests that women are increasingly acting as facilitators, supporters and educators of the movement. Ness (2007) estimates that girls and women now make up 30–40 per cent of the active combatants in numerous ethnic separatist/guerrilla struggles. Gonzalez et al. (2014: 349) also emphasize the active and independent nature of European far-right extremist women, stating that:

> they are more than off-shoots of men's groups ... they are in fact separate entities with different roles and leadership structures that work in partnership with but are not subservient to the men's groups.

It is women's involvement as suicide bombers that is perhaps best documented within the literature. With women's participation expanded both 'ideologically, logistically and regionally' (Dearing, 2010), such engagement warrants some attention. Bloom (2011: 2) reports that between 1985 and 2010, female bombers committed over 257 suicide attacks (representing a quarter of total) and that the percentage of women operatives since 2002 in some countries exceeds as much as 50 per cent. Dearing (2010) goes on to note suicide attacks involving women by groups such as Hamas and Fatah in Israel, Chechen in Russia, Tamil separatists in Sri Lanka, Islamic militants in Uzbekistan, Kurdish separatists in Turkey, Syrian nationals in Lebanon and militant groups in Pakistan. The extent to which such participation demonstrates women's agency remains a contested issue with some scholars keen to draw out the context of broader societal gender relations. Zia (2011), for example, warns against any attempt to 'rescue the subaltern Islamist woman', concluding that given the overall patriarchal discourse and violence against and marginalization of women, it is difficult to read the trend of women suicide bombers in Pakistan as a sign of self-realization and autonomy. Bloom (2009) adds an additional dimension to the debate, suggesting that the recruitment of female suicide bombers can be better understood as a tactical response to the need for more manpower and as a useful tool to shame men into participating. In their analysis of Arab/Palestinian women in Israel, Berko et al. (2010) document the considerable ways in which women's 'troubled' home lives underline many of their deviant activities. Barberet (2014) also situates the widespread participation of women in a range of heinous acts during the Rwandan genocide against a backdrop of clear subordination to men in Rwandan society.

In making sense of the contemporary moral panic over women's participation in terrorist activity, we once again make reference to the importance of taking a historical perspective. There is now a considerable body of evidence to suggest a long history of women's involvement in extremist activity, including their participation in early modern terrorist groups in nineteenth-century revolutionary Russia, the Baader-Meinhof gangs in Germany in the 1960s and 1970s, the Provisional IRA of the 1970s and 1980s, the Zionist Movement in the post-war years and 1970s, the Tupamaros in Uruguay in the 1970s, the Basque separatist group ETA in Spain, the Tamil Tigresses in Sri Lanka and the Chechnya 'black widows' in the 1990s (Berko and Erez, 2007; Bloom, 2011; Hillyar and McDermaid, 2000; Kolinsky, 1988; Porzecanski, 1973; Weinburg and Eubank, 1987, 2011).

The previous section has demonstrated that not only have women offended throughout history but they are actively choosing, though not always under circumstances of their own choosing, to engage in new forms of opportunity. Next we consider the consequences of this for feminist research into females as perpetrators of crime.

Acknowledging women's agency in offending

Identifying women's participation in non-traditional crimes such as violence, terrorism and sexual abuse poses interesting dilemmas for those interested in the study of gender and crime. Barberet (2014: 140) has described this dilemma as the 'feminist criminological perversion'. On the one hand, the discourse of equivalence might act as a useful tool in unshackling women from traditional characterizations of their behaviour and their potential for criminality – this is especially important, given the erasure of much of their agency in criminal activity over time. On the other hand, the identification of women with a will-ingness and capacity to commit crime may also bring with it a raft of repressive state responses. Through emphasizing women's capacity to engage in a range of acts once reserved for men, the conventional idea of what it means to be a woman and of womanhood can no longer be sustained. Indeed we have already argued that there is a need to rethink the dualism that has come to characterize both women and men in the criminal justice system. Broadening the focus and blurring the distinctions between such dualisms as 'women as victims' and 'men as offenders' makes it possible to stand outside traditional criminal justice models. If we were to acknowledge and accept that women are capable of committing serious criminal acts in the same way as their male counterparts, it might follow that those who come before the courts accused of such crimes would be treated with less hostility. While we are keen to observe the very real positive benefits of such investigations, an alternative reading of the search for equivalence suggests a much more dismal outcome for women. Worrall (2002: 64) argues that the 'search for equivalence' which called for the empowerment of women by making them accountable for their deeds has resulted in the inevitable increase in the numbers of women ren-dered punishable.

In trying to make sense of the increased punitiveness directed at the crimi-nal woman, Snider (2003) focuses her attention on how the knowledge generated about the female offender is *heard* and *interpreted* by those officials in power. In doing so she treats the:

> [k]nowledge produced by feminist and non-feminist criminologies as produc-tive and constitutive, as an essential component of changes in the conception of the female offender and in the policies to control, discipline and punish her. (Snider, 2003: 355)

For Snider, feminist criminologists have themselves been complicit in the surge of punitiveness that criminal women receive today. She notes that while a key success of feminist work has been to contribute to a discourse in which the female offender has become more 'self-aware', 'robust' and 'equipped with the languages and concepts of resistance', such a characterization has developed from the claim that female offending arises from female victimiza-tion. This idea has been extensively documented, debated and discussed throughout feminist criminology (Balfour, 2000; Carlen, 1983; Comack, 1996; Kendall, 2000; Pollack, 2000). Victimization discourses are now widely employed by those hoping to improve conditions for the female offender and inmate; indeed, we draw on this script in order to make our own case in this book. Snider (2003: 366) notes that the victims' discourse is a useful 'tool in the kitbag of resistance' and has proved 'pivotal in the constitution of the resilient, resistant female offender'. Herein lies the problem. This knowledge has not been *heard* or *translated* into improving conditions for the female offender. On the contrary, it is this very claim that has generated considerable resistance, fuelling a powerful backlash against all progressive movements, including feminism.

The female offender has now been characterized as someone who no longer 'knows their place' (Snider, 2003: 356). The resulting outcome is that it is not the woman victimized by life's experience that is at the forefront of govern-mental intervention but rather it is the 'mean girl', in all her various forms, discussed above, who has come to preoccupy government thinking as the pun-ishable offender who deserves the increased punitiveness of the state. The 'mean girl' phenomenon is contributing to new forms of regulation, surveillance and discipline that hold serious implications for all girls. Insightfully, Ringrose (2006: 412) notes the differential impact of such regulation on differently positioned girls when she states that:

> [While] new technologies, therapies and educational strategies are being adopted by middle class communities, schools and parents to regulate the risks presented by the powerful mean girl, the effects of this narrative of girl-hood for those girls who lay outside the boundaries of middle-class mean-ness are quite different. New criminal categories like the anti-social behavior bans draw particular girls into growing webs of penal regulation.

It is girls 'whose families and communities do not necessarily have the resources to challenge the criminalization of minor forms of youthful misbehaviour' that bear the brunt of increased social control (Chesney-Lind and Irwin, 2004: 55).

Not only are more women entering the criminal justice system but the move towards accepting the concept of gender neutrality in offending has resulted in the 'unmaking of "women" as a category of offender requiring any special attention at all' (Chesney-Lind and Irwin, 2004: 65). Emphasizing that women can be the same as men has effectively resulted in the denial and erasure of sex and gender from discussions. This is particularly important when thinking about policy interventions. The disastrous effects are highlighted by Worrall (2002: 48) when she states that:

> The apparent realization that women might deliberately sexually harm children, rather than protect them from sexual harm, justified an ideological and moral retreat by professionals and policy makers.

The message then is clear. Through a discourse of gender neutrality and equivalence in offending, the state is better able to rescind its obligation of treating women as a category of offender with distinct needs. Treating women offenders as though they were men, particularly when the outcome is punitive, in the name of equal justice, amounts to nothing more than what Chesney-Lind (2006) terms 'vengeful equity'.

Processing and punishing the female offender

Women's experience of the criminal justice system has been the subject of much academic inquiry over time. As we have already documented in Chapter 2, feminist criminologists have worked hard to expose the complexity of women's experiences and have highlighted the disparity between the rhetoric of leniency and the reality of practice in which women are subjected to a gendered criminal justice system, characterized by gendered organizational logics and gendered agents of power. Since the first edition of this book, there has been a discernible consensus and near acceptance among academic and policy-makers alike that female offenders have been 'shoehorned' into a system designed for men (Fawcett Society, 2006). Suffering from a range and multiplicity of physical and mental health issues, together with the social effects of poverty, histories of addiction, physical and sexual abuse, the overwhelming consensus of research is that women's needs both within and beyond prison are more varied and complex than men's (Carlen, 2002; Carlen and Worrall, 2004; Corston, 2007; Eaton, 1993; Fawcett Society, 2004; HM Chief Inspector of Prisons, 1997; Howard League, 2015a; Prison Reform Trust, 2011; Sheehan et al., 2011).

Following pressure to address the specific needs of women, successive governments have gone some way in addressing the issues raised. The Home Office's (2004d) *Women's Offending Reduction Programme* (WORP 2004–07) is often cited as a starting point from which to make sense of some of the more recent policies aimed at developing more community-based approaches for women offenders as an alternative to incarceration. Aimed at reducing women's offending and reducing the number of women in custody, the programme focused more specifically on improving community-based services and interventions that were better tailored to the needs of women by encouraging collaboration between government departments and other agencies within the framework of the new National Offender Management Service and the new sentencing powers of the Criminal Justice Act 2003 (Gelsthorpe et al., 2007). NOMS was intended to create a more integrated system of offender management in England and Wales, thus ending the 'silo' mentality that was perceived to exist in the probation and prison services respectively.

More recently, the Corston Report (Corston, 2007) was to bring about a renewed vigour and momentum to the study of women offenders. Critical of previous efforts to address the needs of women offenders, Corston (2007) reported little improvement in their treatment and called for a radical change to the way in which women are treated throughout the whole criminal justice system. Emphasizing the need for gender-specific understandings and a community-based support system for women, she called for a more 'distinct, radically different, visibly-led, strategic, proportionate, holistic and woman-centred, integrated approach' to both women who offend and those at risk of offending (Corston, 2007: 79).

The Government accepted 25 of Corston's 43 recommendations for change (including the use of holistic community-based support services for women) and a further 14 in principle or in part (Ministry of Justice, 2008). The Corston Report was pivotal in driving forward support for women-centred approaches in dealing with women offenders (see Gelsthorpe et al., 2007 for a good overview of community-based provision). Early evaluations of such approaches indicate that there is much to be optimistic about. The work carried out by the *Together Women Project* has received much positive feedback and the service has been commended for providing both practical and emotional support within an 'enabling and empowering' culture (Hedderman et al., 2008; Jackson, 2009). Such findings are further echoed in evaluations of the *218 Centre* in Glasgow (Beglan, 2013; Easton and Matthews, 2010) and the *Inspire* project in Northern Ireland (Easton and Matthews, 2011).

In line with Snider's (2003) position, outlined above, we encourage a more cautious reading and appraisal of change. Malloch and McIvor (2011, 2013) suggest that greater attention be paid to the human rights implications of community sanctions, noting that women are more likely than men to receive additional requirements relating to medical/psychiatric/psychological treatment or drug treatment. The notion of 'empowerment' as a guiding principle of women-centred policy has also come under increasing scrutiny. While it may seem counter-intuitive to suggest that the provision of such women-centred services are not empowering for women offenders, the reality may not be as straightforward as it first appears. Easton et al.'s (2010) study on the operation of the women's specific caution (WSC) offers some insight into this paradox. They argue that while it may be the case that the increased requirement to engage with support services over a period of time may result in an overall positive benefit on women offenders' lives, the formal requirements of the WSC were not intended to require women offenders to engage with support but rather to encourage their voluntary engagement. Despite the voluntary nature of engagement with the support services on offer at Together Women's Projects (TWP), some women offenders in their study expressed the 'coercive' element of such support.

Such coercion is echoed in Pollack's (2010: 1275) study of women in prison, in which she argues that women are 'often required to "perform empowerment" in order to gain access to parole, passes and programming'. In this way, she argues: '[m]andated empowerment is a contradiction in terms' (ibid.: 1273). Such practices of empowerment through women-centred approaches have also been described as sites for the construction and perpetuation of idealized forms of femininity and domesticity (Barton and Cooper, 2013). The future of community-based interventions targeting the diverse needs of offenders is currently undergoing ongoing and radical transformational change, initiated by the Coalition government (2010–2015). The Rehabilitation Revolution redefined the nature of such provision through the continued dismantlement of the National Probation Service, creating an open marketplace for a range of private/commercial and third-sector agencies. The emphasis on payment by results is likely to steer providers in a particular direction, specifically crime reduction goals rather than more welfare-oriented ones. Recent findings from the *Inquiry into Preventing Unnecessary Criminalisation of Women* by the Howard League (2015a) report that the private companies now running the majority of community sentences lack knowledge and experience about the importance of gender and providing gender-specific services.

With the future of women's punishment in flux, the final part of this chapter draws on a human rights discourse to further emphasize the plight of the female prisoner.

What can human rights do for women in prison?

In Chapter 2 we documented our rationale for adopting a human rights approach to all offenders (men and women). In this section we focus on three main issues that confront female prisoners more particularly: their over-representation in suicide and self-harm statistics; contact with their children and families; and the experience of girls in prison. In doing so, we consider the relevance of Article 2: The right to life and Article 8: The right to private and family life, alongside the more recent provision made within the Bangkok Rules (2010) and the United Nations Convention on the Rights of the Child.

The Prisons Inspectorate already relies heavily on international human rights standards in setting its 'expectations', against which it measures conditions for prisoners (HM Inspectorate of Prisons, 2004). The Standard Minimum Rules for the Treatment of Prisoners (United Nations, 1955, 1977) are broad-based and incorporate every aspect of prison life, including transportation and reception, healthcare, education, legal rights and protection from harm. They also extend to the need to seek alternatives to custody, through preventative measures, and the reintegration of prisoners into society.

While most of the principles apply to all prisoners, some are gender- or age-specific, and others relate to the issue of **racism** or other forms of discrimination in prison (Scraton and Moore, 2004; Wahidin, 2016). There are some positive procedures within the Minimum Rules that are designed to encourage the special status of women's rights. So far as possible, men and women should be detained in separate institutions (United Nations, 1955: 8). There must also be special provision for pre-natal and post-natal care in women's prison and, where possible, babies should be born outside prison. When babies are permitted to stay with their **mothers in prison**, there should be nursery provision staffed by qualified personnel (United Nations, 1955: 23). Women's prisons should also be staffed predominantly by female officers (United Nations, 1955: 53).

The United Kingdom went on to sign up to the *Optional Protocol to the Convention against Torture and other Cruel, Inhuman or Degrading Treatment or Punishment* (United Nations, 2002), further enhancing the external inspection and monitoring of prisons. In 2010, the United Nations restated its commitment to women through approving the *Rules for the Treatment of Women Prisoners* (otherwise known as the **Bangkok Rules**). Encouraging non-custodial alternatives and gender-specific laws, policies and practices, the rules state that where possible:

- Admission procedures should acknowledge women's vulnerability (Rule 1)
- Women in prison should be in accommodation close to their home (Rule 4)
- Women's hygiene, physical and mental health needs must be met (Rules 5 and 6)
- Health screening should include an appreciation of histories of sexual and violent abuse (Rules 12–18)
- Specific provision should be made for the care of pregnant and nursing mothers (Rules, 22–24)
- Visits between mothers and children are encouraged and should allow for 'open contact' (Rule 28)
- Alternatives to custody should be stressed (Rules 57–62).

Suicide and self-harm

When a person is in the custody of the state, the state has a particular duty to safeguard their right to life. More specifically, the prison service claims to operate the concept of the 'healthy prison'. Drawn from international human rights principles, the prisons inspectorate uses the World Health Organization's four tests of what constitutes a healthy custodial environment to measure and assess the prison regime. In determining whether or not an establishment is 'healthy' it tests whether: prisoners are held in safety; if they are treated with respect and dignity as human beings; if they are able to engage in purposeful

activity; and if they are prepared for resettlement (cited in Scraton and Moore, 2004). Research into the healthcare of women in prison, however, portrays a prison service working at odds with the concept of a 'healthy' environment. Poor regimes, healthcare and hygiene standards; a lack of holistic needs-based programmes for women; an overemphasis on security and discipline; an inappropriate allocation of prisoners; and an overall inadequate standard of care due to staff shortages are all characteristic of the conditions documented in women's prisons (Lowthian, 2002; Malloch and McIvor, 2013; Prison Reform Trust 2011, 2015; Scraton and McCulloch, 2006; Scraton and Moore, 2004).

Maintaining a healthy prison and upholding the right to life is especially significant regarding women prisoners, who are over-represented in the suicide and self-harm statistics (Asthana and Bright, 2004; Coles, 2010, 2013; Liebling, 1994, 1995; Sandler and Coles, 2008). Between 1990 and 2011 there have been 139 deaths of women in prison. Despite constituting only 5 per cent of the prison population, around 50 per cent of all self-harm incidents in prisons are committed by women and the self-injury rates for women in prison rose by nearly 50 per cent between 2003 and 2007 (Coles, 2013). Moreover, in a systematic review of cases between 1990 and 2007, Sander and Coles (2008) found that women who die in prison are disproportionally likely to be young, substance misusers, already identified as at risk of suicide on arrival, on remand or in the early stages of imprisonment, and also mothers. We now know much about the distinctive vulnerabilities of women in prison. Women are nearly twice as likely as men in prison to be identified as suffering from depression (65 per cent versus 37 per cent), and more than three times as likely as women in the general population (19 per cent); almost a third (30 per cent) of women in custody had a psychiatric admission prior to entering prison (Prison Reform Trust, 2015). Over half of women in prison (53 per cent) report having experienced emotional, physical or sexual abuse as a child, compared to 27 per cent of men (Ministry of Justice, 2012); and 46 per cent of women in prison report having suffered a history of domestic abuse (Corston, 2007). The outcomes for women on remand are particularly alarming given that 44 per cent of women on remand have attempted suicide in their lifetimes (Corston, 2007: 18).

With explanations of suicide and self-harm traditionally located within models of individual pathology, a number of damning reports on the penal estate and prison policy have done much to reposition the debate. Following a series of inquiries and reports, most notably those undertaken by Her Majesty's Chief Inspectorate of Prisons (HMCIP), the Corston Report (Corston, 2007) and the report by the Women's Justice Taskforce by the Prison Reform Trust (2011), explanations for women's high rates of suicide and self-harm have been located firmly within the failures of the prison and of penal policy. Findings by Scraton and Moore (2004) on Northern Ireland raised serious concerns about the extent to which the treatment of women and girls in custody is compliant with international human rights law and standards. Their findings point to a prison service operating a disregard for the concept of the 'healthy prison', which at best neglected the needs of prisoners and at worst added to the hopelessness, helplessness, and desperation experienced by many prisoners (Scraton and Moore, 2004: 83).

More recently, INQUEST's casework has highlighted a range of features within the prison system as contributory factors in explaining women's suicide and self-harm, including:

> [a]ppalling conditions; systematic neglect of women's physical and mental health; inadequate health care; use of segregation and isolation for suicidal women; overuse of force; failure to implement suicide prevention guidelines; lack of staff training; and poor communication. (Coles, 2010: 76)

A series of deaths at Styal prison, where six women died between 10 August 2002 and 12 August 2003, did much to draw attention to the institutional neglect and systematic failings in the treatment and care of women suffering from mental health and drug problems (INQUEST, 2005, 2008, 2009, 2010). Emphasizing the lack of institutional and corporate accountability by prison authorities following the repeated warnings made about the inadequacy of mental healthcare, the poor treatment and care of women withdrawing from drugs and the subsequent deaths of women at Styal prison, Coles (2013) develops a convincing case of corporate manslaughter.

Imprisoning mothers

With the majority of women in prison (around two-thirds) being mothers with children under the age of 18, the issue of imprisoning mothers remains high on campaign agendas. Often the sole parent to children, the loss of family relationships and social support systems through incarceration raises further unique effects for imprisoned women. While over 90 per cent of male prisoners' children were cared for by either their partner or the child's mother, only 23 per cent of the children of female prisoners were cared for by their partners (Dodd and Hunter, 1992). When a mother is imprisoned the primary caregiver falls often to grandparents or other female relatives (Caddle and Crisp, 1997; Dallaire, 2007; Mumola, 2000). The ruinous effects on children of having their mother incarcerated add further evidence of women's distinctive pain of imprisonment. The National Association for the Care and Resettlement of Offenders found that a significantly higher proportion of the children of female prisoners than male end up in care, and for those children that are taken into care there is an increased likelihood of them becoming offenders themselves (cited in the *Commission on Women and the Criminal Justice System* – Fawcett Society, 2004). Furthermore, research has found that the children of imprisoned mothers displayed a variety of behavioural problems, including: sleeping and eating problems; bed-wetting; becoming withdrawn; and problems in developing overall social skills (Convery and Moore, 2011; Murray and Murray, 2010; Murray et al., 2012). The dire consequences of imprisonment for women are summed up neatly by the Director of the Prison Reform Trust, Juliet Lyon (2004), when she highlights that imprisonment will cause a third of women to lose their homes and separate more than 17,000 children from their mothers.

Despite their incarceration, prisoners have the 'right to a private and family life' (Article 8 of the HRA). In order to facilitate this, the Bangkok Rules (2010) state that services to incarcerated women must include being sent to prisons close to home. The state also has a duty to provide assistance to a prisoner's children. Further rights for the children of prisoners can be found in the broader United Nations Convention on the Rights of the Child (UNCRC). The UNCRC is important in that it emphasizes that all the rights it identifies apply to *all* children and that there should be no discrimination on the grounds of the activities or status of the child's parents. Article 9 of the Convention states that the child has a right to maintain regular contact with both parents unless it is contrary to their interests. In real terms, however, the structural configuration of women's prisons has very real and detrimental consequences for women's ability to maintain contact with their families. With 13 women's prisons throughout England, the small number of establishments that accommodate women means that they are, on average, more likely to be located further from their families than men are. The Chief Inspector of Prisons reported that 60 per cent of women surveyed were more than 50 miles from home (HMCIP, 2005).

One of the ways in which the prison service has responded to the concept of maintaining family life has been to allow women to keep children with them in prison. There is considerable difference to the age limits of children who accompany their mothers to prison around the world (see Barberet, 2014 for comprehensive list). In the UK, mother and baby units are available for women with a child under 18 months. They are staffed by trained prison officers and employ professional nursery nurses and the prison accepts a duty of care towards the baby in relation to health issues. With restrictions in telephone communication to their children and no special arrangements made for family visits, Scraton and Moore (2004: 143) report that the right of women in prison and their children to a meaningful family life was not respected. International studies by Fleetwood and Torres (2011) and Haney (2013) further point to evidence of 'coercive mothering' and 'penal contradiction'. Defined through idealized notions of womanhood, and in turn 'motherhood', Haney

(2013: 125) argues that 'Parenting in the penal state ... can be quite punishing' and that traditional processes of control and domination do not disappear; they reflect dominant ideas about gender, race and class, and 'mothering' is undermined and subsumed.

The idea that mother and baby units are a progressive attempt to address the specific vulnerability of women offenders with children, then, is not shared by all. With an obligation for sentencers to consider the rights and welfare of the child at sentencing stage, Gelsthorpe (2013) questions the potential impacts of such decisions for women who do not have children, and for women presented in courts as 'unfit' mothers. The concern at sentencing stage is further outlined by Epstein (2014), who found no evidence of any specific consideration of the Article 8 rights of the child. In her analysis of 75 cases, she reported much inconsistency in judicial actions noting that:

- There were some cases where the accused's children were not mentioned
- In some cases the defendant was blamed for the trauma and misery caused to the children
- When the welfare of the children was considered a suspended term of imprisonment was common
- Only in a few 'Court of Appeal' cases did the judge reduce the length of sentence after considering the plight of the defendant's children.

The very idea of imprisoning women with children, together with the current organization of the women's prison estate, hinders and indeed militates against the possibility of achieving the right for private and family life.

The incarceration of girls

Thus far we have argued for a greater appreciation of the complex vulnerabilities of adult women in the criminal justice system. The issue of vulnerability takes on an additional dimension when we come to consider children who come into conflict with the criminal justice system. Goldson (2002: 7) observed that children in prison can be 'innately' and/or 'structurally' vulnerable. They have more often than not suffered family breakdown, poverty, educational failure and various forms of abuse. As a result, he argues that the social circumstances of the children who inhabit our prisons are invariably 'scarred by multiple and inter-locking forms of disadvantage and misery' (Goldson, 2002: 27). With regard to girls more specifically, those who end up in the penal system have often experienced poor parenting, neglect and abuse, resulting in chaotic lives (Howard League, 2012). A more concerted and sustained attention to safeguarding children's human rights then becomes especially pertinent and should form a key objective of any 'humane' criminal justice system. Coming into force in 1990, the UN Convention on the Rights of the Child (UNCRC) is the key global instrument on children's rights. Covering all aspects of children's lives, including family life, education, healthcare, employment, among others, a core principle of the UNCRC is that the 'best interests' of the child should be the primary consideration in all actions and interventions concerning the child (Article 3). Hamilton (2011) points out that, while the term 'best interests' has not been defined precisely, it prioritizes rehabilitation, reintegration and restorative justice as responses to offending behaviour over repressive or retributive measures. Articles 37 and 40 relate more specifically to juvenile justice. Here, the detention of children should be used only as a measure of last resort and for the shortest appropriate period of time. Children must not be put in a prison with adults and they must be able to keep in contact with their family. Furthermore, every child deprived of liberty shall be treated with humanity and respect for the inherent dignity of the human persons and in a manner that takes into account the needs of a person of his or her age.

The importance of human rights becomes even more apparent when we consider the criminal age of responsibility. The minimum age of criminal responsibility (for both boys and girls) is set at 10 years in England, Wales and Northern Ireland. Scotland since 2011 will not prosecute below 12 years. In Europe age 14 or 15 is more usual, with Belgium and Luxembourg as high as age 18. The low age of criminal responsibility in the UK has been subject to much critique for contributing significantly to the growing greater **'responsibilization'** and 'adultification' of children more generally (Children's Commissioner for England, 2010; Goldson, 2009; Goldson and Muncie, 2012; Muncie, 2008; United Nations, 2008). With a greater responsibilization of children, Weber et al. (2014) point to a strong antipathy towards the recognition of children's right as offenders. Cast as distinct from the 'innocent child' represented by mainstream children's rights discourse, together with the tirade of negative political, public and media attitudes to young people's behaviour, there is a lack of empathy and recognition of the vulnerabilities of the young offender (Abramson, 2006; Goldson and Muncie, 2012; Muncie, 2008).

The vulnerability of girls who come into conflict with the criminal justice system is intensified and exacerbated once incarcerated. A report by the Howard League for Penal Reform in 1997, *Lost Inside*, found that 22 per cent of girls had self-harmed, 65 per cent had experienced family breakdown, 40 per cent had been in care and 41 per cent reported drug or alcohol abuse. At the same time, they reported that staff had little or no training in dealing with such vulnerability. These findings were echoed by the **Youth Justice Board** in 2012, where it was found that girls in custody are more likely to be restrained, more likely to self-harm and more likely than boys to be placed in segregation (Youth Justice Board, 2012). Despite the human rights principle that children have a right to family life and that contact with family is crucial in terms of children's rehabilitation, Scraton and Moore (2004) found no evidence of any appropriate provision by the prison service to ensure that children and young prisoners were given as much access as possible to family and friends. It is within this context of vulnerability that 19 children killed themselves in prison in England and Wales between 1993 and 2003 (Joint Committee on Human Rights, 2003).

Following the publication of *Lost Inside* (1997), the Howard League went on to challenge a number of breaches of human rights through the courts. It supported and gave evidence at a judicial review of **Home Office** policy concerning the holding of girls under age 18 alongside adult prisoners. The court ruled that it was unlawful for the Secretary of State automatically to place children in an adult prison. In 2002 the Howard League for Penal Reform successfully challenged the prison service insistence that the protection of the Children's Act 1989 did not apply to children in prison. Since then there have been some important developments regarding the holding of girls in the penal system. Set up in 2009, the All Party Parliamentary Group (APPG) on Women in the Penal System launched a year-long inquiry on girls in 2011. Alongside the work on adult women in prison, it found that girls are 'pigeonholed' into a criminal justice system designed for men, and that there is a lack of understanding about the different needs of girls and little evidence of what works, or programmes designed specifically for girls (Howard League, 2012: 5).

Moreover, it found that contrary to the United Nations Convention on the Rights of the Child, custody is not invariably being used as a last resort for girls. A decline in incarceration rates for young people over the past decade does, however, provide some comfort here. In 2005/06 there were 2615 boys and 200 girls in custody; these figures had reduced to 966 and 38 respectively by 2014/15 (Ministry of Justice, 2015a). While undeniably a positive step in the right direction in reducing the number of young people in custody, concerns about the potential 'net-widening' and 'up-tariffing' effects of contemporary interventions again make for a more cautious reading. To reiterate, girls remain more likely to be criminalized for behaviour that in previous decades would have warranted little attention. Conceptualized as 'wayward' and in need of 'protection', girls are invariably harshly sanctioned for non-violent, non-criminal offences and trivial misdemeanours. Often, girls have broken moral and not legal rules and find themselves being punished for behaviour that flaunts normative expectations (Chesney-Lind and Shelden, 1998; Phoenix, 2002, 2006; Sharpe, 2011; Youth Justice Board, 2012). It follows then that an overly punitive and disproportionate response to teenage girls' behaviour can make it more, rather than less, likely that they will be drawn further into the penal system, leading to poorer outcomes. We also need to be mindful of the way in which the 'welfare' needs of girls often become confused and translated into risks. The APPG (see Howard League, 2012) inquiry heard evidence that some girls were receiving a more restrictive sentence or being 'up-tariffed' because they had higher levels of welfare needs and were seen as being at higher risk of reoffending.

Concluding thoughts

Our knowledge of the female offender and her experience of criminal justice has grown enormously over the past 50 years or so and the female offender now occupies a significant place on both criminological and policy agendas. An unhealthy interest in the emergence of the 'mean girl', the female sex offender and the female terrorist more particularly, has secured a future in which *all* women – and girls – risk being subjected to punishment for behaviour that contradicts normative expectations. In making girls and women offenders central and visible in this chapter, it is not our aim to contribute to the ongoing anxiety about their behaviour, nor do we want to deny their very real presence in presenting historical evidence that suggests that their manifestation as perpetrators of crime is not new. Rather, with girls and women now established and present in a range of criminal categories, the challenge for future research will be to better understand the complex role of both women and men (and in turn of femininities and masculinities). As Barberet (2014: 147) writes, feminist criminology should 'reconsider women as more active than passive and conduct fuller analyses of logical and strategic support undertaken by women offenders'.

At the same time, we have argued for a greater alertness to the gendered nature of criminal justice in contributing to differential experiences for both girls and women. Despite the considerable progress made in developing alternatives to custody for women and girls, we remind readers here that policy does not always necessarily translate into practice easily, nor does the message intended necessarily always translate with its original meaning intact. Hannah-Moffat (2002, 2010) and Hayman's (2006) accounts of failed penal reform in women's prisons in Canada illustrates this well. Despite a well-intentioned, gender-responsive and women-centred strategy of reform, Hannah-Moffat argues that a major barrier to the realization of any meaningful structural reform is its 'denial of the material and legal reality of carceral relations embodied in the prison' (Hannah-Moffat, 2002: 203). This work serves as a powerful reminder of the very real limits of reform within existing penal systems where prisoners are not perceived as deserving of their basic human rights.

Moreover, the integration of the 'healthy prison' concept will not over-come the uneasy relationship that exists between the delivery of care within punitive containment (Sim, 1990). We concur with the idea that prison is rarely a necessary, appropriate or proportionate response to girls and women who come before the criminal justice system. The combination of factors that characterize the female offender underpins our concern of their con-tainment within punitive contexts where the capacity of the prison service to uphold its duty of care to those it imprisons remains questionable. Hence, our attention to maintaining a human rights lens on women's experience of criminal justice. To reiterate our basic position, the language of human rights offers a vocabulary for those interested in understanding the location and operation of power within a gendered criminal justice system. If approached in this way, the vulnerability of girls and women who inhabit our prisons will become glaringly obvious. More broadly, adopting a human rights perspective offers us an opportunity to rethink and fracture our con-ception of the offender, and while offenders may continue to be unpopular and undeserving, we might begin to conceive them as deserving of their human rights.

Summary

- While most crime is committed by men, this chapter described the extent and prevalence of female offending behaviour. Women are responsible for fewer offences and the distribution of offences is different, with women perpetrating less serious crimes than their male counterparts. That said, women are involved across all categories of crime.
- There is evidence of an increased anxiety over the criminality of women and girls, with the emergence of discourses highlighting the phenomenon of the 'mean girl', 'women who sexually offend' and 'women terrorists'. The reality remains that women are far from being equal to their male counterparts, thus perpetuating more insidious forms of criminal injustice.
- This 'search for equivalence' in the criminality of women and men has resulted in a tendency in criminal justice policy to disregard gender and treat women offenders in the same way that men are treated.
- Since the publication of the Corston Report (Corston, 2007), there has been a considerable shift in the way in which women offenders are processed within the criminal justice system, with a concerted move to diverting women from custody into community-based sanctions. Though welcome, we have emphasized that policy does not always necessarily translate into practice easily nor does the mes-sage intended necessarily always translate with its original meaning intact. We provide evidence of the problematic nature of such delivering of well-intentioned 'gender responsive' programmes for women offenders.

- The inequitable treatment of the female offender was examined with reference to human rights discourse, focusing in detail on the experiences of female prisoners. In contrast to men in prison, women and young girls who are locked up are extremely vulnerable. To be specific, they are more likely to self-harm and commit suicide and more likely to experience the painful and damaging consequences of being separated from their children and families.
- A human rights framework offers an opportunity to create a more humane prison environment.

STUDY QUESTIONS

1. Is there such a thing as a 'new female offender'?
2. What are the implications of the current trend to 'search for equivalence' in women's and men's offending?
3. Discuss the idea that women's offending is underpinned by victimization.
4. In what ways are women offenders particularly vulnerable?
5. To what extent have women offenders been denied their agency?
6. Outline and discuss the ways in which the female offender is experiencing greater punitiveness.
7. Outline the advantages/disadvantages of gender-responsive programmes for women offenders.
8. Can a human rights discourse offer anything to the female offender?

FURTHER READING

There are a number of good texts on gender and crime. Though some are dated, they remain classic and essential reading for those wanting to review the history of criminology and the place of the female offender within it. These include: F. Heidensohn (1996) *Women and Crime*, 2nd edn (Macmillan); S. Walklate (2000) *Gender, Crime and Criminal Justice* (Willan); L. Gelsthorpe and A. Morris (eds) (1990) *Feminist Perspectives Criminology* (Open University Press); and F. Heidensohn and N. Rafter (eds) (1999) *International Feminist Perspectives in Criminology: Engendering a Discipline* (Open University Press), who provide a more international discussion of perspectives. A more recent text in this vein includes: R. Barberet (2014) *Women, Crime and Criminal Justice: A Global Enquiry* (Routledge).

For the more focused insight into the rise of the so-called 'new female offender', see the collection of contributions offered in C. Alder and A. Worrall (eds) (2004) *Girls' Violence: Myths and Realities* (SUNY Press) together with L. Snider's (2003) excellent contribution to the *British Journal of Criminology* on 'Constituting the punishable woman: Atavistic man incarcerates post-modern woman (43(2): 354–78).

For an insight into girls more specifically, there is an excellent insight provided by M. Burman and S. Batchelor (2009) 'Between two stools: Responding to young women who offend' (*Youth Justice,* 9(3): 270–85) and G. Sharpe (2011) *Offending Girls: Young Women and Youth Justice* (Routledge).

In relation to the broad interventions for women offenders, see M. Malloch and G. McIvor (eds) (2013) *Women, Punishment and Social Justice* (Routledge); L. Gelsthorpe, G. Sharpe and J. Roberts (2007) *Provision for Women Offenders in the Community* (Fawcett Society); and R. Sheehan, G. McIver and C. Trotter (eds) (2011) *Working with Women Offenders in the Community* (Willan).

6

Men as Offenders

OVERVIEW

Chapter 6 provides:

- An overview of the involvement of men and boys in crime, disorder and anti-social behaviour.
- An account of the response of the criminal justice system to male offenders.
- An assessment of the reasons why boys and men are more likely to offend than girls and women.
- A summary of the main theoretical approaches developed to understand the relationship between masculinity and crime, including structural, psychosocial and discursive schools of thought.
- An analysis of the applicability of a human rights agenda in relation to men. It is argued that men may be beneficiaries of a rights-based agenda with reference to the over-policing of marginal men. By contrast it is suggested that the violent behaviours of men inhibit the human rights of their victims.

KEY TERMS

- criminalization
- gender relations
- hegemonic masculinity
- human rights
- marginalization

- masculinity/masculinities
- patriarchy
- psychosocial approaches
- social divisions

Introduction

The previous chapter shows that prior to the 1960s it was assumed, albeit implicitly, that the offender was either a man or boy. Feminist criminologists have argued quite persuasively that 'malestream' criminology was problematic because it did not render visible the extent to which offending behaviour is gendered (see Chapters 2 and 5 of this volume; Walklate, 2004). Feminist critiques have elicited several responses from male criminologists, including a growing body of writers who have embraced the intellectual, political and practical challenges raised by feminism as well as those who are more sceptical about the essence of the case advanced by some feminists (Collier, 1998; Hall and Winlow, 2015; Jefferson, 1997; Messerschmidt, 2004; Newburn and Stanko, 1994). In short, this chapter reviews some of the complex and unresolved theoretical and methodological debates about men, masculinities and offending that have been conducted over the last two decades or so. Despite the lack of consensus in existing narratives focusing on masculinities and crime, more and more criminologists are accepting that most crimes are mainly committed by males.

In common with the previous chapter, this one also considers the relevance of a human rights agenda. While the HRA 1998 attempts to universalize rights, many of the structural inequalities pre-dating 1998, or to be more accurate 2 October 2000, remain. Above all, certain groups of men continue to be marginalized, disadvantaged and excluded despite interventions in the name of human rights. Wider developments in the political economy may undermine the progressive and liberalizing tendencies of the human rights agenda through perpetuating gendered patterns of inequality.

Key themes in the study of men, masculinities and crime

This chapter is divided into three main sections. The first section on male law-breaking and offending behaviour is quite traditional in its approach and provides a largely descriptive, although not overly statistical, overview of the involvement of men in crime and anti-social behaviour. There are two elements to this part: (i) the relationship between men, masculinities and particular types of offending (e.g. acquisitive crimes such as burglary and theft and violent crime such as rape); (ii) the gendered dimensions of criminal justice agencies and their contact with males. In the previous chapter it was argued that more women than ever before are being brought into the criminal justice system; it is suggested here that offending is still essentially something men do more than women. In this section we revisit the international crime drop debate already outlined in Chapter 4 in order to argue that much of the existing data neglects a lot of crime. The second part of this chapter introduces the work of a number of writers on masculinity, especially the seminal work of Connell, and shows how her structural analysis has been adopted by Messerschmidt (2004).

Other writers have adapted this contribution to take on board psychosocial factors (Jefferson, 1997) and the relevance of discourse (Hearn, 1998) whereas some criminologists have rejected Connell's contribution (Hall, 2002). In the third part the human rights agenda is introduced. It is argued that men may benefit from enhanced appreciation of their human rights, a point illustrated with reference to policing and the tendency of this organization to further marginalize already marginalized men, especially in BME communities. Drawing on the work of Bayley (2002), human rights are equated with the principles of justice and equality, as well as fairness, freedom and dignity. It is also recognized that however marginalized some male offenders are, their behaviour inhibits the human rights of others through victimizing individuals and communities. This is explored with reference to homicide and sex offending (see Chapter 8). Crucially, this section indicates that men may be both the beneficiaries and inhibitors of a more fully developed human rights agenda.

Male offending and criminality – the evidence base

Given that recorded crime statistics obtained by the police do not routinely tell us the gender of the offender, this makes the task of providing an accurate account of the responsibility of men for all offending behaviour problematic. It is only possible to identify the gender of an offender once they enter the criminal justice system. The following paragraphs consider male offending, and the criminalization of men resulting from their interaction with the police service, the magistrates' and Crown courts, and the National Offender Management Service (NOMS), comprising therein the prison and probation services.

General offending

Men and boys are responsible for most offending behaviour, especially violent crime manifested in many different forms, ranging from the masculinities expressed in the form of the 'warrior' instigating warfare between nation states and power blocs, such as the US/UK alliance on a global stage (Goldstein, 2001), corporate and white-collar crime (Beirne and Messerschmidt, 2005; Gottschalk and Glaso, 2013; Klenowski et al., 2011) to the turf wars fought on the streets of ethnically divided communities (Stenson, 2005). Men also occupy a dominant position in relation to women, evidenced by the extent and prevalence of domestic violence and rape and the ways in which men subordinate and exploit women in interpersonal and sexual relationships (Lombard and McMillan, 2013; Renzetti et al., 2010). In point of fact, if we look at court proceedings and convictions 75 per cent are men (Ministry of Justice, 2014a). In terms of offence type, 34 per cent of men are found guilty or cautioned for theft and handling. Other 'popular' crimes among males were drug offences and violence against the person (Ministry of Justice, 2012). Boys and young men who offend are less likely than females to desist from crime by the time they reach the end of their teenage years, with the offending behaviour of the former likely to peak later on in the teenage years and continue into adulthood in comparison to the latter (Farrall and Calverley, 2006; Kazemian and Maruna, 2009). Males are more likely to have extended criminal careers than females. The prospective longitudinal Cambridge study (Farrington, 1994; Farrington et al., 2006; West and Farrington, 1977) provides detailed evidence of this. This research focuses on 411 south London males who were born in 1953 and first studied at the age of 8 in 1961. Farrington et al. (2006) reveal that:

- 41 per cent of this population had a conviction
- The average conviction career was nine years, including five convictions for standard list offences (excluding motoring offences)
- 7 per cent of the population accounted for just over half of all convictions
- Those men convicted earliest (i.e. at the relatively youngest age) had the most convictions and longest criminal careers.

The relationship between men and crime is also evident with regard to place and the number of males in the population (Dixon et al., 2006). For example, it is well known that crime is overwhelmingly concentrated in cities, especially urban areas with a high degree of social deprivation and a large proportion of social housing. Deprivation does not automatically result in crime, however, as is demonstrated by the case of Sedgefield, the seat of a former New Labour Prime Minister (1997–2007) Tony Blair. Sedgefield is an impoverished, ex-mining community with a notably low crime rate due to the low proportion of young men living in this area.

Self-report studies

There are a number of self-report studies where the gender of respondents was known. These studies confirm the disproportionate involvement of males in a range of criminal acts, although they indicate that the variations may not be as profound as sometimes imagined (Flood-Page et al., 2000; Graham and Bowling, 1995; Jamieson et al., 1999). Other research shows that males who are arrested and appear in court are relatively more likely to self-report compared to females (Farrington et al., 2010; Piquero et al., 2014). The aforementioned body of work supports the claim of Farrington et al. (2006) that those males who start to offend relatively early on in their lives are less likely to desist at a later stage in their criminal career than males who first offend when they are older.

The criminalization of men

Chapter 3 set out the processes leading to the criminalization of men throughout the nineteenth century and the different trajectories this process has taken in contrast with women who offend. In the twenty-first century, men are more likely to be stopped and searched and such an encounter is more likely to result in an arrest. This observation is expanded later on in the chapter when the gendered nature of human rights discourse is scrutinized. Out of all arrests made in 2012/13 (1,072,068) 85 per cent were males and 15 per cent females. Between 2008/09 and 2012/13 there was a fall in the number of arrests for both males and females: about 50 per cent for the former and 60 per cent for the latter (Ministry of Justice, 2014b). Females accounted for slightly more arrestees among juveniles (18.3 per cent) compared to adult females (15.8 per cent) (Parity, 2013: 8). In the police station men are less likely to exercise their right to silence (Home Office, 2004a: 9), which means that they run the risk of being treated more harshly in the courts when they face a trial (Ashworth and Redmayne, 2010). There are differences when different types of offending behaviour are scrutinized. In 2003 relatively more men than women were arrested for the **notifiable offences** listed below. The figures in brackets show the number of adult arrests by gender and type of offence.

- Violence against the person (315,508 men and 61,802 women)
- Sexual offences (31,937 men and 947 women)
- Robbery (18,111 men and 1,733 women)
- Burglary (63,365 men and 5,357 women)
- Theft and handling stolen goods (187,968 men and 53,419 women)
- Fraud and forgery (22,164 men and 7,353 women)
- Criminal damage (75,395 men and 10,640 women)
- Drug offences (96,741 men and 26,564 women). (Parity, 2013: 7)

Other Home Office studies show that males account for most violent crime, a figure of about 75 per cent (Office for National Statistics, 2015a), and that they are the main perpetrators of domestic violence and stalking (Myhill and Allen, 2002a, 2002b; Walby and Allen, 2004). In cases of sexual assault the **Crime Survey of England and Wales** showed that victims experiencing such an offence since the age of 16 stated that the perpetrator was a male in 99 per cent of cases (ONS, 2015a: 19). This statistical evidence is supported by criminological studies, which testify to the culpability of boys and men for most domestic abuse (Dobash and Dobash, 2012; Hester, 2013).

Towards the end of the 2000s there were increased concerns about the involvement of boys and young men perpetrating abuse towards their partners and family members. This goes some way towards explaining the addition of 16- and 17-year-olds in March 2013 to definitions of domestic abuse in recognition that victims of domestic abuse include those under 18 years. The disquiet about young people and abuse became an issue due to several reports highlighting a 'hypermasculine' culture among young males under pressure by society, the media, advertising and peer groups into believing that in order to be accepted as a 'man' they have to display sexual assertiveness and be controlling of the females in their lives to establish their masculinity (Crowther-Dowey et al., 2016). This is an ongoing concern for the government and there is growing research that highlights the dangers of the internet for young people, particularly with regard to online pornography. The media often portray women as highly sexualized and men as domineering and this could be one of the reasons why young males feel it is acceptable to treat women as sexual objects. Young males have distorted ideas about women and what the latter are expected to do to seek respect from men. The sexualization of young people through the media has been termed the 'pornification of popular culture' (Coy et al., 2013: 45). A campaign raising awareness of abusive relationships between young people, run jointly by the NSPCC and the government, distributed a leaflet aimed at parents that outlined the characteristics of an abusive perpetrator for those parents suspecting that their children are in an abusive relationship. It states that:

- Masculinity is displayed through physical aggressiveness;
- they [young males] have the right to demand intimacy;
- they will lose respect if they are attentive and supportive towards their partners; and
- men and women aren't equal and women should be treated differently;
- ... they have the right to control their partners if they see fit. (Home Office, 2012a: 9)

We now shift our focus to consider other crime types. In public space and on the streets males are responsible for most burglaries (Mawby, 2012) and street and gang-related crimes (Hallsworth, 2013; Hodgkinson et al., 2009). The influence of drugs (Aldridge and Medina, 2008) and alcohol (Carrabine, 2008; Hadfield, 2009) on male criminality, especially in the context of the 'night-time economy', is well documented (Hobbs et al., 2003; Monaghan, 2004; Winlow, 2001). Alcohol in particular is misused to a greater extent by young men, who when inebriated indulge in crime, anti-social behaviour and other types of 'hypermasculine' behaviour (Royal Geographical Society, 2013: 22). There is also the disproportionate over-representation of men among the population of sex offenders (Ministry of Justice, Home Office and the Office for National Statistics, 2013; Thomas, 2005). The position is remarkably similar for those individuals committing crime in the offices of the commercial and industrial sectors (Steffensmeier et al., 2013). Even the majority of perpetrators of crime in virtual environments tend to be men, demonstrated by a disparate group of offences such as internet **paedophilia** and carousel fraudsters [sic] (Yar, 2006). On those occasions when the police confront groups of protestors, either rioting in socially excluded communities or as part of a new social movement (i.e. anti-capitalism/globalization marches), the people they face tend to belong to the male sex. It is men who have carried out most of the media-reported shootings in rundown areas of London, Manchester, Birmingham and Nottingham (Bullock and Tilley, 2002; Pitts, 2012; Povey, 2004). Interestingly, if we consider crime as a form of social harm, Hearn's (2003) observation that some male criminologists are responsible for 'workplace bullying' does not let academics off the hook either.

Returning to the criminal justice system, overall male arrestees tend to be treated more harshly than females, demonstrated by the finding that men are more likely to be charged (60 per cent compared to 52 per cent) and therefore less likely to be cautioned (Home Office, 2004a: 9). This statement does need some qualification, however, because there is the contested nature of leniency and harshness in the sense that some women enter the criminal justice system for lesser deviancy. Of all the cautions administered in 2011, 76 per cent were to men (the same figure applies for PNDs – penalty notices – for both summary and **indictable offences**) (Parity, 2013: 10–11). While the reasons for this are complex, this occurs in part because men are less likely to admit that they have offended and their arrest is more likely to result from them committing a more serious offence. Despite this, even when seriousness of offence is considered it would appear that men are less likely than women to be cautioned, though the percentage of males cautioned increased from 74 per cent in 2007 to 76.3 per cent in 2011. The equivalent figures for females showed a decline: 26 per cent (2007) and 23.7 per cent (2011) (Ministry of Justice, 2012: 47).

Remand and mode of trial

At the next stage of the criminal justice process men are more likely to be remanded in custody. In 2013 male defendants appearing in **Crown Court** were twice as likely to be remanded in custody than females, and males remanded in custody were more likely to be given an immediate custodial sentence. A similar finding is evident for bail (Ministry of Justice, 2014b). These findings are attributable to the fact that more men have previous convictions, as well as the nature of their offending behaviour (e.g. its seriousness) (Ashworth and Redmayne, 2010). Thus the sex of the accused is not likely to be that significant in isolation from other factors. The same observation applies to the tendency for men to be committed for trial more frequently than women (Home Office, 2004a: iii). Men remanded in custody spend more time under lock and key than women. When it comes to the trial, for **triable-either-way** cases men are far more likely to be committed to Crown Court for trial, although this is partly explained by the generally more serious offences committed by men (Home Office, 2004a: iii). Men (74.1 per cent) who are held on remand are more likely to end up in prison than women (59.4 per cent) (Ministry of Justice, 2014b: 44). Thus there are more men represented at each stage of the criminal justice system considered so far, which is not altogether surprising given their greater propensity to engage in crime than women.

Sentencing and penal policy

In 2010 the Sentencing Council (created by the Coroners and Justice Act 2009) replaced the Sentencing Guidelines Council. It restated the importance of reforming and rehabilitating offenders as one of the five things sentencing sets out to achieve. In Chapter 5 we briefly noted the 'Rehabilitation Revolution' announced by the Justice Secretary at that time, Kenneth Clarke. This did not refer explicitly to men but, as we have shown, due to the disproportionate involvement of men at all stages of the criminal justice system, this will affect men, at least numerically, to a greater degree. The aforementioned Revolution was driven forward by Clarke's replacement, Chris Grayling, who was concerned about reoffending rates, especially prisoners serving short sentences. This was followed by the Offender Rehabilitation Act 2014, which makes it a legal requirement for all offenders, irrespective of the length of their prison sentence, to receive 12 months of supervision in the community. When commencing their custodial sentence each prisoner will have their respective needs and risks assessed, culminating in a bespoke and individualized plan for their time spent in custody and for their resettlement needs when they are released back into the community. Significantly, Section 10 of the Act requires the needs of women offenders to be taken into account when making arrangements for rehabilitation, which shows that offender management is gendered in complex ways. Furthermore, in order to rehabilitate offenders the probation service needed to be reformed by making sure it had to compete with private and voluntary sector agencies – which would be called community rehabilita-tion companies (CRCs) – for contracts to manage offenders. In practice, the CRCs manage low to medium risk offenders and the National Probation Service high and very high-risk offenders, a population largely made up of men (Kemshall, 2008).

While there have been some shifts in sentencing and penal policy since the publication of our first edition of this book in 2008, other aspects have not changed dramatically. The 'fine' is still the most popular sentence for both men and women. As a proportion of men in the criminal justice system compared to the male population as a whole (49 per cent), males account for 75 per cent of convictions, although between 2003 and 2008 the convic-tion ratio was between two and four percentage points lower for males (Ministry of Justice, 2014b: 9). Sentencing outcomes are gendered too, with men being much more likely to be given a custodial sentence for committing an indictable offence (Ashworth and Redmayne, 2010). In June 2014, 95.4 per cent of the prison population were men and on average men served longer custodial sentences for indictable offences: 18.8 months for males compared to 9.9 months for females (Ministry of Justice, 2014a). Two dec-ades earlier, in 1992, the equivalent figure for the prison population was 96.6 per cent, indicating a small decline in the proportion of men impris-oned (Home Office, 2004a). Males are more likely to be received into prison for the following sentences: violence against the person; sexual offences; and burglary (Ministry of Justice, 2012). Male juvenile offenders under the age of 18 are also over-represented in the custodial population and at the end of May 2015 the child custody population was 989, which included 42 girls. This represents an overall fall of 102 compared to May 2014 (Howard League, 2015b).

Regarding community-based penalties, there are offenders who are under supervision following a court order and those supervised due to be given a community sentence or suspended sentence order. According to the Ministry of Justice (2014b), in December 2013, 85 per cent of individuals under supervi-sion as a requirement of a court order were men, a figure which has not notably changed since 2003. Overall, the use of community orders and suspended sen-tence orders has fallen since 2007, with a greater decrease for men (27 per cent) compared to women (23 per cent). This conceivably coincides with the changed climate relating to female offenders following the dissemination of the Bangkok Rules (see Chapter 5).

Inside the prison, in the past, in comparison to women, male offenders have been much more likely to be the beneficiaries of an accredited offender behav-iour programme, e.g. Accredited Enhanced Thinking Skills, the now phased-out Reasoning and Rehabilitation (R&R), Think First, Controlling Anger and Learning to Manage it (CALM), and the Cognitive Skills Booster Programme,

SOTP (Harper and Chitty, 2005). More recently, more of an onus has been placed on designing programmes to address male violence and abuse against women, such as 'Domestic Violence Perpetrator Programmes' (Kelly and Westermarland, 2015). Despite the development of such programmes, men in prison are not as well educated as female offenders (Home Office, 2004a: iv). Male prisoners are also more likely to experience ill health and have an anti-social personality disorder (Harper et al., 2005: 17) and consult a doctor more frequently than their female counterparts (Home Office, 2004a: 38). General conditions inside prison tend to be slightly poorer for men, in particular the time inmates spend on purposeful activity and the length of time they spend in their cells (Home Office, 2004a: 38). Purposeful activity levels in 2014 were at their lowest since 2006 and the quality of teaching and learning provision had declined. In July 2015 the outgoing Chief Inspector of Prisons in England and Wales, Nick Hardwick, delivered his final report, which suggested that the prison service is 'still waiting for the "rehabilitation revolution"' and male pris-oners in particular were experiencing a concentration of factors, which meant the standards of a 'healthy prison' were not being met (HM Chief Inspector of Prisons for England and Wales, 2015). To the list of problems identified in the past Hardwick observed that special accommodation (unfurnished cells used for short-term segregation) was inappropriate, particularly for self-harming men, and that drug and alcohol misuse was more common among men. These diffi-culties are all exacerbated by reduced staffing levels (ibid.). Theoretical work has drawn attention to the extent to which the offender management industry – including the probation and prison services – have regimes which may be oriented towards men, but there is the absence of an explicit understanding of masculinity (Hearn and Whitehead, 2006; Jewkes, 2005; Whitehead, 2005).

From a historical perspective, on release from prison it would seem that men have more chance of being resettled, with nearly twice as many men finding employment or a training course placement than women (Home Office, 2004a: v). This is only part of the story, however, and a report by the Social Exclusion Unit (2002) indicated that prisoners serving short sentences (less than 12 months), where there is no mandatory post-release support, were more likely to reoffend and be reconvicted compared to those who were serv-ing longer sentences. For example, of those men serving up to 12 months inside prison, 62 per cent reoffended within two years of being released com-pared to 60 per cent for females. The percentage of prisoners held for between one and four years were less likely to be reconvicted within two years: 55 per cent of males and 35 per cent of females. If we look at reoffending rates, which have not changed discernibly since 2000, between March 2011 and April 2012 the rates for men and women respectively were 28.3 per cent and 18.7 per cent (Ministry of Justice, 2014c: 12). Young male offenders are at greater risk of reoffending within two years (74 per cent), confirming what criminologists know about the linkages between age and sex/gender. It is also clear that black and Asian males are over-represented in the young offender population (Young Review, 2014). At the time of writing, resettlement is beset with problems, with limited coordination between offender management and the resettlement agenda – partly a consequence of the uncertainty created by the reforms mentioned above. This is demonstrated by the lack of satisfactory and timely assessments of the needs of offenders and the risks they pose, as well as access to programmes designed to address offending behaviour (HM Chief Inspector of Prisons for England and Wales, 2015).

Men's offending and the international crime drop

This is something that we acknowledged in Chapter 4 and although there are contextually specific variations across the world, the relevance of this trend to the UK has been confirmed at a general level by police recorded crime figures and the Crime Survey of England and Wales over the last decade or so (Office for National Statistics, 2015b). This could be attributed to men offending less, especially crimes of an acquisitive nature, although it conceals increases for other offences, such as knife crime, which increased in 2015 for the first time in four years, and the surge in sexual offences, including rape, in the aftermath of Operation Yewtree (see Chapter 7) (Travis, 2015). The identification of this trend and the other statistical sources used above are flawed – not that any criminologist should need reminding – because official statistics are a consequence of 'organizationally defined processes' that record and classify deviant and criminal behaviour (Kitsuse and Cicourel, 1963: 139). Arguably due to the recession and cuts to the police service made since 2010, the police, with its reduced capacity and declining resources, have not investigated all crimes effectively and an increased proportion remain unsolved (HM Inspectorate of Constabulary, 2014a). This is especially pronounced with men's and increasingly boys' violence against women and girls (and boys) in the private sphere, which is significantly higher than estimated (Walby et al., 2014), partly because it is still invisible to the authorities and wider public in spite of governmental commitment to ending this form of violence. Also, Travis (2014) unearthed evidence that the police were calling on the public to solve 'some' volume crimes, which potentially amounts to the decriminalization of some offences. Finally, by focusing exclusively on legally defined offence categories a range of harms and damaging behaviours are neglected. Hall and Winlow (2015: 126) argue persuasively that *non-criminalized harms*, such as multinational companies avoiding paying tax and the intimidation and bullying found on economically deprived estates, remain under or unpoliced.

The material reviewed above does not provide any surprises and confirms common-sense perceptions about men and their involvement in crime and disorder. Explanations of offending behaviour have taken this for granted and there is a tacit presumption in most criminological theory that the criminal is a man or boy. Feminist critiques of the gender blindness of criminological theorizing are well known and there is no need for another rehearsal here but, in short, the discipline of criminology has not fully come to terms with the problems posed by men. On a more positive note, things are starting to change with some important theoretical interventions by writers on masculinity.

Theorizations of men, masculinities and crime

In this section the emergence of criminological theories focusing on men and **masculinity** are outlined. It considers the impact of the 'second wave' of feminism on understanding the involvement of men in crime and how some male criminologists have taken on board the 'transgression of criminology' called for by feminist scholars (Cain, 1990). The seminal work of Connell (2002) and the concept of '**gender relations**' are introduced and some attempts to apply it to explain crime are then described. The scholarly outputs of men writing about the criminality of men falls into two broad categories: sociological and psychosocial. Two things need saying about these perspectives. Firstly, at least in criminological circles, the two are not mutually exclusive and there is some articulation between them. Secondly, more has been written from a sociological perspective, largely because criminology, or at least the way it is studied in Britain, has been more sociological in its conceptual and methodological orientation. Related to the latter point is the fact that one particular individual, Connell (2002), has had a major and enduring influence on thinking about men and masculinity; this macro level, materialist and structural perspective, which is informed by a wealth of empirical evidence drawn from various areas of social life, has been the touchstone for all criminologists in this area (Jefferson, 1997). The writings of Connell are especially interesting because, while they take on board feminism, they do not accept certain early radical accounts where it is evinced that male dominance and patriarchal structures are monolithic and absolute. Masculinity may be intertwined with power and authority, furthering heterosexual and specific class interests, but it can be challenged and is changeable. In short, masculinity appears in different forms in different cultural and historical contexts.

Connell's writings have had critics (Hall, 2002; Hood-Williams, 2001), and while the critics make cogent critiques, they are not able to jettison Connell's framework in its entirety and other approaches have adapted Connell's ideas, in particular discursive (Hearn, 1998) and psychosocial approaches (Gadd and Jefferson, 2007). For the aforementioned reasons, the contribution of Connell (2002) is reviewed in some detail. It is followed by an exploration of one of his most sympathetic critics and occasional co-author, Messerschmidt (1993, 1997, 2000, 2004; Connell and Messerschmidt, 2005), who has made considerable inroads into a bemired area. This is followed by an overview of other criminological work that builds sympathetically on what Connell has done as well as other more sceptical accounts.

Connell – 'gender relations'

Sociological accounts of gender include variants where the focus is, on the one hand, on social identities or identity categories, namely men and women, and, on the other hand, relational approaches like that advanced by Connell (2000, 2002) in her explanation of masculinity. Connell offers a macro-level analysis of these issues, showing that although there are changeable structural hierarchies and multiple masculinities, men are in a dominant position overall because of what has been referred to as '**hegemonic masculinity**'. This concept posits that a certain form of masculinity – one among many – is valued more highly than others at a particular time and place, which in turn legitimates the social domination of masculinity. Such dominance is not automatic and is achieved as part of a struggle, but it serves as a touchstone towards which men position themselves. More than that, there is a tendency for heterosexual women to be 'complicit' with hegemonic masculinity, something that is more often than not achieved through persuasion rather than violence. Hegemonic masculinity is not so much about groups and interests but a socially dominant ideal of manhood. This ideal, supported by effective authority, encourages men to see the dominant ideal of masculinity as something towards which they aspire. This task of identification is far from straightforward because forms of hegemonic masculinity change over time in cultures and even within subcultures.

Connell does not focus much on crime but has produced co-authored work with a criminologist (Messerschmidt, 1993, 2005a, 2005b). The latter has attempted to integrate the structural analysis of the former with the micro sociology of **ethnomethodology**. He shows how social action and practices are accomplished in the context of gender relations in particular social settings. Above all, Messerschmidt shows that attempts to accomplish a masculine identity are a way of dealing with life and are undertaken with reference being given to idealized versions of a dominant masculinity. This ideal is, for far too many men and boys, an unobtainable aspiration in different social settings, such as at home and at work or school. Messerschmidt (1993) is concerned with recognizing a diversity of masculinities, for example by looking at youth crime and its interconnection with wider structural inequalities. He shows how masculinities are related to power and the division of labour in the context of class and race relations. In line with critical, radical and **left realist criminologists**, Messerschmidt (1993) draws attention to those groups marginalized and excluded from labour markets, but rather than arguing that these factors push men into crime, he describes how men who cannot access economic and material resources commit crime as a method of 'doing masculinity' and the assertion of manliness. In short, what Messerschmidt has done is look at particular acts of aggression and relate them to hegemonic masculinity. Crucially, this is not a mechanical link, although the pursuit of hegemony does have a causal influence (Connell and Messerschmidt, 2005: 834).

Collison (1996) deploys such reasoning in his investigation of the linkages between consumption, drugs markets and masculinities. In underclass-type communities which are awash with visual images of the affluent society, and where the chances of obtaining wealth and material goods are all but blocked, the drugs economy is a way out. More than that, the behavioural response to these conditions sometimes involves predatory forms of masculinity, inspired, at least in part, by media narratives. Respect is no longer gained through hard physical labour but through the pursuit of pleasure in a chaotic environment. The physical demands of labour and the cogent images of masculinity it provides, which were so closely related in the world of work, become enmeshed with the reality of, and semi-fulfilled fantasies about, criminality in the workless society (Collison, 1996: 14).

The suggestion that crime is a form of gendered social action that creates opportunities for the maintenance of privileged forms of masculinity is shared by Byrne and Trew (2005) in their research into offender perceptions about their own behaviour and orientation towards crime. They found that a positive orientation towards crime – that is, a greater willingness to offend – was more prevalent among their male than female respondents.

A strength of Messerschmidt's work is that he draws attention to different offences and how different men in different classes and ethnic groups define their experiences of crime differently. For example, white working-class masculinities will be markedly different from black masculinities because of their particular experiences of labour markets and other localized, context-specific socio-economic and political conditions. The nature of the criminal response of these respective groups will also vary as will the nature of the masculine response, although the celebration of toughness and physical power are likely to be present. Messerschmidt has been criticized by Hood-Williams (2001), who remarked that the former is essentially a revised version of Mertonian strain theory.

Hood-Williams (2001) also argues that the concept of hegemonic masculinity covers too much by bringing in class, race and other social divisions when analysing gender.[1] A more damaging criticism is the view that Messerschmidt presents of an evaluation that is tautologous in the sense that crimes committed by men are an expression of masculinity. Related to this, not all men commit crime, which demonstrates that it is not men that are the discriminator between crime and non-crime. Finally, there is a willingness to lump together different types of crime, which are all seen as a response to a threatened sense of masculinity. For instance, the theft of a mobile phone is very different from the sexual assault of a child. The concept of hegemonic masculinity has also elicited considerable criticism from Hall (2002), who suggests that hegemony refers to large-scale, historical changes involving whole classes, and in using this idea the focus is on a relatively narrow construction of masculinity. In a later article, S. Hall (2012) questions the relevance of the concept of hegemonic masculinity as a strategy of domination that men, as well as women who enjoy the 'patriarchal dividend', use to control the social world, on the grounds that the word hegemony refers to the use of non-violent methods (e.g. through the media, legal system and so on) to maintain social dominance and superiority. This effectively means that interpersonal violence, especially that found in excluded and marginalized communities, cannot be understood with reference to hegemony. What is being referred to instead are subordinated masculinities that, as Hall (2002) puts it, are associated with 'useless violence' that do not bring about 'rewards' for hegemonic masculinity and are not an effective strategy of institutionalized dominance (see also S. Hall, 2012: 123–4). There are also questions about the structural determinism and restricted opportunities for change. Connell and Messerschmidt (2005) have responded to Hall and other critics with the retort that their usage of Gramsci's (1971) idea of hegemony emphasizes the 'active struggle for dominance'. Moreover, they also point out that domination is not achieved as a result of imposing force, but rather through persuasion and securing consent. Nonetheless hegemonic masculinity does incorporate subordinate masculinities and it can also fail to achieve its specific projects.

Collier (1998) has remarked that hegemonic masculinity tends to focus on the negative characteristics of masculinity – aggressiveness, a lack of emotionality, independence, non-nurturing – and their association with crime, and that it is necessary to take on board that these characteristics are not displayed by all or even most men. Connell and Messerschmidt (2005: 832) reply by stating that men consent to particular ideologies of masculinity but there are 'tensions, mismatches and resistances', again strongly suggesting the potential for change and that however bleak a situation may appear there is no need to lapse into a sense of impossibilism. Masculinity is a 'configuration of practice' and it is multidimensional because it has its own crisis tendencies. They also consider the influence of 'ideals, fantasies and desires' that are linked to Freudian psychoanalysis, although this aspect is not central to Connell's voluminous outputs (Connell and Messerschmidt, 2005: 832).

Jefferson's (1997) innovative psychosocial approach, which now receives attention, draws some inspiration from psychoanalytical work and a focus on intersubjective factors.

Psychosocial and other approaches to thinking about crime and masculinities

Jefferson (1997) argues that notions of hegemonic masculinity are problematic because they are based on an assessment of a 'unitary subject' who is over-socialized as a result of the deterministic influence of social structural arrangements. To come to terms with masculinities and crime it is necessary to foreground the psyche, which has its own irreducible determinants and its own rules. Contradictory emotions in the subject create anxiety and a threat to the self which need to be handled by the psyche regardless of the class position or ethnic identity adopted by the individual man. By looking at the psyche there is an acceptance of both conscious and unconscious processes, including hidden desires. The human subject is multi-layered and divided and involved in splitting and projecting different parts of their personality. For Jefferson, the key issues are how in reality men deal with their own life histories and psychic formations with regard to masculinities. This is done intersubjectively because of the centrality of 'biographically mediated difference between men' (Gadd, 2003: 333). Each man has his own highly personalized and diverse experiences and trajectories that are made intelligible by taking on board particular discursive positions to deal with or defend against a sense of anxiety and powerlessness.

The above points are illustrated in one of Jefferson's case studies, which focuses on the former world heavyweight boxing champion, Mike Tyson (Jefferson, 1996 1998). Tyson was imprisoned for the rape of Desiree Washington in 1992, followed by the decline of his status as a champion and his psychological disintegration. Some commentators explained Tyson's life in terms of his class (working) and race (black), but Jefferson's analysis considers the ambivalence and contradictions that Tyson's psyche had to deal with. On the surface he was a huge and powerful man, although this concealed a more troubled personality. This is apparent in Jefferson's (1996) account of Tyson's transformation from 'A Little Fairy Boy' to a 'Complete Destroyer', which shows how the biography of this sportsman was full of contradictions. What Jefferson (1996) does is show Tyson as a young man who had a lisp and who lacked the physique he later acquired as a result of years of pumping iron in the gymnasium. Tyson became 'Iron Mike' by splitting-off, or rejecting, his own perceived deficiencies and projecting the resulting violent feelings towards his opponents in the ring. The victim is then blamed for the perceived weaknesses of the perpetrator. In other words, Tyson's life cannot be explained in terms of structural factors alone. Intersubjective factors are important too, especially the irreducibility of the psyche, which has its own determining rules.

The psychosocial approach draws attention towards men's subjectivities and the workings of unconscious processes, a line of argument that has been elaborated by Gadd and Farrall (2004). Their research concentrates on the criminal careers and desistance literature, digging deeper to look at the 'latent or unconscious meanings embedded in offenders narratives' (Gadd and Farrall, 2004: 148). More than this, they call for researchers to ascertain the meanings offenders invest into factors, such as unemployment, social exclusion and drug misuse. In order to understand the criminal behaviour of men it is necessary to be aware of the unique biographies of individual men. An appreciation of men and their subjectivities shows the complex processes whereby they 'identify' and 'disidentify' themselves with particular reference points, including real figures in their lives (e.g. their father, a sibling) and 'cultural stereotypes' (Gadd and Farrall, 2004: 149), such as alcoholics and drug addicts. It is necessary, as Gadd (2000: 431) puts it, to

> ... expose the disparity between what violent men feel, say and do, the interface of men's psychic investment in social discourses and practices.

This is where changes could occur.

Elsewhere, Gadd (2002) questions the view that domestic violence is, as Messerschmidt (1993) insists, an example of 'accomplishing masculinity'. Rather than wife beating being seen as a situational response by men to reassert their damaged sense of masculinity, violence is more likely to culminate in a sense of shame and guilt. Like Jefferson (1997), Gadd scrutinizes emotional and psychic complexity and attends to the dilemmas involved with 'uniting social and psychic processes', which pull in different directions. Drawing on the account of an individual offender, Gadd (2002) suggests that those men who are violent towards the significant women in their lives do not necessarily find their behaviour acceptable when they describe what they have done. While men can consciously and unconsciously invest in discourse that condones their violence, there is also the issue of public condemnation. In another study, men who were violent attempted to distance themselves from identifying with 'violent, dangerous men', thus seeing themselves as different. Violent men also feel persecuted, even if this feeling cannot be expressed orally, a problem that makes difficult-to-handle emotions even more testing. Defences in the psyche allow the splitting of unwanted parts of the self, which are projected onto the victim. Basically, men recognize that their behaviour is problematic and talk about changing their ways but persist with their violent behaviour. Gadd (2002) argues persuasively that the nature of the relationship many heterosexual men have with women is based on ambivalence and contradiction where women are 'idealized' and 'denigrated'. This can be explained, in part, with reference to 'gender relations' but also the multifaceted emotions making up men's subjectivities and their tendency to 'split off' and 'reject' what they dislike or do not understand. Indeed, male offenders end up blaming their female victims for their own weaknesses. Perhaps the most important insight offered by the psychosocial paradigm is that it rests on an understanding of change, so despite the presence of 'stubborn psychic investments' (Gadd, 2000: 445) men can be pushed into changing by representing violence against women in terms of 'emasculating weakness' (Gadd, 2000).

The theme of change is also rehearsed in a later article by Gadd (2006a), in which he draws on Benjamin's concepts of 'identification' and 'recognition'. Here he shows how a 'far-right activist' desisted from his violent past when he recognized that the hostility projected onto his victims was a part of himself that had been projected onto the victim and which was also a part in need of being reclaimed. This important body of work has been applied to interpret masculinities and hate crime by Treadwell and Garland (2011), who conducted interviews with three men who are motivated by anti-Muslim bias and prejudice. They combine structural and psychosocial explanations to show how marginalization and disadvantage result in externalized hostility and fury (e.g. the Islamic 'other'). Holligan and Deuchar (2015) have attempted a similar exercise in their study of incarcerated male teenagers in Scotland. They situate the life histories of their participants in the context of the socio-economic changes impacting on Scottish society.

The psychosocial perspective has faced criticism, not least from Hood-Williams (2001), who posits that psychic processes are not sexually differentiated or, if they are, it is far from straightforward. An alternative way of looking at this dilemma is to ask if there is anything in the psyche that is masculine or should researchers consider masculinity as a presentational or performative phenomenon. Furthermore, the psyche is 'fictional' and a series of 'enactments' inasmuch as masculinity is what the psyche deals with, not what psyches are (Hood-Williams, 2001: 53). In sum,

> Masculinity must be understood phenomenologically, that it is not the exclusive property of men, that it has no essential underpinning in sex or in the intrinsic character of what is to count as masculine. (Hood-Williams, 2001: 53)

Whitehead (2005; see also Hearn and Whitehead, 2006) is also critical of Connell and Messerschmidt and retains a strong sociological focus, resisting the call for a psychosocial explanation like Jefferson's. Whitehead (2005) is interested in what men share in common as a category, such as an involvement in domestic violence and sexual offending. He is critical of Connell's over-concentration on relations between men and women at the expense of men in relation to other men. He concedes that recognition of masculinity in the plural (i.e. masculinities) has cast some light on the diversity of men's identities and experiences but suggests that this leaves a gap, specifically those patterns of behaviour men share in common and women do not. More than that, he refers to behaviours that men share regardless of their race and class. Whitehead argues that the idea of 'manhood' captures the masculinity of all men regardless of their class, ethnicity and sexual orientation. The mythical figure of the Hero, albeit manifesting itself in various forms, is an ideal form of masculinity. Men do not display manliness at all times, if at all, for example at work and in the context of family life. The qualities of heroism are reserved for those occasions where men encounter conflict with other men. Not surprisingly men may sense masculine anxiety or the complete collapse of their self-identity. Men, especially young men, are constantly adjusting their perceptions and behaviour in line with an unobtainable 'Ideal Masculine Self'. A result of this may be the onset of panic and an irrational over-reaction to certain social cues, hence man-on-man violence in pubs and on the street. An illuminating insight granted by Whitehead (2005: 411) is that an individual man may

> demonstrate his masculinity by two categories of violence to other men: violence which includes victims in the category "man" as worthy rivals and violence which excludes victims from the category "man" as unworthy of being there. The latter category is likely to include gay men and men from minority ethnic groups.

This brief overview of debates about masculinity and crime all hold to the view that male behaviour is problematic. It has also shown that feminists have argued that criminology is male-centred and the work reviewed above continues to focus on males. However, this body of work is informed by the feminist critique of malestream criminology. The work of Connell has been particularly influential, especially the study of gender relations. More than that, it attempts to theorize masculinities in a form that is recognizable by men.

Men, masculinities and crime – towards a human rights perspective

Relatively recent writing by a disparate group of social scientists in response to feminist scholars and their respective problematizations of the relationship between men, crime and criminology are to be welcomed, even though they have not fundamentally reoriented the directions taken by criminological theorists and state-funded research agendas. Correspondingly, the man question continues to be largely hidden, although those who have made a contribution have laudably brought to the fore key questions about men, masculinities and criminality. Here we scrutinize the male offender and Chapter 8 moves on to explore these themes with reference to male victims. Much of the work has revisited classical debates in social science about the relative significance of structure and agency or accounts attaching relative primacy, on the one hand, to societal, political economic influences on crime and, on the other hand, to individual and psychosocial influences. Although students of criminology now have a more sophisticated evidence base to think about men as offenders, we are still not clear why men are so inherently crime-prone and why their behaviour causes so much harm and suffering in an increasingly troubled and insecure world. We do not have any answers to this perplexing question and are grateful for the insight gained from the writers discussed in the previous section. Drawing on human rights principles offers another way of seeing the gender and crime debate.

In this part of the chapter, issue is taken with the notion of human rights and its potential to create a universalistic discourse about crime and public policy. Since the passing into law of the Human Rights Act 1998, which came into full effect on 2 October 2000, there has been considerable debate about its impact on the criminal justice system. Without trying to oversimplify what has happened, in the early twenty-first century it would appear that there has been general compliance with the HRA, and that most legislation pre-dating it conformed with its principles anyway (Department for Constitutional Affairs, 2006; Human Rights Watch, 2006; Norrie, 2001). Under the stewardship of the New Labour (1997–2010) and the Coalition (2010–15) regimes, the main exemption to this rule is counterterrorism legislation, best demonstrated by the controversies surrounding the detention of foreign nationals under the Anti-Terrorism, Crime and Security Act 2001 (Martin, 2006), the Prevention of Terrorism Act 2005 and the Terrorism Prevention and Investigation Measures Act 2011. The House of Lords decided that the detention of suspects on the grounds of their nationality or immigration status was incompatible with Article 14. The emergence of terrorist groups such as Al-Qaeda and the Islamic State of Iraq and the Levant (IS) have resulted in yet more intrusive forms of surveillance in society on the domestic front. The previous chapter showed how an appreciation of human rights discourse exposes a range of injustices relating to female offenders. This chapter attempts a similar exercise for male offenders, focusing in particular on the police.

The Human Rights Act 1998 and other related legislation do not openly mention gender, although it is arguably gendered in a way that favours male interests, at least if a macro-level analysis is adopted. The evidence presented elsewhere in this book shows quite clearly that women in general, and female offenders in particular, continue to be disadvantaged despite the aspirations of human rights legislators. Men and those subjects accomplishing a range of masculinities may appear, at least on the surface, to benefit from having their rights shored up, but a closer inspection of males who offend indicates a more complex situation.

Male offenders and human rights discourse: Threats and opportunities

The human rights agenda and the discourses surrounding it offer an opportunity for criminologists to consider the diverse experiences of men as offenders and suspects. Ideally, we would like to focus on this issue in a similar fashion to the previous chapter, but it is our argument that a symmetrical approach is not the most appropriate method of appraising the situation of men and their masculinities. It is argued that the status of the male offender can be studied from two perspectives: either as a *potential beneficiary* of human rights values or as an *inhibitor* of the human rights of others.[2] Although this is a binary approach, some men are likely to be both inhibitors and beneficiaries of any emancipatory discourses, such as human rights. The notion that men may be beneficiaries refers to the experiences of relatively marginalized and powerless masculinities that would benefit from an enhancement of their human rights. The observation about inhibitors is a more tentative attempt to come to terms with the fact that male offending behaviour seriously compromises the human rights of individuals and communities and calls for the 'responsibilization' (Garland, 2001) of some men to address this. The remainder of this section considers these perspectives in turn, focusing mainly on the former. Before that, though, it is necessary to restate explicitly in concrete terms the reasons why human rights is important for coming to terms with men, masculinities and offending.

In accord with our earlier statements, the following points are at stake, in particular our adoption of a human rights framework that observes the three principles of freedom, equality and dignity. Faulkner (2007: 137) and his characterization of a **'classical' view of the offender** underpins this:

> ... as a person empowered by free will, entitled to dignity and respect as a human being capable of change and improvement. It found expression in the European Convention on Human Rights, incorporated into domestic law by the Human Rights Act 1998. How it is interpreted and applied will change over time – the Convention is to be regarded as a living instrument – but the values are permanent and not to be set aside because the 'world has changed'.

These important touchstones are there as a moral imperative to ensure that the equal status of each and every human being – however distasteful or heinous the acts of some men may be – is not only recognized but also protected. We argue that all social relationships in which male offenders and suspects participate need to be based on an appreciation of justice and equality, two core values that complement the human rights agenda. This is far from straightforward, however, because human rights are based on unity and diversity, which can create tensions in attempting to establish equal rights for all. In principle, human rights discourse may be used to unify the experiences of vulnerable groups (i.e. offenders) but in practice criminal justice is gendered in complex ways and there are profound inequalities existing among male offenders, relating to wider social divisions, principally ethnicity, class and age.

In the past, human rights discourse has focused mainly on international violations and it would be possible to continue this tradition with a discussion of masculinities in the context of warfare and militarism, although in this chapter we seize the post-1998 opportunity to consider human rights in a domestic setting, specifically the criminal justice system in the UK. It is also shown that the human rights agenda is premised on the transformation of civil society. In the 2000s attempts to realize this were tried through the so-called 'civil renewal' agenda and by deepening and widening democracy. Under the Coalition government (2010–15) the notion of 'Big Society', though not clearly defined, latched on to the idea that as far as possible communities should be self-governing and create a strong civil society instead of relying on the state and big government (Clear, 2012; Walklate, 2012).

It is necessary to restate one of our introductory observations, namely that human rights are inextricably linked with civil and political rights and a preoccupation with the public sphere. It is now a truism in socio-legal studies and political science that the prioritization of these considerations reflects patriarchal, or at the very least masculine, interests at the expense of women. Also neglected are the economic, social and cultural rights which have impacted the most on women, although these factors also have consequences for our understanding of the human rights of men who offend. This is the stuff of citizenship and the need for reciprocal rights and obligations or responsibilities. It is argued that when it comes to men the application of human rights discourse leads to a certain moral and political ambiguity, which is unique to men. In the forthcoming paragraphs a similar case to the one in the previous chapter will be made to show that certain unitary categories of male offenders are not treated equitably and that their freedom and dignity are compromised. This is not to say that specific articles and principles of the Human Rights Act are routinely contravened, rather that some vulnerable men and their masculinities are marginalized and subordinated due to their powerlessness and their lack of appreciable economic, social and cultural rights. Consequently, these men are denied equal access to resources and an experience of justice that is compatible with our broader understanding of human rights. In short, there is a justice and equity shortfall for some male offenders, resulting in them being marginalized, devalued and denigrated. Such men may be conceived of as *potential beneficiaries* of human rights.

Men as beneficiaries of human rights discourse

Many male offenders are marginalized or kept away from the centre of society, not only at a macro level but also in terms of the communities and the families to which they may or may not belong. It is such men who may be *potential beneficiaries* of a radical human rights agenda that moves beyond the legalistic discourse of the 1998 Act and other conventions. Many men in prison are denied a voice, partly because they are disenfranchised but also because many have been deprived of an adequate education, and indeed some men lack basic literacy and numeracy skills. The mental health of many men in prison is poor and the minds of far too many who are locked up are addled as a result of drug and alcohol misuse. Many men arrive in prison with very little in terms of socio-economic status or cultural capital and they leave with even less (Senior, 2002). The prison estate is not only full of Bauman's (1998) 'flawed consumers', but damaged and disturbed people who are further dehumanized by a punitive system. Research shows that these problems are much worse for some male BME, especially African-Caribbean, prisoners as a result of their experiences of wider structural inequalities and institutionalized racism (Phillips and Bowling, 2012). The issue of imprisonment has been examined in depth already and the observations about Article 2 ('The right to life') and Article 8 ('The right to family and private life') apply to male prisoners too, albeit in different ways. The next section of the chapter takes us to the start of the criminal justice system where offenders meet the police in their capacity as gatekeepers. Based on an observation made by Jefferson (1990: 41) a quarter of a century ago, but one that still resonates today, it is argued that police powers are applied more readily against particular groups. For example, young black males and radical protestors often confront the police due to a breakdown in communication or lack of interaction (this may be a temporary or permanent situation).

To capture developments in the second decade of the twenty-first century this paragraph needs reworking to take stock of the emergence of different conflicts and groups, although the presence of gender and ethnicity remain central to police accountability and legitimacy. It is argued that the police service, in its approach to stop and search, might deny some male suspects their human rights. Crucially, drawing on the work of Bayley (2002), we show how recognition of human rights standards can enhance the experiences of male suspects and offenders. In short, our argument is that an explicit formulation of human rights discourse in Bayley's terms can address many of the injustices affecting marginalized masculinities.

Introducing human rights – the police and discrimination against marginalized men

The police service is charged with many responsibilities, including the prevention and detection of crime and disorder among an expanding remit. Both of these activities, but especially the latter, necessarily involve some compromise of the rights and civil liberties of individual citizens and the police from time to time represent a threat to the rights of some groups of marginal men, especially socially excluded and discriminated against masculinities. However, there is recognition of the need for a balance. As Smith (2002: 12) puts it, there is a perpetual 'search for a balance between the demands of the general interests of the community and the protection of individual human rights'. Thus police officers cannot undertake crime fighting without some limits to what they may do; citizens do have fundamental human rights that need to be protected and safeguarded, if only to avoid the wrongful conviction of the innocent. This has been achieved by the Police and Criminal Evidence Act (PACE) 1984 and the Human Rights Act 1998. Taking the latter as an example, Articles 2 and 3 protect persons from having their life taken away from them (Article 2) and from torture and inhuman or degrading punishment or treatment (Article 3). Article 5 is a limited right that ensures the right to liberty and security. It pertains to the police power to detain a person and the fact that the police need to have sufficient reasons for detaining a suspect, reasons that need to be made transparent to the suspect. Another limited right is Article 6 or the right to a fair trial. This is arguably more closely related to what takes place in the courts, although the police in their gatekeeping capacity do influence developments that occur later on in the criminal justice process. A study of sentencing policy and practice in a sample of West Midlands courts, for instance, evidences some gendered and racialized discrimination which was partly explained in terms of police activities prior to the prosecution process (Hood, 1992). Citizens are given a qualified right to privacy under Article 8, meaning that any surveillance of a person needs to be proportionate. Article 11 refers to the freedom of the individual to associate and assemble with other persons to march or demonstrate.

A key article, at least for the purposes of this chapter, is Article 14, where it is asserted that the individual should be free from discrimination. Significantly, this article actually refers to sex and gender, as well as other variables like race/ethnicity, age and religion. However, Article 14 is not free-standing and must necessarily be set alongside other Articles, such as 5 (Liberty and security) and 8 (Privacy). This can be seen in relation to stop and search where the use of discretion and selective law enforcement is rife (Quinton, 2013); for example, black people were six times more likely to be stopped and searched than white people. Asians – especially following the 7/7 bombings in London – were two times more likely to experience this aspect of policing than whites (HMIC, 2013; Home Office, 2006c: viii; Parmar, 2013, 2014). As noted in the Young Review (2014: 19), although talking about the prison population, there is a situation now where ethnic minority communities are 'perceived through racialized stereotypes; black prisoners through the lens of gangs and drugs and Muslim offenders through the lens of extremism and terrorism'. According to critics, 'stop and search powers allow unjustified interference with Article 5 and, in the way they are used, breach Article 14 as well' (Wadham and Modi, 2004: 222).

Several other studies expressed concern about the use of stop and search, especially the finding that officers do not always observe the 'reasonable suspicion' requirement found in the legislation. Reasonable suspicion can never be supported on the basis of personal factors alone without reliable or supporting intelligence or information or some specific behaviour by the person concerned. For example, a person's race, age, appearance, or the fact that the person is known to have a previous conviction, cannot be used alone or in combination with each other as the reason for searching that person. Reasonable suspicion cannot be based on generalizations or stereotypical images of certain groups or categories of people as more likely to be involved in criminal activity. Most crucially, these studies found that the powers of stop and search were used disproportionately against black people, principally males (Home Office, 2014b; Hurrell, 2013; Rowe, 2013).

Bayley (2002) has written a provocative article, calling police scholars to consider the role of the police in response to interpersonal violent crimes motivated by hatred on the grounds of race, ethnicity and religion. The issue of gender is not an explicit element of his essay yet criminological research shows quite clearly that men mainly carry out this type of offending. More than that, Bayley's ideas are applicable for addressing the policing of marginalized masculinities. The concept of fairness, based on the recognition of human rights standards, is applied in order that the police can formulate accountable, transparent or open and effective interventions. As Bayley (2002: 90) puts it, 'the police need to become a minority group themselves – a minority group dedicated to equality and citizenship'. In the context of England and Wales, Bayley's thoughts are related to diversity, an agenda that requires the police to be open and fair in their treatment of suspects and offenders. The police are not equipped to deal with the subjectivities or structural location of violent men. However, they can perform their duties in such a way that their actions are underpinned by the values of justice and equality. The realization of such an aspiration is not easy, especially among men in marginalized positions where there is a history of discrimination sustained by the state and political elites.

Bayley draws inspiration from the Patten Commission in Northern Ireland, which was convened in 1998 to set up a post-Good Friday police system. Patten concluded that a human rights-based approach should be central to police activity. While the troubles in Northern Ireland at that time are beyond the remit of this chapter, Bayley shows the importance of the police for maintaining human rights and a respect for diversity in multi-ethnic societies. Clearly this is a political issue and the police cannot aspire to achieve this end without the total commitment of central government. Under New Labour, for example, attempts were made to deepen and widen democracy but the human rights of some men have been threatened. In the aftermath of 9/11 and 7/7, Muslim communities have increasingly being placed under surveillance and the stop and search powers of the police have been deployed against young Asian men. The activities of the police are articulated with the war on Iraq and the Bush–Blair axis and the powerful influence of military and political masculinities where human rights abuses are considered at best secondary if not irrelevant in a 'war on terror'. The structured masculinities of state actors, including the politicians and senior police officers, tap into and project public anxieties onto an 'enemy within'. Crowther (2000) notes that in the past this was young black men in the inner cities, whereas since 2001 it has been young Asian men (Webster, 2007, 2014).

A strength of Bayley's (2002: 85) piece is that he situates human rights in relation to discourses about citizenship and the police, who perform a highly visible role in demonstrating that rights are real and evenly distributed. The rights of suspects can be protected in several ways. Firstly, police leaders must demonstrate their commitment to human rights, not only of the general public but also of suspects. Officers who infringe human rights need to face disciplinary measures, based on a code of conduct, to give off an unequivocal message that discrimination will not be tolerated. This needs to be underpinned by robust diversity training. If things go wrong, there needs to be a clear mechanism for remedying failed policies and initiatives.

Unfortunately, there are impediments to these goals, not least the point that the preservation of human rights is out of kilter with the **crime control model** outlined by Packer (1968), which has been prioritized all too often in many modern societies (Bowling et al., 2004). Having said this, police research shows that the use of hard policing styles can be counterproductive because it alienates marginal subcultural groups.

The effectiveness of the police is dependent on recognition of universal needs, although specific communities have their own needs and these need to be considered at the expense of the slavish observance of narrow performance regimes imposed by central government. To counter any human rights deficit experienced by some excluded and marginalized masculinities there is a clear need for consultation. Furthermore, to ensure that policing is compatible with a human rights benchmark it is necessary to make efforts to make sure resources are allocated fairly and effectively with a focus on transparency and accountability. To achieve this:

- Police operations must be lawful and not political
- The rule of law needs to be visible and free from political interference
- Operational strategies need to be evaluated
- Allegations about police misconduct need to be investigated
- There should be independent civilian review of complaints against the police
- Recruitment must reflect diversity
- Covert intelligence should be regulated in line with the European Convention on Human Rights
- Civilian familiarization of policing must occur, either through observing police operations or by attending police civilian training academies. (Bayley, 2002)

Although we have made a case for protecting the rights of suspects and offenders, this needs to be balanced by recognizing the harm caused by these individuals, especially the harm experienced by victims of violence.

Men as inhibitors of human rights discourse

In contrast to our consideration of the female offender in Chapter 5, we argue that it would also make sense to consider the orientation of men with regard to human rights discourse from a markedly different standpoint, namely as *inhibitors*. The fact that men commit most murders (Dorling, 2005) and that they are responsible for most sex offending, including paedophilia (Thomas, 2005), shows the type of suffering they cause. It is the crimes of men that are most likely to compromise the human rights of others. The New Labour mantra (articulated by three governments between 1997 and 2010) that with rights comes responsibilities may be taken as an invitation to men to assume personal responsibility for the victimization they cause, particularly of women and children, and arguably the community more generally. In the next chapter a persuasive case is made to show the parallels between domestic violence and torture. To be more precise, how male violence (including domestic and sexual forms) undermines the freedom and dignity of women and children (see Articles 2, 3, 4 and 5 of the HRA).

More generally, the social and economic costs of male crime and anti-social behaviour can have an indirect effect on other economic and social rights because of the drain their actions have on the increasingly finite resources available for the delivery of crime and public policy. By adopting this stance we make both a political case and a pedagogical case for bringing about change in men to ensure they respect the human rights of others. For example, while men and masculinities are characterized by difference and diversity, there is the potential for a common language to be developed that gives equal respect to the freedom and dignity of all citizens. Some of the insights offered by the psychosocial approach may be instructive here, in the sense that individuals have the capacity to recognize a need to change, although there are 'stubborn psychic investments' (Gadd, 2003). At a macro level there is also the 'subordination and marginalization of some masculinities that are not able to or committed to conforming nor complying with hegemonic patterns' (Connell, 1995: 79).

Concluding thoughts

This chapter has demonstrated that the statement that men and boys are responsible for the bulk of offending behaviour has the status of a truism in criminological debate. Considerable advances have been made in terms of theorizing the relationship between men and criminality, although some confusion and ambivalence still remain in terms of causality. The introduction of an appreciation of human rights discourse has been used as part of an attempt to come to terms with male offending behaviour. Despite the claims to universality underpinning human rights rhetoric, gender is still a vital determinant of differential experiences when it comes to suspects and offenders. By drawing attention to a diversity of configurations of masculinities relating to both men/ boys and women/girls some of the masculinities routinely accomplished by some offenders are subordinated and rendered inferior. The outcome is that all citizens have human rights but that these are compromised by public policy and political economic conditions.

With the exception of certain forms of theft – in particular shoplifting – and offences relating to prostitution, the disproportionate involvement of the male sex is very pronounced. Most anti-social behaviour on street corners and outside shops is linked with groups of teenage boys. In the chapter on males as victims it is argued that some of these boys are, in effect, the victims of over-punitive criminalization by statutory agencies and vocal citizens belonging to 'middle England' and so-called 'respectable' society. Acquisitive crimes such as burglary and the theft of and from motor vehicles tend to be carried out by boys and men, many of whom misuse drugs. Similarly, more violent offences, including street robberies committed in predominantly urban areas, as well as interpersonal violence committed both in public places as well as the private sphere, are all inextricably associated with men.

The first part of this chapter reviewed what we know about offending behaviour and confirmed this picture. It should be noted that crime statistics are socially constructed, sometimes telling us more about the behaviour of those producing the data, and that this information does not necessarily shed much light on the dark figure of crime (e.g. those offences that do not come to the attention of the police service or Home Office statisticians). Despite this observation, it would be fair to say that there is not a hidden reserve of hitherto unknown female offending and that the disproportionate involvement of men in crime and disorder is a reflection of some kind of underlying reality. However, the conventional methods of measuring the correlation between offending behaviour and sex are not without problems. The methods used to render visible gender in relation to offending are based on a physical marker of difference, which in the last analysis is based on differentiation on the grounds of genitalia. Officials responsible for compiling Home Office figures, for example, are not troubled by the deficiencies of looking at sexual difference in this way, nor is there any discernible concern with the concept of gender, especially debates about the problems with collapsing gender into sex. This point is of theoretical significance and was examined in more detail in the second part of the chapter.

Criminology has rightly been criticized for its taken-for-granted **sexism**, and although the field of study has not been redefined as such by feminist critiques there has been a partial reorientation of its subject matter. It would be fair to say, however, that some scholars have been more responsive to the criticisms made by 'second-wave' feminism than others. While most theoretical criminologists have not denied the problem of sexism inherent to criminological theory, in many instances they continue to think in a way that is to all intents and purposes 'gender blind' and essentially androcentric.

Scholars who have started to take seriously the relationship between gender and crime invariably start with a reference to the work of Connell (2002), although many writers question some of its conceptual assumptions (Hood-Williams, 2001; Jefferson, 2002; Whitehead, 2005). Criminological theory has certainly been enriched by this growing body of work and other material has reflected on the practical consequences of such insights for working with male offenders (Gadd, 2003; Whitehead, 2005). These different explanations of masculinities and crime are all-persuasive but the question 'Why is it that not all men offend?', despite seemingly sharing similar psychological and sociological characteristics, remains. This chapter has not been able to answer this question and has taken a detour by considering the linkages between different masculinities in relation to human rights discourse, where an attempt has been made to universalize and equalize the outcomes of human experience.

Early reviews of the anticipated impact of the Human Rights Act 1998 were 'sceptical' and academic and the state evaluations have concluded that the predicted avalanche of appeals in criminal law cases have not materialized (Department for Constitutional Affairs, 2006; Human Rights Watch, 2006; Norrie, 2001). This chapter suggests that the masculinities accomplished by certain male offenders make their human rights more vulnerable. An involvement in crime – or increasingly for some offenders a potential involvement in crime – places people in vulnerable positions as they enter the criminal justice process, where their human rights are likely to be jeopardized. The use of stop and search and its resultant criminalization of African-Caribbean and – increasingly in the post 9/11 and 7/7 universe – Asian men makes their human rights more vulnerable. We should not forget that some male offenders also place victims in a situation where their human rights are fragile or, in extreme cases, nullified.

Summary

- This chapter described the distribution, extent and prevalence of male crime. It is clear that men commit most offences, especially violent crime; they are over-represented in most categories of crime in comparison to their female counterparts.
- Men experience criminal justice agencies, such as the police, courts and correctional agencies, in different ways from women. Inevitably, more men come into contact with the criminal justice system, although they are treated in a gender-neutral way in the sense that masculinity is not problematized. It is shown that current arrangements are not explicitly designed for men yet they effectively deal with the problems caused by, and the needs of, men.
- A question running throughout this chapter is 'Why do people commit crime?' This dilemma has preoccupied theorists since the development of criminology and traditionally the discipline has been gender-blind in its reply. Drawing on the work of writers who have taken seriously the issue of masculinities and crime, we reviewed the contribution of two schools of thought: the structural and the psychosocial. Both approaches provide persuasive accounts of different aspects of the male crime debate, although there are other possible interpretations.
- We argued that a human rights discourse provides a potentially complementary approach to come to terms with the crime and disorder of men. It was argued that men routinely inhibit the human rights of their victims and that they need to assume a greater degree of personal responsibility for their harmful actions. However, there are inequalities existing between men and some masculinities are marginalized, resulting in criminalization and over-policing. This latter group of men may potentially benefit from a human rights-based approach that highlights the salience of equality, fairness and justice.

STUDY QUESTIONS

1. Account for the different nature of male and female offending behaviour.
2. Assess the relevance of the concept of hegemonic masculinity for explaining the crime and disorder of men.
3. Evaluate the contribution that the psychosocial approach can make to our comprehension of male crime and anti-social behaviour.
4. Outline and analyse the different ways in which the human rights of male offenders may be threatened.
5. Critically assess the usefulness of the distinction between men as beneficiaries and men as inhibitors of human rights in relation to the crimes of men.

FURTHER READING

A useful starting point is Chapter 2 in S. Walklate (2004) *Gender, Crime and Criminal Justice* (Willan). Though published several decades ago now, the special issue of the *British Journal of Criminology* published in 1996 (36(3)) introduces the field and although much work has been done since, this captures the main currents of the debate. This should be read alongside T. Jefferson (1997) 'Masculinities and crimes', in M. Maguire, R. Morgan and R. Reiner (eds) *The Oxford Handbook of Criminology*, 2nd edn (Oxford University Press).

For the structural approach developed out of Connell's contribution, a good entry into the field is R.W. Connell and J. Messerschmidt (2005) 'Hegemonic masculinity: Rethinking the concept' (*Gender and Society*, 19(6): 829–59). This should be followed up by reading J.W. Messerschmidt (1993) *Masculinities and Crime: Critique and Reconceptualization of Theory* (Rowman & Littlefield). For an introduction to psychosocial approaches, see D. Gadd and T. Jefferson (2007) *Psychosocial Criminology: An Introduction* (Sage). For a more accessible and lively overview of the topics covered in this field, see the relevant articles in the Autumn 2003 issue (no. 53) of *Criminal Justice Matters*, a magazine published by the Centre for Crime and Justice Studies.

Notes

1. Given Hood-Williams' (2001: 41) insightful observations about the 'et cetera clause', any consideration of the linkages between different structures and social divisions is fraught with difficulties and would require more attention than is feasible in a book of this size.
2. These are not mutually exclusive categories and are separated here for heuristic purposes.

PART III
IN NEED OF CARE

7

Women as Victims

OVERVIEW

Chapter 7 provides:

- An outline of the broad-based nature of women's victimization, including an analysis of women in prostitution/sex work, forced marriage, 'honour'-based violence and female genital mutilation.
- A critical review of the changing official responses to violence against women.
- A discussion on the problem of attrition in rape and domestic abuse cases.
- An overview of the rising global concern over the victimization of women.
- A reconceptualization of domestic violence as a human rights violation.
- A reconceptualization of violence against women as a form of coercive control and torture.
- A critical discussion of state responsibility and accountability with respect to violence against women.

KEY TERMS

- attrition
- coercive control
- consent
- domestic abuse and violence
- female genital mutilation
- forced marriage
- 'honour'-based violence
- human rights

- ideal victim
- prostitution
- rape
- sex work
- state accountability
- torture
- violence against women

Introduction

Victims of crime have increasingly come to occupy a central place within criminal justice proceedings and within broader debates about crime, harm and justice. More particularly, there has been an exponential growth in our knowledge of the gendered nature of victimization in recent years. Feminist-inspired research agendas, analyses of criminal justice policy and practice, and theorizing – all inspired by feminism – have achieved much in naming the abuse and violence in women's lives and, in the process, have assisted in transforming the problem of male violence from a 'private trouble' to a 'public issue' (Hamner and Maynard, 1987; Hester et al., 1996; Kelly, 2014; Stanko, 1990, 1995; Walby et al., 2014; Westmarland, 2015). The recent high-profile revelations of the widespread sexual abuse of girls and women committed by celebrities such as Jimmy Saville, and others identified as part of Operation Yewtree, has firmly cemented the issue of violence against women into the public domain. At the same time, a growth in grassroots feminist activism, as seen in the work of *Everyday Sexism* (Bates, 2014) (**Everyday sexism project**) and *Counting Dead Women* (http://kareningalasmith.com/counting-dead-women/) has done much to enhance visibility of the pervasiveness of harassment and violence against women. This increase in awareness has been accompanied by considerable innovation and reform to the way in which the criminal justice system responds to female victims.[1] A more pronounced commitment by government in its *Violence Against Women and Girls* (VAWG) agenda, together with a raft of policy and legal changes over the past decade, has resulted in a considerably altered landscape.

The chapter is divided into four main parts. The first part reviews the changing policy and legal definitions of violence against women. Since the publication of the first edition, definitions and categories of violence against women have undergone considerable change, with a number of 'new' concerns about violence against women emerging in public discourse. A greater emphasis on the 'coercive' dimensions and '**social harm**' experienced by women has also done much to expand the frame of reference when thinking about women's victimization (Antrobus, 2008; Bose, 2008; Cain and Howe, 2008; Green, 2008; Stark, 2007, 2009).

The second part documents the broad-based nature and extent of women's victimization. We consider a broad spectrum of harms and crimes against women in our analysis, including a focus on: intimate partner violence; sexual violence and rape; prostitution; sex trafficking; **forced marriage**; 'honour'[2]-based violence and female genital mutilation. We are conscious of the partial reading that might result in naming some forms of violence and not others, but hope that readers will appreciate the considerable task of exploring women's victimization within a single chapter.

In reviewing the extent to which things have changed, the third part of the chapter critically reviews the official responses to women's victimization through a consideration of policy and practice within criminal justice over time. We outline the problem of **attrition** and consider the construction of the 'ideal' victim and its consequences for the policing of such crimes.

In the final part we transgress existing debates within criminology and situate violence against women within a human rights framework. With violence against women now recognized throughout the globe as a significant social problem and as a human rights issue, we consider the value of a human rights framework (United Nations, 1995). We develop our analysis of '**coercive control**' through an appreciation of domestic violence as a form of torture – a clear and obvious human rights violation. In developing our argument, we link the local with the global and consider the role of the state and its responsibility with respect to violence against women.

(Re)conceptualizing violence against women

From its early use in the mid-1970s, the term 'domestic violence' originally referred to violence within intimate partner relationships, but since that time the recognition of violence against women has been transformed. The term now recognizes a host of behaviours against other family members, including child-to-parent violence, 'honour'-based violence, forced marriage and female genital mutilation, among others. To acknowledge violence within same-sex relationships, the term intimate partner violence (IPV) has become increasingly drawn upon. The term 'domestic abuse' has also emerged to enable a distinction for many of the behaviours that do not involve physical violence. The first edition of our book was written under the HM Government 'cross-government' definition in 2005 as:

> [any] incident of threatening behaviour, violence or abuse (psychological, physical, sexual, financial or emotional) between adults who are or have been intimate partners or family members, regardless of their gender or sexuality. This includes issues of concern to black and minority ethnic (BME) communities such as so called 'honour based violence', female genital mutilation (FGM) and forced marriage. (Home Office, 2012b)

Since that time, this definition has been developed by the government as:

> [any] incident or pattern of incidents of controlling, coercive, threatening behaviour, violence or abuse between those aged 16 or over who are, or have been, intimate partners or family members regardless of gender or sexuality.

The abuse can encompass, but is not limited to:

- psychological
- physical
- sexual
- financial
- emotional

Controlling behaviour is: a range of acts designed to make a person subordinate and/or dependent by isolating them from sources of support, exploiting their resources and capacities for personal gain, depriving them of the means needed for independence, resistance and escape and regulating their everyday behaviour. *Coercive behaviour* is: an act or a pattern of acts of assault, threats, humiliation and intimidation or other abuse that is used to harm, punish, or frighten their victim. (Home Office, 2013a)

The progressive nature of this change is hugely significant in reframing conceptualizations of violence against women. While reducing the age of responsibility from 18 to 16 has done much to make visible the harms perpetrated against girls, acknowledgment of the 'controlling' and 'coercive' dimensions of such violence offers perhaps the greatest potential for repositioning and reframing the debate (Crowther-Dowey et al., forthcoming). Not only does a focus on these elements provide a more accurate lens within which to describe the realities of violence and harm experienced by women, but it also enables a more complex appreciation of the capacity of women to demonstrate agency within victimization. Moreover, a focus on coercion has much resonance with our stated position of adopting a human rights approach to address violence against women. Drawing on the work of Evan Stark (2007, 2009), we explore each of these briefly before returning to their significance in the final part of the chapter.

As a key proponent of reconceptualizing violence against women as 'coercive control', Stark (2009: 1514) emphasizes the limitations of contemporary analyses which define domestic violence as an 'incident-specific crime', equating abuse with physical and psychological assault. For Stark, coercive control goes beyond the physical and psychological harms of prevailing victimization narratives and draws attention more closely to the diverse humiliations, intimidation, isolation and degradation that violate women's personhood.

The 'technology of coercive control' is better understood here through the 'constraints on women's opportunities to enact their life projects', to 'develop their personhood, utilise their capacity or practice citizenship' (Stark, 2007: 4). Here the 'controller' (violent man) exploits resources, and forces her to defer her hopes and plans, degrades her, and blocks her autonomy and liberty (Stark, 2009: 1524).

While studies of coercive control have been accused of overstating women's victimization and underplaying women's resilience and resistance (Anderson,

2009; Libal and Parekh, 2009; Polletta, 2009), Stark (2009: 1514) reminds us that many of the women in his study did not resemble the stereotypical battered woman; rather, many were in 'successful careers, physically assertive or aggressive rather than passive to their fate'. In describing victims' resilience, however, Stark describes it within a frame of 'self-destruction'; here women's resilience is viewed as having 'control in the context of no control'. The harms perpetrated against women, then, are better understood as broader 'sociopolitical' harms in which women are ultimately denied access to equality, liberty and autonomy. Given the universal language of individual freedoms and equality embedded within human rights discourse, a focus on addressing coercive control has much appeal for those working within a human rights framework. As Stark (2009: 1521) notes:

> Although coercive control occurs in the private sphere, typically with little or no government collusion, it nonetheless merits classification as a human rights violation because of its broader political context, systemic roots, gendered construction, the extent to which it exploits pre-existing inequalities, and particularly because of its consequences, the denial of equal rights to citizenship.

We return to and expand our discussions on the 'coercive' elements of violence against women later in the chapter.

In our first edition, we focused mainly on documenting the prevalence and nature of 'domestic violence' to convey our message about women's victimization. We maintain that the term had validity and currency at the time of writing. Given our increase in knowledge of the range and multiplicity of violence perpetrated against women, in this next section we revisit the knowledge base on 'mainstream' forms of violence against women and go on to extend our focus to incorporate some 'new' and emerging areas of concern.

Violence against women and girls

In Chapter 3 we emphasized the normalcy and everyday nature of violence against women over time. We also emphasized the centrality of *victim blaming* and the *lack of prosecution and conviction* for defendants accused of rape and interpersonal partner violence. In this chapter, we argue that there is much evidence to suggest continuities in the present. We remind readers of the seminal work by Stanko (1990) on 'everyday violence'. Emphasizing the 'hidden' nature of violence against women, she argued that women 'manage' their danger on a daily basis and experience violence as a common occurrence.

Alongside this, Kelly's (1988) notion of the 'continuum of sexual violence', in which many forms of coercion, abuse and assault are experienced by women at different points in their lives, has done much to inform and reshape our understanding of violence against women. Given these analyses, there is now a wealth of data to support the reality that the violence(s) experienced by women are not one-off events occurring in the public sphere between strangers, but rather are more likely to be found in the everyday private sphere between those known to them. Critical of the official count of violent crime, Walby et al. (2014: 187) argue that violent crime against women is both 'under-measured and ubiquitous' and is routinely made invisible in the public sphere.

Against a backdrop of overall crime reduction, official statistics indicate an increase in levels of violence against women. The number of referrals for domestic abuse and violence from the police for prosecution is higher than ever before and in a recent review of the investigation and prosecution of rape in London, Angiolini (2015) reports an increase of 68 per cent in rape offences recorded by the Metropolitan Police Service (from 3079 in 2005/06 to 5179 in 2013/14). Such an increase was not, however, matched by an equivalent number of charged offences (only increasing by 17 per cent from 836 in 2005/06 to 982 in 2013/14). In England and Wales 85 women were killed by a partner or ex-partner in 2013–14. According to a 2013 *Overview of Sexual Offending*, around 90 per cent of complainants of the most serious sexual offences in the previous year knew the perpetrators, compared with less than half for other sexual offences (Ministry of Justice, 2013a). The exposure of the systematic abuse against girls and women by a range of celebrities and within institutional settings, including care homes, in recent years has further restated and re-emphasized the pervasive nature of violence against women over time (Jay, 2014; Westmarland, 2015). The setting up of a website and twitter account by Laura Bates in 2012 on documenting *Everyday Sexism*, suggests that the harassment of women in public spaces remains a daily occurrence – after 20 months since its launch, the site had received 50,000 posts, including cases of unwanted sexual greetings, sexual harassment not deemed serious as well as examples of serious sexual assaults (Bates, 2014). Work by Phipps and Young (2012) on 'lad culture' and a survey by the National Union of Students (2010) also document extensive levels of violence and harassment of women in higher education.

Alongside the more 'mainstream' manifestations of violence against women, a 'new' set of anxieties about the victimization of girls and women has emerged. Although we perceive these concerns as part of the overall agenda on violence against women, our motivation in delineating them is twofold: firstly, we wish to stress them as contemporary anxieties, some of which have been constructed with a particular 'cultural' emphasis; and secondly, we emphasize their emergence in this new edition.

Women involved in prostitution/sex work

The victimization of women involved in prostitution has increasingly come to dominate academic, social and political agendas over the past decade (APPG, 2014; Bindel, 2004; Bindel and Atkins, 2007, 2008; Home Office, 2004c, 2006d, 2008, 2011a; Mayor of London, 2010, 2011). Following the Home Office Review on *Tackling Demand for Prostitution* in 2008, the recent *All-Party Parliamentary Group on Prostitution and the Global Sex Trade Inquiry* (APPG, 2014) has done much to emphasize and restate the gendered imbalance of harm that exists in prostitution. Following 413 submissions of evidence, key findings include: a lack of clarity and consistency in the legislation governing prostitution; a failure to protect vulnerable women; a failure to recognize prostitution as a form of violence against women and girls; a failure to target perpetrators effectively; a lack of prioritization and resourcing in the policing of prostitution; inconsistency in law in supporting women to exit; and a failure to acknowledge the impact of prostitution on gender equality.

In our historical analysis in Chapter 3, we argued that women involved in prostitution have negotiated and straddled a variety of identities, being the recipients of both state 'care' and 'control' through their construction as victims and/or offenders. This complex status continues to have much resonance in contemporary debates and is the source of much tension among feminist scholars. Barberet (2014) reminds us of the importance of definitional issues within criminology, noting that the creation, mention and choice of terms and use is part of the social construction of a social problem.

'Prostitution' and 'sex work' are both terms that are used to describe the selling of sexual services. The past decade has witnessed a significant shift in terminology from 'prostitution' to 'sex work'. While it is not our intention to be drawn into the polarized arguments about prostitution/sex work, we do wish to draw attention to the ways in which women's identities within criminal justice are both fluid and changing. We also want to emphasize the differences within and between feminist campaigners seeking to improve the lives of women, albeit in different ways, and to highlight the ways in which differences in identity impact upon the nature of the criminal justice response invoked.

Those using the term 'prostitution' view the selling of sex as something that women would rather not do, that they are coerced in some way or have little choice. Here, prostitution is understood as a form of gendered exploitation and sits within a wider violence against women agenda – the proponents of this perspective strive for the abolition of prostitution, a greater emphasis on targeting men who buy sex, together with the provision of greater support for women wanting to exit prostitution (Baker et al., 2010; Bindel et al., 2012; Coy, 2012; Coy et al., 2012; Jeffreys, 2009, 2012; Matthews et al., 2014). In the UK, the tragic murders of five women involved in prostitution in Ipswich in 2006 did much to reignite the call for a greater alignment of the experiences of women involved in prostitution with the broader violence against women agenda. Reflecting on more contemporary times, Matthews et al. (2014) argue that we have moved from seeing women involved in prostitution as offenders, then victims, to people with agency who are willing to take control of their lives and leave prostitution.

Alongside the domestic concern about women's involvement in prostitution, a growing anxiety over the number of women being trafficked for sex is gaining increasing prominence in national and international agendas (Breuil et al., 2011; O'Brien et al., 2013; Segrave et al., 2009; Spencer and Broad, 2012). We outline some of these global concerns later in the chapter.

For those utilizing the term 'sex work', such involvement is perceived to be undertaken voluntarily in some way by the worker and not by force. Engaging in sex work is understood as a legitimate form of labour and not as a social problem *per se* (Sanders and Hardy, 2015; Sanders et al., 2009; Weitzer, 2010). Here, sex work can be undertaken domestically or transnationally, and unlike the concerns raised above regarding the global trafficking of women, the 'migrant' sex worker is perceived to be a worker who migrates to engage in sex work. The point of intervention for campaigners, then, becomes important when reviewing the conditions of labour within which women work (Goodyear and Cuisick, 2007; Sanders, 2004, 2005). As O'Connell Davidson (2008: 17) argues, abuse and exploitation are connected to the fact that sex workers do not enjoy the civil and labour rights that other citizens receive.

Scholars of sex work argue that the claims of abolitionists about the nature of sex work, and the definition of sex trafficking, are out of touch with the empirical evidence on sex work (Doezema, 1999, 2005; Weitzer, 2010, 2012, 2014). Under the guise of what Augustin (2007) calls the 'rescue industry' (a coalition of NGOs, 'faith-based' groups, abolitionist feminists, conservative and liberal government officials), commentators also point to a range of increasingly repressive and punitive state responses targeted at sex workers (Bernstein, 2010, 2012; Feingold, 2005).

Forced marriage

While a number of international human rights instruments include the right to freely consent to marriage, including Article 16(2) of the Universal Declaration of Human Rights 1948, the issue of forced marriage in Britain has only recently received formal recognition and is now a central feature of the VAWG agenda in the UK. Defined by the government as a 'marriage where one or both people do not (or in cases of people with learning difficulties, cannot) consent to the marriage and pressure or abuse is used', official discourses have emphasized the issues of 'consent' and 'coercion' in noting the differences between forced marriage and arranged marriages (Anitha and Gill, 2009). It should be noted, however, that by thinking about forced marriage simply as an absence of consent there is the risk that the gender-based violence it involves will be underestimated and that in conceptual terms it treats this practice as something different from other forms of violence against women, such as rape, forced pregnancies and kidnapping, that may occur over the course of a woman's lifetime (Quek, 2013).

In 2005 the Forced Marriage Unit (FMU) was established to lead on policy and to provide support for women and other professionals. Forced marriage in the UK (unlike most of its European counterparts) has subsequently been made a specific criminal offence and can be found in Part 10, Section 121 of the Anti-social Behaviour, Crime and Policing Act 2014. While it may be some-what premature to assess to what extent and in what ways this new offence will be policed and prosecuted, we know that in 2014 the FMU gave advice or support related to a possible forced marriage in 1267 cases. Of these cases, 79 per cent involved female victims and 21 per cent involved male victims. The majority of those seeking support (53 per cent) were aged 25 or under. It handled cases involving over 88 different countries, with over half of the cases (53 per cent) involving Pakistan, India and Bangladesh; 23 per cent of the cases handled by the FMU were domestic and had no overseas element (www.gov.uk/forced-marriage). At the time of writing, it could be added that on 10 June 2015 we saw the first successful prosecution under the 2014 forced marriage laws. An unnamed 34-year-old man from Cardiff in Wales was given a 16-year custodial sentence because he made a woman marry him under duress (see www.bbc.co.uk/news/uk-wales-33076323).

'Honour'-based violence (HBV)

In Chapter 3 we explored the importance of *honour* as a key feature of violence between men in the early modern period. In this section, we refer more spe-cifically to the role of 'honour' in the violence and killing of women by family members. Broadly speaking, **'honour'-based violence** (HBV) encompasses:

- Any form of violence perpetrated against women within a framework of patriarchal family and social structures.
- The main justification for the perpetration of HBV is the protection of a value sys-tem predicated on norms and traditions concerned with 'honour'.
- Different violations of the honour code are associated with different punishments: thus HBV manifests in numerous ways, including physical, sexual, emotional, psychological and financial abuse. (Gill, 2014: 73)

As with domestic violence, there is no specific criminal offence of 'honour'-based violence and incidents are policed and prosecuted using generic offences that already exist, such as homicide, rape, assault and harassment. The killing of Banaz Mahmod in 2006 by her father, her uncle and another male relative did much to raise the profile of HBV in the UK. The case also did much to restate the continued failures and inadequacies of the police service in its handling of violence against women. The revelation by the Independent Police Complaints Commission (IPCC) (2008) report that followed demonstrated a number of serious failings and fundamental misunderstandings and ignorance of the practice of 'honour' killing. In response to such failures, the same year saw ACPO develop an 'honour'-based violence strategy, underlining the need for frontline staff to more adequately protect victims. We return to the failures of policing later in the chapter (HMIC, 2014b).

Despite a lack of official statistics on HBV in the UK, the findings of the Iranian and Kurdish Women's Rights Organizations (IKWRO) are increasingly being cited in public discourse. Based on Freedom of Information requests sent to all 52 police forces across England, Wales, Scotland and Northern Ireland asking how many incidents of HBV they had recorded last year, IKWRO report that 39 police forces responded with a total of 2823 incidents. Twelve of the police forces also provided statistics for 2009, and nine of these showed an increase in 'honour' crime between 2009 and 2010. The overall increase across the 12 forces was 57 per cent. In London 'honour' crime has doubled to more than five times the national average, and in Northumberland it has tripled in a year (see http://ikwro.org.uk/2011/12/nearly-3000-cases-of-honour-violence-every-year-in-the-uk/). For an international overview of HBV see Oberwittler and Kasselt (2014).

Female genital mutilation (FGM)

The issue of female genital mutilation (FGM) comprises broadly of 'any procedure that is designed to alter or injure a girl's (or woman's) genital organs for non-medical reasons' (see www.gov.uk/female-genital-mutilation). Designed to curb sexuality, the procedure can cause lifelong physical and psychological complications. Commonly identified in parts of Africa, in some countries in Asia and the Middle East, the World Health Organization estimated up to 140 million girls and women as having been subjected to FGM. It is at this global level that a human rights approach has been most influential in naming and developing a 'zero tolerance' approach at a European Union level (Brown et al., 2013). Alongside a global concern, there is now considerable anxiety over its increased prevalence in England and Wales. Illegal in the UK since 1985, with the law being strengthened in the Female

Genital Mutilation Act 2003 to prevent children from travelling from the UK to undergo FGM abroad, estimates from the Foundation for Women's Health Research and Development suggests as many as 6500 cases per year (see www.forwarduk.org.uk/). While some commentators have been critical of FGM law as nothing more than 'symbolic' (Phillips, 2010), Westmarland (2015: 87) has stressed that it is precisely this symbolic recognition, i.e. 'a new, state-backed social norm', that has been of paramount importance in developing a consensus within the international community of the need to outlaw such a practice. Indeed, in February 2015, *The Guardian* reported the first FGM prosecution of Dr Dhanuson Dharmasena, a junior registrar in obstetrics and gynaecology. The medic was accused of sewing up a woman's vagina following her giving birth. The procedure 'amounted to the reinstitution of FGM – known as reinfibulation' (*The Guardian*, 2015a). The Serious Crime Act 2015 has gone on to strengthen the law to tackle FGM, including the introduction of civil protection orders.

When taken collectively, there are a number of striking parallels in the ways in which these 'new' sets of anxieties are conceptualized in popular discourse. The importance of the cultural framework within which such crimes often take place is routinely drawn upon to 'mitigate' and 'excuse' both the *actions* of perpetrators and the *inaction* of the criminal justice agents. Scholars have argued persuasively that cases of HBV, forced marriage and FGM are presented in the media and public discourse as a result of a 'clash of cultures' (Gill, 2009; Thiara and Gill, 2010). Violence against women within this frame is attributed primarily to religious and cultural traditions rather than gender (Gill et al., 2012). Moreover, in an analysis of prosecutions for 'honour' killings in the UK, Gill (2009) emphasizes that almost all of the defendants put forward a cultural defence. In this way, cases of 'honour' killings (and forced marriage and FGM for that matter) have become 'ethnicized' in the British multi-cultural context, as belonging only to specific ethnic groups (Meetoo and Mirza, 2007). As Gill et al. (2012: 78) have argued:

> [r]esponses to HBV that focus on culture exoticise the act instead of enabling the issues to be viewed as part of the larger struggle against violence against women.

Responding to violence against women

We have already seen the significant difference brought about by feminist criminology in relation to knowledge production. The very real impacts of such work are perhaps more visibly pronounced within the raft of policy and legal changes that have emerged over recent decades. Before reviewing these changes, however, we wish to contextualize such change within a discussion of the longstanding problem of attrition with regard to addressing violence against women.

The problem of attrition

The attrition of violence against women, particularly cases of intimate partner violence and rape, within the criminal justice system has been a relentless and growing concern to both academics and practitioners working in the field. Attrition refers to the process whereby cases drop out of the criminal justice system at one of a number of potential points of exit from that system. Though somewhat dated now, work by Gregory and Lees (1999) continues to have much resonance today. In their work, they identify four major points in the judicial process at which domestic violence cases are excluded:

- When a case is 'no-crimed' by the police
- When the police fail to refer a case to the Crown Prosecution Service
- When the CPS decides not to proceed or reduces the charge to a less serious offence
- When the court dismisses the case or the jury finds the defendant 'not guilty'.

As the gatekeepers to the criminal justice system, we explore the role of the police more particularly to elaborate our discussion on the treatment of victims. Writing over 25 years ago, Edwards (1989) reported that the police tended to avoid making arrests – of the 93 cases of domestic violence in her study, 83 per cent were subsequently 'no-crimed'. A decade later, Gregory and Lees (1999) found substantial evidence of the re-classification of offences in cases of rape, sexual assault and domestic violence to less serious offences. Despite a series of Home Office circulars (69/1986; 60/1990; 19/2000; 003/2013) laying emphasis on the importance of violence against women as a central policing task, there remains evidence of an ongoing lack of police engagement. In March 2014, the HMIC report *Everyone's Business: Improving the Police Response to Domestic Abuse* (HMIC, 2014b) found that 'Domestic Abuse is a priority on paper but, in the majority of forces, not in practice'. With regard to rape more specifically, the picture is equally alarming. Kelly et al. (2005) found that the highest proportion of rape cases in the UK are lost at the earliest stages, with between half and two-thirds dropping out at the investigative stage. There have been a number of damning reports on both police and prosecutors for failing rape victims by wrongly recording many cases as 'no-crime' and dropping others prematurely without following possible lines of investigation. Collectively, these reports have emphasized the insensitive treatment of victims by police, together with drawing attention to significant variation and inconsistency in the provision of support throughout the country, suggesting a 'postcode lottery' of justice for rape victims (Angiolini, 2015; HMCPSI and HMIC, 2002, 2012; HPCPSI, 2007; Kelly et al., 2005; Stern Review, 2010).

Constructing the 'ideal' victim

In explaining the poor police response to violence against women over time, research has emphasized a series of beliefs based on a range of myths and stereotypes about the 'ideal' victim. It is now been well established that police officers' decision to charge is not restricted to judgements of guilt or innocence of the assailant, nor to the legal seriousness of a sexual and domestic assault, but to a range of extralegal factors (Berk and Loseke, 1981; Stewart and Madden, 1997; Waaland and Keeley, 1985). The role of discretion in relation to the front-line officer who attends any incident is of paramount importance in understanding the under-enforcement of the law in these cases. Commentators have pointed to the ways in which police officers' own attitudes and prejudices about women have a profound impact on the way in which that discretion is used. Officers draw on their own internal belief systems, their own attitudes, prejudices and 'common-sense' notions concerning violence against women (Angiolini, 2015; Edwards, 1989; Ferraro, 1989; Stanko, 1989). In this way, the 'moral' perspective takes dominance over the 'legal' perspective in the policing of such crimes. Here, not all women are equal in the eyes of the law and the concept of 'deservedness' is key to understanding which cases go on to secure a conviction.

For the most part, factors that have been identified as pertinent to the process of attrition include the age of the victim, the relationship between the complainant and the suspect, and the degree of violence used. Cases where a conviction is secured tend to involve young single women attacked by a stranger and physically injured during the attack (Grace et al., 1992). While this 'ideal victim' scenario does have the possibility of being played out in the crime of rape (although, as we have already noted above, this is a serious distortion of who rape victims are), victims of domestic violence, whose experience of violence takes place with intimates within a familial frame, have little chance of demonstrating their deservedness to authorities. Despite a concerted attempt in recent years to address the myths and stereotypes about violence against women and girls, research continues to emphasize their enduring presence. The general perception that rape is predominantly a crime undertaken by a stranger, and that the complainant will have sustained some form of injury and resisted rape, still persists (Angiolini, 2015; Kelly et al., 2005). In providing fresh evidence on the problem of attrition, Hohl and Stanko (2015: 331) emphasize the ongoing reliance of myths about rape when they state that:

> As far as police decisions (but not the victim's decision to withdraw) are concerned, the intractable 'respectable women' image is significant, voluntary alcohol consumption prior to her rape, a history of consensual sex with the perpetrator, mental health problems and learning difficulties, and a woman's 'misunderstanding' of the meaning of consent explain police decisions to discontinue a case.

Such powerful stereotypes undeniably function to limit the definition of what counts as 'real rape' in terms of the contexts and relationship within which sex without consent takes place.

In our historical review of women who come into contact with the criminal justice system in Chapter 3, we emphasized the ways in which women have been constructed as both liars and deceivers and as somehow to blame for their own victimization. Such ideas have much resonance when thinking about the contemporary criminal justice responses to violence against women. The operation of a 'culture of disbelief' within policing was an important finding of Kelly et al.'s (2005) study, in which it was reported that key factors preventing complainants from completing the initial investigative process included being disbelieved and fear of the criminal justice system. High levels of under-reporting continue to be a feature for such crimes. An *Overview of Sexual Offending* by the Ministry of Justice (2013a) reported that among female complainants of the most serious sexual offences, 'around a quarter (28 per cent) had not told anyone about the incident; only 15 per cent had told the police and 57 per cent of females had told someone about the incident, but did not tell the police. Alongside the culture of disbelief rests a discourse that implicates women in their own victimization. Research has indicated that police view victims of domestic violence as being responsible for the crimes committed against them. Victims are blamed because they are seen as provoking the violence which could be avoided by being more accommodating to their assailants (Hart, 1993; Walklate, 1989). The belief among some criminal justice professionals that many complainants are false places further unreasonable requirements on complainants to demonstrate that they are 'real' and 'deserving' victims (Kelly et al., 2005; Stanko, 1990). The notion that victims by their provoking behaviour trigger their victimization by male victimizers – and in fact deserve to be victimized – is part of the patriarchal mindset that lies at the root of such crimes.

The 'private' and 'intimate' nature of violence against women also produces considerable conflict and tension for police officers in negotiating their role in the public and private spheres. Though the policy environments within policing have now been transformed, with the police service now readily accepting its role as fundamental in the policing of IPV, we encourage readers to contextualize such change in relation to earlier studies on policing. Such contextualization provides an important backdrop to understanding how criminal justice agencies have historically dealt with and conceived women as victims of violence. It will also better enable us to speculate about the efficacy of new initiatives to combat violence against women. Studies on the organizational culture of policing have made some important observations here about how the police perceive themselves and the work that they do. Characterized by a **'cult of masculinity'**, the damaging effects of such a culture have now been extensively documented (Dick et al., 2013; Loftus, 2010; Silvestri, 2003). We return to these debates in more detail in Chapter 10 but suffice to say here that the culture of policing has been described as one that is hostile to women and continues to have a strong influence in defining and structuring policing and police work.

Understanding how the police perceive themselves and their role goes some way to accounting for their inadequate response to victims of male violence. Silvestri (2003) argues that through encouraging the imagery and mythology of 'street cop' masculinities to pervade organizational processes, the police organization and its officers continue to subscribe to a crime-fighting mission, as opposed to a more crime prevention, peace-keeping model. Police work continues to be imagined in its mythological form where the crime-fighting role is routinely constructed, negotiated and reconstructed. It is within this crime-fighting model that female victims of violence feel the brunt of inadequate and poor policing. While debates about what the police role is and should be continue to plague the police organization and academics, Waddington (1999: 177) best sums up the police reality when he states that the 'occupational self-image of the police as crime-fighters is not just a distortion of what they do, it is virtually a collective delusion'. Domestic violence accounts for nearly a quarter of all recorded violent crime in England and Wales and the police service in the UK receives a domestic assistance call every minute (Westmarland, 2015). There is further concern over a lack of police engagement in relation to the 'cultural' crimes listed above, i.e. HBV, FGM and forced marriage. The poor attitudes of police officers in particular have come under increasing scrutiny and criticism. The criticism centres on the fact that officers:

> [r]outinely dismiss this form of violence as part of the culture of black and minority ethnic communities, stereotyping both victims and abusers. The police often fail to take HBV seriously and, as a result, they regularly fail to protect women from further violence. (Gill et al., 2012: 83)

Following such sustained criticism, there has been considerable reform to the way in which the criminal justice system now responds to violence against women – we review some key developments below.

A 'specialist' and 'coordinated' approach to violence against women

We have already acknowledged the considerable changes in law and policy that have reformulated definitions of violence against women to incorporate a wider range of victims. The Sexual Offences Act 2003 and the Domestic Violence, Crime and Victims Act 2004 developed an extensive range of policy interventions aimed at reducing the incidence of sexual and domestic violence, with an increase in the protection, support and rights of victims. A more 'coordinated' approach to the investigation and prosecution of such crimes, together with the provision of 'specialist' support systems for women victims, can be seen across a range of interventions.

The work of *Domestic Homicide Reviews* (since 2011) has been aimed at developing a more 'holistic' approach to coordinating the work of multiple agencies on better understanding the gendered nature and circumstances in which homicides take place. By providing protection to victims by enabling the police and **magistrates** to put in place protection in the immediate aftermath of a domestic violence incident, the provision of the *Domestic Violence Protection Order* (DVPO) in 2014 further cements a commitment to supporting the victims/survivors of violence. Alongside this, the introduction of the **Domestic Violence Disclosure Scheme (known as Clare's Law)** was rolled out nationally in 2014 (Home Office, 2013b). Under certain circumstances, the scheme allows women to be told if their partner had perpetrated partner violence in a previous relationship. In 2005 the **Crown Prosecution Service** introduced its **Specialist Domestic Violence Court** (SDVC) programme, in which a partnership approach to domestic violence, enabling police, prosecutors, court staff, the probation service and specialist domestic violence advocates to work together in a 'whole system' approach. The introduction of **Independent Domestic Violence Advisers** (IDVAs) in 2005 was also designed to act as primary point of contact for the victim, offering the services of 'trained specialists providing independent advocacy and support to high-risk victims' (HM Government, 2009: 17).

The same vigour in innovation can be found in relation to victims experiencing sexual crimes. Following the establishment of **Sexual Assault Referral Centres** (SARCs) in 1986, we can see a renewed attempt in recent years to improve both the investigation process and the support provided to victims of rape. One of the key aims of setting up these centres was to encourage victims who might be reluctant to go to a police station – either because they were traumatized by their experience or because they lacked confidence and trust in the police – to report their experience to professionals other than the police, such as a health worker. SARCs provide victims with support at this difficult time and an opportunity to leave forensic evidence that can be used at a later date. In 2007, the Crown Prosecution Service introduced specialist rape units and specialist training for all rape prosecutors (see Angiolini, 2015 for a full review). The police service has also identified the considerable benefits of having specialist police rape teams, with specially trained officers and investigators dedicated to rape and serious sexual assault. The way in which the Metropolitan Police Service investigates rape has evolved significantly over the past 15 years. New teams called *Sapphire Units* were developed independently across London, starting in 2001, at local police stations, utilizing officers who only investigated rape and were trained in dealing with both the investigative and complainant care aspects of this complex crime type. The development of **Sexual Offences Investigative Techniques (SOIT) Trained Officers** and a greater emphasis on the role of the forensics in the investigative process have collectively done much to strengthen the expertise required for the investigation of such offences and have served to strengthen the possibilities of building a strong case for prosecution. The appointment of **Independent Sexual Violence Advisers** (ISVAs) has also done much to provide support to complainants of rape and other sexual offences regardless of whether they have reported to the police.

While we applaud these changes, we remain mindful of the inherent problems identified in the policing of such crimes. A series of recent police failures have led to continued anxieties about the ongoing problems of translating policy into practice. In 2009 John Worboys, a London taxi driver, was convicted of 19 offences, having been found guilty of drugging and raping women in his taxi. Though initially arrested in 2007, Worboys was not charged until 2008. In 2009, Kirk Reid was convicted of 27 offences (though he was believed to have committed 80–100 offences) which had remained undetected by the local Sapphire Unit between 2001 and 2008. The investigation that followed both of these cases found significant failures in the investigative process and standards within the Sapphire teams (IPCC, 2010a, 2010b). More recently, in 2013, the IPCC published a report into allegations of unethical rape reporting practices within Southwark Borough's Sapphire Unit. It found evidence that women reporting rape were pressured by police into providing 'retraction' statements, i.e. when a victim states that the reported incident did not happen. The report also found cases of reported rape that were not recorded or investigated. Since then, the Metropolitan Police Service has centralized the Sapphire response from 32 separate boroughs to one centralized Sapphire Command. The Sapphire Intelligence Unit was disbanded in 2013 and analysis of sexual offence was moved to the separate Met Police Intelligence Bureau (Angiolini, 2015).

In our first edition, we reported evidence of both progression and regression in the way in which the criminal justice system responds to violence against women (Cromack, 1995; Hanmer and Saunders, 1990; Mooney, 1993; Morley and Mullender, 1994; Plotnikoff and Woolfson, 1998; Radford and Gill, 2006). In this second edition, we argue that there is much more to be optimistic about – that is, the issue of violence against women is certainly on the agenda, there is evidence of a more comprehensive and inclusive approach to defining violence against women and there is a strong awareness of the need for a specialist and coordinated approach to deal with the variety of crimes within the umbrella term of violence against women. We do, however, temper this optimism with a degree of caution and concur with Stern's position when she states that 'the policies are right but there is still much to be done to turn the policies into reality everywhere' (Stern Review, 2010: 8). We also add our concerns to those most recently reported by Angiolini (2015: 12) on the potential impact of cuts to policing budgets in 'undermining complainant confidence, increasing attrition and ultimately diminishing reporting'.

Global concerns and responses

In connecting the 'local' with the 'global' (see Chapter 4), while the manifestation of violence against women may differ depending on the economic, social and cultural context, a broad base of research now indicates that the phenomenon is universal and contributes enormously to women's subordination worldwide. Recent analysis of figures from the World Health Organization (WHO) with the London School of Hygiene and Tropical Medicine and Medical Research Council (2013), based on existing data from over 80 countries, found that globally 35 per cent of women have experienced either physical and/or sexual intimate partner violence or non-partner sexual violence. Worldwide, almost one-third (30 per cent) of all women who have been in a relationship have experienced physical and/or sexual violence by their intimate partner. However, some national violence studies suggest that this figure stands at 70 per cent and as many as 38 per cent of all murders of women globally are committed by intimate partners. Around 120 million girls worldwide (slightly more than one in 10) have experienced forced intercourse or other forced sexual acts at some point in their lives. More than 133 million girls and women have experienced some form of female genital mutilation (FGM) in the 29 countries in Africa and the Middle East where the harmful practice is most common (cited in UNICEF, 2015).

A further set of global anxieties about violence against women can be found in studies that chart the increased trafficking of women worldwide. Figures from the International Labour Organization (2012) indicate that women and girls represent 55 per cent of the estimated 20.9 million victims of forced labour worldwide and 98 per cent of the estimated 4.5 million forced into sexual exploitation. The issue of sex trafficking more particularly has generated much academic debate over the past decade (Augustin, 2007; Bernstein, 2012; Doezema, 1999, 2005; Gozdziak, 2014; Segrave et al., 2009; Spencer and Broad, 2012; Weitzer, 2007). It is within this sphere that we can identify a surge of interest in locating new sites of gendered exploitation. Research on the 'border' as a site of exploitation, together with its focus on women's multiple identities as victims of trafficking/migrants/asylum seekers and potentially as offenders, is transforming the boundaries of academic debates about women's victimization (McCulloch and Pickering, 2012; Maher et al., 2013; Pickering, 2010; Pickering and Weber, 2006; Weber and Pickering, 2011). As the trafficking of women assumes an ever more significant role in public discourse, we anticipate this as a considerable growth area in criminological research on women's victimization over the coming decade.

Despite a relatively slow start by the international community, significant inroads have been made over the past 20 years in connecting women's experiences of violence across the globe and reframing this violence as a violation of human rights (Cain and Howe, 2008; Cook, 1994; Kallen, 2004; Roth, 1994). Critical of the way in which international human rights law has ignored and marginalized the concerns of women, feminist activists have lobbied hard to place the issue of violence against women on a human rights platform. Enshrined in the Convention on the Elimination of All Forms of Discrimination against Women (CEDAW 1979) and recognized by the international community as a human rights issue at the Vienna World Conference in 1993, the formal expression of this commitment can be found in the 1993 UN Declaration on the Elimination of Violence against Women (DEVAW). Further developments have gone on to strengthen and progress women's voices at an international level and there is now a range of international and regional human rights instruments (see United Nations for a full review). Couched in a language of 'social harm', more recent human rights directives have emphasized gender inequality as both a root cause and solution to women's rights and freedom. The Council of Europe Convention (2011) on preventing and combating violence against women and domestic violence – known as the Istanbul Convention (2011) – neatly encapsulates this position, noting that violence against women is a

> manifestation of historically unequal power relations between women and men, which have led to domination over, and discrimination against, women by men and to the prevention of the full advancement of women. (Council of European Convention, 2011: 1)

In presenting evidence of a global and 'universal' narrative of violence against women, we are conscious of the considerable criticism that such a position

has attracted. The classic work by Mohanty (1986) has done much to challenge and reject the 'ethnocentric universalism' in which white Western
feminists construct themselves as political subjects while representing
migrant and Third World women as racialized, powerless 'others'. At the same
time, we remind readers that in revisiting her work over a decade later in
2003, Mohanty herself goes on to demonstrate an appreciation of the particularly damning and brutalizing impacts of globalization in 'exacerbating
economic, racial and gender inequalities' and calls for a transnational feminism, informed by an analysis of the effects of corporate globalization
restructuring on the 'raced, classed, national and sexual bodies of women'
(Mohanty, 2003: 509).

We acknowledge the significance of such arguments and restate our alle-
giance to the idea of a human rights framework as offering a unifying lens
within which to identify the persistent structural inequalities and discrimination faced by all women – be that at a local or global level. In thinking about
how we might begin to use human rights law to address violence against
women, we concur with Roth (1994), whose work points to a narrow reading
of the broad language of the International Covenant on Civil and Political
Rights (the Covenant) as a key limitation of attempts to address the problem
of violence against women. He argues that while the Covenant does not explicitly establish a state's duty to combat private violence, its broad language is
fully compatible with this duty. For Roth, the powerful and expansive guaran-
tees provided in Article 6 (1) 'Every human being has the inherent right to life';
Article 7 'No one shall be subjected to torture or to cruel, inhuman or degrading treatment' and Article 1 'Everyone has the right to ... security of person',
all have obvious and potential relevance for the fight against violence against
women and could be read as imposing a duty on the state to address both
official and private violence. In what follows, we explore the potential of
Article 7 in conceptualizing domestic violence/abuse through a framework of
torture. We then go on to outline how we might hold the state more accountable
for violence against women.

Reconceptualizing domestic violence as torture

In 1975 the United Nations (UN) General Assembly unanimously approved
the Declaration on the Protection of All Persons from Being Subjected to
Torture and Other Cruel, Inhuman or Degrading Treatment or Punishment.
Article 3 made clear: 'No State may permit or tolerate torture or other cruel,
inhuman or degrading treatment or punishment'. Though the practice of torture remains ever present in contemporary society, it is simultaneously

universally condemned as one of the most heinous forms of violence against humanity. Despite the knowledge we have on the global violence that women face, intimate violence remains on the margins and is still considered different, less severe, and less deserving of national and international condemnation and sanction than officially inflicted violence. In this section we draw heavily on the work of Rhonda Copelon (1994) in making our case. Copelon's (1994: 117) basic starting point is that 'gender-based violence is no less grave than other forms of inhumane and subordinating official violence'. From such a position she ably demonstrates the commonalities that exist between officially defined torture and domestic violence. By focusing on the infliction of severe **pain** and suffering and the intentionality and purpose of that infliction (both elements of Article 1), we also hope to convince readers of the need to associate the acts of domestic violence/abuse and torture more closely.

When discussing the concept of pain we refer to both its physical and psychological components. The infliction of physical pain is common in the practice of torture. Common methods of physical torture and ill treatment reported by Amnesty International and Human Rights Watch include electric shocks, rape and sexual abuse in custody, suspension of the body, beatings, suffocation, mock execution or threat of death, prolonged solitary confinement, and sleep and sensory deprivation. The powerful effects of inflicting such brutal physical pain are obvious and we need not outline them here except to note that the body is weakened and essentially destroyed. A more critical appreciation of the suffering experienced by the victims of torture require us to transgress the traditional concept of physical pain towards an understanding of more insidious forms of torture that do not involve overt physical brutality. While all forms of physical torture are likely to have psychological aspects and consequences, some forms of torture are primarily psychological in nature. Copelon (1994: 124) argues that the destruction of one's sense of self can easily be accomplished through methods that passively as well as actively attack the body, giving examples of:

- threats to kill, mutilate, or torture the person, or family members or friends
- isolation
- arbitrary and unpredictable punishments
- intermittent rewards
- the alternation of active and passive brutality with kindness.

In this way, we can begin to understand torture as a context and process of domination and not simply as a set of brutal acts. It is through understanding the relationship between the abuser and the abused as one founded upon domination and coercion that we can begin to make the connection between the more traditional victims of torture and the victimization that women experience in a domestic setting. Like officially defined torture, domestic violence/

abuse commonly involves some form of escalating, physical and mental brutality. Victims are subjected to verbal insult, sexual denigration and abuse. The
methods used against women in intimate violence resemble many of the common methods of torture, and routinely include rigorous interrogation and
violence. Women also experience intermittent stages of 'care' and 'control', of
kindness and violence (Stark, 2007). A key feature in the enactment of torture
is the eliciting of information through interrogation. Scarry (1985: 38) argues
that the pain of torture is almost always accompanied by the 'Question'.
Consisting of questions, statements, insults and orders, the interrogation is
'internal to the structure of torture, exists there because of its intimate connections to and interactions with physical pain'. While the content of the
interrogation may appear meaningless, its commission is essential to the torturer's self-justification and a tool in the destruction of the victim (Scarry,
1985). In this way the eliciting of information demonstrates the power dynamics between the torturer and the victim, with the torturer maintaining control
and the victim powerless.

Like torture, Copelon (1994) argues that domestic violence is both physical
and verbal. Whether precipitated by rage, jealousy, or a real or feared loss of
control, domestic violence has its own interrogation-type questions, accusations, insults and orders: 'Where were you today?', 'Who were you with?',
'Why is the house dirty?' are all fairly typical forms of interrogation that those
in abusive relationships face. The goal of such interrogation is not to elicit the
truth necessarily, but rather to instil a sense of dread, humiliation and submission in the victim. Copelon (1994: 131) explains that in both contexts, the
victim/survivor seeks to stop or avert the pain, to protect others from harm
and to pacify the aggressor.

We observe striking parallels between Copelon's position and Stark's (2007)
work on 'coercive control' outlined earlier in understanding the complex
dynamics at play in violence against women. We now turn our attention to
outlining how we might make the state more accountable in relation to violence against women.

Making the state accountable for violence against women

Identifying the 'ultimate perpetrator' in relation to violence against women is
a complex task, leading Cain and Howe (2008: 16) to argue that 'it is necessary
to identify the ultimate as well as intermediate and direct perpetrators'. We
remind readers here that since the perpetrators of violence against women are
by definition 'private', they cannot be treated as appropriate subjects of international human rights law unless the state can in some sense be held

responsible – while anyone can commit a common crime, only a state and its agents can commit a human rights violation under international law. Such a dilemma has forced scholars to rethink the concept of **state accountability**. We draw on the work of Roth (1994) to develop our analysis. In pushing the boundaries of state accountability, he argues that the state can be held responsible under international human rights law for both its *inaction* and its *action* (emphasis added). He writes:

> The state's abdication of its duty to protect citizens from crimes of violence amounts to a tacit endorsement of that violence. That complicity provides the requisite governmental dimension to consider the violence as a human rights issue – this is state responsibility by omission rather than commission. (Roth, 1994: 329–30)

In other words, when the state makes little or no effort to stop a certain form of private violence, it is in effect tacitly condoning that violence. In turn, this 'complicity transforms what would otherwise be wholly private conduct into a constructive act of the state' (Roth, 1994: 330). In this way the theory of liability by omission can be used to treat the state's systematic failure to confront domestic violence against women as a human rights issue. Given the changes in Britain outlined above, we are unable to find the British state complicit in violence against women. And, while there may be various nation states that do continue to omit such crimes from its policy and legislative agendas, Britain's position is far from this. On the contrary, as noted earlier in the chapter, Britain has a well-developed raft of policy and law aimed directly at tackling such crime. Herein lies the paradox. Despite this mounting range of policy and law, violence against women in Britain remains rife, rape convictions are at an all-time low and research presented above continues to represent damning evidence of the way in which women are treated by criminal justice agencies. With the potential explanation of governmental complicity now exploded, how else might we hold the state to account for such forms of violence?

Perhaps we should be asking if it is enough that the state outlaws the practice of violence against women or whether it is enough that those responsible for its regulation make the occasional arrest, launch a periodic prosecution, or secure the occasional conviction. Human rights advocates would argue that such efforts are not enough for a state to avoid being held complicit in domestic violence. Roth (1994: 331) asks: When does a state's failure to stop private violence constitute a human rights violation, as opposed to a mere policy failure? Roth (1994) develops his argument about state accountability further when he notes that where a state is doing the bare minimum in combating domestic violence to escape charges of complicity, a discrimination-based theory of liability allows insistence on greater diligence as a matter of international human rights law. The demand can be made that a state's effort to combat domestic violence be at least on a par with its efforts to fight comparable forms of violent crime. In short, when a state moves beyond the stage of obvious complicity, which Britain has, a discrimination-based theory of state responsibility permits an additional argument: a state can be said to condone a particular form of violence because it pays inadequate attention to prevent it in relation to comparable forms of violence. The textual basis for a discrimination-based theory of liability can be found in several provisions of the Covenant. Article 2(1), for example, states that:

> [e]ach State Party to the present Covenant undertakes to respect and to ensure to all individuals within its territory and subject to its jurisdiction that rights recognised in the present Covenant, without distinction of any kind, such as race, colour, sex, language, religion, political or other opinion, national or social origin, property, birth or other status.

Article 26 states that:

> All persons are equal before the law and are entitled without any discrimination to the equal protection of the law. In this respect, the law shall prohibit any dis-crimination and guarantee to all persons equal and effective protection against discrimination on any ground such as race, colour, sex, language, religion, political or other opinion, national or social origin, property, birth or other status.

The basis of these provisions requires that whatever efforts a state makes to combat private violence, it must do so in a non-discriminatory way. Whatever level of resources a state decides to devote to enforcing criminal laws against private acts of violence, it must ensure that crimes against women receive at least as thorough an investigation and as vigorous a prosecution as crimes against men. Taking this line of reasoning to its logical conclusion suggests that if less attention and less rigour is adopted in the regulation of violence against women than other comparable acts of violence, this could constitute not only a violation of the anti-discrimination provision of the Covenant but could also provide evidence of the complicity needed to make out a substantive violation (Roth, 1994). In the case of Britain, applying this theory of discrimination requires us to establish that the inadequate policing and resulting lack of pros-ecution observed is due to a prohibited form of discrimination. As Roth (1994: 336) argues, these cases of non-prosecution reflect a pattern that is attributable to the state rather than to exceptional behaviour of isolated individuals.

It is here that we can perhaps begin to contextualize the position of the British state and its criminal justice system. There have been a number of welcome changes in the regulation of violence against women and substantial inroads have been made to secure greater protection for its victims. At a policy level, at least, there is much to be cheerful about and we certainly cannot hold the state responsible for its inaction towards the victims of male violence. Yet, despite this optimism we restate the continued serious disjuncture that exists between policy and practice. We have provided substantial evidence of the discriminatory way in which the various forms of violence against women are progressed through the criminal justice system. The persistence of negative stereotypes and myths about female victims of violence, together with the alarming levels of '**no-criming**' and 'downgrading' within policing practice, indicate that the policing of the private sphere does not receive the same degree of rigour as those crimes policed in the public sphere. Moreover, research has also shown us that the problems of policing are not those that reside with individual rogue officers or of 'isolated functionaries', as noted by Roth (1994). Rather, gender discrimination is something best described as a systemic condition and the gendered nature of the criminal justice system can be felt at structural, cultural and individual levels.

Concluding thoughts

In this chapter we have sought to make visible the multifaceted nature of male violence against women and have emphasized their connections at a local and global level. We have also outlined a number of significant and positive transformations in the study of women's victimization. An increased awareness of the pervasive nature of violence against women, together with observable changes in policy and law, have contributed much to a transformed landscape. At the same time, we have reported persistent problems in translating policy into practice and have emphasized the inadequate level of redress for victims of male violence. We reiterate Stern's argument that 'the policies are right but there is still much to be done to turn the policies into reality everywhere' (Stern Review, 2010: 8) and we urge those working in the field not to become complacent about the extent to which violence against women is being tackled.

Indeed, we argue that despite an increased awareness, there is a very real possibility that things might get worse. Radford and Tsutsumi (2004) argue that globalization has brought with it *different* and *more* opportunities for increased violence against women. With systems now in place to police the perpetrators of violence and protect its victims, it is all too easy to give up the fight for improved services. We encourage a more critical dialogue between researchers and criminal justice agencies to make sense of the ongoing inadequacy of protection afforded to victims. We argue that the inadequacies of the criminal justice system and its various agents to 'police' violence against women has much to do with the gendered nature of criminal justice organizations, their work and their workers. The criminal justice system and its agents all work within clearly defined 'gender schemes' which set the boundaries of what is considered appropriate and inappropriate behaviour for men and women (Kelly et al., 2005). Given that criminal justice work remains an overwhelmingly male activity, it is invariably men's attitudes about women that count here. More specifically and in relation to the police organization, with a preponderance of men in policing roles, much of the mandate for policing violence against women rests in the hands and minds of men. We discuss the implications of this in greater detail in Chapters 9 and 10 of this book, but suffice to say here that gender remains a crucial division in and defining feature of the criminal justice system.

We find Stark's (2007, 2009) analysis of coercive control, structural gender discrimination and inequality compelling. And, while we are under no illusion that making the state more responsible and accountable for violence against women will end its practice, we think it an important place to start. Violence against women is complex and has its roots in the structural relationships of power, domination and privilege between men and women in society – adopting a human rights approach, then, requires that gender inequality is addressed as a root cause, and that women's rights and freedoms are upheld.

Summary

- The discovery of victims of crime is closely related to an interest in the victimization of women and the propensity to associate men with offender and women with the status of victim. The experiences of female victims are outlined in detail and it is apparent that women are particularly vulnerable to violent victimization at the hands of men in the private sphere.
- With a number of 'new' concerns about violence against women emerging in public discourse, we chart the considerable change in the definitions and categories of violence against women. A greater emphasis on the 'coercive' dimensions and 'social harm' experienced by women has also done much to expand the frame of reference when thinking about women's victimization.
- We consider a broad spectrum of harms and crimes against women in our analysis, including a focus on: intimate partner violence; sexual violence and rape; prostitution; sex trafficking; forced marriage; 'honour'-based violence; and female genital mutilation.
- Female victims of these crimes are under-protected by criminal justice agencies, demonstrated most tellingly by the high attrition rate, or the low number of offences that result in a successful conviction of an offender. We outline the problem of attrition and consider the construction of the 'ideal' victim and its consequences for the policing of such crimes.
- This chapter also develops an argument stating that domestic violence is a fundamental violation of human rights. With violence against women now recognized throughout the globe as a significant social problem, we develop our analysis of 'coercive control' through an appreciation of domestic violence as a form of torture – a clear and obvious human rights violation. In developing our argument, we link the local with the global and consider the role of the state and its responsibility with respect to violence against women.

- While we agree that violence against women is complex and has its roots in the structural relationships of power, domination and privilege between men and women in society, we have argued that adopting human rights requires that gender inequality is addressed as a root cause, and that women's rights and freedoms are upheld.

STUDY QUESTIONS

1. To what extent has criminology acknowledged the female victim?
2. Outline the ways in which the criminal justice system is said to be taking violence against women seriously.
3. Critically discuss the importance of the changing official definitions of violence against women.
4. Critically consider the tensions that exist when thinking about prostitution/sex work in relation to 'agency' and 'victimization'.
5. Consider the problem of attrition with regard to sexual offences and violence against women.
6. Critically debate some of the dilemmas and tensions that police officers may face when policing violence against women.
7. How useful is the 'coercive' dimension to understanding violence against women?
8. Discuss the importance of linking 'local' concerns about violence with more 'global' concerns.
9. How might we make the state more accountable in relation to such crimes?
10. Is there anything to be gained from reconceptualizing violence against women as a human rights issue?

FURTHER READING

There are a number of important official studies/inquiries listed in the chapter – these all provide up-to-date and important sources of knowledge on the prevalence and nature of women's victimization. Of particular note is E. Angiolini (2015) *Report of the Independent Review into the Investigation and Prosecution of Rape in London* (Metropolitan Police).

N. Westmarland (2015) *Violence Against Women: Criminological Perspectives on Men's Violences* (Routledge) provides an excellent insight into various forms of victimization experienced by women; L. Bates (2014) *Everyday Sexism* (Simon & Schuster) also provides a review of contemporary concerns and see K. Hohl and E. Stanko (2015) 'Complaints of rape and the criminal justice system: Fresh evidence on the attrition problem in England and Wales' (*European Journal of Criminology*, 12(3): 324–41) for a good overview of the ongoing problem of attrition. In relation to emerging concerns about HBV, FGM and FM, read the broad range of works by Aisha Gill.

For a global insight, see M. Cain and A. Howe (eds) (2008) *Women, Crime and Social Harm: Towards a Criminology for the Global Age* (Hart Publishing); S. Pickering (2010) *Women, Borders and Violence: Current Issues in Asylum, Forced Migration, and Trafficking* (Springer); and M.T. Segrave, S.J. Pickering and S. Milivojevic (2009) *Sex Trafficking: International Context and Response* (Willan).

In relation to human rights, we recommend that Copelon (1994) and Roth's (1994) contribution in this text be read alongside E. Stark (2007) *Coercive Control: How Men Entrap Women in Personal Life* (Oxford University Press) and E. Stark (2009) 'Rethinking coercive control violence against women' (*Violence Against Women*, 15(12):1509–25).

Notes

1. While some commentators within the field have consciously renounced the term 'victim' in favour of using the term 'survivor' (for its capacity to promote the agency and the coping strategies adopted by women), we use the term 'victim' throughout this book to acknowledge the persistent, pervasive and broad range of victimization experienced.
2. The word 'honour' is enclosed in speech marks throughout this chapter to stress the problems inherent in using this term – i.e. there is no honour involved in the perpetration of such acts.

8

Men as Victims

OVERVIEW

Chapter 8 provides:

- An audit of the patterns of victimization experienced by men.
- An outline of the needs of male victims and the services they receive.
- A critical review of explanations of the causes of male victimization.
- A consideration of the need to think about the links between victim and offender statuses.
- An in-depth account of the victimization of young boys involved in anti-social behaviour.
- An appraisal of the view that male victims should take more responsibility for their victimization by recognizing the risk factors attached to their behaviour.

KEY TERMS

- anti-social behaviour
- criminalization
- fear of crime
- hate crime
- homophobic violence

- interpersonal violence
- Respect Agenda
- responsibilization
- the rights and needs of victims

Introduction

In the previous chapter we outlined the extent and prevalence of the victimization of women by men, describing domestic violence as a form of torture and coercive control. We also demonstrated that while individual men perpetrate such violence across nation states their law enforcement apparatus is often complicit in privileging and sustaining violent masculinities. Finally, the case for adopting a human rights framework was outlined, based on the premise that violent men do not give due respect to the human rights of their victims. This chapter turns to the male victim to account for the gendering of his treatment and experiences at different stages of the criminal justice process. A cursory glance at victimological research shows the higher profile of the female victim in academic and public policy debate, which has occurred largely as a result of the influence of feminism on **victimology** and the victim's movement more generally (Cook and Jones, 2007). Indeed, it is arguable that in some instances victimology is almost synonymous with the female victim (Goodey, 2005; Walklate, 2004). In contrast to mainstream criminology, where the concern is with the male offender, the study of victims has until relatively recently neglected the victimization of males (M. Hall, 2012; Hoyle, 2012).

The reasons why the male victim has been disregarded are complex, although we suggest there are three main reasons. Socially and culturally constructed ideas about masculinities do not entertain the idea that men can be victims is the first and, as Goodey (1997) observed, an enduring perception about masculinity is that 'boys don't cry', thus denying their vulnerability and emotionality. As Hall and Winlow (2015: 59) put it, '"doing masculinity" is a more reliable predictor of failing to register as a victim than it is of committing acts of violence.' Secondly, most male victims are the *victims* of other men, especially with regard to interpersonal violence, and in some ways male on male victimization is normalized. Thirdly, the discovery of male victims of female violence is an issue that has attracted the attention of researchers but is something that is seldom talked about without a degree of ambivalence.

Key debates

In order that we can develop an understanding of men as victims the chapter consists of three main strands, which although overlapping are rehearsed in discrete sections for the purpose of elucidation. The opening and longest section considers the knowledge base relating to the phenomenon of male victimization, focusing in particular on interpersonal violence. In line with the previous chapter it is suggested that this type of offending behaviour illustrates most the gendered nature of victimization and that gender is less obviously relevant for other types of crime, principally property offences. Because this book is about gender and crime the focus is mainly on men, although it is necessary to avoid reifying masculinities above other social divisions because it is intertwined in myriad ways with ethnicity, age, sexuality and social class. The salience of masculinities in relation to the services victims receive is then rehearsed, showing how the criminal justice system in England and Wales has been oriented towards victims' needs despite the word 'rights' being in circulation.

Secondly, there is a brief review of prevailing explanations of male victimization in light of victimological and masculinities research. A key point emerging from this section is that the distinction between victims and offenders is not hard and fast. Therefore, when we consider boys and men there is a clear need to recognize the intricate linkages between complex patterns of exclusion that marginalize men both as victims and offenders, although spelling out the significance of the former at more length.

Thirdly, we utilize human rights discourse to provide an alternative way of conceptualizing the victimization of men. We argue very briefly that some male victims need to be 'responsibilized' (Garland, 2001), the attainment of which can reduce the risk of violent victimization for some men. Another way of deepening our appreciation of the potential application of human rights discourse is by focusing on how the state has on some occasions unfairly and unjustly criminalized – and victimized – the **anti-social behaviour** of boys and young men. This group represents the enduring problem of youth – along with greater criminalization of girls (see Chapter 5) – and our argument is that their exposure to the criminal justice system at a young and tender age renders them vulnerable. We realize that this is a provocative standpoint, though one that is consistent with a human rights agenda and accepted definitions of the crime victim, such as that promulgated by the United Nations (UN):

> Victims means persons who, individually or collectively, have suffered harm, including physical or mental injury, emotional suffering, economic loss, or substantial impairment of their fundamental rights, through acts or omissions that are in violation of criminal laws, including those proscribing abuse of power. (United Nations, 1998, cited in Goodey, 2005: 10)

It is our contention that crime policy since the late 1990s involved the state mobilizing its political power in a way that not only over-criminalized boys but also led to the partial violation of Articles 6, 7 and 14 of the Human Rights Act 1998. More than that, this links with wider developments involving the subordination of concerns about the mental and emotional well-being of young people in general, but especially boys, to the goals of crime reduction and penal populism.

Men as victims of crime – the knowledge base

It is worth reflecting back on the point that official statistics often reflect police priorities and information about victims can be limited, something known as the 'dark figure of crime' (Crowther-Dowey and Fussey, 2013). What is becoming clear is that this 'dark figure' of unreported crime 'probably contains a significant amount of violence inflicted on men by female or gay partners' (Hall and Winlow, 2015: 59). To start coming to terms with male victimization there are various sources of data although the **British Crime Survey** (BCS) (now the Crime Survey of England and Wales (CSEW)) is that which is most widely used. In 2010/11 the Survey found that in that year 22.6 per cent of men were victims of crimes recorded by the BCS compared to 20.5 per cent of women (Parity, 2013: 4). There is a plethora of other more localized studies that have taken seriously the victimization of men; however, studies of this type seldom explicitly assess masculinities.

An important lesson that can be learnt from studies of crime victims is that clearly any person, regardless of their gender, may become a victim of offences against the person, offences against property and offences against public order. Having said this, gender is more conspicuous with regard to certain types of crime than others. Taking offences against property, such as burglary and theft, as an example there is not necessarily a discernible gender pattern and alternative explanatory factors are more significant. There are some snippets of data showing that 18 per cent of young men lose earnings as a result of being burgled compared to 11 per cent of all burglary victims, for example, but they are just that, snippets (Dixon et al., 2006: 30). Victims of burglary consist of both men and women and other demographics, such as socio-economic status, housing type, the lack of capable guardians, are more accurate indicators of the likelihood of victimization (Davies et al., 2007). This is demonstrated in unequivocal terms by the most innovative research examining the extent and prevalence of burglary where repeat or multiple victimization is studied. The British Crime Survey 2011/12 shows that men were victims (3.8 per cent) more than once more frequently than women (2.1 per cent) (Home Office, 2011b). A search of the repeat victimization and burglary literature results in relatively few hits when searching for the words men, women, male and female (Pease, 2015). Naturally the situation is different with regard to domestic violence where 0.2 per cent of men have been victimized on more than one occasion (the figure for women is 0.5 per cent) (Parity, 2013: 4).

If our attention switches to crimes against the person there is an altogether different story. According to the BSC/CSEW data published since the mid-1980s, which examines violent crime – including domestic violence, mugging and other violence by strangers and acquaintances – a situation that is very much gendered has been consistently portrayed (Parity, 2013). Men are more likely to be victimized by an acquaintance or stranger while women face a greater risk of being the victim of domestic abuse. The 2013/14 CSEW showed that 2.3 per cent of males and 1.4 per cent of females were the victim of a violent crime within a 12-month period prior to them being interviewed (Office for National Statistics, 2015a: 18). To look at this issue from a different angle, overall one in 20 people aged 16 or above stated that they were the victim of a personal crime against the individual (e.g. 'theft from person', 'other theft of personal property', 'all violence with and without injury' and 'personal and acquisitive crime') in the previous 12 months. Before the end of the 2000s females were less likely to be a victim, but now there is no statistically significant difference between males and females. Age is important too and 11.4 per cent of men and 11.3 per cent of women aged 16–24 were victims of personal crime. The equivalent figures for men and women aged over 75 are 0.8 per cent and 1.5 per cent respectively. If violence is scrutinized, males aged 16–26 are at more risk of being a victim (6.4 per cent) than females (3.6 per cent) in the same age group (Ministry of Justice, 2014b). If we look at violence overall, young men experience the greatest risk of becoming a victim of violent crime (Brookman and Robinson, 2012; Ray, 2011) so the intersection between gender and age is important. Boys aged 10–15 are more likely to be a victim of personal crime than girls. Boys aged 10–12 are twice as likely to be a victim of violence than their female counterparts (Ministry of Justice, 2014b: 28). Thus, like offending behaviour, the risk of becoming a victim reduces as men age (Hird, 2006: 16).

It is not just age; other characteristics are connected with the gendering of violent victimization, in particular disability and marital status (Ministry of Justice, 2014b).

The aforementioned points are made at a very high level of generality so the category of violent crime needs to be deconstructed carefully. This reveals a situation that is perplexing if factors such as different types of violent crime (e.g. rape, robbery), age and victim–offender relationships, to name but a few, are considered. The nature of the relationship between the victim and offender is very significant, with male victims stating that they were more likely to be the victim of violence in general terms (referring to violence in general) than their female counterparts (ONS, 2015b: 18).

If we look at intimate personal violence ('different forms of physical and non-physical abuse consisting of partner abuse, family abuse, sexual assault and stalking') more closely, the following pattern is discernible.

> Women were more likely than men to have experienced intimate violence since the age of 16, with women twice as likely as men to have reported being a victim of non-sexual partner abuse (the most commonly experienced type of intimate violence) and seven times as likely as men to have reported being a victim of sexual assault. Women were also more likely than men to have experienced intimate violence in the previous 12 months. (Ministry of Justice, 2014b: 10)

In 2013/14 the CSEW showed that over the previous year 8.5 per cent of women and 4.5 per of men reported that they had experienced domestic abuse and sexual assault or stalking where the perpetrator was known to or acquainted with the victim. In real numbers this equates to an estimated 700,000 male victims compared to 1.1 million female victims. The Survey also looks at victims' experiences over time, revealing that 14.7 per cent of males experienced domestic abuse since the age of 16 (ONS, 2015b: 1). The Crown Prosecution Service in England and Wales published a report assessing the *Violence Against Women and Girls* (VAWG) agenda (see Chapter 7). It should be recognized that although men are not a visible element of this strategy, they are victims of the offences it covers (domestic abuse, rape and sexual offences) in 16 per cent of cases, although the data that is available relating specifically to rape is not robust (CPS, 2015).

The difference between the genders is perhaps not as pronounced as students often initially think, which supports Karmen's (2004: 26) observation that '... in some couples the presumed victim offender relationship is reversed: the woman is the aggressor and the man the injured party'. Thus even though 'battered husbands' are, just like women, slapped, kicked, bitten and have objects thrown at them, men are less likely to be injured by their partner and even less likely to suffer frightening threats. Given that domestic abuse consists of the diverse acts just listed, it would seem that the cumulative nature of domestic abuse is reflected by this finding in the sense that men are likely to be less fearful of their violent partners than female victims. For example, domestic abuse refers to 'any incident or pattern of incidents of controlling, coercive, threatening behaviour, violence or abuse between those aged 16 or over who are, or have been, intimate partners or family members regardless of gender or sexuality' (Home Office, 2013d: 29). The fact that women are between three and four times more likely to be victimized on a repeat basis, are more likely to be upset and frightened in their day-to-day lives and are more likely to seek medical help relating to domestic assaults also adds weight to this supposition. This dimension of the offender–victim relationship has been largely 'hidden' until relatively recent times but criminologists have debated whether abusive relationships, especially those involving domestic violence, are either 'gender symmetrical' in the sense that men and women are equally culpable of violence or 'gender asymmetrical', meaning that male and female perpetrators behave differently when they are violent (Dobash and Dobash, 2012; Hester, 2013). We concur with Hester (2013) that in heterosexual relationships domestic abuse is asymmetrical because males are more controlling, coercive and violent than their female counterparts. Furthermore, compared to female victims, male victims endure less severe abuse and are less likely to use services provided by the police, NHS and other statutory and voluntary community sector agencies. Indeed, it has been found that males are less likely than females to be victims of abusive relationships; males are also viewed as suffering a lesser emotional impact from abuse than females (Hickman et al., 2004). Nevertheless, one study found that 10 per cent of young women and 8 per cent of young males who participated in a survey reported that their partner had tried to force them to have sex (Burman and

Cartmel, 2005). However, the onus is mainly placed on female victims where they are often blamed for being abused, as there is a 'widespread acceptance of forced sex and physical violence against women' (Berelowitz et al., 2013). As there is this prevailing tolerance of domestic abuse against women, there is a perception that it is in some way their own fault for being abused. There is no implied lessening of severity of physical or emotional abuse on young male victims, but there is simply a higher likelihood of young females being or becoming victims.

Despite the points made in the above paragraph other researchers, in a ground-breaking study in Scotland, evaluated the 'unmet needs' of those men who are victims of domestic violence (Gadd et al., 2002). The Ministry of Justice (2014b: 31) corroborates some of the key findings of this research, indicating that men were less likely to tell someone about their experiences of abuse, including some-one they knew personally and the authorities. Chapter 7 rehearsed those factors that made women reluctant to report any abuse they might have suffered to the police but men were less likely to do this: 27 per cent compared to 10 per cent. Gadd et al. (2002) conducted interviews with 44 men out of the 90 who reported to the Scottish Crime Survey that they were the victim of domestic violence. The qualitative interviews involved some reinterpretation of their responses in the questionnaire, specifically a tendency to downplay or, as Cook (1997: 91) put it, *deny* to varying degrees what had happened.

Following closer investigation it also seems that male victims are also per-petrators, although this may sometimes be seen as an act of retaliation. This illustrates the importance of the perception of the victim. While there were 'harrowing' accounts of serious violence comparable to those routinely described by women, there are clear gender variances. On the whole, and echoing the research findings cited above, in contrast with women, men are less likely to be victimized on a repeat basis and their injuries are of a less serious nature. Consistent with the latter point men (one out of three) are less likely to recognize their abuse than women (four out of five), but like men in England and Wales, the men in Scotland reported that they are less fearful of potential abuse and the impact of this form of violence is less severe regard-ing their general health and well-being (Gadd et al., 2002). Crucially, the long-term control and intimidation violent men exert over victimized women is not as evident and while men suffer from the equivalent of 'battered woman syndrome', they are less likely to be 'immobilized' by a sense of help-lessness and perception that there is no other option (Wallace, 1998: 151). Men are not, in our view, subjected to the torture and coercive control sketched in our narrative on women as victims. To this, Gadd et al. (2002) add that male victims are financially better off, in full-time employment and less likely to live in rented accommodation, which is in contrast to the predicament of many female victims.

Another type of interpersonal violence where there are gender differences is *sexual violence*, which may or may not include domestic violence. The CSEW include rape, sexual assault and unlawful sexual activity against adults and children, sexual grooming and indecent exposure under this category (ONS, 2015a). Males are less likely to experience *indecent assault* (including buggery) committed by a stranger (27 per cent compared to 37 per cent of females) and 70 per cent of male victims of this type of offence were aged 16 years and under; for females the equivalent figure is about a half. Fewer men than women are raped and in 2002–03, for example, Home Office figures showed that the police recorded 11,441 rapes of females compared to 825 (6.5 per cent) male rapes (Home Office, 2004a: 45). This is an old yet important example of why a historical perspective on gender and crime is invaluable because it registers how changes in legislation create new categories of victim. For male rapes an equivalent figure did not exist before the Criminal Justice and Public Order Act 1994, when male rape was first made a statutory offence, the first case being upheld in 1995. Prior to that, 'the unwanted penetration of the male body was not considered as problematic as the unwanted penetration of the female body' (Graham, 2006: 201). Research co-authored by the HMCSPI and HMIC (2002) reviewing 1741 crime reports of rape taken from 10 police forces provides some pertinent information about victims of male rape. In its study it showed that 7 per cent of victims were male, adding that between 1996 and March 2001 there was an 'enhanced reporting rate' of 192.5 per cent as more men reported their victimization. The rather limited research literature scrutinizing the policing and prosecution of male rape shows that relatively few suspected rapists are actually detected but, interestingly, the percentage of detections is slightly higher for male victims (37 per cent) than it is for female victims (36 per cent) (Home Office, 2004a: 45). The other study referred to above demonstrates that there is also a gender-specific difference if conviction rates are taken into consideration because 37.5 per cent of suspects accused of male rape are convicted compared to 21.8 per cent of suspects accused of female rape (HMCPSI and HMIC, 2002: 36). Angiolini (2015) suggests that all is not well for victims of this offence, which would appear counter-intuitive in light of the previous sentence. Evidence suggests male victims of rape experience feelings of isolation and alienation, in part because their experiences are not encapsulated in the terminology of the VAWG agenda (noted above). These feelings are much more acute for gay men and transgendered people who have to counter heterosexist myths. Angiolini (2015) suggests that male victims encounter obstacles that prevent them from reporting their suffering to the criminal justice system. The influence of stereotypically gendered perceptions, which potentially shape the experiences of male victims of rape, is illustrated starkly in the words of a provider of specialist support services quoted in Angiolini (2015: 56):

All of the PTSD (post-traumatic stress disorder), shame, guilt, excess of com-plexity that are going on, multiply that by a hundred ... You know if you're a man, society has told you from infancy that you have to be certain things. One of them is able to protect yourself, because if you can't protect yourself, you can't protect anyone around you, and your role is protector. So you're not telling people. You make the call, a male police officer turns up. You've just been 'de-maled', that's what your experience is. Everything about your masculinity has been shattered, and a representative of the most alpha masculine part of the world turns up, dressed in a most alpha masculine way, and you're expected to explain to them how you've been made less of a man.

The inability of the police to accommodate their specific needs accounts for the preference of male victims to go to accident and emergency departments and sexual assault clinics to allay their anxieties about health-associated com-plications resulting from their assault. There are Havens (specialist centres providing specialist services for people who have been raped or sexually assaulted) in place for victims of sexual violence and 6 per cent of their visitors are males seeking a medical or psychotherapeutic response. The informal deci-sion at the time of writing by the police to rename their Rape and Sexual Offence Units to Violence Against Women and Girls Units adds to the sense of isolation among male victims (Angiolini, 2015).

An under-researched issue is rape and sexual assault in prisons, and follow-ing research published in the USA that exposed the extent and prevalence of this problem, the Howard League explored the issue of coercive sex in England and Wales. Drawing on data made available by HMIP, it shows that 1 per cent of prisoners – or between 850 and 1650 – reported that they had been sexually abused while inside. Male victims, but especially gay and transgendered pris-oners, were particularly susceptible (Howard League, 2014). This study cites work by Turchik and Edwards (2012) asserting that the perpetuation of myths about male rape (i.e. a 'real' man can defend himself unlike a gay man) are used to explain the low visibility and marginal status of male sexual assault (Howard League, 2014: 3).

O'Donnell (2004) is one of a small number of researchers who has focused on the act of male rape that has been evidenced inside prison, an environment characterized by 'rampant homophobia'. Rather like in the outside world, the perpetrators of male rape are, at least in their own eyes, heterosexual, and their violently aggressive behaviour is seen not as a homosexual act but rather as a way of asserting dominance over a passive victim. The motivations behind the offender's actions and the experiences of the victim are similar to the rape of women carried out by heterosexual men, although in a prison setting rape is one stage in an ongoing process and is a '...form of persistent sexual slavery' resulting in the long-term control of the victim. The victims of this crime are emasculated and labelled as 'girls', 'pansies' and 'fairies' (O'Donnell, 2004: 243).

While rape is a form of sex offending, it is the victim who is subjected to degradation and humiliation and, in contrast to other sex offenders, in particular paedophiles and predatory rapists, the prison rapist is likely to have a high status among other men.

Researchers have also evaluated gendered patterns of victimization in relation to 'intimate violence', which includes partner abuse that is not sexually motivated, family abuse that is not sexually motivated, sexual assault and stalking. It is shown that like female victims of sexual assault the perpetrator is more often than not known to the male victim: 83 per cent of males compared to 89 per cent of females (Jansson, 2007: 56). Thus the dynamics of interpersonal violence are gendered. Taking the issue of victim–offender relationships further, women are more likely to be assaulted by a stranger (63 per cent) than men (51 per cent), indicating that men are more likely to know the offender. For serious sexual assault, more male victims (65 per cent) know the perpetrator than females (40 per cent) either as a friend or acquaintance. A partner or ex-partner is less likely to victimize a man (36 per cent) than a woman (54 per cent) and strangers are more likely to victimize a male (17 per cent) than a female (11 per cent) victim (Jansson, 2007: 60). However, these statistics are rather limited due to the relatively small numbers of male victims.

Another form of sexually motivated victimization is **homophobic violence**, a variant of 'hate crime', which consists of verbal abuse, damage to property as well as threatened and actual physical assaults (Chakraborti and Garland, 2009; Hall, 2013). In the UK there are five recognized and monitored strands of hate crime: race, religion, disability, sexual orientation and transgender. Significantly, gender is not one of these strands but research surrounding this type of victimization does refer to the gender of victims.

Homophobic violence is an expression of intolerant attitudes towards gay and homosexual people or individuals who are perceived to be of this sexual orientation. This crime is the materialization of **heterosexist ideologies** which promulgate heterosexuality as the preferred sexual norm and deny and calumniate any behaviour or identities that are non-heterosexual (Herek and Berill, 1992). Heterosexism is similar to racism and other ideologies that legitimate oppression and it is sustained and reproduced by state institutions as well as in civil society. Thus the heterosexual norm is hegemonic masculinity whereas homosexuality is marginalized and subordinated. Given that such assumptions are entrenched in the social structure, it is not altogether surprising that homosexuals are subject to exclusionary processes in some areas of economic, social and political life, a sense of exclusion that may be exacerbated by a fear of homophobic hate crime.

Dixon et al. (2006: 15) demonstrate that two-thirds of gay men have been the victim of a homophobic crime. Reviewing Metropolitan Police Service figures gathered between January and June 2001, Stanko (2002: 34) shows that for every female victim of this type of crime there were seven male victims. Of the incidents reported to police three out of five received no physical injuries and in two-thirds of cases the victim had no prior relationship with the perpetrator. Over half of the offences (53 per cent) occurred in the vicinity of or in the home of the victim, with 17 per cent being reported as occurring on the street. Another study carried out in Edinburgh showed that 50 per cent of gay men had experienced harassment, with one in four men becoming the victim of violent crime (four times the national average for heterosexual men) (Morrison and Mackay, 2000, cited in Stanko, 2002: 34). Stonewall (2005, cited in Dixon et al., 2006: 15) shows that young gay men under 18 are especially vulnerable, with 48 per cent having experienced violence, 61 per cent reported being harassed and 90 per cent said they had experienced verbal abuse because of their sexuality.[1]

The Leicester Hate Crime Project (Chakraborti et al., 2014) shows that men are more likely than women to be verbally abused, harassed on a regular basis and experience violent crime (Chakraborti et al., 2014: 18). Regarding victim–offender relationships, the victim knew the perpetrator in one-third of cases (ibid.: 54). An innovative feature of this study is its attempt to broaden existing definitions of hate crime by including victims who are 'peripheral' or 'invisible', hence the inclusion of 'gendered hostility' – or prejudice based on the perception that a victim does not conform to stereotypical gender roles such as traditional notions of masculinity. The crimes experienced by these victims ranged from verbal insults, online abuse through to sexual assault (University of Leicester, 2014).

What about other violent crimes, such as homicide? Below we show that this is a crime that is overwhelmingly committed by men but some official statistics do problematize the 'masculine excess of' crime and 'anti-social behaviour' (Oakley and Cockburn, 2013). We say more about the latter later, but what is immediately evident from the statistical material relating to homicide that has been published since the mid-2000s is the gendered nature of this offence has not changed. Men are more likely to be killed. When they are killed their demise is more likely to be caused by a friend or acquaintance in contrast with women, where just over half of victims are murdered by a current or ex-partner (Ministry of Justice, 2014b: 10). Understanding homicide is difficult because victims are quite clearly unable to give an account of events but there has been some pioneering research, providing an insight into those factors leading to a fatal incident. Because most victims are located and the cause of death identified through forensic science, the evidence base tends to be reliable – probably more than any other form of crime victimization (Hall and McClean, 2009). Drawing on an analysis of data gathered between January 1981 and December 2000 looking at 13,140 victims of homicide in Britain, Dorling (2005: 27) states that:

- ...the rate [of murder] for men, at 17 per million per year is roughly twice that for women (at nine per million per year).
- The single age group with the highest murder rate are boys under the age of one (40 per million per year).
- A quarter of all murders are of men aged between 17 and 32.
- A man's chance of being murdered doubles between the age of 10 and 14, doubles again between 14 and 15, 15 and 16, 16 and 19 and then does not halve again until age 46 and again by age 71 to be roughly the same then as it stood at age 15.

The above quotation shows indubitably that the gender of homicide victims is relevant and in the region of seven out of 10 known victims are male (Ministry of Justice, 2014b). Most victims know their killer and circumstances resulting in a fatality are, unsurprisingly, often emotionally charged (Innes, 2003). According to figures covering 1995–2000, on most occasions the victims of homicide are men (68 per cent) (Coleman and Reed, 2007: 7; Francis et al., 2004: 9). This figure is remarkably consistent and in 2012/13, for instance, 70 per cent or 380 of the 551 homicide victims were men (Ministry of Justice, 2014b: 32).

In 2012, 13.5 per cent of both females and males were shooting victims (Ministry of Justice, 2014b). There is an association between shootings carried out by BME males, especially young black men: between 1995 and 1999 in 32 per cent of incidents where either the suspect or victim was black a firearm was used. In cases of so-called black-on-black male crime a firearm was evident on 27 per cent of occasions (Brookman and Maguire, 2003: 34). This is important because of the perceived inter-relationship between race and masculinity in relation to gangs. For instance, Williams' (2014) research in Manchester, UK, found that the Manchester Police gang data base registered 89 per cent of people were from a black, Asian and minority background. In his view this is much to do with a 'racialized construct of the "gang"'. Joseph and Gunter (2011) have called for further research into non-stereotypical representations of youth cultures and the identities of young people that explores their day-to-day lives in more depth without over-stating the presence of 'gangs' and 'violence'. We would add that such racialized stereotypes detract from the victimization of young black males.

Brookman and Maguire (2003) cite evidence showing that victims of homicide share other factors in common. As well as being predominantly male they tend to occupy a relatively lowly socio-economic status, with 40 per cent of victims being unemployed and of the remainder a significant proportion are employed in unskilled manual jobs. Indeed, Dorling (2005) offers a compelling account that exposes the close mapping of murder rates and structurally generated inequalities. This demonstrates that male victims are similar to male offenders, reinforcing a point made throughout this chapter about the inextricable links between men and their identities as victims and victimizers.

Among the victims of infant homicide, a higher number of boys are victimized and between 1995 and 1999 102 boys were murdered compared to 70 girls (Brookman and Maguire, 2003: 17–18). There are other lifestyle and situational factors connected with an increased risk of victimization, particularly alcohol consumption, which is an issue for 50 per cent of victims, including not only those murdered in public houses but also in or in close proximity to their homes (Brookman and Maguire, 2003).

In addition to actually becoming a victim of crime in concrete terms, **fear of crime**, which is essentially being worried about becoming a victim, is also gendered. Research into the fear of crime indicates that even accounting for macho attitudes men are less fearful of victimization (see Hale, 1996), although on the basis of using an innovative methodological device, known as the 'lie scale', Sutton and Farrall (2004: 221) surmise quite persuasively that because of a 'macho concealment of fear' men are actually more afraid than women. This scale is able to sift out the effect of men giving socially desirable responses – answers that conform with prevailing forms of 'hegemonic masculinity' – when they are questioned about their fearfulness. They observe that there are considerable variations between crime types and that men are able to justify to themselves a fear of assault (Sutton and Farrall, 2004: 220). Given such attitudes, we can anticipate that the unwillingness of men to become victims may push them into offending. This theme is followed up after statutory response to victims has been discussed.

The criminal justice response to male victims

Once a victim of crime has been recognized or acknowledged what does society do in response to this experience and their particular needs? Unlike the offender who is drawn into the criminal justice system and who enjoys various rights to safeguard them from any abuses of power by statutory agencies like the police and the courts, victims have no rights and the kind of response they receive is something of a lottery (Ashworth and Redmayne, 2010). Unfortunately, from time to time victims of crime may be victimized again by the criminal justice system. The police may disbelieve a victim or a victim may have their character assassinated in the courtroom. This is known as 'secondary victimization' (Hoyle, 2012). There have been various criticisms directed at this tendency, resulting in fundamental reforms and gradually the enhanced status of crime victims.

Since the early 1990s successive British governments have introduced so-called Victims' Charters in 1990 and 1996 (Home Office, 2001), followed by the Code of Practice for Crime Victims (the Victims' Code), coming into effect in 2006 with the passing into law of the Domestic Violence, Crime and Victims Act

2004. In 2013 the Ministry of Justice (2013c) published a consultative document looking to improve this Code. As a result of these developments, victims may not be centre stage but they are now entitled to basic support in the form of information and in some instances this may be backed up with services.

The aforementioned changes have been welcomed by many organizations campaigning on behalf of victims as well as by victims. However, it is quite clear that the delivery of services and support to victims is uneven and lacking equity. This is partly explicable by the fact that the victim does not have formal rights and therefore has limited scope for questioning the treatment they may receive.

There is more to it than that, though, as a distinction is frequently drawn between two types of victim: on the one hand, there is the 'deserving' victim; and on the other hand, a victim who is designated 'undeserving' (Mawby and Walklate, 1994). This differentiation of victims is based on the personal characteristics of the victim and any putative relationship this may have to their victimization. Early victimologists (Von Hentig, 1948) adopted the concept '**victim precipitation**' to explain how some victims brought about their own victimization. If any evidence of this was found then the victim would be deemed 'undeserving'. Another example is the treatment received by victims of rape in the courtroom. A woman who was a sex worker with a drug misuse problem is much more likely to be cast as an 'undeserving' victim, in contrast to another victim who is an educated professional woman, who is well spoken and gives off the impression of coming from an affluent background. The latter is more likely to be characterized as 'respectable' and subsequently a 'deserving' victim (Zedner, 2002) or the 'ideal victim' (Christie, 2015).

Let us now consider the relevance of the above points for understanding male victimization. While men are more likely to consider that the rights of the accused are respected by criminal justice authorities, they are less confident in the criminal justice system in general than women and, most crucially, male victims are less satisfied with the effectiveness of the police response than their female counterparts (Allen et al., 2006).

Angiolini (2015), like the HMCSPI and HMIC (2002) study, found that the police were struggling to come to terms with the investigation of male rape, with regard to a relatively new group of crime victims, although the constabularies involved in the study had all made a concerted effort to encourage male victims to come forward and report their experiences. A number of possible reasons were given for the reluctance of male victims to report their victimization to the police. Some did not know that what they had experienced was a criminal offence whereas some victims who did know this were reluctant to tell the police because of a fear of being disbelieved or anxiety about their own sexuality and/or the views of a third party about their sexuality.

Female victims of rape express similar worries although male victims seem to be much more worried about how their sexuality is perceived, reflecting cultural attitudes about rape and male sexuality (Graham, 2006; Turchik and Edwards, 2012). There is notable under-reporting of **homophobic violence** due to a lack of trust and confidence in the police and a perception that the police may end up charging the complainant with a 'gay' offence. There are also anxieties about retribution and possible outing, as well as an acceptance of violent victimization as normal (Dixon et al., 2006: 15).

George and Yarwood (2004: 9) show that male victims of **domestic violence** are not always taken seriously by the police, who may be sceptical about the veracity of the reported incident. It is not surprising, therefore, that they remark that 'current policies thus generally do not appear to deal at all with the large extent of female violence or abuse against male partners' (George and Yarwood, 2004). Such a finding is not out of kilter with the kind of attitudes female victims experienced when they contacted the police and it would appear that the police could take heed from the lessons they learnt. What is more, on some occasions the male victim was treated by officers as if they were the perpetrators, resulting in the police threatening to arrest them for breach of the peace. Men reporting abuse or violence experience prejudicial and discriminatory treatment not just from the police, but from the courts and other agencies as well. This is apparent from the police response to emergency calls and the finding that 35 per cent of respondents said that the police did not take much notice of the information they received (George and Yarwood, 2004: 12). Due to this, such victims were reluctant to report their experiences and this reluctance influenced wider reporting to friends or family due to a fear of being mocked, embarrassed and disbelieved (Karmen, 2004: 247). An obvious consequence of this is gross under-reporting of this type of victimization. Gadd et al. (2002) also argue that the response to male victims of domestic violence needs to pay attention to the difficulty of distinguishing victims and perpetrators. Above all, though, recognition of the fact that men have different needs from women and that different types of service need to be provided is imperative. Having said that, the lack of hostels and other voluntary sector provision for men is a notable gap in service provision.

Explaining patterns of male victimization: Masculinities and the fluidity of victim–offender statuses

Victimology is renowned for some of its more controversial theories about the factors and processes leading to victimization. Mendelsohn (1956) is among the founders of this field of study and his typology of victims claims that victims of crime to some degree are responsible for what happens to them and in actual fact provoke their own victimization. Research published by the Institute for Public Policy Research makes this point about the 'huge numbers' of young males who are victims of violent crime, stating that:

> ...some of these victims may not have been entirely blameless – they may well have unreasonably provoked the offender. ... In England and Wales together these figures suggest that nearly 450,000 young men were attacked by a stranger in 2004–5 (GAD, 2005). Lifestyle undoubtedly plays a part here: people who visit a pub at least three times a week are more than twice as likely to be victims of violent crime as those who never go. (Nicholas et al., 2005, cited in Dixon et al., 2006: 16)

Clearly, this problematically reduces the responsibility of the offender and apportions more blame to the victim yet it requires us to take seriously the fact that relationships do exist between the victim and their assailant and that associations arise to varying degrees on the basis of mutual consent.

There is another important point to this section. It is almost a truism, although one that is not always acknowledged in all accounts of victimization, that many victims are also offenders and that this is related to masculine identities. The linkage of these two statuses is explored by Winlow and Hall (2006), who describe a state of affairs in the 'post-industrial pleasure dome' where men need to demonstrate a capacity for violence as well as recognizing the perennial threat of victimization to their 'social status and psychic security'. Interestingly, in this work, the men involved do not exclusively belong to underclass populations and many are employed, albeit under economically insecure conditions. Men engage in an internal dialogue where they are characterized simultaneously as potential victims as well as 'victors'. Indeed, victimization is perversely sometimes perceived as part of an initiation ritual leading a person into manhood. Being beaten up, for instance, is just part of 'growing up' and actually toughens up some individuals. Victimhood is never far away and men need to show that they can take violence but in doing so this must avoid 'excessive damage or humiliation' to their social and psychological status (Winlow and Hall, 2006: 158–9). In a habitus where violence is accepted as the norm and a near inevitability, men must accept their predicament with stoicism and 'fortitude'. Consequently, they position themselves in order that they can avoid humiliation, a pose maintained by an emphasis on physicality, survival, honour and respect. Violence is therefore used defensively to control a status that is dependent on the vilification of victimization. There is a reluctance to report violence, especially if the physical condition of a victim shows that they came off worse. The hazard of violent victimization is just an aspect of the fun and entertainment sought in the liminal spaces belonging to a burgeoning night-time economy. Overall, when the different interpretative strands are synthesized we are left with an impression of victims with 'stoical, fatalistic and reactionary attitudes to violence [and] a deeply entrenched and highly productive form of "survivalism" that infuses the localised culture and the habitus of its male members' (Winlow and Hall, 2006: 161).

Reilly et al. (2004) describe the relationship between victims and offenders, which is especially glaring in situations of serious armed conflict, such as the situation in Northern Ireland where it was difficult to distinguish and separate the involvement of young men as victims and offenders. In referring to the inevitability and ubiquity of violence and the fluidity of offender–victim status, Reilly et al. (2004: 474) express this unambiguously:

> All discussions generated consensus that in Northern Ireland, and more generally, violence is a major factor in the lives of young men. One discussion generated a list of groups of people they associated with violence, including paramilitaries, skinheads, bullies, Hoods (local gang members), Combat 18, the Klu Klux Klan, and the police. Violence was mentioned in relation to a lot of contexts such as school, clubs and bars, the street, the home, drugs and alcohol, domestic violence, sectarian violence, kneecappings, shootings, and riots. In all discussions there was complete acceptance that whether as victim or perpetrator, violence was an issue that all young men must negotiate.

Both of the accounts reviewed above are interesting inasmuch as they are both tainted with a fatalistic acceptance of the threat and actual reality of violent victimization.

Male victims and their human rights: A critical framework

The section before the last one shows that there is a commitment on the part of criminal justice agencies to respond to **the rights and needs of victims** of crime and that this orientation is based on an assumption that the rights of victims are partly met by adopting more punitive and exclusionary practices towards the offender (Spalek, 2006). We have already acknowledged an inherent problem with this type of approach, specifically the fluidity of victim and offender identities, especially among men and boys. We argue that this dilemma is clearly exposed when the policy response to the victims is considered with reference to the:

1. responsibilization of victims;
2. the anti-social behaviour of predominantly excluded youthful masculinities is considered.

'Responsibilizing' male victims

The point we wish to make here follows up our observations in the chapter on male offenders which argued that the behaviour of some men inhibits the human rights of others. Here we suggest that men who engage in behaviour that runs a high risk of victimization, in particular alcohol misuse, need to be challenged. The reasoning behind this claim is that men who offend when drinking are also more likely to be victimized at the same or other times. In other words, certain lifestyle choices are intimately related to victimization, especially regular visits to pubs. Avoidance of risky situations or changing certain elements of personal lifestyle can limit those situations where human rights are compromised. More importantly, refraining from heavy drinking will reduce the costs of the response to this type of behaviour, freeing up more resources for responding to the human rights and needs of a wider range of crime victims. Clearly there are powerful vested interests and a modicum of 'hypocrisy', especially in the night-time economy, that would need convincing, but this may be a fruitful way of reducing some gendered forms of victimization that impact most on men (Hobbs et al., 2005).

Anti-social behaviour (ASB) and masculinities

Our argument in this section chimes with the work of Haines and Case (2015; see also Case and Haines, 2015), who suggest that juvenile justice policy includes an eclectic mix of welfare-oriented and justice-based policies and interventions, yet there is a marked tendency to treat juveniles as offenders rather than children. It was Senior (2005) who remarked that the government conflated essentially the sub-criminal conduct constituting anti-social behaviour (ASB) with the global threat of terrorism and serious and organized crime. In line with a **left realist** approach (Matthews, 2014), we do not wish to minimize or trivialize the degrees of anxiety and suffering ASB can cause for communities, rather that the disproportionately 'punitive' ethos underpinning crime policy in this area (Muncie, 2008) treads perilously close to disregarding the rights of children, in particular boys, who are responsible for most incidents of ASB. This admittedly controversial argument is based on the premise that the legislative and policy framework in place for responding to ASB can result in powerful state actors and agencies victimizing vulnerable masculinities.

Below there is a brief history of the origins of ASB and its main characteristics, followed by a contextualization of this phenomenon in New Labour's youth and criminal justice policy (1997–2007). The principal strategies implemented to tackle ASB are then sketched, including anti-social behaviour orders (ASBOs) and dispersal orders, as well as the more recent Anti-Social Behaviour, Crime and Policing Act 2014, which was introduced by the Coalition government (2010–14). This is followed by an evaluation of the antipathetic nature of these policies towards the human rights of the insecure and precarious masculinities of the young.

The origins and definitions of ASB

ASB is not exclusively about young boys in particular or youth in general but under New Labour the connection was axiomatic. ASB includes a range of general issues such as: criminal and sub-criminal behaviour; disorder and incivilities; **community safety**/public protection, fear of crime, and quality of life issues, as well as, more specifically, drinking, vandalism, noise (i.e. nuisance neighbours and 'neighbours/families from hell'), threatening behaviour, joy-riding, violence, racial harassment, dropping litter and verbal abuse. These problems are not new and have been around in one form or another in all societies, although the frames used to think about and respond to them are contextually specific (Pearson, 1983, 2009). In the nineteenth century ASB was more likely to be associated with fears about social revolution whereas in the early twenty-first century there is an underlying concern with the perceived moral and behavioural deficiencies of the young (Waiton, 2001). In 2000 the Home Office funded the British Crime Survey which identified drug dealing/misuse, litter, teenagers hanging around (rude or abusive behaviour) and disputes between neighbours (especially on low-income housing estates). Even the aforementioned behaviours refer to many different activities. For example, ASB related to drinking may occur in subways and public parks in the daytime, but outside pubs and clubs in the context of the night-time economy. In short ASB refers to a diversity of behaviours.

In the 1990s, the term ASB was used to focus on behaviour in relation to housing, but this definition was broadened to encompass a variety of civil disobediences and criminal activities. ASBOs, for example, were used as a measure to tackle prostitution, racial abuse, verbal abuse, criminal damage and vandalism, graffiti, noise nuisance, threatening behaviour in groups, begging, kerb crawling, throwing missiles, assault and vehicle crime (see www.renewal.net). Whitehead et al. (2003), in attempting to produce a universal definition of ASB, said that it must be defined with reference to harm caused to others and by types of behaviour and activity (from those that directly harm people, to the damage of property, to things that are just a nuisance). They also highlighted the diversity of definitions in use: 'Most definitions of ASB involve some overlap with definitions of crime. Some indeed include all crimes' (Whitehead et al., 2003: v). They therefore conclude that 'Given the difficulties of definition ... it is hardly surprising that measurement of the extent of ASB presents considerable difficulties' (Whitehead et al., 2003: v).

Concern about ASB and young people is inextricably linked to the policy agenda of the Conservative government in office in the mid-1990s, mainly the response to the Jamie Bulger case. In 1993 two young boys abducted Jamie Bulger, a toddler, in a shopping centre in Bootle, Merseyside, and later on they murdered him beside some railway tracks. The crime itself was particularly brutal and horrific, made even more disturbing by CCTV footage showing Jamie with his hand being held by one of his abductors as he was walked away from a crowded shopping mall. This murder led to an overhaul of public policy regarding young people who, according to government officials, were acting with impunity because of a 'soft' and lenient criminal justice system. The government's view was that a concern with the welfare of children had created an excuse culture where children were not encouraged to assume personal responsibility for their actions (Audit Commission, 1996, 2004; Fionda, 2005).

On being elected in May 1997 New Labour signalled the potential for a more thoughtful approach to young people, especially with its assurance to tackle the exclusionary outcomes of previous government policies via joined-up and evidence-based policies, which were, according to the oft-quoted mantra popularized by then Prime Minister Tony Blair, *tough on crime, tough on the causes of crime*. More specifically, the Blair regime placed the onus on preventing offending by targeting young people and their families. For example, Hughes and Muncie (2002: 10) cite the government as stating in 1999 that 'if a child has begun to offend they are entitled to the earliest possible intervention to address that offending behaviour and eliminate its causes'. This pledge was welcomed by many who prioritized the welfare and human rights of young people but a preoccupation with ASB started to permeate discourses about crime and disorder so the two become barely distinguishable from each other (Squires, 2009; Squires and Stephen, 2005). Indeed, ASB featured in the Crime and Disorder Act 1998, where it is defined in terms of people 'acting in a manner that caused or was likely to cause harassment, alarm or distress to one or more persons not of the same household as (the defendant)' (Home Office, 1998). At a later date the Anti-Social Behaviour Act 2003 broadened the definition to include any behaviour that 'is capable of causing nuisance or annoyance to any person'. Consequently, ASB is very much about the reaction or possible reaction to people based on subjective criteria and giving scope for the boisterous, noisy, irritating behaviour of young people to be labelled as distressing, alarming and annoying. Moreover, it can lead to the '"quasi-criminalization" of the normal behaviour of children [and youth]' (Fionda, 2005: 243).

ASB, youth and crime policy under New Labour: Enforcement strategies to tackle ASB

Early responses to ASB are rooted in the **Respect Agenda**, introduced in 2006 by Tony Blair, which draws on the vague definitions of ASB rehearsed above and employs civil law measures, including ASBOs, parenting contracts and orders and dispersal orders. Although the Agenda was quite short-lived, and replaced and driven forward by the activities of the Department for Children, Schools and Families (2007–10), the thinking underpinning it and some of the measures it introduced reconfigured certain aspects of youth policy (Millie, 2009).

ASBOs

ASBOs were first introduced to protect communities from ASB and included conditions stopping a person behaving in certain ways and from entering particular geographical areas for at least two years. Early research showed the dominance of a housing management perspective in the response to ASB (i.e. Housing Act 1996 injunctions, etc.). Burney (2002) points out, however, that young people and their rowdy and unruly behaviour were treated as a priority by key agencies on the ground, largely in response to calls from members of the general public. For example, the UK government published a White Paper, *Building Communities, Beating Crime* (Home Office, 2004b), which called for crime reduction partnerships to respond more effectively to anti-social behaviour (Squires and Stephen, 2005). In addition, the *National Policing Plan 2003–2006* directed chief officers and local authorities to include in their local plans a strategy to address youth nuisance and anti-social behaviour (Home Office, 2005a: 9).

As a result of the Bulger case, which abolished the presumption of *doli incapax*, the ASBO could be enforced against any person aged 10 years or more. As a civil order, a breach of its conditions was made an indictable offence, meaning that a person could receive a custodial sentence of up to five years. A potential penalty for a juvenile (i.e. over 15 years of age or a persistent offender aged 12–14) breaching the conditions of an ASBO was a two-year detention and training order, a sentence including a year spent in custody with the remainder of time being a community-based punishment managed by a **Youth Offending Team**. Younger children between the age of 10 and 11 could be given a community penalty. A fundamental problem at the heart of the ASBO was its nebulousness in the sense that the distinction between civil and criminal law is fuzzy. It criminalized non-criminal behaviour and Smith (2007) shows that on 10 September 2003 over half of 66,107 recorded incidents of ASB were already defined as criminal. Furthermore, the ASBO was sometimes used to tackle criminal activity when substantial evidence was not available to demonstrate criminal responsibility. This happened because as a civil order the standard of proof ('balance of probabilities') is lower than it would be for criminal cases ('beyond reasonable doubt'). Effectively, Article 6 of the Human Rights Act 1998 is not observed because the right to a fair trial is foregone. An overarching problem is that ASBOs can lead to criminal charges through the 'back door' (Burney, 2005) without any reference to the principles of '**due process**' (Packer, 1968). Breaches can lead to criminalization and, with specific reference to young people, in the first four months of 2005 some 200 receptions into young offender institutions were of people breaching their ASBOs (Smith, 2007).

The enforcement of ASBOs is dependent on increased levels of surveillance to ensure banned youths are not doing the things they are prohibited from doing. This is ensured by publicizing specific details – including photographs – about the reasons why an order was meted out and the restrictions imposed on the young person. This is essentially a form of 'naming and shaming', arguably out of proportion with the seriousness of the behaviour in question. The net widening of mechanisms in social control was further epitomized by the creation of 101 non-emergency call centres, set up to provide information and advice to deal with ASB and community safety matters (Home Office, 2006a, 2006b). This surveillance based in communities consisted of preventive and exclusionary practices and conflicting concerns with care, control and enforcement, although it appeared that enforcement was prioritized above care and welfare, evidenced by the following Home Office (2006a: 11) statement:

> The ASBO legislation does not require an assessment of the needs of a child before an order is made. Where an assessment is considered appropriate, this should be carried out, but should not delay the ASBO process. ASBOs issued to young people can be reviewed annually to assess how they are working, whether the prohibition in ASBO needs to be reviewed or whether there is a case for varying or discharging it.

Again, there is the targeting of actual and potential behaviour without sufficient reference to the needs of and mitigating circumstances of 'offenders'.

An outcome of this punitive atmosphere was a heightened sense of fear and anxiety, especially in those social spaces where young people gather, and there was the social construction of a dangerousness and representations of a criminal 'Other' (Reiner, 2007; Young, 2007). A tool that has been implemented to prevent people from socializing in public places is the 'dispersal order', including the power to take children home, which can be used alongside fixed penalty notices, ASBOs and anti-social behaviour contracts.

Dispersal orders

The dispersal order was used by police to disperse groups of two or more people if they had reason to 'believe their presence or behaviour has resulted, or is likely to result, in a member of the public being harassed, intimidated, alarmed or distressed' (Home Office, 2010: 18). Significantly, it was only necessary for a police officer to believe that the possibility of the above existed, hence the police engaged in prediction based on crude profiles assessing the risk of offending rather than guilt proven beyond reasonable doubt. The police, including Police Community Support Officers (PCSOs), received additional powers for dealing with children under 16 who were out on the streets unaccompanied by an adult after 2100 hours and they could take a child home, using reasonable force if necessary (Home Office, 2007a, 2007b). This intervention was justified, by appealing to welfarist principles, as a form of child protection, although we suggest that an outcome was the penalization of normal behaviour among children. Just 'hanging out' and 'chilling' was treated as suspicious, abnormal and ultimately anti-social. Most crucially, though, the safeguards protecting people on the street from abuses of power is limited and the authorities and members of the public more or less had a licence to determine what they regard to be troublesome. Once again, the rhetoric surrounding dispersal orders was premised on caring for young people yet in reality there was room for exclusion and social control to the extent that the cultural rights of children and their right to associate in particular places was outlawed as part of an attempt to 'sanitise public space' (Burney, 2005, 2009) and reclaim and/or re-impose the respectable values of civil society. The parents of anti-social children were also made more responsible for the behaviour of their protégés through parenting contracts and parenting orders.

Thus, the Respect Agenda and the ASB framework were all about changing how people behave in line with acceptable modes of conduct defined along the lines of respectability. This was undertaken by appealing to the rights of all, but in actual fact already marginalized and vulnerable groups were further victimized, including in this instance young boys. Despite government rhetoric *to be tough on crime and tough on the causes of crime*, the Respect Agenda resulted in the criminalization of incivilities and the twin objectives of caring for and controlling young people produced contradictions, not least a willingness to divorce an understanding of social problems from a material social context.

In October 2014 with the passing into law of the Anti-Social Behaviour, Crime and Policing Act 2014, police, councils and landlords – among others – were given new powers and measures to deal with ASB and to make sure victims and communities felt safer. Victims are placed at the heart of the process by making it possible for them to trigger action (the 'Community Trigger') and the 'Community Remedy' gives victims more say in how low-level crime and ASB should be dealt with in the form of out-of-court punishment. The new powers are more flexible with fewer bureaucratic structures blocking their application, for example, the Criminal Behaviour Order (CBO) and Public Spaces Protection Order (PSPO). The CBO can be issued by the courts after a person has been convicted for a criminal offence, and who is persistently anti-social, to ban them from certain places and engaging in particular activities. The PSPO imposes conditions on the use of an area to tackle particular behavioural orders. The dispersal order (outlined above) is augmented by the 'police dispersal power', which allows the police to disperse people from a specific place for a specified time, up to 48 hours (Home Office, 2014c). At the time of writing no systematic evaluation of the Act was available. On the one hand, there is no reason to believe there will be any deviation from the general pattern outlined above and regulation and control of the spaces and activities that occupy boys remain the primary objective. On the other hand, the Act does call for informal interventions for young people, where possible, and it is cognizant of human rights principles.

Compromising the human rights of children: Victimizing boys

At the centre of the policy response to ASB is a degree of compulsion to bring about change in people's behaviour. With reference to the Human Rights Act 1998 and the Convention on the Rights of the Child 1989 the emphasis on the ASB of male youth does not give sufficient attention to their cultural rights with regard to freedom of thought, association and assembly. As Waiton (2001) shows, ASB is 'adult-centric' in the sense that the ASB of children is defined in opposition to the norms of adulthood. Due respect is not always given to the interests of children, who are not only discriminated against on the grounds of their age and gender, but also on the basis of the social and behavioural attributes of their parents. In particular, the anti-social behaviour order (ASBO) (described above) as a civil response could be used against any person aged 10 years or over who behaves anti-socially. As Hopkins Burke and Morrill (2004) show, ASBOs concern civil matters where 'behaviour need only be proved on the balance of probabilities' rather 'than beyond reasonable doubt', as is in criminal cases. Crucially, an ASBO can be imposed against people who have not done anything criminal, but it is a criminal offence to breach an ASBO, possibly leading to a five-year prison sentence. There are five themes that need to be considered.

1. Definitions of ASB are ambiguous and many discussions of this phenomenon concern the acceptability of behaviour rather than behaviour that is criminal. Defining acceptable behaviour is a subjective exercise and actions that are acceptable for

one person may not be acceptable for another person. For example, there are certain types of behaviour, which are acceptable to young people (e.g. 'hanging around') which are not acceptable to older people. Acceptability not only concerns behaviour but factors such as dress codes. The clothes young people wear (i.e. hooded tops) may symbolize ASB. In the last analysis, this can infringe on the cultural rights of children and their capacity to associate freely.

2. This brief history of ASB has shown that the emphasis of successive governments is full of contradictions. When ASB legislation was passed into law the New Labour government at that time was concerned with addressing poverty and neglect among young people. At the same time, ASBOs were being used to target young people. Rather than addressing their problems, young people were at greater risk of being labelled as criminals. Thus children experience discrimination on the grounds of their age.

3. The ASB agenda tends to concentrate mainly on the individual offender, thus ignoring wider social and economic factors (Cook, 2006). The thinking behind ASBOs is an example of being tough on crime. ASBOs can be used to coerce people to conform to wider expectations about behaviour. A consequence of paying too much attention towards controlling the people who act anti-socially is that the wider, socio-economic causes of this behaviour are not addressed.

4. The civil standard of proofing effectively opens a back door to criminal conviction (Hopkins Burke and Morrill, 2004: 236) where the right to a fair trial is effectively renounced. The ASBO is a civil order, which means that the anti-social person is not necessarily arrested and read their rights. They are also not required to attend the court for a hearing. If an 'offender' does not comply with this order there is a law enforcement sanction. As such, civil law can be used as a crime reduction tool.

5. Some of the trends outlined in 1–4 are still germane regarding the Anti-Social Behaviour, Crime and Policing Act 2014, in the sense that by 'putting victims first' the criminalization of boys as vulnerable victims is neglected. However, guidance given to practitioners states that powers need to be used reasonably and proportionately in a way that is compatible with human rights (Home Office, 2014c).

Concluding thoughts

This chapter has outlined the multifaceted experiences of men as victims of crime. In the first part we argued that in considering victimization it is necessary to avoid reifying gender by showing that it is not necessarily significant in relation to all types of offending behaviour and a distinction was drawn between offences against property and offences against the person. We argued along similar lines to the chapter that focused on women as victims that it is violent crime, especially interpersonal violence, where gender differences in victimization are most evident. As a result of the influence of second-wave feminism on victimology, most attention is quite rightly directed towards women and girls as victims of violent masculinities that are not tackled head on at a structural level by the state and the law enforcement and correctional agencies within its purview. However, more recently writers have started scrutinizing the complex pattern of victimization and its impact on men. Most of this victimization, especially the alcohol and drug-fuelled turf wars that sometimes culminate, in the most extreme cases, in murder, is carried out by men. More than that, the distinction between offenders and victims is rarely clear-cut because men and boys in certain marginalized milieu are both victims and offenders. We also showed that some men are victimized by women, which goes against the grain of some preconceptions that have been held by feminist scholars. Despite the existence of male victimization by women, this is statistically negligible and men are culpable for most of the victimization that impacts on men.

We then addressed the salience of human rights discourse for coming to terms with the victimization of men. We followed up a discussion introduced in the chapter on male offenders, which called for such men to take on board personal responsibility for their actions, by suggesting that the evidence base shows that some men do tend to engage in risky behaviour that brings about their own victimization. This allusion to the notion of victim precipitation is likely to attract considerable criticism but there is conceivably a case for responsibilizing victims, especially those who also victimize, and to convince them of the need to accept a rights-based agenda. A visit to casualty and A&E departments at a weekend reveals the consequences of the brutalizing effects of the carnivalesque on all young people, but mainly men. To counter any potential victim-blaming we argued that certain masculinities are criminalized as a result of over-punitive policies. This argument was fleshed out in relation to the anti-social behaviour of boys and male youths where we argued that legislation has been introduced which renders vulnerable the human rights of this group. It is argued that young men in all walks of society, especially those from poorer socio-economic groups, need their rights buttressing if they are to respect so-called civilized values.

Summary

- It goes against the grain of deeply embedded cultural attitudes that men can be victims and when men report victimization it is often said that it is an affront to their sense of what it is to be a man. However, men are frequently victimized and this chapter outlined the extent and prevalence of the types of victimization they experience. An important point is that many men and boys occupy the status of both offender and victim and that the two can from time to time become indistinguishable.

- In contrast to women, who are much more vulnerable in the private sphere, men have a higher risk of becoming a victim in public space. Most officially recognized interpersonal violence is perpetrated against men and boys by other men and it was suggested that male victims can actively avoid some risky criminogenic environments.
- While victimology has rightly highlighted the appalling treatment of female victims by criminal justice agencies, the male victim has also not fared particularly well. The factors underlying the neglect of the male victim are different, though, and are related in part to masculine identities and a lack of understanding of the needs of male victims by the police, courts and wider society.
- The causes of male victimization were reviewed and it was suggested that certain unpopular victimological concepts, such as victim precipitation, have perhaps been jettisoned prematurely with regard to violent crime in the night-time economy.
- There are established ways of looking at crime victims and this chapter attempted to contest some of our preconceptions about the victimization of men. It is our view that young men and boys can be victimized by the effects of state power and through a consideration of the policy response to ASB we described how this group can be perceived as victims, as well as offenders. A human rights agenda is one way of recognizing the unfair and unjust treatment of young people, as well as being a means to counter punitive policies.

STUDY QUESTIONS

1. What does criminology and victimology tell us about men as victims of crime?
2. Assess the adequacy of the criminal justice response to the specific needs of male victims of crime.
3. Critically explore the reasons why young men are so vulnerable when it comes to becoming the victim of violent crime.
4. Assess critically the claim made in this chapter that we ought to recognize the anti-social behaviour of boys as a form of victimization.
5. What practical steps can be taken to reduce the victimization of men?

FURTHER READING

In addition to the general introductions to victimology authored by J. Goodey (2005) *Victims and Victimology: Research, Policy and Practice* (Longman) and B. Spalek (2006) *Crime Victims: Theory, Policy and Practice* (Palgrave), various studies commissioned by the Home Office cited in this chapter provide important sources of knowledge on the prevalence and nature of men's victimization, especially of interpersonal violence. However, there are some excellent studies looking at the fear of crime and male rape respectively, including:

J. Goodey (1997) 'Boys don't cry: Masculinity, fear of crime and fearlessness' (*British Journal of Criminology*, 37: 401–18) and R. Graham (2006) 'Male rape and the careful construction of the male victim' (*Social and Legal Studies*, 15: 187–208). Also use the index to find the relevant pages in S. Walklate (2004) *Gender, Crime and Criminal Justice*, 2nd edn (Willan) and T. Newburn and E. Stanko (eds) (1994) *Just Boys Doing Business: Men, Masculinities and Crime* (Routledge). S. Winlow and S. Hall (2006) *Violent Night* (Berg) focus on the inter-relatedness of victimization in relation to men and masculinity. Overall, there are a limited number of readings dedicated to the victimization of men and it will be necessary to search carefully through the indexes of various victimological texts looking under men and masculinity.

Note

1. Lesbians and bisexuals were combined with gay men in this statistic.

PART IV
IN CONTROL

9

Gender and Criminal Justice Workers

OVERVIEW

Chapter 9 provides:

- A discussion of the differential employment of men and women in the criminal justice sector.
- An evaluation of the quantitative and qualitative dimensions of gendered patterns of employment.
- An analysis of gender-based discrimination in the criminal justice system.
- A critical assessment of the impact of heterosexist and hegemonic masculinities on the policing functions of police officers and private security workers.
- An initial explanation of the influence of power on the gendered dynamics of work in the criminal justice sector. It is shown that power weakens the influence of human rights-based values, thus perpetuating gendered patterns of inequality.

KEY TERMS

- cult of masculinity
- diversity
- elitism
- equal opportunities
- hegemonic masculinity
- heterosexist ideology
- ideology

- pluralism
- police and policing
- police culture
- power
- sexism
- Third Way

Introduction

In the next two chapters the gendered nature of criminal justice organizations is considered. We depart from the symmetrical approach utilized in the chapters focusing on offenders and victims, introducing a number of themes relating to the experiences of men and women workers throughout the sector. The next chapter explores the theme of career progression to show how discriminatory ideas and practices obstruct the mobility of female professionals and how this tendency is out of kilter with the rights-based approach we have been advocating.

As a precursor to this, the specific aim of this chapter is to examine the location of men and women in the criminal justice system in terms of the numbers employed by different agencies and their respective positions of power and influence in these organizations. Unlike the arguments made when we looked at offenders, in particular to reduce their inclusion in the criminal justice system, here we are making a case for the greater representation of women so they have an equal status with men. We start from the premise that there are inequalities existing between men and women, confirmed incontrovertibly in 2007 by the publication of the final report by the now disbanded Equal Opportunities Commission (EOC), where it is observed that there are stark gender gaps and that sex discrimination is rife for women in the workplace and at home.[1] The pattern of inequality is far from straightforward, however, and it is necessary to look behind the numbers to show how organizational cultures produce and sustain sexist attitudes, beliefs, processes and practices. By the end of the chapter it is demonstrated that the effective power of hegemonic masculinities underpin the workings of the professional groups operating in an increasingly pluralized criminal justice system. This network of agencies behaves in such a way that privileges the interests of men at the expense of women and shows how this state of affairs is diametrically opposed to a human rights agenda, which values the principles of equality, opportunity, diversity, fairness, dignity and balance. For example, in 2008 the United Nations Committee on the Elimination of Discrimination Against Women (CEDAW) (mentioned in Chapter 1 and followed up in Chapter 10) made several recommendations for a cross-governmental strategy to progress women's rights. The government is a signatory of this Convention, which is viewed by some as an international charter for women's equality (*The Guardian*, 2013). This Convention contains several articles, some of which are potentially relevant to criminal justice workers, to gauge discrimination against women (Fawcett Society, 2010). These benchmark principles were supposedly enshrined in the Equality Act 2010 where organizations must show 'due regard' to the **Public Sector Equality Duty**. The Act states that:

A public authority must, in the exercise of the functions, have due regard to the need to: a) eliminate discrimination, harassment, victimisation and any other conduct that is prohibited by and under this Act; b) advance equality of opportunity between persons who share a relevant protected characteristic and persons who do not share it; c) foster good relations between persons who share a relevant protected characteristic and those who do not share it.

This statement needs to be situated into a structural context and we need to be mindful that gender is side-lined by other equality objectives and human rights values, which is possible under conditions of austerity. Britain has experienced profound political, economic and cultural changes, which have occurred in response to the global recession and economic meltdown. On entering office the Coalition government (2010–14) argued that public expenditure on state-funded services, including those in the criminal justice system, was not sustainable and that cuts were necessary. Many of these cuts had a particularly negative effect on women, especially due to austerity measures targeting public sector jobs, which is where relatively more women are employed (*The Guardian*, 2013). The previous New Labour regime had overspent and evidence was cited to show that police budgets increased by 50 per cent from 2004 to 2009 and between the same dates the increase for NOMS was 36 per cent. This view was shared by the former New Labour Prime Minister, Tony Blair, who was critical of the creation of the 'Big State' by his successor Gordon Brown (Blair, 2010). As part of its austerity measures the Coalition embraced neo-liberal aspirations to reduce the scale and size of the state, which was partly achieved by reducing expenditure, but also by encouraging the voluntary and community sector and individual citizens to take on more responsibility for their own security and safety, or the strategy of 'responsibilization' (Garland, 2001).

The Coalition prioritized economic growth, by making it clear that cuts were needed, not more spending on a bloated public sector. For example, in the autumn of 2010 it was announced that the Home Office and Ministry of Justice faced 23 per cent cuts by 2014. Up to 150 courts were to be closed and government funding of the police reduced by one-fifth between 2010 and 2014, with 18,000 fewer officers (KPMG, cited in *The Financial Times*, 21 October 2010). The links between these changes and gender are not clear-cut, but under fiscal conditions like this there is the danger that human rights values might be of declining importance.

To achieve the aforementioned aims the chapter is split into two main sections beginning with an 'audit' of the criminal justice system, which counts the number of men and women working in the staple or core professions: the police, courts, probation and prison services. As well as these organizations, we consider the Ministry of Justice, Youth Justice Board, Forensic Science Service, the Parole Board, Independent Monitoring Boards (formerly Board of Visitors) and the Serious Fraud Office. We also very briefly draw attention to an under-researched group of para-professionals, or those people brought into the criminal justice sector who lack the full expertise and powers of professionals (i.e. the police, probation and prison officers) yet who are proving influential. This group of para-professionals is largely an effect of the pluralization of criminal justice, and they are playing an increasingly pivotal role in crime policy yet remain unresearched, especially the gendered nature of their activities (Senior et al., 2007). There is also the expansion of the voluntary and community sector (VCS) and private security where gender is also salient. For the latter we show masculinist ideologies permeate the organizational cultures of door security staff, often referred to as door supervisors or 'bouncers'. This group of workers pose a unique set of challenges because unlike police officers they are not publicly accountable and evade monitoring and scrutiny. While this part is mainly descriptive, there are discernible patterns requiring some elucidation. In particular, the higher positions within the justice system tend to be held by men. We argue that this can make the system less representative of the diversity of society than it might be if women were to have a more prominent profile in senior positions, which raises questions about justice and fairness. The limitations of relying on statistical data are acknowledged and the properties of the relationship between numerical and other hidden inequalities are identified.

In the second part we account for the apparent failure of equal opportunities policies, despite the production of various statements of good intent and seemingly positive anti-sexist initiatives. We utilize the Shadow report from the UK CEDAW Working Group to make sense of the effectiveness of legislation on reducing gender-based discrimination (Women's Resource Centre, 2013). We apply the concept of power to convey how attitudinal and institutionalized forms of sexism preserve male interests within and between professional groups. It is argued that despite damning criticisms of male dominance it has not been fundamentally challenged in some areas of crime and public policy and that its local workings lead to more subtle and insidious forms of discrimination and injustice. Over the last three decades or so, but especially from 2000 onwards, there is clearly a higher degree of compliance with a rights-based discourse, but full commitment to it is less easy to evidence. We argue that deeper structural and attitudinal changes are needed to address gendered inequalities in the criminal justice professions, a point followed up in the next chapter.

A gender audit – men and women working in criminal justice

The activities of criminal justice agencies are gendered in myriad ways and their external orientation towards gender issues, which has been traced thus far in this volume, is intimately related to their internal orientation. In other words, the differential and inequitable treatment of men and women as gendered subjects is in some ways mirrored by what goes on inside the police, the courts and correctional agencies. There is a numerical dimension but later on we show there is a qualitative angle too. Statistical data can be rather dull to look at but numbers are becoming increasingly important as a result of Public Sector Equality Duty, which came into force on 5 April 2011, as they are used as a measurement of equality.

The police service

As gatekeepers to the criminal justice system it has already been noted that police work is gendered in terms of the differential treatment of male and female offenders and victims. In the case of sexual and domestic violence police attitudes are ambiguous and the devaluation of women can be routinized and, despite reforms, sexist assumptions still remain in some areas of police work. This externally gendered orientation is, at least hypothetically, intimately related to the number of practitioners who are women, although that is clearly only part of the story. Historically, the number of women joining and staying in the police service has been low and the numbers did not grow appreciably until the 1970s (Heidensohn, 2003). Overall, there are more male than female police officers, an over-representation most glaringly obvious at the senior levels of the force hierarchy. In the first edition of our book, we noted that on 31 March 2005 there were 142,795 full-time police officers in the 43 forces of England and Wales, including central services. Of this number 30,162 were female, which is the equivalent of 21 per cent. In the previous year 20 per cent of officers were women (Bibi et al., 2005: 5). By March 2006 the female population in the police service was 22 per cent (31,273 of 143,271) (Fawcett Society, 2007: 29), suggesting some enhanced, albeit negligible, representation. Over the course of 10 years there has been a decline in numbers – especially between 2010 and 2013 – and on 31 March 2015 there were 126,818 officers in 43 police forces (there were an additional 292 officers seconded to central services and the British Transport Police employed 2,877 officers). This decline can, in part, be attributed to the austerity measures implemented by the Coalition government (2010–14). In terms of gender, in March 2015 the number of female officers was 35,738 (an increase of 85 (0.2 per cent) compared to 2014). Since 2006 there has been a gradual increase in the proportion of female officers: 22.3 per cent in 2006 to 28.2 per cent in 2015 (Woods, 2015), but at the same time there has been a fall in the number of men occupying these posts (Ministry of Justice, 2014b).

In the police service there is a clearly demarcated hierarchical rank structure and the service is organized in a quasi-military style (Walklate, 2004).

At the top are the chief police officer ranks, with the chief constable being the highest ranking officer (the equivalent for the Metropolitan Police Service is Commissioner) followed in ascending order by superintendents, inspectors, sergeants and the police constable. Table 9.1 shows the distribution of officers in terms of their gender and position in the rank structure, focusing on the variation between 2005 and 2015.

Table 9.1 demonstrates clearly that there has been a significant percentage increase in the proportion of female officers. What is significant about the trend captured above is that the increase is most notable among senior officers (the rank of inspector and above) whereas in the past there was a relatively higher proportion in the junior ranks (e.g. police constables). The situation is a long way off equal representation of men and women, though, and using figures available in 2006, according to an Equal Opportunities Commission (EOC, 2006, cited in Fawcett Society, 2007) report it was estimated that 101 out of 269 senior officers (i.e. the ACPO ranks) should be female if there is to be a higher degree of equity. Moreover, workforce data also shows that proportional advances for women police disguise considerable variation in the number of women in policing across jurisdictions, with a number of service areas indicating less than 27 per cent (Home Office, 2013c). Findings from Laverick and Cain (2014) provide a further powerful critical reading of the suggested upwards trend in women's representation within policing, noting a real loss in the number of women in policing against a rhetoric of proportional advances being made.

Table 9.1   The rank of police officers in England and Wales by gender

Rank	% of male officers in 2005	% of male officers in 2015	% change between 2005 and 2015	% of female officers in 2005	% of female officers in 2015	% change between 2005 and 2015
Chief Officers	90	78.6	−11.4	10	21.4	+10.6
Chief Superintendents	93	78.7	−11.3	7	21.3	+10.7
Superintendents	90	80.8	−9.2	10	19.2	+9.2
Chief Inspector	90	77.4	−12.6	10	22.6	+12.6
Inspector	89	79.8	−9.2	11	20.2	+9.2
Sergeant	87	79	−8	13	21	+8
Police Constable	76	69.8	−6.2	24	30.2	+6.2
Total ranks	79	71.8	−7.2	21	28.2	+7.2

Source: Adapted from Bibi et al., 2005: 5; Woods, 2015

In addition to police officers there is police staff, a body consisting of relatively fewer male employees, and on 31 March 2005 there were 49,856 female police staff (Bibi et al., 2005: 19). As a percentage in 2005, 36 per cent of police staff employees were men and by 2015 there were 40 per cent (Woods, 2015). If we consider ethnicity as a factor, 2886 BME staff were female out of a total of 4181 (Bibi et al., 2005: 19). Females accounted for 30.7 per cent of 13,066 special constables, which is a higher figure than for police officers. Among Police Community Support Officers (PCSOs), of which there were 13,022 in 2015, 44.9 per cent were female. The percentage of female leavers is 22.2 per cent (Woods, 2015). This shows that there is a higher proportion of women working in this role in contrast to fully sworn-in police officers. In 2006, 58 per cent of PCSOs were men (Fawcett Society, 2007: 30) compared to 55.1 per cent in 2015 (Woods, 2015).

Thus women are concentrated in the less senior and influential positions in the world of policing, which indicates that there is potentially a problem with their progression, an issue followed up in the next chapter. When looking at the numbers of police officers the key issues are recruitment and retention. In 2015, 30.8 per cent of recruits were female, which is a positive development in the sense that this number is higher than the percentage of existing officers (Woods, 2015). Despite this there is a relatively low turnover of police officers and police careers tend to be long so the impact of this, if it continues, is not likely to be conspicuous for some time. ACPO has said 'it will take between 17 and 23 years to achieve the Home Office target for 2009 of 35 per cent for women police officers' (ACPO, cited in Fawcett Society, 2007: 29). Significantly, this is only likely to be achieved if a course of 'affirmative action' is driven forward by the government. Police officers do leave the organization and Woods (2015) shows in the 12 months leading to March 2015 that 22.2 per cent of this group (6988) were female.

More recently the role of the Police Authority was replaced by Police and Crime Panels, which advise directly elected Police and Crime Commissioners in England and Wales. Six of the 41 people elected into this post were female (14.6 per cent). The Panels, on average, consist of no more than 20 per cent women (Centre for Women and Democracy, 2013: 13).

The Crown Prosecution Service (CPS)

It is only in relatively recent times that the police have not been responsible for prosecuting individuals. Since 1986 the Crown Prosecution Service, or the CPS as it is known now, decides whether or not a case should be taken to court so people can be prosecuted. Nowadays the police are only responsible for the investigation of an alleged offence and preparing a case for the CPS, which at least speculatively reduces the impact of the **police culture** and its 'cult of masculinity' (this is elaborated below: see Waddington, 1999). The CPS, in comparison to the police, has a higher proportion of female employees (66 per cent) compared to males (34 per cent), although there is a higher proportion of men

(52 per cent) employed in positions of relative seniority compared to women (48 per cent). Women are over-represented in most pay bands but they lag behind in positions of seniority, and 13 of the 42 Chief Prosecutors are female (Fawcett Society, 2007: 28). The CPS is committed to gender equality and it issued an Equality and Diversity Expectations Statement to ensure that members of the Bar working with or seeking work with the CPS will have equal opportunities policies in place. It is also committed to creating more gender friendly and **flexible working** arrangements (ibid.). Women might be under-represented among the higher echelons, but over the last few years there has been a gradual and small increase in their numbers (Ministry of Justice, 2014b).

The Ministry of Justice

This government department is responsible for running the courts, tribunals, legal aid, sentencing policy, prisons, the management of offenders, and also issues relating to law and rights. The Ministry assumed responsibility for the Department for Constitutional Affairs, which we examined in the first edition. Overall it employs 62,370 staff with 51 per cent of them being men. Within the Ministry the representation of men and women varies and 36 per cent of NOMS employees are female whereas in Her Majesty's Courts and Tribunals Service (HMCTS) 71 per cent are female (Ministry of Justice, 2014d).

National Offender Management Service (NOMS)

The ideas behind NOMS were introduced by the Carter Review (Carter, 2003) with the aim of creating an integrated corrections agency joining together community-based and custodial penalties; thus it includes both the prison and probation service. NOMS became an Executive Agency of the Ministry of Justice in 2008 and it currently commissions and delivers prison and probation services – and more recently, Community Rehabilitation Companies – in an integrated fashion. NOMS employed 43,390 staff at June 2014 (including 8270 National Probation Service staff). It is worth noting that overall numbers have declined since 2010 (Ministry of Justice, 2014e).

The prison service

We already know from the chapters on offending behaviour that most prisoners are men, although the proportion of women in this population started to increase from the late 1990s (Gelsthorpe, 2006). This is mirrored by the gendered pattern of employment where male officers outnumber females significantly. The prison service is structured like a militaristic organization and its working practices are heavily imbued with aggressive masculinities where security and control are of tantamount importance. The focus in this section is exclusively on public sector prisons, thus omitting data about private establishments. Operational staff employed in prisons are mainly male. On 31 March 2014, 28 per cent of prison officers were female. The equivalent figure for Operational Managers was 34 per cent. For both sets of employees there has been a slight increase in the number of female staff. If we look at those posts found in the non-operational below-manager grade, then there is a higher proportion of females (56 per cent) and at NOMS HQ the equivalent figure is 51 per cent (Ministry of Justice, 2014d). Hence, just like the police service, men occupy the more senior positions in the prison service.

The probation service

The probation service has changed fundamentally over the years in terms of its structure as well as its organizational values. Its links with the social work profession have disappeared and probation officers, recast as offender managers, are more punitive in their approach and subject to the growing influence of managerialism, especially with the introduction of competency frameworks to measure staff performance. Another change is the transition from an organization dominated by male officers to one where there are relatively more women than men. The reasons for this are unclear but research suggests that women have in part seen this as a positive development, although the increased workloads, relatively low pay and the uncertainty of the probation service's future undermine this positivity (Annison, 2013). Since the publication of the first edition the probation service's has been further transformed and from 1 June 2014 the National Probation Service (NPS) was given the responsibility for managing the most high-risk offenders in the community. Other categories of offender are now managed by Community Rehabilitation Companies (CRCs), which will eventually be contracted out to the private or voluntary (third) sectors.

The representation of females in the NPS is higher than it is in NOMS in general (Ministry of Justice, 2014e). The Ministry of Justice (2014b) records 72 per cent of probation service staff being women, which is the highest number since 2010. Due to the changes that have recently occurred, here we rely on historical data to show how this organization was gendered in the past.

According to one survey, the National Probation Service (2005) employed a total of 22,873 staff, of which almost two-thirds were women. Altogether, women outnumber men by an approximate ratio of 2:1. In other words, in contrast to the police service, there is in statistical terms an under-representation of men as 64 per cent of Probation Officers (POs) and 74 per cent of Trainee Probation Officers (TPOs) are women. There is a smaller proportion of female Senior Probation Officers (53 per cent), but they are still numerically better represented. Of the 42 chief officers of probation, half are women. At an even more senior level, five out of 10 Regional Offender Managers are women, including the Chief Executive (Fawcett Society, 2007: 30). If we look at this information in more detail, women have a greater representation in the operational job category and other roles and there is a reduced representation of men in Probation Service Officer and Senior Practitioner roles. This is consistent with the higher representation of women as POs and TPOs noted above, and it is reasonable to assume that people in these posts will progress through the seniority structure. Women do not dominate all areas of probation, though, and there has been an increase in the number of men employed in the Psychologist job group.

Taking the staff population, 76.44 per cent of staff were female, although this figure is skewed by the fact that there were 90.45 per cent women staff working in the Support Staff Administration job group. Turning to more senior staff support roles, there was a higher proportion of men, averaging out at 56 per cent (National Probation Service, 2005: 5). These disparities could be explained with reference to the higher proportion of older men employed in this category, although women in this category tended to have a greater length of average service, another criteria widely used by employers to determine promotion prospects. In the National Probation Directorate (NPD), the civil service arm of the NPS, 57.39 per cent of staff were men (National Probation Service, 2005).

Probation Officers have always been placed under tremendous pressure and staff sickness is a significant problem, but most importantly probation has been unable to resist radical reforms to its organizational structure and functions, for example, the introduction of the principle of contestability in the National Offender Management Service. As Senior et al. (2007) demonstrate, this is an idea that has its origins in economics and was taken up by Martin Narey, a former head of correctional services. Narey described contestability as a mechanism that may be used to raise the standard and quality of services by opening up major areas of work for competition. Functions and roles typically carried out by state agencies could also be delivered by the private and voluntary and community sectors. It signalled the end of state monopoly of crime and public policy. The issue here is that the gendered nature and ethos of organizations in the private and voluntary sectors could be very different from the probation service, and the commitment of the NPS to 'advise, assist and befriend' offenders could be further abandoned by organizations motivated more by a need to demonstrate economic rather than ethical viability.

Other criminal justice agencies

The judiciary

Information about judicial officers shows that in the past there is a clear bias with women being under-represented in all positions (see Table 9.2).

The Judicial Appointments Commission was launched as part of an attempt to redress this stark gender imbalance but, as the Fawcett Society (2007: 4) rightly observes, even if the number of women who become judges increases, it will take a long time to have a significant impact on the gender balance as the pace of change is slow.

In more recent times the representation of women has increased and between 2009/10 and 2013/14 there were annual increases in the proportion of female staff from 21 per cent to 25 per cent. This increase has been evident across both senior

Table 9.2   Judicial officers in England and Wales by gender

Position	Total	Men	Women
Lord of Appeal in Ordinary	12	11	1
Head of Division (excluding the Lord Chancellor)	4	3	1
Lord Justice of Appeal	37	35	2
High Court Judge	108	98	10
Circuit Judge	643	576	67
Recorder	1358	1172	186
Recorder in Training	17	13	4
District Judge (including Family Division)	433	349	84
Deputy District Judge (including Family Division)	823	620	203
District Judge (**Magistrates Courts**)	128	101	27
Deputy District Judge (Magistrates Courts)	168	130	38
Total	**3731**	**3108**	**623**
% of total	**100**	**83.3**	**16.7**

Source: adapted from www.dca.gov.uk/deptreport2005/pdf/dca2005a.pdf (accessed 30 April 2007)

(including Justices of the Supreme Court, Heads of Division, Lord Justices of Appeal and High Court Judges) and junior positions (Ministry of Justice, 2014b). For example, by 2010, 15 out of 109 High Court Judges were women, which is an increase compared to the number in Table 9.2 (see above) (Fawcett Society, 2010).

The magistracy has a slightly higher proportion of females (52 per cent) than males (Ministry of Justice, 2014b). The legal profession more generally is a male-dominated profession, especially at higher levels, and this is elaborated in Chapter 10.

In addition to the core criminal justice agencies there are other players where details about the gender of employees are collated.

The Youth Justice Board (YJB)

The YJB is an executive non-departmental public body and it was created to oversee the youth justice system in England and Wales, including Youth Offending Teams (YOTs), which are multi-agency teams set up by the Crime and Disorder Act 1998 to deal with youth justice matters. YOTs vary in size, with some having 20 members whereas others have 500. On 30 June 2013, 14,292 people worked for YOTs, including volunteers and part-time staff, not just full-time employees. Like many of the other agencies considered in this section, there has been a reduction in staffing levels. Information about gender is limited and data published on 30 June 2013 only considered full-time equiv-alent members and 69 per cent of staff were female (Ministry of Justice, 2015b).

In 2015 the Board employed approximately 231 staff. On 31 March 2015, 135 were women and 96 men, but a relatively lower proportion of women occupy senior posts. For example, the YJB Board is composed of four women and seven men and the Executive Management Group has two women and four men. If we look back to the first edition, it is apparent that although women remain under-represented in senior positions, they did not have a pres-ence in 2006 in the most senior grades (Home Office, 2006d).

The Parole Board

This takes decisions about when and if to release prisoners. The Board employs relatively few staff and of 241 employees 59 per cent were male (Home Office, 2006e: 21). In 2015 the Board was much smaller and employed 104 full-time members of staff, and at this time the number of women exceeded men: there were 62 females and 42 males. Even the Management Committee, which includes 12 members, had a higher proportion of women (7) compared to men (5) (Parole Board, 2015).

The Independent Monitoring Boards (formerly Board of Visitors)

This organization monitors the treatment of people held in custody, such as prison, immigration removal centres and some short-term holding facilities at airports, to make sure those being detained are treated fairly and with respect (www.imb.org.uk/). Of the 1785 staff who are unpaid, 51.71 per cent of staff are men (Home Office, 2006e: 21).

Forensic Science Service

This organization employed 2595 staff in March 2006 with 42.5 per cent male employees, although the issue of seniority is relevant because there are slightly more men (50.7 per cent) in managerial posts (Home Office, 2006e: 21). This Service was closed on 31 March 2012 and its work is contracted out to the private sector.

Victim Support

This charitable organization is there to offer help and assistance for crime victims, possibly following a referral by the police. In 2004–05 it employed 6162 staff, of which 1593 were male. Volunteers working for Victim Support cannot be forced into reporting their gender and for this reason there is missing data in some 5000 cases (Home Office, 2006e: 22).

Criminal Injuries Compensation Authority

This is in place to compensate some victims of violent crime. Since 2010 staff levels shrunk by 40 per cent and by 2015 the Authority employed 148 male and 157 female staff (Criminal Injuries Compensation Authority, 2015). The Chief Executive and Deputy Chief Executive were both female.

Serious Fraud Office

The function of this body is to deter, investigate and reduce fraud and corruption. It works in partnership with other government departments and regulatory bodies, including the National Crime Agency and Her Majesty's Revenue and Customs. It employs 229 male and 182 female staff. Senior Civil Service staff include 11 men and four women (Serious Fraud Office, 2015).

NACRO

This organization has charitable status and is dedicated to reducing crime and making society a safer place. It aims to reduce crime in order to give actual offenders and those at risk of becoming offenders a stake in society. It is committed to reducing various forms of disadvantage and social exclusion. In terms of its staff profile, 38.5 per cent of its workers are men with 61.5 per cent being women (NACRO, 2005).

Para-professionals

A group of employees who are becoming increasingly influential in criminal justice policy are what Senior et al. (2007) call para-professionals, which is part of a trend towards the pluralization of providers of criminal justice services. From the 1990s onwards there were new opportunities for a range of players and stakeholders, not least the expansion of the Voluntary and Community Sector (VCS) (see below) and private enterprises in the commercialized sector of the crime reduction industry. To give an example of pluralization and deprofessionalization, a raft of posts have been created in the anti-social behaviour industry. In addition, the core players in criminal justice are also being transformed by the de-professionalization of their status. There has effectively been 'downward hierarchical theft' where the roles and responsibilities of criminal justice professionals are being handed down to those whom professional groups perceive to be relatively under-qualified or unqualified and inexperienced people, such as unqualified justice workers and posts in the legal profession. The point is that the gendered nature of these rising organizations is yet to materialize, although it could transform gender relations and the machinations of the criminal justice professions.

The Voluntary and Community Sector (VCS)

The VCS has always existed in one form or another yet it is difficult to quantify the number of agencies in existence. The kind of numerical data included above does not exist for this sector, but there are some important themes to acknowledge. The size of organizations in the sector vary profoundly, ranging from small community-based to large international organizations, including some where volunteers receive no income as well as those that are run like commercial businesses. Organizations in the sector focus on a range of issues and may concentrate their crime reduction work on offenders and/or victims. In the first decade of the twenty-first century the VCS has been moved to centre stage by successive governments, in part through the injection of the principles of competition and contestability into criminal justice, especially when it comes to determining the roles, responsibilities and workloads of offender managers (prison and probation officers) (Senior et al., 2007). The impetus behind the activities of the VCS may be charitable and altruistic but there are other motives. The Coalition government (2010–15), for instance, promoted the idea of the 'Big Society', and although its chief architect, David Cameron, did not always have a coherent vision, its core aim was to realign the relationship between the citizen and state by increasing the role of the former and reducing as far as possible the role of the latter: the buzz words were public sector reform, social action and community empowerment (Morgan, 2012). This raises questions about whether or not the underlying objective is to get people to take more responsibility with fellow citizens in their neighbourhood/community by making them less reliant on the state. The VCS is also a relatively under-researched area and there are few systematic studies of how such organizations are gendered, but evidence suggests that women tend to be 'more public spirited than men' and more active in local, community-based organizations, especially the non-profit sector (Themudo, 2009). Research in the field of social work draws attention to the theoretical significance of an influx of men entering the sector and how their masculinities are reshaping the philosophy and practice of some organizations (Baines et al., 2014). There are also organizations employing women volunteers, such as Rape Crisis, which provide gender-specific services. This particular organization came into being to provide services that were not made available by the statutory sector (Jones and Cook, 2008).

Policing: The gendered nature of the police and private security

Jones and Newburn (1998: 18–19) argue that policing consists of 'organized forms of order maintenance, peacekeeping, law enforcement, the investigation and prevention' of crime (which can involve 'coercive power') carried out by 'individuals or organizations', where their activities are viewed as a 'central part of their purpose'.

Take another example from Bowling and Foster (2002: 980):

> 'Police' refers to a particular kind of social institution, while 'policing' implies a set of processes with specific social functions. 'Police' are not found in every society, and police organisations and personnel can have a variety of shifting forms. 'Policing', however, is arguably a necessity in any social order, which may be carried out by a number of different processes and institutional arrangements. A state-organised specialist 'police' organisation of the modern kind is only one example of policing.

The idea of policing is therefore not restricted to what the police do and is concerned with a set of processes and practices rather than an institution. The police, in other words, perform a policing function but policing can be undertaken by non-police agencies as well. Indeed, the police are, in historical terms, a relatively new phenomenon with a more specific role: 'the police are nothing else than a mechanism for the distribution of situationally justifiable force in society' (Bittner, 1974: 39).

As the quotations taken from Jones and Newburn (1998) and Bowling and Foster (2002) cited above both show, there are a range of individuals and organizations drawn from the public and private/commercial sectors that are involved in policing. At this stage it is still not any clearer what policing *is*, however. In essence, policing is a form of social control and security, related to the surveillance of particular geographical areas but, above all, specific populations or groups of people. Examples of surveillance include the CCTV cameras installed more or less everywhere, private security staff at shopping centres and night-club bouncers (Hobbs et al., 2003). The list is endless and it soon becomes clear that the police are just one provider of control, security and surveillance. The underlying aim of these activities is to make sure society is disciplined and orderly and that any unruliness and disorder are kept to a minimum. It is in this context that various masculinities are played out, which have a ruinous effect on the working lives of many women and, in actual fact, men too. An argument that is developed is that the heterosexist orientations of both the public police and private security are inhibitors of a fully-fledged human rights remit for employees. However, the publicly funded police are potentially more amenable to regulation and censure, whereas the violent masculinities of the private sector are less easily channelled in such a direction.

Because the core functions of police work, especially the symbolic and actual physical use of force, require 'male' attributes, such as force and strength, there are issues relating to embodiment (Collier, 1998). Although policing has undergone something of a transformation in relation to some activities, other masculine roles remain sacrosanct and the 'masculinity' or 'masculinities' of specialisms such as firearms remain under the control of male officers. Similar tendencies can be seen in the commercial sector. It is not just the public police where masculinity is an issue demonstrated by an emergent literature examining door supervisors, which is part of the trend described as the pluralization of policing. This is most evident in the area of commercial security, an expanding sector that provides policing for areas of 'mass private property' (Shearing and Stenning, 1981), such as shopping centres, sports stadia and gated communities. Private security firms who employ door security staff, often 'bouncers', also effectively police the night-time economy – the pubs and clubs in town and city centres (Hobbs et al., 2003). It is here that we can observe the work of predominantly men who are in control of mainly intoxicated people in a hedonistic and chaotic environment, exemplified by the subtle, rich and thick ethnographic description found in the works of Winlow (2001) and Monaghan (2004). Although the subject matter was similar, these two writers adopted a different critical stance in their respective analyses, with the former referring to political economic change and deindustrialization and the latter looking at embodiment.

This is not the place to review in detail their methodologies, but this work does reveal some illuminating information for our understanding of the gendering of criminal justice workers. Door supervisors perform an increasingly important function in maintaining order in an unruly night-time economy and their work complements the work done by the police as well as that work which the police do not do. It is an overwhelmingly male occupation and most men working in this role conform to notions of 'hegemonic masculinity'; they are heterosexual and their sense of embodiment is central to their work. The research shows that the banter of bouncers is remarkably similar to police officers and both groups of workers celebrate a cult of masculinity where there is talk about women, drinking and violence. At one level of analysis the nature of their work is very much alike, although the bouncer lacks the legal status that is enjoyed by the police officer. As an individual who needs to be able to look after himself, or at least give off that impression, the bouncer is rather vulnerable, especially because his actions are sometimes illegitimate – how much violence can be acceptably used to maintain order in a pub or club is the question they face routinely. More importantly for the purpose of our analysis, the bouncer occupies two statuses: (1) as a potential perpetrator of unlawful violence and (2) as a victim of violence from a reveller who is a customer.

Other work has explored the involvement of female bouncers in violence work, again using ethnographic approaches to gain an insight into the work they do. The fact that there is demand for women to work in this area challenges preconceptions about hypermasculinity and toughness being prerequisites for controlling violence, which are at odds with traditional notions of femininity and perceptions about the female body and its capacity for physical violence (Hobbs et al., 2007). O'Brien et al. (2008: 162) show that demand for female bouncers does lead to the reproduction of '"traditional" notions of femininity' by women adopting 'conciliatory styles of conflict management'. At the same time these women rework the gendered order of things and use violence as a resource to maintain control and manage violence and aggression. In Chapter 10 we expand on the idea that women police officers make some difference to the outcome when it comes to the use of force.

As far as a human rights agenda goes, this is of limited relevance to employees in this area of the economy, yet the work they do infringes very much on the rights of the people they encounter.

The preceding pages in this section have explored how masculinities have been enacted in various organizational settings. The usage of public and private forms of policing as exemplars shows that heterosexism pervades these

occupations, although they are not occupationally specific and similar attitudes will be found among corporate and political elites. What is especially
interesting is that the police service is subject to various government and state-
led initiatives that are in place to ensure compliance and to outlaw and stamp
out sexism. The pervasiveness of the police culture continues to be registered
by administrative and critical criminologists alike and gendered discrimination
is therefore an obdurate feature of contemporary policing. There are many
explanations for this, although the concept of power is illuminating for our
purposes (Lukes, 1986). Before that we consider some of the limitations of the
material reviewed in this section of the book.

The limitations of statistical information

The figures compiled for this section provide, if not a contradictory then a
rather confusing picture. At a simplistic level it may be argued that the criminal justice system is sexist and that it systematically disadvantages the women
it employs. If we take the police and prison services, then this argument would
have some veracity but other agencies, such as probation and the CPS, employ
more women. Thus if the outcomes of the various activities of different agencies are assessed according to the number of men and women employed, then
the probation service does not appear to be discriminatory. However, despite
the appointment in June 2007 of the first ever female Home Secretary, we
know that men occupy many senior positions and that hegemonic masculinity
can be evidenced in a number of areas. The form of hegemonic masculinity
varies from agency to agency, although we have a fuller picture of how masculinities are manifest in relation to policing. The gendered dynamics of
working in the probation, prison and court services are less well documented
and for that reason the next part draws on the voluminous literature on policing and its gendered organizational cultures.

Addressing human rights: The gendered
working of power

Thus the concept of power is potentially very useful for coming to terms with
conflicts and contradictions arising when we study gendered organizations and
the ascendancy of particular value frameworks, such as hegemonic masculinity.

An understanding of the power of governments at a macro level is essential for grasping the dynamics of organizational cultures at a micro level and the mediating influence of players at a meso level. More specifically, it is contended that some conceptions of power are useful because they offer a preliminary explanation of some of the reasons why men and women remain in unequal positions in criminal justice. At a superficial level things should be equal, or at least more equal, now. Equal opportunities legislation and a range of anti-discriminatory initiatives have been introduced, most recently the Equalities Act 2006, the CEHR and the Equality Act 2010. Regardless of calls for affirmative action to reduce sexist discrimination in the workplace, inequalities still exist. An appreciation of the concept of power and its workings in organizational settings can go some way towards appreciating this contradictory state of affairs. While legislators and campaigning reformers have counselled that legislation and policy are the most appropriate mechanisms for instigating meaningful change, the predominance of a cult of masculinity at levels of institutions, and a preponderance of men in influential and powerful positions, is still an obstacle to equality. It is argued that the political agency exercised by governmental elites preserves the existing status quo in the criminal justice sector. Economic goals such as the financial probity of agencies and their ability to meet over-simplified and inappropriate performance targets (i.e. 'what gets measured, gets done') are prioritized above progressive politics, such as the human rights agenda. Since the late 1990s the government has pledged that it will modernize the public sector, although this has occurred without any fundamental changes to the social structure, in particular gendered inequality. How does the concept of power help us to understand this?

There are several conceptions of power, or more accurately, 'effective power'. Power may be channelled through many outlets and can be exercised diffusely (pluralists) or centrally (elites) (Dahl, 1958; Wright Mills, 1956). In addition to these perspectives, which put social agents at the centre of their analytical frameworks, there is also a structural dimension (Lukes, 1974, 1986). It is not feasible to do justice to the literature on power, and only a few issues are selected here for our purposes (see Clegg, 1989 for a detailed overview). Power is distributed inequitably among various social, economic, political and cultural groups, not least men and women. Numerous commentaries imply that power is simply imposed from above, but one must also account for the fact that in the policy-making process, if anything is to happen at all, some kind of consent and consensus is required from below, however tacit that may be. This is fully in accord with the Gramscian argument that the dominance of one group needs to be accepted by subordinate groups (Gramsci, 1971).

How is this consensus and consent constructed? Bachrach and Baratz's (1970: 16) 'two dimensional view of power' (Lukes, 1974, 1986) elaborates on

Dahl's (1958) pluralist 'one dimensional' view of power. The pluralist conception of power held by the latter focuses on the conduct of decision-takers, which entail observable conflicts between the different groups (e.g. men and women police officers), who are each aiming to further their interests. The actual route or course of action that they take reflects the interests of each of these groups. In other words, 'where the interests [of groups] are seen as equivalent to revealed preferences' (Lukes, 1986: 9). In their critique of Dahl's (1958) pluralist model, Bachrach and Baratz (1970) introduce the second face of power. As they put it:

> ...in conceiving of elite domination exclusively in the form of a conscious cabal exercising the power of decision making and vetoing, he overlooks a more subtle form of domination; one in which those who actually dominate are not conscious of themselves simply because their position of dominance has never seriously been challenged. (Bachrach and Baratz, 1970: 16)

The 'overlooked' form of domination in decision-making they refer to is:

> ... non-decision making, that is the practice of limiting the scope of actual decision making to 'safe' issues by manipulating the dominant community value, myths and political institutions and procedures. To pass over this is to neglect one whole face of power. (Bachrach and Baratz, 1970: 18)

This second face of power describes covert conflicts between actors over actual as well as potential issues. Thus, non-decisions, whereby particular issues like the proliferation of heterosexist occupational cultures are kept off the agenda, are as significant as actual decisions. It reveals the ability of the players involved to determine what is on the agenda so that any of the decisions taken do not threaten the position of the dominant political groups.

Lukes (1974) describes a third face of power, which shows that even if a group is unaware of a conflict of interests, this does not deny the existence of conflict. This disputes the hypothesis that power is only exercised where conflict is observable. This does not dispense with overt and covert conflicts, but illustrates how power may operate to shape and adjust aspirations and beliefs in order that they do not reflect people's interests. This third dimension of power, known as 'latent conflict', is used to question the view that if consensus exists, power is not being exercised.

The key issue here is ideology and it would appear that in light of the continued inequality experienced by female employees working in criminal justice occupations, heterosexist and masculinist ideologies downplay this fact. The existence of legislation and initiatives is misrecognized as an equivalent of equality in practice.

Ideology is enmeshed in the policy process, both at a macro level and micro level. The former includes the dominant political and economic values of the day, such as social democracy and neo-liberalism, elements of which both underpin government policy in the early twenty-first century. According to the mission statements and founding goals of recent governments, there is an emphasis on human rights, and words such as equality, opportunity, diversity and fairness are in circulation, though in practice these principles do not necessarily materialize.

Hewitt (1992: 44–5) referred to the elasticity of ideologies, which helpfully illustrates how different as well as similar values, or 'contrasting but complementary principles', are arranged in such a way that a 'coherent logic' is developed to justify a particular course of social action or inertia. At a micro level there are operational ideologies which are sometimes in conflict with those at macro and meso levels. For example, competing ideological perspectives can be mobilized between and within these levels of analysis. The ideas which acquire, in the words of Gramsci, the 'solidity of popular beliefs' (Gramsci, 1971: 423) in organizational cultures and practices are explicitly different from the government's rhetoric or political ideology. Furthermore, the occupational cultures of street-level bureaucrats (such as police officers, security staff) forms part of an all-encompassing agency culture which includes other levels, ranging from middle to senior managers. The diverse range of ideas underscoring representations of gender, including masculinity and femininity, belong to street-level bureaucrats, as well as senior, albeit more *streetwise* bureaucrats who network with influential civil servants and powerful government officials. It is at such points that the ambiguities in sexist and heterosexist banter come into play.

At a macro level, policies and initiatives are created step-by-step, reacting to changing societal, economic, political and ideological conditions. Firstly, we look at the impact of structural factors mentioned above, and secondly, the ways in which these impinge on actors at a micro level. If individual Home Secretaries are taken as an example, there is little to unify them in terms of diversity of their individual intellectual standpoints, foibles and idiosyncrasies. Individuals are undoubtedly relevant but there are other important factors such as the influence of political ideology, of which a recent example is the **Third Way**, an idea developed through the influential writings of the social theorist Anthony Giddens (1990, 2007). The 'Third Way' signalled an attempt to move beyond the distinction drawn between the political left and right, and refers to a raft of social democratic reforms and programmes intended to update or modernize government and public sector activities. Martin (2003: 165) provides a nice précis of the situation in the UK:

A fundamental component of New Labour's Third Way is the emphasis on modernizing government. This is sold as a package of reforms and programmes, which can be used to update government and public services, and which works as a means to move beyond the assault on public services that occurred under the Conservatives.

The 'Third Way' is a project that has not been fully realized but it does have
some distinctive features that are closely related to the restructuring of state
forms, in particular Jessop's (2003) account of the ongoing and incomplete
transition from a Keynesian Welfare National State (or KWNS) to the
Schumpeterian Workfare Post-National Regime (or SWPR) (Hay, 1999; Jessop,
2003). This partial transformation has been achieved through a response to
the neo-liberal and New Right-led reforms of the state and government. For
example, the Third Way is partly a continuation of managerialism or the New
Public Management (NPM), including the '3Es' (economy, effectiveness and
efficiency), privatization, quasi-markets, organizational restructuring, down-
sizing and contracting (Clarke and Newman, 2004; Martin, 2003; Newman,
2000). The modernizing imperatives underlying the Third Way are not simply
about adopting these earlier reforms but also the introduction of other value
frameworks to compensate for the worst excesses of the free market ethos
held by neo-liberal conservatives. Politicians belonging to the social democratic left subscribe to social values such as equality of opportunity and social
solidarity evidenced by the Human Rights Act 1998, and in the areas of childcare, schooling and education, social security and income maintenance.

The resources made available to different agencies in different policy areas
vary substantially and the social problems identified as priorities may be counterproductive, largely because economic interests override social interests.
Due to the obsession with 'what gets measured, gets done', criminal justice
agencies will dedicate time and energy to activities that are prioritized by government, and gender-based discrimination and the human rights of employees
is not necessarily one of them. Even if there is a rhetorical commitment, this
does not necessarily become a guiding principle of policy and practice. Also,
as an upshot of neo-led reforms of the public sector, the welfare state no longer
has available the resources and government support needed to deal with the
needs of a diversifying and fragmented society. The subordination of social
policy to the requirements of economic policy can result in the neglect of some
social issues and even in some cases politicians can evade responsibility for
particular policies that their government had devised. Moreover, they can
blame policy failure on other levels by invoking the ideologically determined
distinction between policy and operations as a way of abnegating responsibility. There is also the matter of 'delegated discretion', described by Hill (1993:
11) as 'sinister' in the sense that responsibility is left in the hands of subordinates, where their actions are accepted but will not be publicly condoned.

Further down the organizational hierarchy the codified statements issued
by policy-makers and legislators are not necessarily translated into practice,
highlighting the difference between policy as it is written and policy in action.

The ideological perspectives which characterize the relationship existing
between the Home Office, Ministry of Justice and powerful criminal justice

policy-making bodies such as ACPO, NAPO and APO also impact on relations between other levels of the criminal justice policy-making machinery. Due to its 'elasticity', ideology can accommodate conflict, inconsistencies and contradictions, and yet still be bound by a coherent logic (Hewitt, 1992: 44–5). The divergent forces at work at macro, meso and micro levels may therefore meet. The government's ideology and rhetoric interacts with the attitudes and popular beliefs which exist in other social organizations and among other social groups. If individual views and the perspectives of culture collectivities alone are considered to be important, then there is little in the way of continuity. If they are interpreted as the outcome of individuals and groups giving their 'spontaneous consent ... to ... the general direction imposed on social life by the dominant fundamental groups' (Gramsci, 1971: 12) that is an entirely different narrative.

In a society in which all things are equal the likelihood of explicitly sexist statements in the mission statement of either the Home Office or any agency is, if not unthinkable, certainly very unlikely. The Human Rights Act and **Gender Equality Duty**, for example, codify a commitment to equality and opportunity where diversity is celebrated. The impact of such seemingly unambiguous statements on the criminal justice system and wider society is less obvious. The criminal justice system is diffuse and macro ideologies interact with operational ideologies, which is the point where an organizational culture comes into prominence. There is no single and unified outlook, say in the police culture, but at this level street-level bureaucrats do attempt to simplify a complex environment. Representations of particular hegemonic masculinity are a useful tool to help practitioners minimize occupational and environmental uncertainty. It is under these conditions that gender stereotypes sustain sexist beliefs, thoughts and, occasionally, deeds. This occurs at various levels where ambiguous 'popular convictions' become institutionalized in such a way that even though policy statements may purportedly cancel out such bias, in effect they become an unwitting feature of policy and practice. The observations Macpherson (1999) made about institutional racism, we feel, are potentially germane to enrich our understanding of gendered inequalities affecting criminal justice workers. To quote Macpherson (1999: para. 6.34), institutional racism:

> ... is the collective failure of an organisation to provide an appropriate and professional service to people because of their colour, culture or ethnic origin. It can be seen or detected in processes, attitudes and behaviour which amount to discrimination through unwitting prejudice, ignorance, thoughtlessness, and racist stereotyping which disadvantage minority ethnic people.

There is insufficient space here to review the strengths and weaknesses of Macpherson's findings and recommendations and the key point we extract from him is the often unwitting nature of prejudice, which indicates that discrimination may be unintentional because it is so deeply ingrained either in the minds of practitioners or in their mundane activities. In some instances it can almost lead to people denying personal responsibility for their attitudes and actions, which are seen as an effect of belonging to a specific organization. This kind of reasoning is almost evident when we consider the heterosexist culture of the police, which in the view of one respondent in Foster et al.'s (2005: 44) study is almost 'inevitable' because of the 'macho external culture in the region'.

Finally, we will briefly look at the impact of legislation on gender equality under the Coalition government, which has occurred since the publication of the first edition of this book.

> The UK may be seen as providing an example of achievement in terms of laws and regulations supporting women's human rights and equality in general. However, the reality for women living in the UK is that there is incomplete reali-sation of these rights and serious attitudinal and behavioural barriers to sub-stantive equality for all women. (Women's Resource Centre, 2013: 7)

These words can be found in a report published by the Women's Resource Centre (2013) which explored the extent to which the Coalition government (2010–15) had made any progress in implementing the United Nations Convention on the Elimination of All Forms of Discrimination Against Women (CEDAW), paying close reference to a number of articles: discrimination against women (Articles 1 and 2), the advancement of women (Article 3), sex role stereotyping (Article 5), political and public life (Articles 7 and 8), and employment and economic (Article 11). The evidence compiled in the report by 42 women's and human rights groups indicates that some progress has been made in terms of achieving equality and human rights, but overall women have not fared well. Matters were made worse by the government committing itself to the abolition of the Human Rights Act 1998. Women have experienced a loss of jobs and income, which is evident from the cuts made across the publicly funded components of the criminal justice system. The spectre of discrimination against women in the labour market means there are limited opportunities for promotion and equal, let alone enhanced, pay.

Articles 1 and 2 relate to discrimination and the Equality Act 2010 has been ineffectual because of a lack of commitment to creating substantive equality for women. As Vivien Hayes, Chief Executive of the Women's Resource Centre put it, 'Evidence in our report raises serious questions about the UK's commitment to women's equality. Austerity is not an excuse for discrimination' (*The Guardian*, 2013). As with legislation more generally, the Equality Act and Public Sector Duty are difficult to uphold and bring about meaningful change. Moreover, the cuts experienced by the Equality and Human Rights Commission, as well as the discussion calling for the abolition of the Public Sector Duty have rendered women vulnerable. Similarly, there is a lack of robust data to assess the extent of women's advancement (Article 3) yet our overview of the gendered nature of employment in the police and prison service indicates this has been limited and that men still dominate the top positions in the government and criminal justice professions (Articles 7 and 8: public life and leadership). The seniority of an employer's status in the labour market equates with higher pay and women remain disadvantaged in terms of employment and economic rights (Article 11), especially as women are concentrated in the public sector where redundancies have been endemic. Chapter 10 investigates sex roles and stereotyping (Article 5), which are enduring features of police and legal cultures. Thus the Coalition government was not fully committed to gender equality, which was articulated explicitly by the Prime Minister, David Cameron, who resisted calls to reinstate 'equality impact statements' to monitor gender and other protected characteristics on the grounds that they were 'bureaucratic nonsense' (*The Guardian*, 2013).

Restating the importance of power

The above analysis has contemplated some of the reasons why men occupy more powerful positions as workers in criminal justice than their female counterparts. It has been shown that effective power maintains inequality between the sexes through the use of ideology. Although legislation has been introduced to improve the status of women, this has largely been ineffective because the government is unwilling to dedicate scarce economic resources towards a gender equality and human rights agenda. Because there is not the political will to drive forward human rights, the rhetoric survives but its material impact is tragically limited as women continue to be paid less and experience various forms of sexualized harassment. Although this analysis is rather negative in tone, the next chapter offers some room for optimism because women may not experience career advancement that parallels that of men but changes have occurred and there is room for further transformation.

Concluding thoughts

In this chapter we have quantified the differences existing between men and women in terms of their representation among different professional groups employed across the criminal justice sector. The pattern is not clear-cut in the sense that while men do tend to be numerically predominant, principally in policing, the prison services and the **judiciary**, they do not outnumber women in all agencies. Despite this, the agencies where there are more men than women are those that exert the most influence on the general tenor of criminal justice policy. The latter point is especially salient with regard to the positions of seniority occupied by men, and the fact that it took until 2007 for the first female Home Secretary to be appointed is just the 'tip of the iceberg' when it comes to gendered inequality. There is far more to gender differences than hard numbers and we concentrated on how gender is played out on a daily basis, claiming that hegemonic masculinity subordinates women through attitudinal and systemic practices. The organizational culture of the police service was used to show how sexist and **heterosexist ideologies** perpetuate structured inequalities that shape the experience of practitioners, both those employed by the state and increasingly the private sector too. It was shown that a cult of masculinity is central to social control where the physical qualities of masculinity are seen to be fundamental prerequisites for a craft that is heavily dependent on the ability to actually deploy, or symbolically demonstrate a capacity for the use of, physical violence. Attempts to reform the functions of employment in criminal justice have not altered this underlying commitment. We then attempted to explain the obdurate features of a sexist orthodoxy with reference to the concept of power. The literature is replete with examples of sexist and heterosexist banter but these attitudes in themselves do not constitute a sufficient explanation of why women are systematically disadvantaged throughout the criminal justice system, hence our allusion to the sociological literature on power. This shows that power operates in hidden ways that are not easy to change, although in line with what we have said about the male offender and male victim there is a pedagogical issue: men must become fully responsibilized and recognize their autonomy as social agents. More than that, governments must not deny their political agency for driving forward agendas for change and, with this thought in mind, the disbanding of the Equal Opportunities Commission is not a particularly inspired or desirable piece of policy-making. The following chapter elaborates this analysis of gendered forms of inequality with an examination of career progression, which is frequently used as an indicator of sexist discrimination. In acknowledging women's potential for transformational change to bring about positive opportunities for career advancement in the context of the criminal justice professions their career aspirations are repeatedly blocked and thwarted.

Summary

- Employment patterns in the criminal justice system for the most part mirror those found throughout the labour force. While there may be more male than female police officers and more female than male probation officers, these quantitative measures tell only part of the story. A more significant factor is the status of male and female professionals, and in more or less all instances men are relatively more powerful and exert a greater influence.

- In addition to describing male dominance across the criminal justice sector the factors underlying this gendered discrimination were investigated. By referring to the police culture thesis we illustrated the pervasive influence of a cult of masculinity on the experiences of both male and female police officers. Evidence suggests that heterosexist and hegemonic masculinities influence the behaviour of both the police service and private security outfits.
- The concept of power was employed to show how hegemonic masculinity is sustained in criminal justice organizations and how it operates against a human rights-based agenda. Power functions at various levels and enables state actors to say one thing but do another. Consequently, legislation and policy statements belonging to the HRA and the CEHR are effectively ignored or subverted. A key point is that gendered inequality is central to the workings of criminal justice agencies and that well-intentioned reforms are seldom as progressive as they seem.

STUDY QUESTIONS

1. Outline the main trends in terms of the distribution of jobs by gender in the criminal justice system.
2. Critically explore the main reasons why the proportion of men and women working in the criminal justice system is important for the study of gender and crime.
3. Assess the relevance of the police culture for understanding the gendered nature of police work.
4. What, if anything, can be done to address gendered forms of discrimination in criminal justice?
5. Evaluate the usefulness of the concept of power for explaining the patterns of gendered discrimination in the criminal justice system.
6. What can a human rights perspective tell us about the experiences of men and women working in the 'crime control industry'?

FURTHER READING

There are not many books which focus exclusively on masculinities in relation to the criminal justice professions. A helpful starting point, written from a feminist perspective, is the work of the Fawcett Commission, which highlights the main issues relating to female – and indirectly male – employees (see, in particular, Fawcett Society (2007) *Women and Justice: Third Annual Review of the Commission on Women and the Criminal Justice System* (Fawcett Society). However, see the relevant chapter in S. Walklate (2004) *Gender, Crime and Criminal Justice*, 2nd edn (Willan). S. Winlow (2001) *Badfellas* (Berg) is an excellent ethnographic study of bouncers and masculinities in the night-time economy. Also see the work of J.W. Messerschmidt (1993) *Masculinities and Crime: Critique and Reconceptualization of Theory* (Rowman & Littlefield) for some comments on gender and the criminal justice professions.

Note

1. As mentioned earlier in the text, the EOC was replaced in 2007 by the Commission for Equality and Human Rights, an all-purpose organization set up to deal with all aspects of inequality and discrimination on the grounds of sex, race, disability, sexual orientation, etc.

10

The Criminal Justice System: A Gendered Site

OVERVIEW

Chapter 10 provides:

- An overview of the broad movement towards developing diversity in society.
- A critical review of the rationale for gender representation in organizations, with particular attention to the business case, the case of difference and social justice.
- An insight into the call for gender diversity within the police service and the legal profession.
- A framework for understanding the gendered nature of organizations through an analysis of Acker's (1990) gendered organization theory.
- An overview of the gendered nature of policing (tasks, identities and culture).
- An overview of the gendered nature of the judiciary (selection processes, Feminist Judgement Project).

KEY TERMS

- cult of masculinity
- feminist judgements
- gender equality
- gender representation
- gendered judiciary
- gendered law
- gendered organizations
- gendered policing
- organizational culture
- organizational diversity
- policewomen
- secret soundings

Introduction

The stark imbalance of men to women in positions of power, as outlined in the previous chapter, confirms the extent to which the field of criminal justice is gendered. The reality is that the administration and delivery of criminal justice remains firmly within the remit of (white) men. We emphasize this as a key and defining feature of the criminal justice system and one that holds much significance for many of the arguments raised within this book thus far. Gender matters significantly to the experiences of those who come into contact with the criminal justice system – both in relation to women and men as offenders and/or victims. It also matters to the way in which criminal justice work is imagined, enacted and experienced by the criminal justice workforce. In the preceding chapter, we outlined the role and work of the voluntary and community sector, together with an appreciation of the increased commercialization of criminal justice work. In this chapter we focus more particularly on the police service and the judiciary to develop our arguments. Not only is there a greater literature to engage with, but we have emphasized the significance of these specific agencies in their gendered interactions with both offenders and victims throughout the book. Exploring the continued male dominance of the police service and the judiciary in particular provide us with a useful framework within which to make sense of our arguments thus far. It also offers us an opportunity to speculate about how we might improve things in the future.

The chapter is divided into two parts. The first part contextualizes the call for greater equality in criminal justice work within a broader narrative calling for greater diversity within organizations more generally. We outline the rationales that have and continue to underpin the drive to recruit more women into work and go on to consider in more detail the narratives that characterize the call for more women to join and progress within the police service and the legal profession. The second part builds on the material presented in Chapter 9 by addressing women's continued lack of progress within criminal justice organizations. The poor retention and progression of women working within policing and the law remains a key cause for concern among policy-makers. It is no longer fair to suggest that the principle of equality is not embedded within workforce policy and agendas. Indeed, as we have already argued, the equalities architecture has grown significantly over recent decades. In making sense of this disjuncture between policy and practice, we draw on the theory of gendered organizations to drive forward our analysis (Acker, 1990, 1992). We outline the way in which criminal justice work is deeply gendered at structural, cultural and individual levels. We reflect on the cultural concept of the 'ideal worker' and develop a more structural account of the way in which the career structure within policing and the law itself acts as an inhibitor to women's progression.

The rationale for gender representation

The need to develop a fairer and more equitable workplace has been the concern of reformers for some time now. Employment equality legislation has expanded considerably since the 1970s to include more groups and to cover more aspects of employment. More than 40 years since the Sex Discrimination Act 1975 came into force in Britain women have made significant inroads in the workplace and are now visible in public life and in areas that were previously closed to them. In the first edition of our book, we noted the appointment of Britain's first female Home Secretary, Jacqui Smith, in 2007 as a much-needed and welcome milestone for women tasked with overseeing issues in criminal justice. Following the appointment of two further governments since then and at the time of writing, the post holder remains female – Theresa May was appointed as Home Secretary both in 2010 and again in 2015. The gender audits provided in the previous chapter also point to an improved picture for the representation of women working in criminal justice overall. Despite such progress, we remind readers that the representation of women in leadership positions across the broader work sector remains disappointingly low. Findings from the annual survey *Sex and Power 2014: Who Runs Britain?* makes for dismal reading and points to the slow pace of change at the top, and in some cases reports on cases of regression in relation to the representation and treatment of women (Centre for Women and Democracy, 2014).

Before we tackle the persistent lack of gender balance within criminal justice work, we explore in brief three key rationales for improving the gender balance within organizations: (1) the *business case*; (2) *making a difference;* and (3) a case *of social justice*. While these narratives are often inextricably linked, it is important to stress here that they begin from different starting points and have different motivational drivers. We then go on to outline the narratives that have shaped the call for more women to join both policing and the law.

The business case

The business case for greater diversity tends to focus on the potential costs and benefits associated with having (or lacking) equality practices; or the potential for benefits from having a diverse workforce (Litvin, 1997; Ozbilgin and Tatli, 2011; Shen et al., 2009; Swann et al., 2004; Urwin et al., 2011; White et al., 2004). Inherent in this is the idea that having a more diverse workforce produces better results and therefore having a workforce that is unbalanced, such as consisting primarily of men, is one that is not realizing its full potential. Former Chair of the Equal Opportunities Commission, Jenny Watson (2007), states:

> We all pay the price when Britain's boardrooms and elected chambers are unrep-resentative. Our democracy and local communities will be stronger if women from different backgrounds are able to enjoy an equal voice. In business, no one can afford to fish in half the talent pool in today's intensely competitive world.

From this perspective there is some specific interest in proving the economic value of gender diversity. Here, unequal opportunities are not only a matter of injustice but become primarily a matter of wasted talent. Developing the principle of equality within a business case is premised on achieving a 'modern' workforce, enabling employers to recruit and retain the best people for the job; maximize the productivity of staff through a commitment to employee well-being; mitigate organizational risks – effective diversity management limits the risk of legal challenges and costly compensatory awards (Government Equalities Office, 2013). The business case has assumed greater prominence in recent years and especially so within a competitive and global workplace. The growth in technological communications has further revolutionized the workplace and has transformed the way in which employers and employees think about work, encouraging 'new', 'creative' and more 'flexible' ways of working. While the introduction of part-time and flexible modes of work were introduced primarily as a response to addressing work/life balance issues for women, the current drive to developing more 'flexible' ways of working is perhaps best conceptualized as an attempt to improve the 'efficiency' of an organization rather than the 'equality' of it – of particular appeal in times of economic crisis and austerity.

Making a difference

The idea that women bring and make a difference to the workforce has also been a key driver in diversity agendas. In claiming greater diversity, this idea rests firmly upon the idea that increasing the number of women in the workforce will lead to a better balance in decision-making, improved policy and democracy. Improvements brought about by the presence of women relates both to their capacity to draw attention to the 'woman question', exposing the male bias inherent in existing frameworks, but also to the idea that women bring with them 'alternative' ways of working (Bartlett, 1990; Graycar and Morgan, 2002). Inherent within this position is the idea that there are basic differences between the sexes. As a result, they essentially define a dichotomous model of behaviour in which 'feminine' behaviour is posited against 'masculine'. The origins of the difference-based justice arguments can be found in the work of Carol Gilligan (1982), whose work centres on the idea that women are more likely than men to bring with them an 'ethic of care' in their interactions with others. The assumption here is that women will bring with them a 'different' and 'improved' approach to the workforce. On this issue, we state our position at the outset.

While it may seem counter-intuitive for those of us seeking better gender repre-sentation to take issue with such a position, in presenting the considerable body of data that suggests positive difference, we are mindful of the problematic impli-cations of such a rationale. The problem here is that it is all too easy to fall into the trap of essentializing the 'feminine' and 'masculine' into single categories, thus failing to acknowledge the diversity that exists between and among women and men. Such studies run the risk of perpetuating many of the myths that have dominated discourses about women and work, further entrenching and sustain-ing the often simplistic and sexist justifications for excluding women's participation in organizations, particularly in leadership roles. It also places an unfair burden on women to bring not only something 'different' to the job but to bring something 'better' – we take up these arguments later in the chapter.

Social justice

Also known as the 'moral' perspective, and in line with the ethos of this book, gender equality here is related to fundamental notions about the quality of **social justice**, human rights and the nature of democracy. With women's right to participate in work freely and without discrimination established clearly within human rights law, achieving a gender balance in a democracy is concep-tualized as an important way to improve the quality of society with the viewpoints of different groups taken into account. Motivations based on social justice have particular resonance for a criminal justice context. Given that the business of criminal justice professionals is the administration and delivery of justice and fairness, it follows that if those working in the criminal justice sys-tem were more representative of society as a whole, the criminal justice system would have a greater chance of securing greater fairness for all – offenders, victims and practitioners alike. As former Lord Chancellor Falconer notes, con-fidence in justice rests too on confidence in those dispensing justice and justice cannot be done unless it carries broad support.

The call for more women in policing

While changes brought about by equalities policy and legislation has done much to improve the position of women in policing, a number of commentators have argued that women's entry and progression within policing has often been trig-gered by a 'crisis' (Brown, 2007; Natarajan, 2008; Prenzler and Sinclair, 2013; Silvestri and Paul, 2015). In their analysis of women and police leadership,

Silvestri and Paul (2015) note that the race to appoint a new London Metropolitan Police Commissioner in September 2011 was underpinned by much media speculation about the possible appointment of a woman chief to address the 'crisis in policing' brought about by various corruption scandals at the time. They also cite the appointment of South Africa's first female police chief, Mangwashi Victoria Phiyega, in 2012, as firmly located within such a discourse of 'crisis', being hailed as 'South Africa's hope, the saviour of the nation's corruption-riddled, scandal-plagued police service' (*The Guardian*, 13 June 2012). In moments of crisis, Heidensohn (1992) argues that the police service often turns to women as 'a desperate remedy' to offset staffing shortages, avert criticism, as an antidote to corruption, or symbolically to demonstrate a softer side to policing. Given the ongoing 'crises' faced by the police service, the influence of such 'crisis'-based discourse continues to hold much resonance for contemporary calls to recruit more women into policing, particularly into leadership roles.

The idea that women can bring greater legitimacy to the police organization in such times rests principally on the premise that policewomen have 'different' and 'improved' styles of working than their male counterparts. Indeed, the idea that women (and diversity more broadly) make a positive difference to the work of policing has become a key feature of both academic and official discourse. A joint report by ACPO, APA and the Home Office entitled *Equality, Diversity and Human Rights Strategy for the Police Service* (2010) recently reported on a number of gains to be made from employing a more diverse police workforce. Drawing on both 'external' impacts with communities and 'internal' impacts with organizational members, the report outlines the capacity to achieve: a broader range of information for decision-making and a wider range of possible solutions; a willingness to challenge established ways of thinking and consider new options; improvements in the overall quality of the team; better staff management, leading to improvements in staff satisfaction; a reduction in the number of employees leaving the service, and fewer grievances and complaints; and better relationships with the community, resulting in a more effective service and better quality services, leading to increased public confidence.

Academic research suggests that in an era where the emphasis on service in policing has become paramount, women may have a positive impact on shifting policing philosophy away from a crime-control approach to a more community and citizen-focused approach. Women officers demonstrate a strong 'service-oriented' commitment to policing, emphasizing communication, familiarity and the building of trust and rapport with communities (Brown and Woolfenden, 2011; Brown et al., 2009; Davies and Thomas, 2003; Fleming and McLaughlin, 2010; Heidensohn, 1992; Miller, 1999; Patten Report, 1999). In relation to their enactment of everyday practices, specifically, interacting with potential or actual perpetrators of crime, research shows that, when compared to men, women police appear to be less 'trigger happy' and much less likely to use deadly force, utilize threats, physical restraint, force and arrest (Brown and Langan, 2001;

McElvain and Kposowa, 2008; Rabe-Hemp, 2008; Schuck and Rabe-Hemp, 2005). In a study of conflict management, Braithwaite and Brewer (1998) found that male officers were twice as likely as female officers to engage in threatening behaviour and physical contact with members of the public, which in turn elicited greater resistance and aggression. Such findings appear to provide explanations for evidence which demonstrates that women are less likely to abuse their power and attract complaints and allegations of misconduct and corruption (Corsianos, 2011; Fleming and Lafferty, 2003; Lonsway et al., 2002).

Positive outcomes in relation to policewomen's enactments of police practices can also be found in relation to their interactions with victims of crime, particularly those who have experienced sexual offences and domestic violence. Research by Brown and King (1998), Page (2007) and Schuller and Stewart (2000) found that women police officers are more likely to believe victims, attribute less blame to the victim and be less accepting of rape myths than their male counterparts. Research also suggests that women officers bring a high level of empathy in serving the needs of women and children, especially those who have been subject to violent or sexual abuse (Rabe-Hemp, 2008, 2009; Sun, 2007). Such findings are echoed in a review of global policing which has emphasized the positive effects of women for police conduct and police–community interactions, in the management and de-escalation of conflict situations and in the support for victims of crime (Brown, 2012).

Academic research also emphasizes the considerable gains to be made through women's presence on the internal dynamics of policing. In relation to women working in police leadership, research has emphasized women's greater association with adopting a transformative leadership style, with some commentators theorizing that the employment of more senior policewomen will lead to new forms of cooperative, transformative management and leadership (Brown, 2003; Dick et al., 2013; Heidensohn, 1992; Rabe-Hemp, 2008; Silvestri, 2003, 2007; Silvestri et al., 2013; Whittred, 2008). The benefits of such a style have been emphasized by a number of police commentators, who argue that the use of participatory transformative leadership styles is more likely to bring about successful long-term change in policing and move the service in line with a greater 'ethical' and 'quality of service' culture (Adlam and Villiers, 2003; Casey and Mitchell, 2007; College of Policing, 2015; Densten, 1999; Dobby et al., 2004; Hassell and Brandl, 2009; Marks and Fleming, 2004; Neyroud, 2011; Villiers, 2003; Wood et al., 2008).

In short, the idea that women make a 'difference' to the work of policing has been a principal driver in the rationale to recruit women. Indeed, this rationale of *difference* is increasingly being drawn upon as evidence in the *business case* for their greater recruitment, integration and promotion. Not only is it evidence of a 'modern' workforce, but an unwritten yet embedded expectation is that, through their presence, women will enable the police service to better mitigate organizational challenges and risks encountered.

The call for more women in law

There is also a considerable body of academic scholarship that suggests that women make a difference to law (Allen and Wall, 1987; Boyd et al., 2010; Choi et al., 2011; Collins et al., 2010; Cox and Miles, 2008; Feenan, 2008; Kenney, 2008, 2013; McCall, 2008; McCall and McCall, 2007; Martin and Pyle, 2005; Peresie, 2005; Segal, 2000; Songer and Crews-Meyer, 2000). In her analysis of gender and the judiciary, Kenney (2013: 41) argues that the scholarly evidence suggests that researchers have assumed women judges are more likely to be feminist, noting that it is assumed they will not only be more inclined to mediate solutions and raise women's issues in speeches but that they will also be:

- more concerned with children and better at juvenile justice
- pro-plaintiff in sex-discrimination cases
- pro-choice in abortion cases
- pro-women in divorce cases
- pro-plaintiff in family and medical leave cases.

Yet in her comprehensive review of the literature across a number of jurisdictions, she argues that the overall findings are mixed and inconclusive. Those studies that do indicate difference argue that women offer alternative and positive improvements to the quality of justice dispensed (Goldman, 1979; Grant and Smith, 1991; McGlynn, 1998; Menkel-Meadow, 1986). The basis of such a claim is that women bring a 'new dimension of justice' (Goldman, 1979: 494) to the bench, namely that women 'enhance the likelihood that a certain perspective (the symbolically female one) is brought to bear' (Grant and Smith, 1991: 73). This line of argument suggests that women might practise law differently from their male counterparts. Ultimately, confrontational adversarial processes might give way to more mediational forms of dispute resolution (Menkel-Meadow, 1985, 1987, 1988; Rifkin, 1984). Bartlett (1990: 863) supports this idea by noting that women approach the reasoning process differently from men, resisting universal principles and generalizations, approaching 'problems not as dichotomised conflicts, but as dilemmas with multiple perspectives, contradictions and inconsistencies'. While much of the research focused on difference rests on the outcome of judicial decision-making in relation to judgements made, Feenan (2008: 493) argues for a much more nuanced understanding of the 'concepts, pathways to and practices of the judge' when measuring the concept of difference.

Demonstrating and proposing such 'difference' remains a contested issue and a considerable source of tension for scholars, particularly for those seeking to improve the representation of women. Malleson (2003: 1) warns of the perils of such difference-based approaches, noting that they are 'theoretically weak, empirically questionable and strategically dangerous'. She challenges the idea that women bring with them a 'feminine voice' and suggests that this has more to do with the nature of work that women judges tend to be given and their career profiles in general than with an expression of their biology. Women judges are, for example, more likely than men to have worked in areas such as family law and employment law where issues of discrimination are more familiar and which tend for the most part to use less aggressive and adversarial techniques. As a result, she argues:

> It has become commonplace for commentators on women in the legal profession to argue that the greater presence of women will bring out a reorientation of the legal system away from formalism, objectivity, universalism and adversarial methods of conflict solving towards the subjective needs to individuals and a greater use of alternative dispute resolution such as mediation. (Malleson, 2003: 3)

Sceptical and critical of the assumption that more women will lead to an improved delivery of justice, Malleson (2003: 8) reviews a number of international studies on the relationship between sentencing decisions and gender. Overall, she concludes that there is no clear or consistent difference between men and women on the bench, but rather that the research is 'contradictory and inconclusive'. Indeed, she notes some instances where women were more likely to impose a custodial sentence on women than their male counterparts (Steffensmeier and Herbert, 1999, and Gruhl et al., 1981, cited in Malleson, 2003: 6).

The reluctance to drive forward the idea that women might bring something different to the administration of law goes beyond the potentially distorting essentialist arguments raised above and rests on a more serious issue that may see women legitimately excluded from taking their place in law. The dangers of presenting women's approaches as 'different' from men on the bench are emphasized by Baroness Brenda Hale, a keen advocate of gender equality in law, when she notes that any claim that women look at things differently from men would be partly inaccurate in many cases and would also make women appear less qualified to be judges (Hale, 2001: 13).

Here, Hale (2001) is referring to the fundamental concept of judicial impartiality. The judicial oath requires that judges do justice to all manner of people without 'fear or favour, affection or ill-will'. If a **judge** was seen to be taking a more favourable or empathetic view of women's perspectives, values and interests, this would raise serious questions about their capacity for upholding the principle of impartiality. While this argument should not hold much weight, given that judicial partiality is commonplace today among male judges (Malleson, 2003), it is a powerful argument and one that will easily jeopardize women's attempts to join the judicial elite.

While we concur with scholars who exercise caution over such difference-based approaches, recent work carried out by the various **Feminist Judgement Projects** in Australia, Canada, the USA and the UK make it difficult to ignore such a position. In these projects, academic and feminist lawyers were invited to rewrite selected legal decisions, imagining they were a feminist judge sitting on the court alongside the original judges, and writing the judgement a feminist judge might have written – see Hunter et al. (2010) for a comprehensive overview of 23 judgements. While many of the feminist judgements argue for different results, others reach the same conclusions but for different reasons, highlighting details of women's lives and raising arguments that the courts overlooked. In some cases, they reveal different feminist views on a particular issue. The important point to stress here is that all of the decisions reached could have been legitimately reached within the existing framework of law. Hunter (2015:131) reminds us that such feminist judging does not:

> [s]imply involve deciding for the woman (especially when there are women on both sides, or no women in the case), nor does it constitute a singular programme. It is informed by feminist theories and an understanding of gender experience, but this may result in a range of approaches, including noticing the gender implications of apparently neutral rules and practices, challenging gender bias in legal doctrine and judicial reasoning, or promoting substantive equality ... A feminist understanding of the issues may inform the characterization of the facts, the interpretation of statute and precedent, the development of doctrine, and/or the exercise of discretion.

Despite the strength of such 'difference'-based arguments, Kenney (2013) has argued that the drive for greater gender representation within the UK has not been based on this, nor has it been located in feminist grassroots mobilization or any surge of public awareness of gender inequality (as it was in the USA and Canada). Rather, she argues that feminist scholars in the UK seized upon various opportunities that presented themselves during the New Labour government (1997–2010) with its commitment to modernization. She argues that feminists were able to capitalize on several trends that had little to do with gender, including:

- changes in the Labour party's philosophy toward courts and law
- a decline in public confidence in the courts
- an increased recognition that the role of the Lord Chancellor in appointment was problematic.
- Several decades worth of momentum of effort to reform the judiciary. (Kenney, 2013: 88)

We go on to explore some of the concern around the judicial appointments system later in the chapter. For now we emphasize the ways in which feminists ably capitalized on New Labour's concerns about judicial power to introduce discussion about women and representation and to persuade well-placed government officials and policy-makers of the need to recruit more women judges 'not so much for gender equality in itself, but because gender equality signalled a modern judiciary' (ibid.). Despite characterizing such actions as instrumental in putting gender on the agenda, Kenney (2013) maintains that while attaching the issue of gender equality to modernization may have been enough to eliminate the largest obstacles for women in the judicial appointments process, it has been insufficient to generate a deeper commitment to gender equality, which is necessary to move women from token to parity.

To sum up briefly, the cumulative and resounding message of many of the studies cited above is that women may be engaged in the project of delivering criminal justice in a distinctly different way from their male counterparts. They also lend further support to the idea that increasing the number of women working in the police and in law may do much to transform and improve the workings of the criminal justice system. This rationale of *difference* is increasingly being drawn upon as evidence in the *business case* for their greater recruitment, integration and promotion. We see this as a risky and misguided strategy and one which will ultimately undermine the key basis upon which we call for greater representation of women – that is, as a human right. In making our **plea** for a better gender balance, it is not simply suggested that an increase in the number of women in criminal justice work (indeed in any organization) will result in organizational change – we do not believe this to be the case. We do, however, contend that through being present – by 'being there' – women may bring new and different perspectives on employment issues and so may become catalysts for change within their organization (Colgan and Ledwith, 1996). More women working as criminal justice professionals will not automatically lead to instances of asking the 'woman question', but a better gender balance may present more opportunities to ask. We believe that increased gender representation will have a powerful effect on both the lives of workers and on those who come into contact with criminal justice agencies. The positive accounts of women's engagement with criminal justice work noted above offer considerable opportunities for building greater trust, confidence and, ultimately, greater consent and legitimacy in the criminal justice system. That said, we support the idea of more women in criminal justice work as a matter of **social justice**. The rationale for the equal participation of women and men in the criminal justice system should not be based on women's potential contributions as women, but rather that their presence be viewed as an inherent and essential feature of a democratic society. It is inherently unfair that men enjoy a near monopoly of power in criminal justice work. As Hale (2001: 18) reminds us, in a democratic society it is wrong in principle that such authority is wielded by such an unrepresentative group.

With the rationale for greater gender balance now firmly established, we turn our attention to exploring why, despite numerous attempts to introduce equality, gender balance continues to be an unattainable goal for criminal justice organizations. In developing our analysis of criminal justice work, we begin with a brief outline of the theory of gendered organizations (Acker, 1990).

The gendered organization

In order to understand the gendered nature of criminal justice work and work-ers, we branch out into the field of organization studies. Out of a growing dialogue between feminist theory and organization theory, a concern with the way in which organizations are themselves gendered has emerged (Acker, 1990, 1992; Baron and Davis-Blake, 1986; Bielby and Baron, 1986; Boyd et al., 1991; Cockburn, 1991; Ferguson, 1984; Hearn and Parkin, 1987; Mills and Tancred-Sheriff, 1992; Reskin and Hartman, 1986). This work demonstrates the systematic attempts to theorize the processes through which organiza-tions and occupations are gendered at both institutional and individual levels. In her influential paper 'Hierarchies, jobs, bodies: A theory of gen-dered organisations', Acker (1990) argues that organizations are arenas in which both gender and sexuality have been obscured through gender-neutral, asexual discourses, concealing the embodied elements of work. As a result, job positions and management hierarchies assume there is a universal, disembod-ied worker. One of the key features of this approach is that it provides an understanding of the ways in which gender divisions are actively created and sustained in the processes of organizational life. Her approach emphasizes that men and women encounter gender meanings, relationships and identities which are embedded in the social setting itself, as part and parcel of the roles and scripts deemed appropriate for that setting. Hence gender is defined here as a contextually situated process and is conceived as an emergent property of social situations rather than as an individual characteristic. Instead of a char-acteristic that people have, gender is something that individuals *do* with their behaviour and organizations *do* through the gendering processes and struc-tures. Such gendering processes mean that:

> [a]dvantage and disadvantage, exploitation and control, action and emotion, meaning and identity, are patterned through and in terms of a distinction between male and female, feminine and masculine. (Acker, 1990: 146)

Through the creation of symbols and images that explain and justify gender divisions, organizations further perpetuate and sustain the gendered order. Here interactions between individuals are crucial as they enact dominance and subordination and create alliances and exclusions; images here are constructed and confirmed. In so doing, individuals consciously construct their own understandings of the organization's gendered structures of work and hence provide the appropriate gender response, in terms of behaviours and attitudes (Acker, 1992: 252–3). This may, for example, include the creation of the correct gendered persona with roles and scripts deemed appropriate for that setting (Hall, 1993). Consisting of both a cognitive element (inferences that permit understanding and comprehension) and a behavioural element (activated performances) in a particular social setting, the concept of scripts describes a 'predetermined, stereotyped sequence of actions that defines a well known situation' (Schank and Abelson, 1977, cited in Hall, 1993: 457). It is through being organizational members that workers inhabit a world of shared meanings, of shared rituals, symbols, languages, practices, rationales and values. In turn, these shared meanings easily translate into scripts that workers draw on in their day-to-day work and interactions. For Acker, the bureaucratic organization has a **'gendered substructure'**, that is, the social practices that are generally understood to constitute an 'organization' rest on certain gendered processes and assumptions. In defining this substructure, she notes:

> The gendered substructure lies in the spatial and temporal arrangements of work, in the rules prescribing workplace behaviour and in the relations linking work places to living places. These practices and relations, encoded in arrangements and rules, are supported by assumptions that work is separate from the rest of life and that it has the first claim on the worker. (Acker, 1992: 255)

It is within this gendered substructure that the 'ideal worker' is routinely constructed and reproduced. Here, Acker is arguing that organizational designs and established norms are far closer to men's lives and assumptions made about men than to women's lives and the assumptions made about women. It is men's bodies, men's sexuality and men's relationships to procreation and production that are subsumed in the image of the disembodied worker. We draw on Acker's ideas below to explore some of the ways in which ideas about femininity and masculinity are embedded in the construction of the 'ideal' worker and in the organizational arrangements that govern a career in policing and law.

Gendered policing

The police organization is a powerful site where symbols, images and forms of consciousness that explicate and justify gender divisions are created and sustained. To suggest that the nature and substance of police work and identity are characterized by a 'cult of masculinity' (Fielding, 1994) remains uncontested within the police literature. In a more recent review of the police culture, Loftus (2010) reaffirms the centrality of 'masculinity' as an enduring aspect of the police culture in the twenty-first century. Other commentators have extended this analysis of gender to incorporate a broader appreciation of 'masculinities' within policing. Silvestri (2003, 2007), for example, outlines the significance of the 'smart macho' culture in an analysis of masculinity within police leadership, and Jones (2014) emphasizes the multiplicity of masculinities in his work on exposing the heterosexist nature of policing.

In thinking about the construction of the 'ideal' police officer, research signifies the importance that rank-and-file officers attach to strength, physicality and the capacity to use legitimate force (Heidensohn, 1992). Studies on women in police leadership also point to 'idealized' constructions of workers. Here the police leader is a 'tough and forceful leader, symbolized by aggressive, competitive and performance traits' (Silvestri, 2007: 49). Across the rank structure, then, police officers are engaged in a number of ways in performing gendered scripts associated with masculinities. Given the emphasis placed on these attributes, female police officers are often made to feel uneasy and as 'outsiders' to the main task of policing. Research has emphasized the considerable resistance to their presence, in which they are not fully accepted by their male colleagues and continue to be subject to sexual harassment, discrimination and differential deployment (Brown and Heidensohn, 2000; Brown et al., 2014; Dick et al., 2013; Hassell and Brandl, 2009; Martin and Jurik, 2007).

A study by Foster et al. (2005) documents widespread sexism in the British police. It delineates the calamitous consequences of this sexism for the future of policing a diverse society. The research was primarily interested in the impact of the Macpherson (1999) inquiry on race and policing, although this was situated in the context of wider forms of discrimination, such as those experienced by women and LGBT groups. The research revealed that toleration of racism, especially prejudicial banter in the 'canteen', had declined post-Macpherson (1999), whereas sexist and homophobic attitudes and beliefs were more likely to go unchallenged. Changes in these areas were superficial, and while officers were anxious about potential disciplinary action being taken against their racism, this did not apply so readily to heterosexist talk. It was found that derogatory attitudes and beliefs about women and gay men and women were not confined to the rank and file and that some senior police officers also articulated or indirectly and implicitly sanctioned these perceptions. Westmarland (2001) echoes the above findings, although there are some novel twists and turns in her ethnographic work, based on unprecedented access to frontline operational police work. It remains a compelling study, which revisits the police culture literature in light of traditional concepts of male and female. More than reproducing plentiful evidence reinforcing what is already known about the behaviour of men at work, Westmarland scrutinized other aspects of police work, such as ideals about professionalism and competence, where there is evidence showing that policing is still perceived to be an essentially male activity.

Although policing has undergone something of a transformation in relation to some activities, findings from the recent Independent Police Commission on *Policing for a Better Britain* (2013: 14) reveals that 24 per cent of women reported experiencing harassment on the grounds of gender, with a further 11 per cent related to pregnancy or maternity issues. The recent high-profile employment tribunal case of PC Carol Howard in 2014, which found discrimination against her as a black woman and further victimization for complaining about that discrimination, is further evidence that not all is as equal as we might have anticipated. PC Carol Howard was a firearms officer and the 'face' of the Olympics 2012: hailed as a symbol of change, not only is she a black woman but, as a firearms officer, her presence was used as a sign of a transformed police service in which women had broken the bar on entry into such specialisms. While acknowledging greater gender equality for women in policing, Westmarland's (2001) study reminds us of the sacrosanct nature of specialisms such as firearms, which remains under the control of male officers. As a result, women are enabled to participate in policing but in many respects remain on the 'outside' of some of its core functions.

The importance of historical insight is of considerable value here. We remind readers that from the very outset, women have been positioned 'outside' the police career. At the turn of the century, women began their career in a separate women's police service. As the century progressed, the appointment of women police in England and Wales continued on a piecemeal basis and women moved from a separate women's sphere to integration into mainstream policing in 1973. Histories document considerable resistance towards their entry and progression within policing, which was vigorously fought, resisted and undermined on legal, organizational, informal and interpersonal levels (Carrier, 1988; Martin, 1980; Miller, 1999; Schulz, 1995; Segrave, 1995). And, though the police service has gone some way to addressing the inequalities within its ranks, the evidence presented here suggests that it still has some way to go in addressing the fundamental cultural belief that the function of crime control is one that rests ultimately with men. The rationale to recruit more policewomen on the grounds that they bring something 'different' to the role is also increasingly being positioned alongside the narrative of their contributions to policing violence against women. Once again, we remind readers that it was within this sphere of work that policewomen were located at the beginning of the twentieth century. And while we do not deny that women may play a central role in the policing of violence against women, we argue that using this as a rationale for their greater representation risks undoing many of the considerable gains that women have made thus far. It may also serve to reinforce the separation of such crimes from the 'core' business of policing. Moreover, it overlooks and denies the considerable contribution that men may make to the policing of violence against women.

A focus on unpacking the 'temporal' arrangements of work within policing also tells us much about the 'gendered substructure' within the police organization. Notwithstanding the recent changes enabling direct entry to the rank of superintendent (Winsor Review, 2012) and the recently implemented 'fast track' career options for identified officers, the police organization in England and Wales remains attached to the idea of a strict linear organizational career model, with progression achieved through climbing a highly structured career ladder through a series of ranks. At first glance the police service appears to offer its members a gender-neutral career ladder within which to advance, with all officers, male and female, beginning their careers at the bottom of the organization. On closer inspection, however, it becomes clear that the ideology of internal recruitment, together with a rank-governed progression system, has particularly damning consequences for women wanting to progress. With the majority of police officers congregating at the bottom of the police structure, it should come as no surprise that the chances of promotion in such an organization become severely limited (Bayley, 1994). While female and male officers both experience the effects of such a system, by its very nature, there is a high degree of predictability about male promotion prospects built into a linear organizational career structure (Halford et al., 1997).

Our focus on the temporal dimension has particular relevance for wider contemporary debates about women, work and rights. The issue of how best to achieve an improved work–life balance is a key part of the human rights agenda for improving the position of women in employment. Article 11 (2c) of CEDAW states:

> In order to prevent discrimination against women on the grounds of marriage or maternity and to ensure their effective right to work, States Parties shall take appropriate measures to: (c) encourage the provision of the necessary supporting social services to enable parents to combine family obligations with work responsibilities and participation in public life, in particular through promoting the establishment and development of a network of childcare facilities.

Developing a better work–life balance has also been at the forefront of broader governmental thinking and policy development for some time now and the inclusion and movement towards more flexible working practices incorporating an improved work–life balance continues to be hailed as indicative of organizations that are serious about developing and managing diversity successfully within their organizations (Tipping et al., 2012). The positive effects of alternative working practices are wide and far-reaching and raise important questions for the career progression of women in criminal justice occupations. Since 1990, the police service has taken an active role in trying to improve the recruitment and retention of women police officers. In line with other organizations, it has been working towards developing part-time and flexible working practices for its employees. In assessing the success of such structural changes, commentators have emphasized the difficulties of translating policy to practice, with a number of studies pointing to a poor uptake and resistance to developing alternative ways of working (Davies, 1998; HMIC, 1995; Laverick and Cain, 2014; Silvestri, forthcoming; Tuffin and Baladi, 2001). The police career is premised on an 'ideal' type of worker in which the possession of a 'full-time, long and uninterrupted career profile' reigns (Silvestri, 2003, 2006). In an increasingly competitive organizational culture, visibly working long hours has come to be an indicator of commitment and stamina, and 'time-serving' remains a fundamental resource for building the identity necessary of the police leader (Silvestri, 2003). Utilizing alternative working patterns do not count towards the profile of earning or demonstrating either credibility or commitment. On the contrary, the police career is one that tends to define the career as at odds with domestic responsibilities. If women in policing choose to limit their working hours or opt to undertake them in an alternative configuration, they do so in the knowledge that they may also be limiting their career opportunities (Adams, 2001; Silvestri, 2003; Stone et al., 1994; Whittred, 2008). Writing in 2000, the then President of the **British Association of Women Police (BAWP)**, Julie Spence, summed up these fears well, stating that 'part-time work continues to be characterized by a mentality that constructs those who assume flexible forms of working as part-able and part-committed' (cited in Jenkins, 2000: 23). Over a decade later, findings from the Independent Police Commission on *Policing for a Better Britain* (2013) also give further cause for concern over the retention of women police, with four in 10 women having considered leaving the force because of low morale and concerns regarding flexible working and childcare considerations.

Gendered judiciary

Although Parliament outlawed the exclusion of women from the legal profession in 1919, the Lord Chancellor did not appoint the first woman English High Court judge, Elizabeth Lane, until 1965. Despite a rapid increase in the number of women in the legal profession, the next 20 years saw only five more women added to the High Court bench, leading Kenney (2013: 97) to argue that composition of the judiciary does not evolve in line with the pool of candidates.

Despite recent increases in the proportion of women, the judiciary remains a male-dominated institution in many respects. Although on the face of it women working in law have made real progress and some perceived glass ceilings are being shattered, there are a number of areas which give cause for concern. In particular, as the previous chapter has shown, women tend to remain clustered at the lower levels of the legal profession. Britain is not alone here. In their overview of 19 countries, Malleson and Russell (2006) demonstrate that achieving diversity within the judiciary has become a key concern of legal systems across the world. Women working as solicitors and **barristers** continue to experience deeply entrenched cultural, structural and practical barriers to career progression with large numbers of them leaving the profession (Fawcett Society, 2006; Mack and Roach Anleu, 2012).

Examining the selection procedure of an organization tells us much about the gendered patterning of jobs, tasks and hierarchies. In this section we explore some of the structural issues that impact on the retention and progression of women within law. There has been considerable criticism directed at the way in which judges are appointed. Before 2006, there were no advertisements for judicial office. Applications were subject to being invited to the post. Selection processes lacked any clearly defined selection criteria. Rather, the selection process for judges in the High Court involved the Department for Constitutional Affairs gathering information about potential candidates over a period of time by making informal inquiries, seeking personal opinions (known as '**secret soundings**') from leading barristers and judges. It was the role of these 'secret soundings' that proved controversial among legal commentators for their discriminatory impact on women and other under-represented groups wishing to join the ranks of the judiciary (Mack and Roach Anleu, 2012; Malleson, 1999, 2002; Malleson and Banda, 2000; Rackley, 2007). Essentially, the process of secret consultations has meant that being 'well qualified' is not necessarily enough to secure selection for senior rank. Rather, the candidate needs to be 'well known' among the group of judges and senior members of the profession whose personal opinions are sought. Those lawyers outside the so-called 'magic circle' of elite chambers are disadvantaged by the process, as are many lawyers from minority backgrounds, and many women lawyers (particularly those with family responsibilities), given their under-representation at the senior bar (Malleson and Banda, 2000). In this way the secretive and discriminatory nature of the selection process ensured that women were unlikely to have equal access to the promotions process. The continuing need to be 'known' in order to be appointed and the role of social networking in the consultation process were cited as key factors in deterring women lawyers from applying from Silk or Judicial Office (Malleson and Banda, 2000).

We have already pointed to the drivers that led to changes to the system on the appointment of the New Labour government in 1997. It was under the former Lord Chancellor, Lord Falconer, that some of the greatest strides towards achieving **judicial diversity** were introduced. Under his leadership, a number of important changes were proposed, including opportunities of job sharing, career breaks and a mentoring scheme (Falconer, 2005). In 2005 he introduced the judicial diversity programme, expanding these developments by encouraging applications and raising awareness, removing barriers to appointments and meeting the needs of a more diverse judiciary. The Constitutional Reform Act 2005 went on to establish a new and independent body to oversee judicial appointments, the Judicial Appointments Commission (JAC). The judicial appointments system was changed in 2006, replacing the old system of 'secret sounding' described above, and moving towards a system that would ensure judicial appointments be made on merit, with greater fairness and transparency (Rackley, 2007). Some of the main changes introduced include a new, simplified definition of merit, with core qualities and abilities required to make a good judge; a fairer system for filling High Court vacancies, in which all candidates must now apply for vacancies, and short-listed candidates have to participate in face-to-face discussions to explore their qualities and abilities, and references will be sought fairly and openly; a more streamlined and objective application process, in which the length of the old application form has been reduced from over 20 pages to nine; and an improved marketing of vacancies, in which advertising will be better targeted to encourage more people to apply (Rackley, 2007). Describing the new system, JAC Chairman Baroness Usha Prashar noted:

> The days of 'secret soundings' and 'taps on the shoulder' are long gone. Today's judicial applicants will be assessed on who they are, not who they know. (www.judicialappointments.gov.uk)

Since then, there has been further movement in relation to developing greater judicial diversity. An Advisory Panel on Judicial Diversity, chaired by Baroness Neuberger, was appointed in 2009 and reported in 2010, making 53 recommendations for progressing the objective of achieving a more diverse judiciary (Ministry of Justice, 2010). A *Judicial Diversity Taskforce* was subsequently appointed to oversee the implementation of the recommendations, which has since published three annual reports (Ministry of Justice, 2011, 2012, 2013b). In 2013, the Crime and Courts Act introduced a new statutory duty on the Lord Chancellor and the Lord Chief Justice to encourage judicial diversity. And in 2014, a report commissioned by the Shadow Secretary of State for Justice made recommendations as to what a Labour government might have done (were it elected in May 2015) to better enhance the diversity of the judiciary (Hunter, 2015).

While such changes provide a much-needed source of optimism for the future of the judiciary – indeed, application figures for **Queen's Counsel** show that the number of women applying has increased from 15 per cent in 2006 to 19 per cent in 2014/15 (see www.gov.uk/government/news/queens-counsel-in-england-wales-2014–to-2015) – we should remain attentive to Acker's (1992) work on the way in which organizations are gendered. For Acker (1992), gendered processes operate on many levels from the explicit and institutional to the more subtle, cultural forms that are submerged in organizational decisions. They include the way men's influence is embedded in rules and procedures, formal job definition, functional roles and the accumulation of competence, skill and merit. Ideas about femininity and masculinity are embedded in organizational arrangements and the opportunities to accumulate 'merit' are structured along gender lines (Burton, 1992). With 'merit' at the forefront of changes to the judiciary, there is growing concern and cynicism among commentators about the extent to which such changes will benefit women. The extent to which 'merit' is a neutral standard by which to judge applicants to the profession is highlighted by Davis and Williams (2003: 11) when they argue that it is of minimal help as the sole criterion and may mask (conscious or unconscious) bias in decision-making.

In this way 'merit' is seen to contain what Thornton (1996) terms an 'essential subjectivity'. Here, decision-makers have the power to construct what they deem to be meritorious using their own frameworks of understanding. The argument then follows that, given that decision-makers are by and large men, the criteria of merit tend to reflect the attributes and concerns stereotypically seen as 'male'. As Thornton (1996: 33) notes:

> [T]he 'best person' to occupy a position of authority has tended to be unprob-
> lematically defined in masculinist terms that reflect the values of the public
> sphere.

We have already emphasized the 'masculine' cultural ideals that underpin police identities – with women positioned as 'outsiders' to the job of policing. Work on the legal profession echoes this, with scholars pointing to the ways in which constructions of the judge and judicial authority are 'male'. Research has described the constitution of judicial office as 'masculine' and a prevailing construction of the woman judge as subverting the fraternal values of the legal culture (Moran, 2009; Rackley, 2002, 2006; Resnick and Curtis, 2011; Thornton, 1996). Feenan (2008) points to the reproduction and reaffirmation of the image of the male judge through a variety of cultural channels, including the media, film and portraiture. Baroness Hale (2005) has emphasized the ideal of the judge as anonymous, dehumanized, impartial and authoritative as 'intrinsically male'. The male judge then becomes synonymous with the 'authoritative knower' (Thornton, 1996). As a result, women are 'othered' and positioned 'outside' judicial authority. Women judges in Northern Ireland interviewed by Feenan (2008) point to a powerful masculinized culture within the law, describing it as: 'ultra-conservative', 'male-oriented', 'an old boy's network' and 'antagonistic and patronising'. In reflecting on the situation in Australia, Justice Catherine Branson emphasizes a culture of exclusion for women, noting that 'we [women] are made to feel that we are outsiders – not of the mainstream' (cited in Feenan, 2008: 504).

The aim of increasing diversity, then, becomes a much more complex task than simply modifying the appointments process – though we think this a good starting point. We concur with Rackley's (2006: 86) assessment when she asserts that Lord Falconer's belief that there is 'no conflict between merit and diversity, is at best, somewhat optimistic, and, at worse, deliberately naïve'. Without an acknowledgment of the gendered nature of 'merit', it is all too easy to join in with the mantra that assumes that 'all things are equal now'. This approach continues to foster the myth that if women work hard(er) to accumulate 'merit' they will succeed and be rewarded (Silvestri, 2003).

Concluding thoughts

We have demonstrated the powerful way in which the police service and the legal profession systematically discriminate against and achieve social closure for women. Bringing about change in any organization is a difficult and often protracted process (Chan, 1997) and despite a wide range of attempts to increase gender balance throughout the criminal justice system progress towards integration and gender equity has been 'glacially slow' (J. Brown, 1998). The police service and the legal profession have demonstrated much resistance towards any potential modification of their career structures. In this sense, pushing for alternative ways of working may appear a fruitless exercise. On the contrary, questioning existing arrangements presents a radical challenge to criminal justice organizations and its agents. Any strategy that offers the potential to fracture and break down the hierarchical nature and loosen the stronghold that men hold in positions of social control is a project worth pursuing. Unlawful discrimination and harassment within the workplace holds serious implications, not only for those in power, but also for those at the receiving end. To restate our position, unlawful discrimination is an important human rights issue. The values of equality, opportunity, diversity, fairness and balance are at the very heart of delivering good and effective justice. The aim, then, should be to turn these values into tangible differences to the lives of women and men working in criminal justice professions. Whether the criminal justice system will be changed by the presence of more women remains to be seen – we are a long way off from achieving diversity.

We do not believe that change will come about simply with the recruitment of more women in criminal justice. To achieve meaningful change within organizations we need to think beyond the numerical. Such an approach will not impact upon the deep-rooted gendered assumptions that characterize the criminal justice system. By concentrating efforts on how best to improve the number of women in criminal justice work, strategies have been directed at helping women to cope with discriminatory policy and structures. Little if no effort has been directed at critiquing or dismantling those structures that constrain women's progression. Ideas about criminal justice work continue to operate within existing parameters and remain characterized as 'men's work'. With regard to the legal profession, initiatives have not fully confronted the

extent to which familiar yet particular images of the judge and judging continue to infuse and distort current discourses on adjudication (Rackley, 2007).
As a result, the woman judge is characterized as a:

> [S]uspicious interloper or dangerous outsider. Her inescapable deviance from
> the judicial norm disrupts the homogeneity of the bench, revealing the unavoid-
> able, yet largely unacknowledged, gender dimension to traditional understand-
> ings of adjudication. (Rackley, 2007: 76)

The same can be said of the female police leader. Perceived as an 'outsider' to
the project of policing, she remains the 'ultimate oxymoron' (Brown and
Heidensohn, 2000). Heidensohn (1992: 215) sums up men's resistance to
women in criminal justice work as:

> ... emanating from a struggle over the ownership of social control ... it may also
> reflect a deeper concern about who has a right to manage law and order.

The increased presence of more women (and indeed greater representation from
other groups whose background differs from that of the majority) has the potential to bring about change in both the substantive law, the interpretation and the
application of law and may work to secure a radical overhaul of criminal justice
professions more generally. Gender matters, and it matters for both women for
men and for justice (Kenney, 2013). Achieving a greater diversity across the
broad spectrum of criminal justice workers will increase the level of public confidence and legitimacy in those who administrate the delivery of social control
and justice (Dick et al., 2013; Malleson, 2003; Rackley, 2007). It will also move
a step closer to assuring compliance with the spirit of non-discrimination at
work in human rights law. In order to expose and address the gendered
nature of criminal justice, however, we emphasize the immeasurable benefits
of harnessing a greater gender awareness and gender activism among criminal justice agents. This transcends the conventional reliance on women to make
a difference – not any woman will do. Rather, we are pushing for a greater
feminist awareness among criminal justice practitioners. Kenney (2013: 15–16)
defines what we mean here well – we need more feminist judges who:

- ask gender questions (i.e. How might this law or statute affect men and women
  differently?)
- interpret equal protection and discrimination in law within their broader social
  change purposes
- value women's lives and women's work
- question their own stereotypes and predilections
- simply believe in equal justice for all.

We expand her position to include all criminal justice professionals.

Summary

- The imbalance of men to women in positions of power confirms the extent to which the field of criminal justice is gendered – the reality is that the administration and delivery of criminal justice remains firmly within the remit of (white) men.
- Gender matters significantly to the experiences of those who come into contact with the criminal justice system – both in relation to women and men as offenders and/or victims. It also matters to the way in which criminal justice work is imagined, enacted and experienced by the criminal justice workforce.
- The need for greater diversity (and increased gender representation) within organizations is now well established. The rationale within the police service and the legal profession for the appointment of more women tends to be located within the 'business case' or that of 'making a difference' rather than a position of 'social justice'.
- While we provide much evidence to suggest that women *can* and *do* make a difference to the administration of criminal justice (research shows that women make a positive difference to the way in which they undertake policing with those who come into contact with the criminal justice system and a gender-aware judiciary has also been seen to make a difference to sentencing outcomes through the feminist judgement project), we argue that calling for more women through such a rationale is a fundamentally flawed position from which to achieve greater diversity. Rather, we argue that more women should be recruited on the grounds of 'social justice' – that it is a fundamental human right to be able to work free from discrimination.
- We draw on Acker's **gendered organization theory** to explain the gendered nature of criminal justice work, the disjuncture between policy and practice, organizational structures and culture and the ongoing lack of women working in the police service and the legal system. Through such an analysis, we argue that criminal justice work is deeply gendered at structural, cultural and individual levels and operates with a conception of an 'ideal worker'.

STUDY QUESTIONS

1. What are the benefits of a more gender diverse criminal justice workforce – why should we employ more women?

2. In what ways is the police service gendered at structural, cultural and individual levels?

3. Why are there so few senior policewomen?

4. Critically discuss the barriers to progression that women working in the legal profession experience.

5. Outline the problems with adopting the principle of 'merit' to the selection of judges.

6. Outline the possible impact of having social control reside in the hands and minds of men.

7. Are there any rational reasons why the ratio between women and men working in the criminal justice system should not be 50:50?

8. Critically discuss the problems with recruiting more women on the grounds that they bring something 'different' to the work of criminal justice.

FURTHER READING

The journal *Gender, Work and Organisations* provides a good source of related articles on the general nature of gender and organizations. J. Acker (1990) 'Hierarchies, jobs, bodies: A theory of gendered organisations' (*Gender and Society*, 4(2): 139–58) provides an essential starting place for those interested in understanding the gendered nature of organizations.

S.E. Martin and N. Jurik (2007) *Doing Justice, Doing Gender* (Sage) provide an overview of the general gendered nature of criminal justice professions. For those particularly interested in policing, see J. Brown and F. Heidensohn (2000) *Gender and Policing* (Macmillan); F. Heidensohn (1992) *Women in Control: The Role of Women in Law Enforcement* (Oxford University Press); F. Heidensohn (2000) *Sexual Politics and Social Control* (Open University Press); and M. Silvestri (2003) *Women in Charge: Policing, Gender and Leadership* (Willan). Readers should also consult the array of literature covered within P. Dick, M. Silverstri and L. Westmarland (2013) 'Women police: Potential and possibilities for police reform' [in J. Brown (ed.) *The Future of Policing* (Routledge)].

For those interested in women working in the legal profession, see S. Kenney (2013) *Gender and Justice: Why Women in the Judiciary Really Matter* (Routledge) and numerous articles by Kate Malleson and Erika Rackley. For work on the feminist judgement projects, see R. Hunter, C. McGlynn and E. Rackley (eds) (2010) *Feminist Judgements: From Theory to Practice* (Hart) and R. Hunter (2015) 'More than just a different face? Judicial diversity and decision-making' (*Current Legal Problems*, 68(1): 119–40).

11

Conclusions

We have covered a lot of ground in a relatively short space, drawing attention to the continued, if not growing, significance of gender in relation to our understanding of crime, victimization and social control. The book shows the differential experiences and inequitable treatment of men and women as offenders, victims and criminal justice workers. While the discrimination might not always be as obvious as it was in the 1970s, it is still there in increasingly complicated and subtle forms. Criminologists have made major empirical and conceptual advances since the 1960s, when feminist scholars first exposed the institutionalized sexism of academic and administrative criminology. All students of the discipline will nowadays be familiar with, or at least aware of, the contrasting experiences of men and women in the criminal justice system, however superficial that knowledge may be. Also, and quite perversely, gender differences exist in a society that has been committed to a human rights agenda, which presented politicians and policy-makers with a largely unrealized opportunity to treat all citizens equitably, especially in the sense that their freedom and dignity are respected. It is also a chance to create a more equal and just society, where fundamental human rights co-exist with wider economic, social and cultural rights. In reality, none of these opportunities is actually enjoyed by everyone in the criminal justice system or, crucially, in the wider socio-economic context in which it is embedded. Currently there is an apparent tension between internationally recognized declarations and statements about human rights and the UK Conservative government, which by contrast has pledged to repeal the Human Rights Act 1998.

Trying to anticipate what will concern students and scholars of criminology in the future is difficult. At the moment crime is, as always, a popular and interesting topic. An important debate currently taking place focuses on the 'crime drop' that has been happening across the globe for well over a decade. If this trend continues, will this mean the subject matter becomes less relevant and not really worth studying? Our view, addressed in the book, is that the study of criminology will need to expand so it is well positioned to confront new forms of offending behaviour and victimization. As society evolves, new criminal threats and opportunities will emerge and the innovative and creative behaviour of perpetrators of crime and deviance will require more sophisticated responses from policy-makers and practitioners in the field of crime control. Criminology will become even more important for coming to terms with these challenges.

In our final chapter, the convoluted pattern of inequality existing among men and women as offenders, victims and professionals is reviewed, and is followed by some reflection about the future debates relating to gender and crime.

An overview of key debates

This book was organized in a way that has hopefully lent some coherence to a complex set of issues and debates about gender and crime taking place in criminology and criminal justice. The main themes covered included offending behaviour, victimization and criminal justice policy and practice, the latter focusing in particular on employees in the criminal justice sector. Throughout this text we have endeavoured to tap into the tension existing between, on the one hand, the clear divisions that exist between men and women in each of these areas, and, on the other hand, attempts to introduce a framework that recognizes the potential unifying features of difference, which is underpinned by a commitment towards repairing the damage done by divisive ideas and practices. This is where the human rights agenda comes into play. As noted earlier on in this book, our ambition is to take us further than the 'black letter law' approach to human rights, opening up the debate to the wider theoretical and empirical concerns of students of criminology. In line with the relevant conventions and protocols first mentioned in Chapter 2, human rights is all about respecting the freedom, equality and dignity of everyone based on an appreciation of justice. Each and every human being possesses an equal moral status on the grounds that they share in common their humanity. Having said that, as well as these universals, there is also social diversity, for example gender, class, race and ethnicity, which can place pressure on the universal. There is a tension between unifying human qualities while recognizing multiple forms of division and differentiation.

Let us review our attempts to achieve the above aims before moving on to consider the intellectual and practical difficulties confronting scholars in the future.

Historical and theoretical debates on gender and crime

Chapter 2 scrutinized the emergence and impact of feminism on the discipline of criminology from the late 1960s onwards. This body of work critiqued existing criminology because it had either excluded or provided distorted representations of women who offend. More than that, it exposed the often invisible experiences of women who were subjected to male violence. It also accounted for growing interest in women working in the field of criminal justice. On the surface feminist criminology might appear to share a common set of assumptions about the cause of inequality, yet the meaning of feminism is contested, which presents a number of challenges. One concern is that gazing on the female offender leads to the unintended consequence of further control and coercion of women. Another is that feminists have sometimes overlooked intersectionalities, which mean women experience multiple inequalities arising primarily from their class, ethnicity and sexual orientation. These criticisms have not diminished the powerful arguments made by feminists over the course of five decades and they continue to provide an insight into the inequalities impacting on offenders, victims and professionals. It is at this juncture in the book that we elaborated our view that a human rights framework is a useful heuristic to interpret the diverse experiences of women, crime and control. We identified as a way forward the need to analyse connections between local and global concerns and the role of nation states in responding to gender-based injustice and inequalities.

In Chapter 3 we revisited the history books – now easier because of the availability of digital archives – to show how the criminologists are committed to rediscovering and recounting new and different stories about the past. This makes it possible to make sense of the connections between contemporary social problems and the past. This is no easy task because of the methodological dilemmas contemporary scholars confront when interpreting historical material. The important lessons that can be learnt from the past are that men are responsible for most offending and that while women do offend it is to a lesser degree, both in quantitative and qualitative terms. The anticipation that, over time, as women became more equal they would become more criminal has not been supported by historical evidence. For example, recent debates about the 'new' female offender and girl gangs are not in fact new and society has always been preoccupied with deviant and criminal women and girls who pose a threat to norms about respectable conduct. There are also certain myths deeply embedded in our culture about the linkages between female crime and notions of dangerousness and insanity, which show that women and girls are in need of both care and control.

In Chapter 4, which focused on globalization, crime and gender, we argued that there are several drivers in global crime, which create a number of paradoxes in criminal justice policy. For example, it is suggested that the principles of the New Public Management (NPM) and modernization, emphases on victim-centred justice, penal populism and public protection, decline of the rehabilitative ideal, the prioritization of the assessment and management of risk and the commercialization of crime control all have a bearing on the gender and crime debate (Senior et al., 2007). The links are not always obvious and need to be teased out but it is argued that these factors contribute towards the shaping of gendered relations in criminal justice and ultimately wider society. These broad brush developments may perpetuate existing inequalities between men and women, in addition to creating new opportunities for change. It is not our intention to bemoan the current situation without there being some recognition of the scope for making progress towards a more humane society in which there is mutual respect and tolerance, and where gender relations are not based solely on conflict and discrimination. Most crucially, we make our final statement about the relevance of the human rights agenda as an antidote to gendered inequality with reference to a political economy of crime (Reiner, 2007. At the time of writing, the British Prime Minister, David Cameron, indicated that there will be a British Bill of Rights embedded in the constitution. Again, whatever the outcome of these deliberations a rights-based agenda provided opportunities and, paradoxically, obstacles for the offenders, victims and employees all caught up in the criminal justice web.

Out of Control

The female offender

Chapters 2, 3 and 5 scrutinized the experiences of women as offenders, tracing from a historical perspective the status of this actor in criminological inquiry. Historically, the study of crime has been male-centred and a range of sexist assumptions have tainted criminological theorizing and the workings of the criminal justice system. When the female offender is not being ignored she is being pathologized and treated as abnormal and aberrant. Feminist scholars rendered the gendered subject visible, redefining the nature of the discipline and calling for a more nuanced account of crime and disorder where the differential experiences of male and female offenders are made explicit. The key point is that women do not offend as much as men and that their offending behaviour is of a less serious nature. There have periodically been moral panics about female crime, embodied in the form of the 'mean girl', but all reliable sources of information about offending behaviour show clearly that female offending is relatively minor. Despite this the woman offender finds herself in an increasingly punitive environment, demonstrated tellingly by the dramatic increase in the number of women being given custodial sentences and the net-widening that places them under more control in the community. Chapter 5 illustrated in painstaking detail the gender-specific problems experienced by female inmates in an environment designed with men in mind, drawing attention to the dehumanizing practices in contemporary penal policy. The deleterious effects of prison life on women's psychological and physical health, their unsettled as opposed to resettled futures on release from custody, and the indirect harm caused to children deprived of the guardianship of their mothers contribute towards a denial of their human rights. We argued that while the National Offender Management Service more or less complies with the Human Rights Act 1998, there are limitations to the black letter law approach inasmuch as human rights defined more widely are not appreciated by all people in society and that the indignities faced by women in prison are inconsistent with human rights principles more generally.

The male offender

Chapter 6 moved on to explore the male offender. Consistent with certain aspects of the feminist critique of criminology, we acknowledge the greater degree of involvement of men in crime. Official statistics and other forms of criminological research show unequivocally that crime, especially violent crime, is more likely to be committed by men and boys than women and girls. The work of the police, courts, probation and probation services all confirm males are more crime prone compared to females. An attempt was also made to consider the contribution of some male criminologists who foreground gender in their respective analyses of criminal behaviour through various adaptations of the concept of masculinity/masculinities, including structural and psychosocial versions. This body of work provides a range of complementary, although not always compatible, explanations of criminality at various levels of analysis, ranging from the individual psyche to structural and global processes. We argued that structural approaches in particular, which draw attention towards marginal working-class and under-class masculinities, show how male offenders experience discriminatory forms of policing, resulting in a denial of their citizenship and human rights. Notably, this approach is consistent with certain variants of **critical criminology** and there is the danger that male offenders are treated as victims of an unjust criminal justice system, which is far from our actual intention. While we recommend that the human rights of unpopular and sometimes undeserving individuals are protected, there is also a need for male (often minority ethnic group) offenders – and some critical criminologists – to recognize that offenders, but especially violent men, inhibit the human rights of others, especially their individual victims and the fearful communities in which they live. Psychosocial approaches which focus on the potential for change in the male subject offer some limited scope for optimism with this aim in mind, although in the last analysis structural and psychic factors restrict the nature of change that can be instigated by individual men.

In Need of Care

Criminology has traditionally been concerned with understanding and responding to offending behaviour and in doing this the victim has been neglected. Nowadays the victim is at the centre of academic and policy debate and in the next part of the book our attention turned towards the victim of crime. Although crime victims were in the past under-studied by criminologists, following two important interventions it is not possible to think about crime without full consideration of this important component of the so-called square of crime formulated by **left realist criminologists** (Lea, 2002). Firstly, there emerged a new field of inquiry, namely victimology, although this perpetuated many of the sexist mythologies associated with criminology, resulting in victim blaming. Secondly, the work of pioneering feminist criminologists highlighted the plight of the female victim, especially women who were victimized by the violence of some men.

The female victim

State-funded and independent research shows that victimization is not distributed evenly among men and women and that women are particularly vulnerable to the worst excesses of male violence, mainly in the private sphere. Evidence reviewed in Chapter 7 also shows that while chivalrous attitudes do exist in the criminal justice system, female victims consistently say that they experience secondary victimization in the form of relatively poor treatment by the police when they report that they are the victims of domestic and sexually motivated violence. The dreadful situation first highlighted by feminist researchers from the 1970s onwards has brought about some changes to police policy and practice, although there is still a long way to go to ensure that there is adequate protection of and care for victims of male violence. In Chapter 7 it was also argued that the victims of domestic violence share much in common with victims of torture, not least because of the coercive control experienced and the repeat/multiple victimization that takes place. Indeed, the main characteristics of the latter are all evident and we suggest that the human rights-based remedies developed to tackle torture are also appropriate for domestic and sexual violence. Above all, both violent men and an unsympathetic or non-responsive criminal justice system need to be called to account for their routine disregard of the fundamental human rights of some of their victims. Thus, male offenders are responsible for most victimization and many of the more serious harms experienced by women are perpetrated by men, but this does not mean that men are not victims too.

The male victim

While criminologists quite rightly tend to focus on the violence experienced by women, Chapter 8 states that men are also victims of violent acts. As the journalist Madeline Bunting (2007) put is, 'Being male carries real penalties, and these are deeply written into understandings of masculinity'. This observation is especially pertinent in relation to victimization. Chapter 8 showed that men are frequently victimized by other men, especially in the context of the night-time economy, although this is often under-reported. The reasons for this are complex, although a significant factor is that, when looking at this category of men, their status as victims and offenders is fluid and interchangeable. Men are also victims of domestic violence carried out by female partners and this chapter accounted for the relative dearth of knowledge about this aspect of victimization. It is necessary for men who victimize, in particular those that are both *victimized* and *victimizers*, to be responsibilized by taking stock of the fact that their behaviour inhibits human rights. In this chapter we also suggested, quite controversially, that young males whose behaviour is labelled as anti-social are actually victims of a process of criminalization. Under successive governments, especially since 1997, boys and juveniles involved in anti-social – invariably sub-criminal – behaviour have been demonized. We argue that while their actions may create fear and distrust, they are in actual fact victims of neglect and stereotyping, especially as a result of a lack of economic, but especially emotional, investment in their uncertain futures. We suggest that often vulnerable young people need to be treated in a way that is respectful of their social and human rights and that the imposition of the British state-led punitive anti-social behaviour agenda and school exclusions is not necessarily the most appropriate solution.

In all of the above chapters a key actor is the criminal justice professional and we have seen how their activities create and/or sustain gender-specific outcomes in their dealings with the wider public, either as suspects and offenders or victims and witnesses.

In Control

The criminal justice practitioner: A gendered perspective

Chapter 9 outlined the gendered dimension of the police, courts, probation and prison services to show how gender is also salient for the people working in the system. The number of practitioners who are men and women in each of these sectors is pertinent: the numerical dominance of men in the police and probation services is of interest, but in itself it does not tell us much about how these organizations operate. For that reason we scrutinized the cultures of masculinity that pervade these organizations to show how women and some men and their masculinities are subordinated. We introduced some of the work that shows how the commercialization of social control means that private sector agencies, such as 'bouncers', are integral elements required for the maintenance of a gender imbalance in crime reduction. The overarching aim of this chapter is to show that power is important for understanding the division of labour across the criminal justice sector and that this compromises the human rights not only of offenders and victims but also employees. Masculine power, for example, facilitates overt forms of sexual discrimination and less visible discrimination that can restrict the realization of women's full potential in the workplace.

Chapter 10 examined in depth the criminal justice system as a gendered site, showing how the respective careers of men and women are played out in the police service and legal profession. Changes in organizational policy and in law have made significant and positive changes to the way in which women and men are recruited and achieve progression. Women and men working in the police service and the legal profession do so within what appear to be gender-neutral systems. Outwardly, there are no visible and apparent restrictions to the progression of men and women within organizations. Yet research has shown us that despite a number of reform initiatives, women continue to be under-represented in criminal justice work, especially at senior levels. Women continue to experience discrimination, albeit in a less blatant and visible form. The 'gendered substructure' in which gendered assumptions about criminal justice work and workers can be found remains a fundamental and defining feature of criminal justice agencies. If we look behind the guise of gender neutrality we see a criminal justice system subscribing to and work-ing within the parameters of an 'ideal worker' – this ideal worker continues to be male. While women have equal opportunity to participate in and com-pete for positions of authority, they do so within existing 'male' systems. The chapter demonstrated the considerable gap that exists between policy and practice. At a cultural level, women remain 'outsiders' in the project of social control and the delivery of justice. The increased presence of more women (and indeed greater representation from other groups whose background differs from that of the majority) has the potential to bring about change in both the substantive law, the interpretation and the application of law, and may work to secure a radical overhaul of criminal justice professions more generally. Above all, achieving greater diversity is a matter of equity and social justice (Diamond, 2007).

The bulk of this book has addressed the central issues covered in the gender and crime debate and we have added our own, hopefully original, albeit exploratory, take on the topic.

Future debates about gender and crime

Predicting the future is always fraught with difficulties, a task not made easier by our argument that historical research can sometimes tell us more about the contemporary situation than we would perhaps like to imagine. Also, many of the core arguments about the causes and nature of gendered inequalities and injustice outlined in the first edition remain in place. New crimes have emerged and there have been adjustments to, and adaptations of, criminal justice policy–makers' responses to them, but the global drivers (itemized above) shaping this reaction are essentially the same. There are three points we would like to make about some of the dilemmas that lie ahead of us before closing, including a short statement about the linkages between crime, offend-ing and victimization; gender; and human rights.

Firstly, if we look at crime and offending behaviour there is a view that there has been an international 'crime drop', which we argue has been over-stated. The claims made for this case are largely based on research evidence provided by the kind of administrative criminology favoured by many govern-ments across the world, especially quantitative evidence derived from crime surveys. Although such sources do provide us with invaluable insights into the extent and prevalence of crime and how there has been a reduction in the number of reported and recorded offences, this neglects how, as argued in Chapter 8, there is still a 'dark figure' of unreported and unrecorded crime. Crime is not always being reported for many reasons, but principally because some victims, especially men, are either refusing to accept victim status or because they do not have any faith in the criminal justice system to take seriously the harm they have experienced. Added to this is the ongoing relative invisibility of violence against women and girls. The recording of crime is also not an accurate measure of its reality and there is evidence to show that the police do not have the capacity to respond to all crime, which is not the same thing as a genuine decline in the number of crimes committed. These two trends have a differential impact on males and females, both as offenders and victims, and further conceptual and empirical work is needed to assess the uneven experiences of both genders. The relationship between political economy and crime needs further research to consider the impact of deepening and widening socio-economic inequality and its criminogenic tendencies, and how these shape the experiences men and women have of crime and disorder. At the time of writing it was forecast that the recession and socio-economic austerity are abating, with signs of economic growth on the horizon, although this optimistic reading is likely to be of benefit to a global power elite rather than the general population, who will continue to inhabit a criminogenic environment with a diminished criminal justice system, which cannot always respond to the diverse, gendered needs relating to care and control.

We also need to be aware of the emergence of new types of crime or, to be more accurate, the official discovering and labelling of behaviour as criminal. Forced marriage and female genital mutilation are not necessarily new offences, but they have only been recognized relatively recently as issues in need of a response. Trafficking has been characterized as a modern form of slavery but globalization has altered the nature of this crime, especially the ease with which it is committed. Global communications such as the internet, though far from new, continue to be exploited by innovators to find alternative methods of committing novel as well as traditional crimes.

Secondly, gender remains a key predictor of offending and victimization. Historical and contemporary research is telling us much more about the female offender and by providing insightful accounts of the often mundane nature of their behaviour (an observation that applies to men too) it helps to dispel many of the populist myths about the purported madness and badness of criminal women and girls. There is still more work to do and social scientific research must continue to explore the gendering of crime.

An issue recognized in the past, and one that is attracting renewed interest, is intersectionality, a theme that we have touched on, but this should be at the heart of future research into gender and crime. We have also shown that domestically – and globally – gender-based equality is on the agenda of policy-makers and there now exists legislation and policy instruments to create a more just and fair society for women as offenders, victims and workers. It would appear that there is plenty of rhetoric surrounding these themes and, while some progress has been made, this is uneven and there are signs that regression may be taking place.

Thirdly, the latter point can be seen when we look at human rights principles and values. Both domestically and internationally there has been some consensus about the fundamental importance of human rights to any civilized society as a means to offer safeguards and protection for its citizens. We call for governments and policy-makers to see these advances as a positive development. Progress has undoubtedly been made and there have been improvements in terms of gender equality, perhaps demonstrated best by the global commitment to tackling violence against women and girls. At the same time, there is also resistance to a human rights agenda, sometimes viewed as an unnecessary and bureaucratic hindrance, and there is the danger that progress has stalled. The accounts we have given of the female offender, victim and worker are a testament to the intractability of gender-based inequality. Indeed, the biggest barrier to progress is the growing inequality in general, but between men and women in particular. Whatever is in store for the future of human rights values – including the Human Rights Act 1998 in the UK – they are an essential benchmark and touchstone for coming to terms with debates about all aspects of the relationship between gender and crime.

Glossary

Agency – The capacity of individuals to act independently and to make their own free choices. By contrast, structure is those factors of influence (such as social class, religion, gender, ethnicity, customs, etc.) that determine or limit an agent and his or her decisions.

Anti-social behaviour – Behaviour that is not necessarily criminal but disorderly and causing people to be fearful.

Arrest – This is when a suspect is lawfully detained, usually by a police officer.

Attrition – The process resulting in criminal cases being dropped at various stages of the criminal justice system because of one of the following factors: (a) a case is **no-crimed**; (b) a case is not referred by the police to the **Crown Prosecution Service** (CPS); (c) the CPS decide that they will not proceed with a case; (d) if a defendant is found not guilty in a court of law.

Bangkok Rules – This refers to the adoption of the United Nations Rules for the Treatment of Women Prisoners and Non-custodial Measures for Women Offenders (known as the Bangkok Rules) in December 2010. They represent an important step forward in recognizing the gender-specific needs of women in criminal justice systems and providing the standards that should be applied in the treatment of such women. The Bangkok Rules are also the first international instrument which specifically addresses the needs of the children of women prisoners.

Barrister – A professional lawyer acting as an advocate in the courts.

British Association of Women Police (BAWP) – A network for policewomen.

British Crime Survey – A survey set up by the Home Office to measure crime victimization throughout England and Wales. This survey complements the recorded crime statistics gathered by the police (i.e. **notifiable offences**). This later became the **Crime Survey of England and Wales**.

Circuit Judge – The individuals in this role are full-time judges who are appointed by the Lord Chancellor. In most instances they are barristers and solicitors who belong to what is called the circuit bench.

Classical view of the offender – According to this view, the offender is a rational person who makes a conscious decision to commit crime. The possible threat of punishment is there to try to put off a person from committing a crime.

Coercive control – Coercive control is a term developed by Evan Stark to help us understand domestic abuse as more than a 'fight'. It is a pattern of behaviour which seeks to take away the victim's liberty or freedom, to strip away their sense of self. It is not just women's bodily integrity which is violated but also their human rights.

Commission for Equality and Human Rights (CEHR) – Set up in 2007 the CEHR drives forward human rights and equality agendas and replaced the Equal Opportunity Commission (EOC), Commission for Racial Equality (CRE) and the Disability Rights Commission. It has a legal role to enforce equalities legislation in relation to sex and gender, as well as race/ethnicity, age, sexuality, disability, etc.

Community safety – This concept refers to the general well-being of a community and focuses on a range of hazards and threats beyond crime.

Comparative criminology – This is the study of crime in different jurisdictions or nation states, which makes it possible for criminologists to learn lessons about the nature of crime and how it is controlled in different contexts.

Continuum of violence – The concept of a continuum of violence against women was developed by Liz Kelly in 1988. Her concern was to change the standard approach from analysing violence against women as episodic and deviant incidents of extreme cruelty and harm, to recognizing that it is normative and functional; an everyday context for the lives and experiences of women and girls all over the world.

Conviction – This refers to when a person is found guilty in a criminal court.

Corston Report – The Corston Report published in 2007 is a review of vulnerable women in the criminal justice system. The Report made 43 recommendations and outlined the need for a distinct, radically different, visibly led, strategic, proportionate, holistic, woman-centred, integrated approach for women in the criminal justice system and women at risk of offending.

Crime – There are many definitions of crime, but one commonly used is the breaking of the law or the violation of a legal code.

Crime control model – In this approach a priority is arresting, charging, prosecuting and sentencing offenders effectively and efficiently. Advocates of this approach assume a suspect is guilty and that this is not something that must be proven beyond reasonable doubt.

Crime prevention – In general terms, this is all about methods of stopping crime from occurring.

Crime reduction – Put simply, this is any method that aims to cut the number of crimes committed.

Crime Survey of England and Wales – See the British Crime Survey.

Criminal justice agencies – The police, crown prosecution, court, probation and prison services (the latter two belong to the National Offender Service (NOMS).

Criminal justice system – **Criminal justice agencies** (see above) are seen to work together in an integrated fashion in the wider context of the **state** and society.

Criminalization – This is the process which leads to particular groups being labelled as crime prone, which means they experience differential treatment by the police, courts and correctional agencies. A person is criminalized when their criminal status is dominant.

Criminology – This is the study of crime, including a focus on its causes and ways of reducing it.

Critical criminology – Society in general and the criminal justice system in particular is oppressive and discriminates against minority groups, such as women.

Crown Court – In this court, trials on indictment (i.e. more serious sentences) are heard in front of a judge and jury.

Crown Prosecution Service (CPS) – The main function of this service is to prosecute most criminal cases.

Cult of masculinity – Masculine values are celebrated and seen as more worthy than other values. This cult tends to be associated with heterosexuality, physical power and risk-taking behaviour, and is strongly associated with what men do.

Custody – To be in custody a person is either given a prison sentence or is detained by the police.

Dark figure – This refers to the number of offences that are either not reported to the police or not recorded by the police when they are reported.

Defendant – This is someone who is put on trial because they are accused of committing a crime.

Determinism – An explanation of criminal behaviour that assumes offending is strongly influenced by social (structural), biological or psychological factors that are beyond the control of the individual.

Discharge – Those occasions when sentencers in the courts take no further action against a suspect.

Discretion – The selective application of legislation or policy.

Discrimination – This refers to the ways in which people are treated differently on the grounds of their sex, race/ethnicity, sexuality, age, etc. This differential treatment is typically negative and results in inequality.

Diversity – This refers to social differences, such as sex and gender, race/ethnicity and recognizes the different needs and wants of various groups or categories of people. Difference is celebrated rather than being seen as a problem.

Domestic abuse – This refers to any incident or pattern of incidents of controlling, coercive, threatening behaviour, violence or abuse between those aged 16 or over who are, or have been, intimate partners or family members regardless of gender or sexuality. The abuse can encompass, but is not limited to, psychological, physical, sexual, financial and emotional.

Domestic violence – This is violence between current or ex-partners in the context of a personal relationship. The violence used may be physical as well as including psychological and emotional forms of abuse.

Domestic Violence Disclosure Scheme (known as Clare's Law) – This is intended to provide information that could protect someone from being a victim of attack. The scheme allows the police to disclose information on request about a partner's previous history of domestic violence or violent acts. The initiative is named after 36-year-old Clare Wood, who was murdered by her ex-boyfriend in 2009.

Due process – In contrast to the **crime control model**, the criminal justice system must prove beyond reasonable doubt that the accused is guilty. Criminal justice agencies must observe all the rules and procedures to safeguard suspects.

Electronic tagging – The use of technological devices, such as an electronic tag, to monitor the movement of offenders.

Equal opportunities – This idea assumes that all people should be given equal opportunities in all walks of life and that their gender, race, sexual orientation, etc. should not result in them experiencing any **discrimination** or be prevented from doing things that most people do.

Ethnicity – The culture, attitudes and beliefs of a particular social group. This is sometimes used interchangeably with **race** (see below).

Ethnomethodology – A sociological approach that focuses on the individual social actor and their attempts to produce meaningful social interaction with other social actors.

Everyday sexism project – An online project set up by Laura Bates in 2012 to catalogue instances of sexism experienced by women on a day-to-day basis.

Family life – Article 8 of the Human Rights Act (1998) states that each person has a right to a private and family life. Evidence shows that this is not always observed and in this book this can be seen by looking at prisoners.

Fear of crime – While crime impacts on many people, it is also clear that people worry about becoming a victim of crime. Such fears are now taken as seriously as actual victimization because it can cause significant harm and distress.

Female genital mutilation – Female genital mutilation (sometimes referred to as female circumcision) refers to procedures that intentionally alter or cause injury to the female genital organs for non-medical reasons. The practice is illegal in the UK.

Female offender – More than describing females who offend, this idea draws attention to changing representations of this phenomenon, such as 'girl gangs', and the association of female crime with masculine forms of behaviour. The female offender is contrasted with stereotypical ideas about female passivity.

Female sex offender – In relation to the female offender this notion concerns attempts to **search for equivalence** between male and female offenders, showing that females are capable of committing the most heinous crimes committed by men.

Feminist backlash – Refers to the negative and/or hostile reaction to feminist ideas.

Feminist criminology – Approaches which highlight the differential and inequitable treatment of women in society.

Feminist empiricism – Broadly speaking, feminist empiricism is empiricism with internalized feminist values. It critiques what it perceives to be inadequacies and biases within mainstream research methods, including positivism, and presumes that knowledge is fundamentally social and implicated in power relations.

Feminist Judgements Project – This is a dynamic and innovative research project in which a group of feminist socio-legal scholars have written alternative feminist judgements in a series of significant cases in English law. Rather than simply critiquing existing judgements, the participants have put 'theory into practice' by engaging in a practical, 'real world' exercise of judgement-writing, subject to the same constraints that bind appellate judges.

Feminist standpointism – Refers to knowledge that is explicitly generated from a 'point of view' or positionality; in this case, women are at the centre of inquiry.

Fine – A sentence of court involving a financial penalty.

Flexible working – Instead of rigid working patterns, such as the 9–5 routine and long, unsociable hours, this approach recognizes a need for different ways of working. Part-time working and 'flexi-time' are examples, but most significantly there is an appreciation that work needs to be balanced with other life commitments (e.g. parenting and other caring relationships).

Forced marriage – This is a marriage conducted without the valid consent of one or both parties and where duress is a factor.

Gender – The socially constructed categories of male and female.

Gender Equality Duty – This makes public authorities legally responsible for promoting gender equality and for tackling unlawful sex discrimination. Agencies need to be proactive rather than relying on members of the public making a complaint.

Gender gap – This refers to the persistent research finding within criminology that men commit much more crime than women.

Gender relations – This idea was developed by Connell (2002). Rather than looking at gender in terms of static categories, such as men and women, she draws attention to the interaction between men and women, which produces more dynamic relationships between the two sexes.

Gendered organization theory – It is widely assumed that organizations such as the police service are gender-neutral organizations where men and women experience organizational activities in the same ways. By contrast, this perspective shows that men and women have markedly different experiences at individual, cultural and structural levels.

Gendered substructure – In any organization there are social practices and arrangements that are influenced by gender. For example, workplace behaviour, including the interaction between men and women and attitudes to work, are based on gender-specific assumptions.

Globalization – The economic and cultural processes that are making different nation states both physically and virtually closer to each other in time and space. It is also a process that leads towards the concentration of wealth and power in the hands of an elite group, thus increasing inequality across the world.

Guilt – In criminal cases this needs to be established beyond reasonable doubt.

Hegemonic masculinity – Drawing on Gramsci's (1971) concept of hegemony, this refers to a dominant form of masculinity which is used to organize **gender relations**. Hegemonic masculinity is the most highly valued form of masculinity towards which people orientate themselves. Crucially, it changes over time and there is no single hegemonic masculinity.

Heterosexist ideologies – A set of attitudes and beliefs that promote heterosexuality (e.g. sexual relations between adult men and women) as the most acceptable and normal type of relationship. Homosexual and lesbian relationships are treated as inferior.

Home Office – This is a government department responsible for the criminal justice system and law and order policies. In 2007 this department was changed, with the creation of the Ministry of Justice, which assumed responsibility for probation, prisons and preventing reoffending.

Home Secretary – The Minister in charge of policy at the Home Office.

Homophobic violence – This is violent crime motivated by negative feelings towards homosexual people. Like domestic violence, this can include emotional and psychological forms as well as physical harm.

'Honour'-based violence – 'Honour'-based violence is a form of domestic abuse which is perpetrated in the name of so-called 'honour'. The honour code which it refers to is set at the discretion of male relatives and women who do not abide by the 'rules' are then punished for bringing shame on the family.

Human rights – These are enshrined in various covenants and pieces of legislation, most notably the Human Rights Act (1998). The different articles making up the HRA rest on the premise that all people should be treated equally, fairly and with dignity. Our argument is that there needs to be a human rights framework that goes beyond legislation or the 'black letter law' perspective to consider wider debates about equality, justice and fairness, in particular citizenship.

Ideology – This is a set of ideas and beliefs that constitute a coherent view of the social world and justify particular courses of social actions, such as sexist **discrimination**.

Incarceration – The imprisonment of sentenced prisoners and persons awaiting trial.

Independent Domestic Violence Advisers – These advisers address the safety of victims at high risk of harm from intimate partners, ex-partners or family members to secure their safety and the safety of their children. Serving as a victim's primary point of contact, IDVAs normally work with their clients from the point of crisis to assess the level of risk. They also discuss the range of suitable options leading to the creation of a workable safety plan.

Independent Sexual Violence Advisers – The Independent Sexual Violence Adviser specializes in the care for victims of sexual crime, to help in the support of these individuals.

Indeterminate sentence – A sentence that does not have a fixed period (e.g. a life sentence). This is in contrast to a determinate sentence.

Indictable offences – Crimes that are tried in the Crown Court.

Interpersonal violence – Crimes against the person, such as **domestic violence** and **homophobic violence**.

Intersectionality – There is an important and increasingly acknowledged recognition that individual women and social structures are affected in distinctive ways by the intersections of oppressions and circumstances (disability, sexuality, age, class, ethnicity, nationality/status, poverty, beliefs/ideologies).

Judge – In the Crown Court this person sums up the court proceedings and provides direction relating to the necessary points of law.

Judicial diversity – Criminologists have shown over the years that the judiciary is dominated by men and that it is necessary for the judiciary to be more representative of the population it serves, thus including a more diverse population comprising a greater representation of women and minority ethnic groups.

Judiciary – Is used to refer collectively to the personnel, such as judges, magistrates and other adjudicators, who form the core of a judiciary (sometimes referred to as a 'bench'), as well as the staff who keep the system running smoothly.

Kleptomania – Refers to a recurrent urge to steal, typically without regard for need or profit.

Ladette – The behaviour of some girls is described as if they are adopting behavioural traits usually associated with boys, such as violence and aggression and heavy drinking.

Left realist criminology – A holistic explanation of crime that considers the complex causes of crime and solutions to offending behaviour.

Magistrate – This person passes sentence in the Magistrates' courts.

Marginalization – Some social groups, such as the **underclass**, are socially excluded and pushed to the edges of mainstream social life so that they do not experience the same rights as *included* individuals.

Masculinity/masculinities – Certain types of attitude and behaviour are associated with men (e.g. masculinity), but it is recognized that there are many different types of masculinity that change over time and space. Hence masculinity needs to be seen in the plural (e.g. there are many masculinities). While masculinity is conventionally associated with men, women may adopt specific masculinities.

Mean girl – Rather like the **ladette**, this refers to aggression and substance misuse, drawing attention towards the cruelty of female offenders who are failing to conform to prevailing cultural expectations about what it is to be a girl.

Modernity – A set of ideas claiming that science and rational thought can be used by human beings to shape the external social world.

Moral panic – A reaction to a crime that is blown out of all proportion in comparison to its actual seriousness.

Mothers in prison – This group of prisoners is particularly vulnerable and the right to private and family life (Article 8, Human Rights Act 1998) is not always fully observed.

New Public Management (NPM) (Managerialism) – A method of public sector reform where there is an emphasis on economy, effectiveness and efficiency.

No-criming – A police practice where it is decided that an incident reported to them does not constitute a criminal offence.

Offence – Any behaviour which is prohibited by the criminal law.

Paedophilia – The sexually motivated abuse of children.

Pain – Victims of domestic violence experience physical and emotional suffering over an extended period.

Parole – The early release of prisoners from custody (i.e. prison).

Parole board – Takes decisions about if, and when, to release prisoners.

Patriarchy – This word means the 'rule of the father' and radical feminists have adopted this idea to explain male dominance in social relations.

Plea – Defendants are able to say if they are guilty of committing the offence with which they have been charged.

Police and policing – These two words are often used interchangeably but they relate to different things. The police is a specialist, bureaucratic organization that exercises legitimate force within a given territory to prevent crime and maintain the rule of law. Policing is a set of practices concerned with social control and surveillance that can be undertaken by a range of agencies (i.e. private security, individual citizens), not just the police.

Police culture – An outlook or world view which belongs specifically to police officers. It is usually connected with negative factors, such as sexism and racism, and tends to be concentrated among the rank and file. It is often described as something blocking effective police reform.

Positivist paradigm – An epistemological position influenced by the natural sciences that posits a belief that there are clear and objectively observable processes that impact on various social phenomena.

Postmodern – Postmodernism challenges modernity and the values of scientific reason and rationality. The emphasis is on deconstructing social reality and recognizing the fragmentation of social life.

Power – In short, this is the capacity to effectively influence society and bring about change. Power can represent the interests of the many (pluralism) or the few (**elitism**) and for our purposes we show how power results in **discrimination** against women.

Probation – The activities performed by probation officers and the National Probation Service.

Psychosocial approaches – To understand masculinities it is necessary to consider psychic influences, in particular the irreducibility and rigidity of psychic identities. The psyche includes conscious and unconscious processes that are shaped by desire. Each person is engaged in splitting and projecting different parts of their personality, which may result in **interpersonal violence**.

Public Sector Equality Duty – Under the Equality Act 2010 organizations are required to show 'due regard' to the Public Sector Equality Duty. This means organizations need to address discrimination and harassment against people with protected characteristics and create equality of opportunity for such people.

Puerperal insanity – A term that covers a group of mental illnesses with the sudden onset of psychotic symptoms following childbirth.

Punitiveness – Policies that are influenced by ideologies that promote punishment as the most appropriate method of crime reduction. The greater the use of custodial penalties in any society, the more punitive it is.

Queen's Counsel – Also known as QC and refers to a limited number of senior barristers who receive 'silk', thereby becoming Queen's Counsel, as a mark of outstanding ability. They are normally instructed in very serious or complex cases. Most senior judges once practised as QCs.

Race – Usually this refers to the use of physical markers (i.e. the colour of a person's skin) to categorize people (e.g. white, black). In actual fact biological differences such as skin colour lack scientific credibility yet despite this race is treated as a real category, hence **racism**.

Racism – Some social groups are discriminated against because they are perceived not only to be different but as inferior too. In other words, groups are arranged hierarchically, including dominant and subordinate groups. Racism can be seen at both an individual and an institutionalized level.

Rape – A form of sexual violence involving unwanted penetration, invariably carried out by men against women and other men against their will. It is widely seen as an expression of individual, invariably male, power.

Rehabilitation – It is assumed by some criminologists that an offender can be reformed and eventually returned to normal life.

Remand – Depending on the seriousness of an offence, a suspect can be held in custody until the trial takes place.

Respect Agenda – Introduced by New Labour governments in the 2000s this argues that the lack of respect for the values held by the decent and respectable majority, which are manifest in the form of crime and anti-social behaviour, pose a threat to civilized society.

Responsibilization – The **criminal justice system** cannot tackle crime and disorder on its own and it is necessary for more responsibility to be given to private and voluntary sector agencies, as well as individuals and communities. We are all in some way responsible for our own welfare and ensuring that we are not victimized.

Restorative justice – An offender may be required to meet with their victim in an attempt to right the wrong they have committed.

Retribution – A principle stating that criminals must be punished in order that they can appreciate that their actions are unlawful and wrong.

Search for equivalence – The view that men and women engage in crime in the same way and for the same reasons.

Secondary victimization – Following a person's initial victimization by an offender, some victims go on to experience further victimization at the hands of the criminal justice system, for example, insensitive cross-examination of rape victims by the defence.

Secret soundings – This is that part of the selection process used to appoint barristers and judges that involves informal, off-the record communication to seek personal opinions about the suitability of a candidate.

Sentence(s) – These are passed by the courts and include fines, custodial or non-custodial (community-based) sentences.

Sexism – An ideology that treats men and women differently on the grounds of discriminatory assumptions.

Sexual Assault Referral Centres – A Sexual Assault Referral Centre (SARC) provides specialist services to victims of rape or sexual assault regardless of whether the victim reports the offence to the police or not. SARCs are designed to be comfortable and multi-functional, providing private space for interviews and examinations, and some may also offer counselling services.

Sexual Offences Investigative Techniques Trained Officers – Police officers who are highly skilled and trained in rape investigation using the Sexual Offences Investigative Technique (SOIT).

Social class – A method of allocating people to socio-economic groups based on an individual's occupation.

Social divisions – The markers which make people different, including sex and gender, **social class**, **race** and **ethnicity**.

Social exclusion – A concept used to describe those people who are not able to participate in the social activities enjoyed by most people. Invariably it is used to describe the poorest members of society.

Social harm – This encompasses social, economic, psychological and environmental injury or damage inflicted on society either intentionally or unintentionally. It is a concept that enables criminology to move beyond legal definitions of 'crime' to include immoral, wrongful and injurious acts that are not necessarily illegal.

Social justice – This is the view that everyone deserves equal economic, political and social rights and opportunities.

Specialist Domestic Violence Court – Specialist Domestic Violence Courts were established as part of a pilot initiative in 2006. They represent a partnership approach to domestic violence by the police, prosecutors, court staff, the probation service and specialist support services for victims. They provide a specialized way of dealing with domestic violence cases in Magistrates' courts. Agencies work together to identify, track and risk-assess domestic violence cases, support victims of domestic violence and share information better so that more offenders are brought to justice.

State – A complex idea that generally describes the more or less permanent legal and organizational framework which is there to control and manage society. Most crucially, the state defines the competencies and powers of its actors (e.g. judges) and agencies (e.g. the police).

State accountability – The activities of states need to be answerable to the wider community. In other words, the state cannot do what it wants without reference to legal principles like the Human Rights Act 1998.

Suicide and self-harm – These behaviours are prevalent in prisons, affecting women and men in different ways. It is our view that they both violate Article 2 of the HRA (1998), namely the right to life.

Surveillance – The mechanisms used to systematically observe and regulate places, people and things, e.g. closed circuit television (CCTV).

Suspect – An individual who is believed to be responsible for a criminal offence. A person remains as a suspect until their guilt is proved beyond reasonable doubt.

The rights and needs of victims – In contrast to offenders who have the right to be presumed innocent until proven guilty beyond reasonable doubt, victims of crime do not have such formal rights. Indeed the status of victim is assumed by the state. Towards the end of the twentieth century there was talk about giving crime victims rights, but in practice victims have certain recognized needs for which there are available services.

Third Way – A political project set in motion, which suggests that the distinction between right and left in politics is no longer tenable. It also claims that there is no alternative to capitalism, although the system needs some regulation.

Torture – The use of torture goes against the grain of Article 7 of the HRA. In this book it is argued that **domestic violence** is a form of torture, thus adding to analyses that tend to see torture as something inflicted by the state and its agencies.

Transnational crime – Crime or criminal behaviour that has an impact across national geographical territories. Because individual states cannot always address such crime on their own there are transnational forms of policing where different nation states work together.

Triable-either-way (T-E-W) – These offences may be tried either in the Crown Court or at a Magistrates' court.

Underclass – The poorest and most deprived social groups; often alleged to be involved in criminal activity.

'Vanishing female' thesis – Refers to a decline in women's participation in criminal behaviour during the nineteenth century.

Victim – This is a person who has been affected by crime.

Victim precipitation – Early victimological research suggested that some victims of crime, especially of **interpersonal violence**, were to some degree responsible for their own victimization.

Victimization – The processes associated with the creation of a victim.

Victimology – The study of crime victims.

Vulnerability – Many offenders and victims are in a position of relative weakness, which means they are more susceptible to exploitation and discriminatory treatment.

Witness – A person who has either actually observed a crime being committed or who can provide information about an offence.

Women in prison – A population that expanded dramatically in the late 1990s and 2000s despite calls immediately prior to that period to restrict the imprisonment of women to the most violent. This population experience different needs from their male counterparts.

Youth Justice Board – The agency overseeing youth justice policy and practice.

Youth Offending Team – Teams set up to work exclusively with young people.

References

6, P. and Peck, E. (2004) 'New Labour's modernization in the public sector: A neo-Durkheimian approach and the case of mental health services', *Public Administration*, 82(1): 83–108.

Aas, K.F. (2013) *Globalization and Crime* (2nd edn). London: Sage.

Abramson, B. (2006) 'Juvenile justice: The unwanted child – why the potential of the Convention on the Rights of the Child is not being realised and what we can do about it', in E.L. Jensen and J. Jepsen (eds), *Juvenile Law Violators, Human Rights and the Development of New Juvenile Justice Systems*. Oxford: Hart Publishing.

Acker, J. (1990) 'Hierarchies, jobs, bodies: A theory of gendered organisations', *Gender and Society*, 4(2): 139–58.

Acker, J. (1992) 'Gendering organisational theory', in A. Mills and P. Tancred (eds), *Gendering Organisational Analysis*. London: Sage.

ACPO (Association of Chief Police Officers) (2011) *ACPO Strategy & Supporting Operational Guidance for Policing Prostitution and Sexual Exploitation*. London: ACPO.

ACPO, APA and Home Office (2010) *Equality, Diversity and Human Rights Strategy for the Police Service*. London: ACPO, APA and Home Office.

Adams, K. (2001) *Women in Senior Police Management*. Payneham, South Australia: Australasian Centre for Police Research.

Adlam, R. and Villiers, P. (eds) (2003) *Police Leadership in the Twenty-First Century: Philosophy, Doctrine and Developments*. Winchester: Waterside Press.

Adler, S. (1975) *Sisters in Crime*. New York: McGraw-Hill.

Adshead, G., Howett, M. and Mason, F. (1994) 'Women who sexually abuse children: The undiscovered country', *The Journal of Sexual Aggression*, 1(1): 45–56.

Aebi, F. and Linde, A. (2015) 'The epistemological obstacles in comparative criminology: A special issue introduction', *European Journal of Criminology*, 12(4): 381–5.

AHRC (Australian Human Rights Commission) (2013) *Historic International Violence Agreement Reached*. Sydney: Australian Human Rights Commission.

Ainsworth, P. (2001) *Offender Profiling and Crime Analysis*. Devon: Willan.

Aldridge, J. and Medina, J. (2008) *Youth Gangs in an English City: Social Exclusion, Drugs and Violence*. Full Research Report ESRC End of Award Report, RES-000-23-0615. Swindon: ESRC.

Allen, D. and Wall, D. (1987) 'The behaviour of women State Supreme Court Justices: Are they tokens or outsiders?', *Justice Systems Journal*, 12: 232–56.

Allen, J.A. (1990) *Sex and Secrets: Crimes Involving Australia Women since 1880*. Oxford: Oxford University Press.

Allen, J., Edmonds, S., Patterson, A. and Smith, D. (2006) *Policing and the Criminal Justice System – Confidence and Perceptions: Findings from the 2004–5 British Crime Survey*. Home Office Online Report 07/06. London: Home Office.

Amussen, S.D. (1994) '"Being stirred to much unquietness": Violence and domestic violence in early modern England', *Journal of Women's History*, 6: 70–89.

Anderson, K.L. (2009) 'Gendering coercive control', *Violence Against Women*, 15 December: 1444–57.

Anderson, O. (1987) *Suicide in Victorian and Edwardian England*. New York: Oxford University Press.

Angiolini, E. (2015) *Report of the Independent Review into the Investigation and Prosecution of Rape in London*. London: Metropolitan Police.

Anitha, S. and Gill, A. (2009) 'Coercion, consent and the forced marriage debate', *Feminist Legal Studies*, 17: 165–84.

Annison, J. (2013) 'Change and the Probation Service in England and Wales: A gendered lens', *European Journal of Probation*, 5(1): 44–64.

Anti-Slavery Day (2014) *What is Human Trafficking?* Available at: www.antislaveryday.com/what-is-human-trafficking (accessed on 4 March 2015).

Antrobus, P. (2008) 'Globalisation, human security, fundamentalism and women's rights', in M. Cain and A. Howe (eds), *Women, Crime and Social Harm: Towards a Criminology for the Global Age*. Oxford: Hart Publishing.

APPG (2014) *All-Party Parliamentary Group on Prostitution and the Global Sex Trade Inquiry*. Available at: https://appgprostitution.files.wordpress.com/2014/04/shifting-the-burden1.pdf.

Aronowitz, A. (2009) *Human Trafficking, Human Misery: The Global Trade in Human Beings*. London: Praeger.

Ashworth, A. and Redmayne, M. (2010) *The Criminal Process* (4th edn). Oxford: Oxford University Press.

Asthana, A. and Bright, M. (2004) 'Suicides rise as weekend jail fails women', *The Observer*, 11 August.

Audit Commission (1996) *Misspent Youth*. London: Audit Commission.

Audit Commission (2004) *Youth Justice 2004: A Review of the Reformed Youth Justice System*. Wetherby: Audit Commission Publications.

Augustin, L.M. (2007) *Sex at the Margins: Migration, Labour Markets and the Rescue Industry*. London: Zed Books.

Bachrach, P. and Baratz, M. (1970) *Power and Poverty*. New York: Oxford University Press.

Baines, D., Charlesworth, S. and Cunningham, I. (2014) 'Changing care? Men and Managerialism in the nonprofit sector', *Journal of Social Work*, 15(5): 459–78.

Baker, L., Dalla, R. and Williamson, C. (2010) 'Exiting prostitution: An integrated model', *Violence Against Women*, 16(5): 579–600.

Bakirci, K. (2009) 'Human trafficking and forced labour: A criticism of the International Labour Organisation', *Journal of Financial Crime*, 16(2): 160–5.

Balfour, G. (2000) 'Feminist therapy with women in prison: Working under the hegemony of correctionalism', in K. Hannah-Moffat and M. Shaw (eds), *An Ideal Prison? Critical Essays on Women's Imprisonment in Canada*. Halifax: Fernwood Press. pp. 94–102.

Balfour, G. (2006) 'Reimagining a feminist criminology', *Canadian Journal of Criminology and Criminal Justice*, 48: 735.

Bangkok Rules (2010) *United Nations Rules for the Treatment of Women Prisoners and Non-custodial Measures for Women Offenders*. Available at: www.un.org/en/ecosoc/docs/2010/res%202010-16.pdf.

Barak, G., Leighton, P. and Flavin, J. (2010) *Class, Race, Gender and Crime*. Lanham, MD: Rowman & Littlefield.

Barberet, R. (2014) *Women, Crime and Criminal Justice: A Global Inquiry*. London: Routledge.

Baron, J.N. and Davis-Blake, A. (1986) 'The structure of opportunity: How far promotion ladders vary within and among organisations', *Administrative Science Quarterly*, 31: 248–73.

Barry, J. and Davies, O. (eds) (2007) *Witchcraft Historiography*. Basingstoke: Palgrave Macmillan.

Bartlett, K.T. (1990) 'Feminist legal methods', *Harvard Law Review*, 103: 829–88.

Bartley, P. (2000) *Prostitution: Prevention and Reform in England 1869–1914*. London: Routledge.

Barton, A. and Cooper, V. (2013) 'Hostels and community justice for women: The semi-penal paradox', in M. Malloch and G. McIvor (eds), *Women, Punishment and Social Justice*. Abingdon: Routledge.

Batchelor, S. (2005) '"Prove me the Bam!" Victimization and agency in the lives of young women who commit violent offences', *Probation Journal*, 52(4): 358–75.

Batchelor, S. (2009) 'Girls, gangs and violence: Assessing the evidence', *Probation Journal*, 56: 399–414.

Batchelor, S.A., Burman, M.J. and Brown, J.A. (2001) 'Discussing violence: Let's hear it from the girls', *Probation Journal*, 48(2): 125–34.

Bates, L. (2014) *Everyday Sexism*. London: Simon and Schuster.

Bauman, Z. (1998) *Work, Consumerism and the New Poor*. Buckingham: Open University Press.

Bayley, D.H. (1994) *Police for the Future*. New York: Oxford University Press.

Bayley, D.H. (2002) 'Policing hate: What can be done?', *Policing and Society*, 12(2): 83–91.

BBC (2015) *Delhi Rapist says Victim should not have Fought back*, 3 March. Available at: www.bbc.co.uk/news/magazine-31698154 (accessed 18 May 2015).

BBC News (2014) 'Human trafficking for labour on the increase', 13 October (www.bbc.co.uk/news/uk-29593086).

Beattie, J.M. (1975) 'The criminality of women in eighteenth-century England', *Journal of Social History*, 8: 80–116.

Beattie, J.M. (1986) *Crime and the Courts in England, 1660–1800*. Oxford: Clarendon Press.

Beattie, J.M. (2001) *Policing and Punishment in London, 1660–1720: Urban Crime and the Limits of Terror*. Oxford: Oxford University Press.

Beck, U. (1992) *Risk Society*. London. Sage.

Beck, U. (2015) *The Metamorphosis of the World*. Cambridge: Polity Press.

Beech, A.R., Parrett, N., Ward, T. and Fisher, D. (2009) 'Assessing female sexual offenders' motivations and cognitions: An exploratory study', *Psychology, Crime & Law*, 15: 201–16.

Beglan, M. (2013) 'The 218 experience', in M. Malloch and G. McIvor (eds), *Women, Punishment and Social Justice*. Abingdon: Routledge.

Beijerse, J. and Swaaningen, R. (2006) 'The Netherlands: Penal-welfarism and risk management', in J. Muncie and B. Goldson (eds), *Comparative Youth Justice*. London: Sage.

Beirne, P. and Messerschmidt, J.W. (2005) *Criminology* (4th edn). Los Angeles, CA: Roxbury.

Bellamy, J.G. (1998) *The Criminal Trial in Late Medieval England*. Toronto: Toronto University Press.

Bennett, T. and Holloway, K. (2007) 'Gender, drugs and crime', in T. Bennett and K. Holloway (eds), *Drug-Crime Connections*. Cambridge: Cambridge University Press.

Berelowitz, S., Clifton, J., Firimin, C., Gulyurtlu, S. and Edwards, E. (2013) *'If only someone had listened': Office of the Children's Commissioner's Inquiry into Child Sexual Exploitation in Gangs and Groups*, Final Report, November 2013. Available at: www.childrenscommissioner.gov.uk/content/publications/content_743 (accessed 2 January 2014).

Berk, S. and Loseke, D. (1981) '"Handling" family violence: Situational determinants of police arrest in domestic disturbances', *Law and Society Review*, 15(2): 317–46.

Berko, A. (2012) *The Smarter Bomb: Women and Children as Suicide Bombers*. Lanham, MD: Rowman & Littlefield.

Berko, A. and Erez, E. (2007) 'Gender, Palestinian women and terrorism: Women's liberation or oppression?', *Studies in Conflict and Terrorism*, 30: 493–519.

Berko, A., Erez, E. and Globokar, J. (2010) 'Gender, crime and terrorism', *British Journal of Criminology*, 50: 670–89.

Bernard, A. (2013) 'The intersectional alternative: Explaining female criminality', *Feminist Criminology*, 8(1): 3–19.

Bernstein, E. (2010) 'Militarised humanitarianism meets carceral feminism', *SIGNS: Journal of Women in Culture and Society*, 36(1): 28–40.

Bernstein, E. (2012) 'Carceral politics as gender justice? The "traffic in women" and neoliberal circuits of crime, sex and rights', *Theoretical Sociology*, 41: 233–59.

Bibi, N., Clegg, R. and Pinto, R. (2005) *Police Service Strength, England and Wales 31 March 2005*, Home Office Statistical Bulletin 12/05. London: Home Office.

Bielby, W.T. and Baron, J.N. (1986) 'Men and women at work: Sex segregation and statistical discrimination', *American Journal of Sociology*, 91(4): 759–99.

Bindel, J. (2004) *Paying the Price: Eaves' Response to the Home Office Consultation on Prostitution*. London: Eaves.

Bindel, J. and Atkins, H. (2007) *Streets Apart: Outdoor Prostitution in London*. London: Eaves.

Bindel, J. and Atkins, H. (2008) *Big Brothel: A Survey of the Off Street Sex Industry in London*. London: The Poppy Project.

Bindel, J., Brown, L., Easton, H., Matthews, R. and Reynolds, L. (2012) *Breaking Down the Barriers: A Study of How Women Exit Prostitution*. London: London South Bank University.

Bittner, E. (1974) 'Florence Nightingale in pursuit of Willie Sutton: A theory of the police', in H. Jacobs (eds), *Potential for Reform of Criminal Justice*. Beverley Hills, CA: Sage.

Blair, T. (2010) *A Journey*. London: Hutchinson.

Blakeborough, L., Pierpoint, H., Bennett, T., Maguire, M., Pinto, C., Wredford, L. and Smith, D. (2007) *Conditional Cautions: An Examination of the Early Implementation of the Scheme*, Research Summary 7. London: Ministry of Justice.

Bloom, M. (2007) 'Female suicide bombers: A global trend', *Daedalus*, 136(1): 94–102.

Bloom, M. (2009) 'Chasing butterflies and rainbows: A critique of Kruglanski et al.'s "Fully committed: Suicide bombers' motivation and the quest for personal significance"', *Political Psychology*, 30(3): 387–95.

Bloom, M. (2011) 'Bombshells: Women and terror', *Gender Issues*, 28(1–2): 1–21.

Bochel, H. and Duncan, S. (2007) *Making Policy in Theory and Practice*. Bristol: Policy Press.

Bohstedt, J. (1992) 'The myth of the feminine food riot: Women as proto-citizens in English community politics, 1790–1810', in H. Applewhite and D. Levy (eds), *Women and Politics in the Age of Democratic Revolution*. Michigan: University of Michigan Press.

Bose, B. (2008) 'Dangerous liaisons: Sex work, globalization, morality and the state in contemporary India', in M. Cain and A. Howe (eds), *Women, Crime and Social Harm: Towards a Criminology for the Global Age*. Oxford: Hart Publishing.

Bottoms, A.E. (1977) 'Reflections on the renaissance of dangerousness', *Howard Journal of Penology and Crime Prevention*, 16: 70–96.

Bowling, B. and Foster, J. (2002) 'Policing and the Police', in M. Maguire, R. Reiner and R. Morgan (eds), *The Oxford Handbook of Criminology* (3rd edn). Oxford: Clarendon Press.

Bowling, B. and Sheptycki, J. (2012) *Global Policing*. London: Sage.

Bowling, B., Phillips, C., Campbell, A. and Docking, M. (2004) *Policing and Human Rights: Eliminating Discrimination, Xenophobia, Intolerance and the Abuse of Power from Police Work*, Identities, Conflict and Cohesion Programme Paper Number 4. Geneva: United Nations Research Institute for Social Development.

Boyd, C., Epstein, L. and Martin, A. (2010) 'Untangling the causal effects of sex on judging', *American Journal of Political Science*, 54(2): 389–411.

Boyd, M., Mulvihill, M. and Myles, J. (1991) 'Gender, power and post-industrialism', *Canadian Review of Sociology and Anthropology*, 28: 407–36.

Braithwaite, H. and Brewer, N. (1998) 'Differences in conflict resolution of male and female police patrol officers', *International Journal of Police Science and Management*, 1(3): 276–87.

Breuil, B., Siegal, D., Reenan, P., Beijer, A. and Roos, L. (2011) 'Human trafficking revisited: Legal, enforcement and ethnographic narratives on sex trafficking to Western Europe', *Trends Organised Crime*, 14: 30–46.

Brookman, F. and Maguire, M. (2003) *Reducing Homicide: A Review of the Possibilities*, Home Office Online Report 01/03. London: Home Office.

Brookman, F. and Robinson, A. (2012) 'Violent crime', in M. Maguire, R. Morgan and R. Reiner (eds), *The Oxford Handbook of Criminology* (5th edn). Oxford: Oxford University Press.

Broom, D. (1994) *Double Bind: Women Affected by Alcohol and Other Drugs*. Australian National University: National Centre for Epidemiology and Population Health.

Broomhall, S. and Van Gent, J. (2011) *Governing Masculinities in the Early Modern Period: Regulating Selves and Others*. Burlington, VT: Ashgate.

Brown, D. (1998) *Offending on Bail and Police use of Conditional Bail*, Home Office Research Findings 72. London: Home Office.

Brown, D. (2002) 'Losing my religion: Reflections on critical criminology in Australia', in K. Carrington and R. Hogg (eds), *Critical Criminology: Issues, Debates, Challenges*. Uffculme, Devon: Willan.

Brown, J. (1998) 'Aspects of discriminatory treatment of women police officers serving in forces in England and Wales', *British Journal of Criminology*, 38(2): 265–83.

Brown, J. (2003) 'Women leaders: A catalyst for change', in R. Adlam and P. Villiers (eds), *Leadership in the Twenty-first Century: Philosophy, Doctrine and Developments*. Winchester: Waterside Press.

Brown, J. (2007) 'From cult of masculinity to smart macho: Gender perspectives on police occupational culture', in D.A. Sklansky (ed.), *Police Occupational Culture: Sociology of Crime, Law and Deviance*. Bingley: Emerald.

Brown, J. (2012) *Facing the Future*, Police Magazine. Available at: www.policemag.co.uk/ editions/709.aspx (accessed 28 April 2015).

Brown, J. and Heidensohn, F. (2000) *Gender and Policing*. London: Macmillan.

Brown, J. and King, J. (1998) 'Gender differences in police officers' attitudes towards rape: Results of an exploratory study', *Psychology, Crime and Law*, 4(4): 265–79.

Brown, J. and Langan, P. (2001) *Policing and Homicide, 1976–98: Justifiable Homicide by Police, Police Officers Murdered by Felons*. Washington, DC: US Department of Justice.

Brown, J. and Woolfenden, S. (2011) 'Implications of the changing gender ratio amongst warranted police officers', *Policing*, 5(4): 356.

Brown, J., Fielding, J. and Woolfenden, S. (2009) *Added Value? The Implications of Increasing the Percentages of Women in the Police Service by 2009*, A report Commissioned by the British Association for Women Policing.

Brown, J., Prenzler, T. and Van Ewijk, A. (2014) 'Women in policing', in R.G. Bruinsma and D. Weisburd (eds), *Encyclopedia of Criminology and Criminal Justice*. New York: Springer. pp. 5548–60.

Brown, K., Beecham, D. and Barrett, H. (2013) 'The applicability of behaviour change in intervention programmes targeted at ending female genital mutilation in the EU: Integrating social cognitive and community level approaches', *Obstetrics and Gynaecology International*. Available at: http://dx.doi.org/10.1155/2013/324362.

Brownmiller, S. (1975) *Against our Will: Men, Women and Rape*. New York: Fawcett Books.

Brundage, J. (1982) 'Rape and seduction in medieval canon law', in V. Bullough and J. Brundage (eds), *Sexual Practices and the Medieval Church*. Amherst, NY: Prometheus Books.

Brunson, R.K. and Stewart, E. (2006) 'Young African American women, the street code, and violence: An exploratory analysis', *Journal of Crime and Justice*, 29(1): 1–19.

BSIA (2001) *Interesting Facts and Figures in the UK Security Industry*. Available at: www.bsia.co.uk/industry.html (accessed 26 October 2015).

Bullock, K. and Johnson, P. (2012) 'The impact of the Human Rights Act on the police service in England and Wales', *British Journal of Criminology*, 52(3): 630–50.

Bullock, K. and Tilley, N. (2002) *Shootings, Gangs and Violent Incidents in Manchester: Developing a Crime Reduction Strategy*, Home Office Research Series Paper 13. London: Home Office.

Bunting, L. (2007) 'Dealing with a problem that doesn't exist? Professional responses to female perpetrated child sexual abuse', *Child Abuse Review*, 16: 252–67.

Bunting, M. (2007) 'This equality road map must now apply to men', *The Guardian*, 24 July.

Burgess-Proctor, A. (2006) 'Intersections of race, class, gender and crime', *Feminist Criminology*, 1(1): 27–47.

Burman, B. and Cartmel, F. (2005) *Young People's Attitudes towards Gendered Violence*. Edinburgh: NHS Scotland.

Burman, M. (2004) 'Turbulent talk: Girls' making sense of violence', in C. Alder and A. Worrall (eds), *Girls' Violence*. New York: SUNY Press.

Burman, M. (2009) 'Breaking the mould? Patterns of female offending', in G. McIvor (ed.), *Women Who Offend*. London: Jessica Kingsley.

Burman, M. and Batchelor, S. (2009) 'Between two stools: Responding to young women who offend', *Youth Justice*, 9(3): 270–85.

Burnard, A. (2008) 'Right to a fair trial: Young offenders and the Victorian charter of human rights and responsibilities', *Current Issues in Criminal Justice*, 20(2): 173–88.

Burney, E. (2002) 'Talking tough, acting coy: What happened to the anti-social behaviour order?', *The Howard Journal*, 41(5): 469–84.

Burney, E. (2005) *Making People Behave: Anti-social Behaviour, Policy and Politics*. Cullompton: Willan.

Burney, E. (2009) 'Respect and the politics of behaviour', in A. Millie (ed.), *Securing Respect: Behavioural Expectations and Anti-Social Behaviour in the UK*. Bristol: Policy Press. pp. 23–40.

Burton, C. (1992) 'Merit and gender: Organisations and the mobilisation of masculine bias', in A. Mills and P. Tancred, *Gendering Organisational Analysis*. London: Sage.

Bush, M. (2004) 'The women at Peterloo: The impact of female reform on the Manchester Meeting of 16 August 1819', *History*, 89: 209–34.

Byrne, C. and Trew, K. (2005) 'Crime orientation, social relations and improvement in crime: Patterns emerging from offenders' accounts', *Howard Journal*, 44(2): 185–205.

Caddle, D. and Crisp, D. (1997) *Imprisoned Women and Mothers*, Home Office Research Study 162. London: Home Office.

Cain, M. (1990) 'Towards transgression: New directions in feminist criminology', *International Journal of the Sociology of Law*, 18(1): 1–18.

Cain, M. and Howe, A. (eds) (2008) *Women, Crime and Social Harm*. Oxford and Portland, OR: Hart Publishing.

Caldwell, D. and Williams, R.E. (2011) *Seeking Security in an Insecure World* (2nd edn). Plymouth, MA: Rowman & Littlefield.

Canton,R. (2013) 'The point of probation: On effectiveness, human rights and the virtues of obliquity', *Criminology and Criminal Justice*, 13(5): 577–93.

Carlen, P. (1983) *Women, Crime and Poverty*. London: Routledge and Kegan Paul.

Carlen, P. (1988a) *Women, Crime and Poverty*. Milton Keynes: Open University Press.

Carlen, P. (1988b) *Women's Imprisonment*. London: Routledge and Kegan Paul.

Carlen, P. (ed.) (2002) *Women and Punishment: the Struggle for Justice*. Cullompton: Willan.

Carlen, P. and Cook, D. (1989) *Paying for Crime*. Milton Keynes: Open University Press.

Carlen, P. and Worrall, A. (eds) (1987) *Gender, Crime and Justice*. Milton Keynes: Open University Press.

Carlen, P. and Worrall, A. (eds) (2004) *Analysing Women's Imprisonment*. Cullompton: Willan.

Carrabine, E. (2008) *Crime, Culture and Media*. Cambridge: Polity Press.

Carrier, J. (1988) *The Campaign for the Employment of Women as Police Officers*. Aldershot: Avebury Gower.

Carrington, K. (2006) 'Does feminism spoil girls? Explanations for official rises in female delinquency', *The Australian and New Zealand Journal of Criminology*, 39(1): 34–53.

Carrington, K. and Death, J. (2014) 'Feminist criminologies' contribution to understandings of sex, gender and crime', in R. Gartner and B. McCarthy (eds), *The Oxford Handbook of Gender Sex and Crime*. Oxford: Oxford University Press.

Carrington, K. and Hogg, R. (eds) (2002) *Critical Criminology: Issues, Debates, Challenges*. Portland, OR: Willan.

Carter, P. (2003) *Managing Offenders, Reducing Crime: A New Approach*. London: Cabinet Office.

Casburn, M. (1979) *Girls will be Girls: Explorations in Feminism*. London: WWRC.

Casburn, S. (2010) 'Flappers, amateurs and professionals: The spectrum of promiscuity in 1920s Britain', in K. Hardy, S. Kingston and T. Sanders (eds), *New Sociologies of Sex Work*. Aldershot: Ashgate.

Case, S.P. and Haines, K.R. (2015) 'Children first, offenders second: The centrality of engagement in positive youth justice', *The Howard Journal of Criminal Justice*. Available at: http://onlinelibrary.wiley.com/enhanced/doi/10.1111/hojo.12099/.

Casey, J. and Mitchell, M. (2007) 'Requirements of police managers and leaders from Sergeant to Commissioner', in M. Mitchell and J. Casey (eds), *Police Leadership and Management.* Sydney: Federation Press.

Caulkins, J.P., Kleiman, M.A. and Kulick, J.D. (2010) *Drug Production and Trafficking, Counterdrug Policies, and Security and Governance in Afghanistan.* New York: Centre on International Cooperation.

Cavadino, M., Dignan, J. and Mair, G. (2013) *The Penal System: An Introduction* (4th edn). London: Sage.

Centre for Women and Democracy (2013) *Sex and Power 2013: Who Runs Britain?* London: Centre for Women and Democracy.

Centre for Women and Democracy (2014) *Sex and Power 2014: Who Runs Britain?* London: Centre for Women and Democracy.

Chakrabarti, S. (2005) 'Rights and rhetoric: The politics of asylum and human rights culture in the United Kingdom', in L. Clements and P.A. Thomas (eds), *Human Rights Act: A Success Story?* Oxford: Blackwell Publishing.

Chakraborti, N. and Garland, J. (2009) *Hate Crime: Impact, Causes and Responses.* London: Sage.

Chakraborti, N., Garland, J. and Hardy, S.-J. (2014) *The Leicester Hate Crime Project: Findings and Conclusions.* Leicester: University of Leicester.

Chan, J. (1997) *Changing Police Culture: Policing in a Multicultural Society.* Cambridge: Cambridge University Press.

Charlesworth, H. (1994) 'What are women's international human rights?', in R. Cook (ed.), *Human Rights for Women: National and International Perspectives.* Philadelphia: University of Pennsylvania Press.

Chesney-Lind, M. (1973) 'The judicial enforcement of the female sex role: The family court and the delinquent', *Issues in Criminology,* 8: 51–70.

Chesney-Lind, M. (2006) 'Patriarchy, crime, and justice: Feminist criminology in an era of backlash', *Feminist Criminology,* 1(1): 6–26.

Chesney-Lind, M. and Shelden, R.G. (1998) *Girls, Delinquency and Juvenile Justice.* Belmont, CA: Wadsworth.

Chesney-Lind, M. and Irwin, K. (2004) 'From badness to mean-ness: Popular constructions of contemporary girlhood', in A. Harris (ed.), *All About the Girl: Culture, Power and Identity.* New York: Routledge. pp. 45–56.

Chesney-Lind, M. and Irwin, K. (2008) *Beyond Mad Girls: Gender, Violence and Hype.* New York: Routledge.

Chesney-Lind, M. and Morash, M. (2013) 'Transformative feminist criminology: A critical re-thinking of a discipline', *Critical Criminology,* 21: 287–304.

Chesney-Lind, M. and Pasko, L. (2013) *The Female Offender: Girls, Women and Crime* (3rd edn). London: Sage.

Children's Commissioner for England (2010) *Response to The Ministry of Justice on Bill of Rights and Responsibilities.* Available at: www.childrenscommissioner.gov.uk/publications/response-ministry-justice-bill-rights-and-responsibilities.

Choi, S., Guati, M., Holman, M. and Posner, E. (2011) 'Judging women', *Journal of Empirical Legal Studies,* 8(3): 504–32.

Christie, N. (2015) 'The ideal victim', in J. Shapland and M. Hall (eds), *Victimology.* Farnham: Ashgate.

Chuang, J. (2010) 'Rescuing trafficking from ideological capture: Prostitution Reform and anti-trafficking law and policy', *University of Pennsylvania Law Review,* 158(6): 1655–728.

Clark, A. (1987) *Women's Silence, Men's Violence: Sexual Assault in England 1770–1845.* London: Pandora Press.

Clarke, J. and Newman, J. (2004) 'Governing in the modern world', in D.L. Steinberg and R. Johnson (eds), *Blairism and the War of Persuasion*. London: Lawrence and Wishart.

Clear, T. (2012) 'The Big Society in the context of a changing justice system', *Criminology and Criminal Justice*, 12(5): 500–5.

Clegg, N. and Branson, R. (2015) 'We have been losing the war on drugs for four decades – end it now', *The Guardian*. Available at: www.theguardian.com/commentisfree/2015/mar/03/war-on-drugs-british-politicians-nick-clegg-richard-branson (accessed 7 July 2015).

Clegg, S. (1989) *Frameworks of Power*. London: Sage.

Clements, L. and Young, J. (1999) 'Human rights: Changing the culture', *Journal of Law and Society*, 26: 1–26.

Clout, L. (2008) 'Violent women: Binge drinking culture fuels rise in attacks by women', *The Telegraph*, 31 July 2008.

Cobbina, J.E., Like-Haislip, T. and Miller, J. (2010) 'Gang fights versus cat fights: Urban young men's gendered narratives of violence', *Deviant Behavior*, 31(7): 596–624.

Cockburn, C. (1991) *In the Way of Women: Men's Resistance to Sex Equality in Organizations*. London: Macmillan.

Coleman, M. and Reed, E. (2007) 'Homicide', in K. Coleman, K. Jansson, P. Kaiza and E. Reed (eds), *Homicides, Firearm Offences and Intimate Violence 2005–2007*, Home Office Statistical Bulletin 02/07. London: Home Office.

Coles, D. (2010) 'Protecting the human rights of vulnerable women: A spotlight on deaths of women in prison', *Probation Journal*, 57(1): 75–82.

Coles, D. (2013) 'Deaths of women in prison: The Human Rights issues arising', in M. Malloch and G. McIvor, *Women, Punishment and Social Justice*. Oxon: Routledge.

Colgan, F. and Ledwith, S. (1996) 'Women as organisational change agents', in S. Ledwith and F. Colgan (eds), *Women in Organisations: Challenging Gender Politics*. London: Macmillan.

College of Policing (2015) *The Leadership Review*. Available at: www.college.police.uk/What-we-do/Development/Promotion/the-leadership-review/Pages/The-Leadership-Review.aspx.

Collier, R. (1998) *Masculinities, Crime and Criminology*. London: Sage.

Collins, J., Paul, M., Kenneth, L. and Carp, M.R. (2010) 'Gender, critical mass, and judicial decision making', *Law and Policy*, 32: 260–81.

Collins, P. (2000) *Black Feminist Thought: Knowledge, Consciousness and the Politics of Empowerment*. New York: Routledge.

Collison, M. (1996) 'In search of the high life: Drugs, crime, masculinities and consumption', *British Journal of Criminology*, 36(3): 428–44.

Comack, E. (1996) *Women in Trouble*. Halifax: Fernwood Press.

Comack, E. (1999) 'New possibilities for a feminism "in" criminology? From dualism to diversity', *Canadian Journal of Criminology*, 4(2): 161.

Conley, C. (2007) *Certain Other Countries: Homicide, Gender and National Identity in Late Nineteenth Century England, Ireland, Scotland and Wales*. Columbus: Ohio State University Press.

Conley, C. (2014) 'Sexual violence in historical perspective', in R. Gartner and B. McCarthy (eds), *The Oxford Handbook of Gender Sex and Crime*. Oxford: Oxford University Press.

Connell, R.W. (1995) *Masculinities*. Berkeley, CA: University of California Press.

Connell, R.W. (2000) *The Men and the Boys*. Sydney: Allen and Unwin.

Connell, R.W. (2002) *Gender*. Cambridge: Polity Press.

Connell, R. (2009) *Gender: In World Perspective*. Cambridge and Malden: Polity Press.

Connell, R.W. and Messerschmidt, J. (2005) 'Hegemonic masculinity: Rethinking the concept', in *Gender and Society*, 19(6): 829–59.

Convery, U. and Moore, L. (2011) 'Children of imprisoned parents and their problems', in P. Scharff-Smith and L. Gampell (eds), *Children of Imprisoned Parents*. Denmark: European Network for Children of Imprisoned Parents.

Cook, D. (2006) *Criminal and Social Justice*. London: Sage.

Cook, K. and Jones, H. (2007) 'Surviving victimhood: The impact of feminist campaigns', in S. Walklate (ed.), *Handbook of Victims and Victimology*. Cullompton: Willan.

Cook, P.W. (1997) *Abused Men: The Hidden Side of Domestic Violence*. Westport, CT: Greenwood Press.

Cook, R. (ed.) (1994) *Human Rights for Women: National and International Perspectives*. Philadelphia: University of Pennsylvania Press.

Coomaraswamy, R. (1999) 'Reinventing international law: Women's rights as human rights in the international community', in *Debating Human Rights: Critical Essays from the United States and Asia*. London: Routledge.

Coomaraswamy, R. and Kois, L. (1999) 'Violence against women', *Women and International Human Rights*, 1: 177–217.

Copelon, R. (1994) 'Intimate terror: Understanding domestic violence as torture', in R. Cook (ed.), *Human Rights of Women: National and International Perspectives*. Philadelphia: Pennsylvania Press.

Corsianos, M. (2011) 'Responding to officers' gendered experiences through community policing and improving accountability to citizens,' *Contemporary Justice Review*, 14: 7–20.

Corston, J. (2007) *The Corston Report: A Review of Women with Particular Vulnerabilities in the Criminal Justice System*. London: Home Office.

Cortoni, F. (2010) 'The assessment of female sexual offenders', in T.A. Gannon and F. Cortoni (eds), *Female Sexual Offenders: Theory, Assessment and Treatment*. Chichester: Wiley-Blackwell.

Costigan, R. and Thomas, P. (2005) 'The Human Rights Act: A view from below', in L. Clements and P.A. Thomas, *Human Rights Act: A Success Story?* Oxford: Blackwell Publishing.

Council of European Convention (2011) *Council of Europe Convention on Preventing and Combating Violence Against Women and Domestic Violence*. Strasbourg: Council of Europe.

Cox, A. and Miles, T. (2008) 'Judging the Voting Rights Act', *Columbia Law Review*, 108(1): 1–54.

Cox, P. (2003) *Gender, Justice and Welfare: Bad Girls in Britain, 1900–1950*. Basingstoke: Palgrave Macmillan.

Cox, P. (2012) 'Marginal mothers, reproductive autonomy and repeat losses to care', *Journal of Law and Society*, 39(4): 541–61.

Coy, M. (ed.) (2012) *Prostitution, Harm and Gender Inequality: Theory, Research and Policy*. Aldershot: Ashgate.

Coy, M., Hovarth, M. and Kelly, K. (2012) 'Troubling notions of male entitlement: Men consuming, boasting and confessing about paying for sex', in M. Coy (ed.), *Prostitution, Harm and Gender Inequality: Theory, Research and Policy*. Aldershot: Ashgate.

Coy, M., Kelly, L., Elvines, F., Garner, M. and Kanyeredzi, A. (2013) *"Sex Without Consent, I Suppose That is Rape": How Young People Understand Sexual Consent*, a report commissioned by the Office of Children's Commissioner's Inquiry into Child Sexual Exploitation in Gangs and Groups. London: Office of the Children's Commissioner.

Coyle, A. (2003) *A Human Rights Approach to Prison Management: Handbook for Prison Staff*. Oxford: Blackwell.

CPS (2015) *Violence Against Women and Girls Crime Report*. London: CPS.

Crawshaw, R., Cullen, S. and Williamson, T. (2007) *Human Rights and Policing* (2nd edn). Leiden: Martinus Nijhoff Publishers.

Creek, S. and Dunn, J. (2014) 'Intersectionality and the study of sex, gender and crime', in R. Gartner and B. McCarthy (eds), *The Oxford Handbook of Gender Sex and Crime*. Oxford: Oxford University Press.

Criminal Injuries Compensation Authority (2015) *Criminal Injuries Compensation Authority Annual Report and Accounts 2014–15*, HC 200. London: CICA.

Cromack, V. (1995) 'The policing of domestic violence: An empirical study', *Policing and Society*, 5: 185–99.

Crowther, C. (2000) 'Thinking about the underclass: Towards a political economy of policing', *Theoretical Criminology* 4(2): 149–67.

Crowther, C. (2004) 'Over-policing and under-policing social exclusion', in R. Hopkins-Burke (ed.), *Hard Policing/Soft Policing: Dilemmas and Debates in Contemporary Policing*. Cullompton: Willan.

Crowther-Dowey, C. and Long, M. (2011) 'TINA and crime policy in the context of the modernisation agenda', paper presented at the Alternative Futures: Issues for the Social Sciences in the Twenty-First Century, Nottingham Trent University, 16 February.

Crowther-Dowey, C. and Fussey, P. (2013) *Researching Crime: Approaches, Methods and Application*. Basingstoke: Palgrave.

Crowther-Dowey, C., Gillespie, T. and Hopkins Burke, K. (2016) 'Building healthy relationships for young people and the prevention of domestic abuse', in S. Hilder and V. Bettinson (eds), *Domestic Violence: Inter-disciplinary Perspectives on Prevention, Protection and Intervention*. Basingstoke: Palgrave.

Cunningham, K. (2003) 'Cross-regional trends in female terrorism', *Studies in Conflict and Terrorism*, 26: 171–95.

Custer, P.A. (2007) 'Refiguring Jemima: Gender, work and politics in Lancashire 1770–1820', *Past and Present*, 195: 127–58.

Dabhoiwala, F. (1996) 'The construction of honour, reputation and status in late seventeenth and early eighteenth century England', *Transactions of the Royal Historical Society*, 6: 201–13.

Dahl, R.A. (1958) 'A critique of the ruling elite model', *American Political Science Review*, 52(1): 463–69.

Daily Mail (2008) 'Feral sex: The terrifying rise of violent girl gang', 16 May.

Daily Mail (2011) 'Escalating thuggery perpetrated by girls', 11 February.

Daily Telegraph, The (2015a) 'Terrifying rise of the all-girl gang', 11 May.

Daily Telegraph, The (2015b) 'The female face of terror', 28 January.

Dallaire, D.H. (2007) 'Incarcerated mothers and fathers: A comparison of risks for children and families', *Family Relations*, 56: 440–53.

Dalton, A. and Asal, V. (2011) 'Is it ideology or desperation: Why do organisations deploy women in violent terrorist attacks?', *Studies in Conflict and Terrorism*, 34: 802–19.

Daly, K. and Chesney-Lind, M. (1988) 'Feminism and criminology', *Justice Quarterly*, 5: 497–538.

Daly, K. and Maher, L. (1998) 'Crossroads and intersections: Building from feminist critique', in K. Daly and L. Maher (eds), *Criminology at the Crossroads: Feminist Readings in Crime and Justice*. New York: Oxford University Press.

Datesman, S. and Scarpetti, F. (1980) 'Unequal protection for males and females in the juvenile court', in S. Datesman and F. Scarpetti (eds), *Women, Crime and Justice*. Oxford: Oxford University Press.

Davidson, J. (2008) *Child Sexual Abuse: Media Representations and Government Reactions*. Abingdon: Routledge-Cavendish.

Davies, A. (1998) *The Restructuring of Police Forces: Implications for Command Resilience*. Pangbourne: Police Superintendent's Association of England and Wales.

Davies, A. (1999) 'These viragoes are no less cruel than the lads; Young women, gangs and violence in late Victorian Manchester and Salford', *British Journal of Criminology*, 39: 72–89.

Davies, A. (2008) *The Gangs of Manchester*. Preston: Milo Books.

Davies, A. (2014) 'Glasgow: City of gangs', *History Scotland*, 14(6): 30–4.

Davies, A. and Thomas, R. (2003) 'Talking COP: Discourses of change and policing identities', *Public Administration*, 81(4): 681.

Davies, H., Nutley, S. and Smith, P. (eds) (2000) *What Works?: Evidence-based Policy and Practice in Public Services*. Bristol: Policy Press.

Davies, P., Francis, P. and Greer, C. (2007) *Victims, Crime and Society*. London: Sage.

Davis, R. and Williams, G. (2003) 'Reform of the judicial appointments process: Gender and the bench of the High Court of Australia', *Melbourne University Law Review*, 27: 910-63.

D'Cruze, S. and Jackson, L. (2009) *Women, Crime and Justice in England since 1660*. Basingstoke: Palgrave Macmillan.

Dean, T. (2001) *Crime in Medieval Europe, 1200-1550*. London: Longman.

Dearing, M.P. (2010) 'Like red tulips at springtime: Understanding the absence of female martyrs in Afghanistan', *Studies in Conflict and Terrorism*, 33(12).

Defoe, D. (1922) *Moll Flanders*. Harmondsworth: Penguin.

DeHart, D. and Lynch, S. (2013) 'Gendered pathways to crime: The relationship between victimisation and offending', in C. Renzetti, S. Miller and A.R. Gover (eds), *Routledge International Handbook of Gender and Crime Studies*. New York: Routledge. pp. 120-38.

Denov, M. (2004) 'The long-term effects of child sexual abuse by female perpetrators', *Journal of Interpersonal Violence*, 19(10): 1137-56.

Densten, I.L. (1999) 'Senior Australia law enforcement leadership under examination', *Policing: An International Journal of Police Strategies and Management*, 26(3): 400-18.

Department for Constitutional Affairs (2006) *Review of the Implementation of the Human Rights Act*. London: Department of Constitutional Affairs.

Diamond, P. (ed.) (2007) *Public Matters: The Renewal of the Public Realm*. London: Methuen Politicos.

Dick, P., Silvestri, M. and Westmarland, L. (2013) 'Women police: Potential and possibilities for police reform', in J. Brown (ed.), *The Future of Policing*. London: Routledge.

Dixon, M., Reed, H., Rogers, B. and Stone, L. (2006) *Crime Share: The Unequal Impact of Crime*. London: IPPR.

Dobash, R.P. and Dobash, R.E. (1979) *Violence against Wives*. New York: The Free Press.

Dobash, R.P and Dobash, R.E. (2001) 'Violence against women: A review of recent Anglo–American research', *Journal of Conflict and Violence Research*, 3: 5–22.

Dobash, R.P. and Dobash, R.E. (2012) 'Women's violence to men in intimate relationships: Working on a puzzle', *British Journal of Criminology*, 44: 324–49.

Dobash, R.P., Dobash, R.E. and Gutteridge, S. (1986) *Imprisonment of Women*. London: Basil Blackwell.

Dobby, J., Anscombe, J. and Tuffin, R. (2004) *Police Leadership: Expectations and Impact*, Home Office online report 20/04. London: Research Development and Statistics Office. Available at: http://collection.europarchive.org/tna/20080205132101/homeoffice.gov.uk/rds/pdfs04/rdsolr2004.

Dodd, T. and Hunter, P. (1992) *The National Prison Survey*. London: HMSO.

Doezema, J. (1999) 'Loose women or lost women? The re-emergence of the myth of white slavery in contemporary discourse of trafficking in women', *Gender Issues*, 18(1): 23–50.

Doezema, J. (2005) 'Now you see her, now you don't: Sex work at the UN trafficking protocol negotiation', *Social and Legal Studies*, 14(1): 61–89.

Dorling, D. (2005) 'Prime suspect: Murder in Britain', in D. Dorling, D. Gordon, P. Hillyard, C. Pantazis, S. Pemberton and S. Tombs, *Criminal Obsessions: Why Harm Matters More than Crime*. London: Crime and Society Foundation.

Downes, D., Rock, P., Chinkin, C. and Gearty, C. (2007) *Crime, Social Control and Human Rights: From Moral Panics to States of Denial*. Cullompton: Willan.

Durston, G. (2007) *Victims and Viragos: Metropolitan Women, Crime and the Eighteenth Century Justice System*. Suffolk: Arima Press.

Dyer, C. (2007a) 'Ministers face legal challenge over jails crisis'. *The Guardian*, 4 June. Available at: www.theguardian.com/uk/2007/jun/04/prisonsandprobation.ukcrime (accessed 26 October 2015).

Dyer, C. (2007b) 'Sentencing change leads to a £10m jail backlog.' *The Guardian*, 23 June. Available at: www.theguardian.com/uk/2007/jun/23/ukcrime.humanrights (accessed 26 October 2015).

Eagleton, T. (2011) *Why Marx was Right*. New Haven, CT: Yale University Press.

Easton, H. and Matthews, R. (2010) *Evaluation of the 218 Centre*. Glasgow: Glasgow City Council.

Easton, H. and Matthews, R. (2011) *Evaluation of the Inspire Women's Project*. Belfast: Northern Ireland Department of Justice.

Easton, H., Silvestri, M., Evans, K., Matthews R. and Walklate, S. (2010) 'Conditional cautions: Evaluation of the women specific condition pilot', *Ministry of Justice Research Series, 14/10*.

Easton, S. (2013) 'Protecting prisoners: The impact of international human rights law on the treatment of prisoners in the United Kingdom', *The Prison Journal*: 1–18.

Eaton, M. (1986) *Justice for Women? Family, Court and Social Control*. Milton Keynes: Open University Press.

Eaton, M. (1993) *Women after Prison*. Buckingham: Open University Press.

Eaton, M. (2000) 'A woman in her own time: Frances Heidensohn within and beyond criminology', *Women and Criminal Justice*, 12: 9–28.

Edwards, S. (1989) *Policing Domestic Violence: Women Law and the State*. London: Sage.

Eisner, M. (2003) 'Long-term trends in violent crime', *Crime and Justice: A Review of Research*, 30: 83–142.

Elias, N. (1994) *The Civilising Process: The History of Manners and State Formation and Civilisation* (single integrated edn). Oxford: Blackwell.

Elliott, I., Eldridge H., Ashfield, S. and Beech, A. (2010) 'Exploring risk: Potential static, dynamic, protective and treatment factors in the clinical histories of female sex offenders', *Journal of Family Violence*, 25: 595–602.

Emsley, C. (2005) *Hard Men: Violence in England since 1750*. London: Hamledon.

Epstein, R. (2014) 'Mothers in prison: The sentencing of mothers and the rights of the child', *What is Justice: Re-imagining Penal Policy*, working paper. London: Howard League for Penal Reform.

Ericson, R. and Haggerty, K. (1997) *Policing the Risk Society*. Oxford. Clarendon Press.

Evans, K. and Jamieson, J. (2008) *Gender and Crime: A Reader*. Maidenhead: Open University Press.

Falconer, Lord (2005) *Increasing Judicial Diversity: The Next Steps*. Available at: www.dca.gov.uk/speeches/2005.

Farrall, S. and Calverley, A. (2006) *Understanding Desistance: Theoretical Directions in Resettlement and Rehabilitation*. Milton Keynes: Open University Press.

Farrington, D.P. (1994) 'Human development and criminal careers', in M. Maguire, R. Morgan and R. Reiner (eds), *The Oxford Handbook of Criminology*. Oxford: Oxford University Press.

Farrington, D.P. and Morris, A. (1983) 'Sex, sentencing and reconviction', *British Journal of Criminology*, 23(93): 229–48.

Farrington, D.P., Coid, J.W., Harnett, L., Joliffe, D., Sorteriou, N., Turner, R. and West, D.J. (2006) *Criminal Careers up to Age 50 and Life Success up to 48*, Home Office Research Study No. 299. London: Home Office.

Farrington, D.P., Jolliffe, D., Hawkins, J.D., Catalano, R.F., Hill, K.G. and Kosterman, R. (2010) 'Why are boys more likely to be referred to juvenile court? Gender differences in official and self-reported delinquency', *Victims and Offenders*, 5: 25–44.

Faulkner, D. (2007) 'Prospects for progress in penal reform', *Criminology and Criminal Justice*, 7(2): 135–52.

Fawcett Society (2004) *Commission on Women and the Criminal Justice System*. London: Fawcett Society.

Fawcett Society (2006) *Justice and Equality*. London: Fawcett Society.

Fawcett Society (2007) *Women and Justice: Third Annual Review of the Commission on Women and the Criminal Justice System*. London: Fawcett Society.

Fawcett Society (2009) *Engendering Justice: From Policy to Practice*, final report of the Commission on Women and the Criminal Justice System. London: Fawcett Society.

Fawcett Society (2010) *What about Women?* London: Fawcett Society.

Feeley, M. and Little, D. (1991) 'The vanishing female: The decline of women in the criminal process, 1687–1912', *Law and Society Review*, 25: 719–57.

Feeley, M. and Simon, J. (1994) 'Actuarial justice: The emerging new criminal law', in D. Nelken (ed.), *The Futures of Criminology*. London: Sage.

Feenan, D. (2008) 'Women judges: Gendering judging: Justifying diversity', *Journal of Law and Society*, 35(4): 490–519.

Feingold, D. (2005) 'Think again: Human trafficking', *Foreign Policy*, 150: 26–30.

Ferguson, K. (1984) *The Feminist Case against Bureaucracy*. Philadelphia: Temple University Press.

Ferraro, K. (1989) 'The legal response to woman battering in the US', in J. Hanmer, J. Radford and E. Stanko (eds), *Women, Policing and Male Violence*. London: Routledge.

Fielding, N. (1994) 'Cop canteen culture', in T. Newburn and E. Stanko (eds), *Just Boys Doing the Business: Men, Masculinity and Crime*. London: Routledge.

Findlay, M. (1999) *The Globalization of Crime*. Cambridge: Cambridge University Press.

Fink, N.C. (2010) *Bombs and Ballots: Terrorism, Political Violence and Governance in Bangladesh Working Paper*. New York: International Peace Institute.

Finkelhor, D. (ed.) (1984) *Child Sexual Abuse: New Theory and Research*. New York: Free Press.

Fionda, J. (2005) *Devils and Changes: Youth Policy and Crime*. Oxford: Hart Publishing.

Fisher, T. (1997) *Prostitution and the Victorians*. Stroud: Sutton.

Fitzpatrick, J. (1994) 'The use of international rights norms to combat violence against women', in R. Cook (ed.), *Human Rights for Women: National and International Perspectives*. Philadelphia: University of Pennsylvania Press.

Fleetwood, J. (2014) *Drug Mules: Women in the International Cocaine Trade*. Basingstoke: Palgrave Macmillan.

Fleetwood, J. and Haas, N.U. (2011) 'Gendering the agenda: Women drug mules in Resolution 52/1 of the Commission of Narcotic Drugs at the United Nations', *Drugs and Alcohol Today*, 11(4): 194–204.

Fleetwood, J. and Torres, A. (2011) 'Mothers and children of the international drug war', in D. Barrett (ed.), *Children of the Drug War*. New York: International Harm Reduction Association. pp. 125–41.

Fleming, J. and Lafferty, G. (2003) 'Equity confounded: Women in Australian police organisations', *Labour and Industry*, 13(3): 37–49.

Fleming, J. and McLaughlin, E. (2010) '"The public gets what the public wants?" Interrogating the "public confidence" agenda', *Policing*, 4(3): 199.

Flood-Page, C., Campbell, S., Harrington, V. and Miller, J. (2000) *Youth Crime: Findings from the1998/1999 Youth Lifestyles Survey*. London: Home Office.

Foster, J., Newburn, T. and Souhami, A. (2005) *Assessing the Impact of the Stephen Lawrence Inquiry*, Home Office Research Study 294. London: Home Office.

France, A. (2007) *Understanding Youth in Late Modernity*. Milton Keynes: Open University Press.

Francis, B., Barry, J., Bowater, R., Miller, N., Soothill, K. and Ackerley, E. (2004) *Using Homicide Data to Assist Murder Investigations*, Home Office Online Report 26/04. London: Home Office.

Frawley, P. and Naylor, B.G. (2014) 'Human rights and people with disabilities in closed environments', *Law in Context*, 31: 48–83.

Fussey, P. (2005) Installing CCTV: A Study of the Networks of Surveillance Policy. Unpublished PhD thesis, Brunel University.

Gadd, D. (2000) 'Masculinities, violence and defended social subjects', *Theoretical Criminology*, 4(4): 429–49.

Gadd, D. (2002) 'Masculinities and violence against female partners', *Social and Legal Studies*, 11(1): 61–80.

Gadd, D. (2003) 'Reading between the lines: Subjectivity and men's violence', *Men and Masculinities*, 5(4): 333–54.

Gadd, D. (2006a) 'The role of recognition in the desistance process: A case study of a far right activist', *Theoretical Criminology*, 10(2): 179–202.

Gadd, D. (2006b) 'Masculinities and violence against female partners', in S.M. Whitehead (eds), *Men and Masculinities: Critical Concepts in Sociology*. London: Routledge.

Gadd, D. and Farrall, S. (2004) 'Criminal careers, desistance and subjectivity: Interpreting men's narrative of change', *Theoretical Criminology* 8(2): 123–56.

Gadd, D., Farrall, S., Lombard, N. and Dallimore, D. (2002) *Domestic Abuse against Men in Scotland*. Edinburgh: Scottish Executive.

Gadd, D. and Jefferson, T. (2007) *Psychosocial Criminology*. London: Sage.

Gamble, A. (2009) The *Spectre at the Feast: Capitalist Crisis and the Politics of Recession*. Basingstoke: Palgrave.

Gannon, T. and Rose, M. (2008) 'Female child sexual offenders: Towards integrating theory and practice', *Aggression and Violent Behaviour*, 13: 442–61.

Garland, D. (2001) *The Culture of Control: Crime and Social Order in Contemporary Society*. Oxford: Oxford University Press.

Garside, R. (2006) *Right for the Wrong Reasons: Making Sense of Criminal Justice Failure*. London: Crime and Society Foundation.

Gartner, R. and McCarthy, B. (eds) (2014) *The Oxford Handbook of Gender Sex and Crime*. Oxford: Oxford University Press.

Gaskill, M. (2007) *Witch Finders: A Seventeenth-Century English Tragedy*. Cambridge, MA: Harvard University Press.

Gavin, H. (2009) "Mummy wouldn't do that": The perception and construction of the female child sex abuser', *Evil, Women and the Feminine*, 1–3 May, Budapest, Hungary.

Gelsthorpe, L. (2006) 'Counterblast: Women and criminal justice: Saying it again, again and again', *The Howard Journal*, 45(4): 421–4.

Gelsthorpe, L. (2010) 'Women, crime and control', *Criminology and Criminal Justice*, 10(4): 375–86.

Gelsthorpe, L. (2013) 'Legitimacy, law and locality: Making the case for change', in M. Malloch and G. McIvor (eds), *Women, Punishment and Social Justice: Human Rights and Penal Practices*. London: Routledge.

Gelsthorpe, L. and Morris, A. (eds) (1990) *Feminist Perspectives in Criminology*. Buckingham: Open University Press.

Gelsthorpe, L., Sharpe, G. and Roberts, J. (2007) *Provision for Women Offenders in the Community*. London: Fawcett Society.

George, M. and Yarwood, D. (2004) *Male Domestic Violence Victims Survey 2001: Main Findings*. Available at: http://dewar4research.org/DOCS/mdv.pdf (accessed 10 January 2007).

Giddens, A. (1990) *The Consequences of Modernity*. Cambridge: Polity Press.

Giddens, A. (2007) *Over To You, Mr Brown*. Cambridge: Polity Press.

Gill, A. (2009) 'Honour' killings and the quest for justice in black and minority ethnic communities in the UK', *Criminal Justice Policy Review*, 20: 475–94.

Gill, A. (2014) *'Honour' Killing and Violence: Theory, Policy and Practice*. London: Palgrave Macmillan.

Gill, A., Begikhani, N. and Hague, G. (2012) 'Honour-based violence in Kurdish communities', *Women's Studies International*, 35(2): 75–85.

Gillespie, A. (2016) *Globalisation: Key Issues and Debates*. London: Routledge.

Gilligan, C. (1982) *In a Different Voice: Psychological Theory and Women's Development*. Cambridge, MA: Harvard University Press.

Glueck, S. and Glueck, E. (1934) *Five Hundred Delinquent Women*. New York: Knopf.

Godfrey, B. (2014) 'A historical perspective on criminal justice responses to female and male offending', in R. Gartner and B. McCarthy (eds), *The Oxford Handbook of Gender Sex and Crime*. Oxford: Oxford University Press.

Godfrey, B., Farrall, S. and Karstedt, S. (2005) 'Explaining gendered sentencing patterns for violent men and women in the late Victorian and Edwardian period', *British Journal of Criminology*, 45: 696–720.

Goldman, S. (1979) 'Should there be affirmative action for the judiciary?', *Judicature*, 62: 489.

Goldson, B. (2002) *Vulnerable Inside: Children in Secure and Penal Settings*. London: The Children's Society.

Goldson, B. (2009) 'COUNTERBLAST: Difficult to understand or defend – a reasoned case for raising the age of criminal responsibility', *The Howard Journal*, 48(5): 514–21.

Goldson, B. and Muncie, J. (2012) 'Towards a global "child friendly" juvenile justice?', *International Journal of Law, Crime and Justice*, 40: 47–64.

Goldstein, J.H. (2001) *War and Gender: How Gender Shapes the War System and Vice Versa*. Cambridge: Cambridge University Press.

Goldwin, C. (1990) *Understanding the Gender Gap*. New York: Oxford University Press.

Gonzales, A., Freilich, J. and Chermal, S. (2014) 'How women engage home-grown terrorism', *Feminist Criminology*, 9(4): 344–66.

Gonzalez-Perez, M. (2008) *Women and Terrorism: Female Activity in Domestic and International Terror Groups*. New York: Routledge.

Goodey, J. (1997) 'Boys don't cry: Masculinity, fear of crime and fearlessness', *British Journal of Criminology*, 37: 401–18.

Goodey, J. (2005) *Victims and Victimology: Research, Policy and Practice*. London: Longman.

Goodyear, M. and Cuisick, L. (2007) 'Protection of sex workers', *British Medical Journal*, 334: 52–3.

Goold, B.J. (2004) *CCTV and Policing: Public Area Surveillance and Police Practices in Britain*. Oxford: Oxford University Press.

Gottschalk, P. and Glaso, L. (2013) 'Gender in white-collar crime: An empirical study of pink-collar criminals', *International Letters of Social and Humanistic Sciences*, 4: 22–34.

Government Equalities Office (2013) *The Business Case for Equality and Diversity: A Survey of the Academic Literature*, BSC Occasional Paper 4. Available at: www.gov.uk/government/organisations/department-for-business-innovation-skills.

Gowing, L. (1996) *Domestic Dangers: Women, Words and Sex in Early Modern London*. Oxford: Oxford University Press.

Gozdziak, E. (2014) 'In search of research on human trafficking', in R. Gartner and B. McCarthy (eds), *The Oxford Handbook of Gender Sex and Crime*. Oxford: Oxford University Press.

Grace, S., Lloyd, C. and Smith, L. (1992) *Rape: From Recording to Conviction*, Research and Planning Unit Paper 71. London: Home Office.

Graham, J. and Bowling, B. (1995) *Young People and Crime*, Home Office Research Study 145. London: Home Office.

Graham, R. (2006) 'Male rape and the careful construction of the male victim', *Social and Legal Studies*, 15: 187–208.

Gramsci, A. (1971) *Selection from the Prison Notebooks*. London: Lawrence and Wishart.

Grant, I. and Smith, L. (1991) 'Gender representation in the Canadian judiciary', in *Appointing Judges: Philosophy, Politics and Practice*. Ontario: Ontario Law Reform Commission.

Graycar, R. and Morgan, J. (2002) *The Hidden Gender of Law* (2nd edn). Sydney: Federation Press.

Grayston, A.D. and De Luca, R.V. (1999) 'Female perpetrators of child sexual abuse: A review of the clinical and empirical literature', *Aggression and Violent Behavior*, 4: 93–106.

Green, A.H. (1999) 'Female sex offenders', in J.A. Shaw (ed.), *Sexual Aggression*. Washington, DC: American Psychiatric Press.

Green, P. (2008) 'Women and natural disasters: State crime and discourse in vulnerability', in M. Cain and A. Howe (eds), *Women, Crime and Social Harm: Towards a Criminology for the Global Age*. Oxford: Hart Publishing.

Gregory, S. and Lees, S. (1999) *Policing Sexual Assault*. London: Routledge.

Guardian, The (2006) 'British girls among most violent in world, WHO survey shows'. Available at: www.theguardian.com/uk/2006/jan/24/schools.pupilbehaviour (accessed 26 October 2015).

Guardian, The (2012) 'South Africa's corruption-tainted police force gets first female chief', 13 June. Available at: www.theguardian.com/world/2012/jun/13/south-africa-police-female-chief

Guardian, The (2013) *Government Cuts Threaten Gender Equality Gains, Warns Report*. Available at: www.theguardian.com/society/2013/may/13/government-cuts-reversing-gender-equality-gain (accessed 14 February 2015).

Guardian, The (2014) 'Schoolgirl jihadis: The female Islamists leaving home to join Isis fighters', 29 September. Available at: www.theguardian.com/world/2014/sep/29/schoolgirl-jihadis-female-islamists-leaving-home-join-isis-iraq-syria (accessed 26 October 2015).

Guardian, The (2015a) 'First FGM prosecution: How the case came to court', 4 February. Available at: www.theguardian.com/society/2015/feb/04/first-female-genital-mutilation-prosecution-dhanuson-dharmasena-fgm.

Guardian, The (2015b) 'India approves rule requiring one-third of Delhi police to be women', 20 March. Available at: www.theguardian.com/world/2015/mar/20/india-one-third-of-delhi-police-women.

Guardian, The (2015c) 'Summer budget 2015 represents new centre of UK politics, says Osborne', 9 July. Available at: www.theguardian.com/uk-news/2015/jul/09/summer-budget-2015-working-tax-credits-cuts-work-penalty-labour-chris-leslie (accessed 26 October 2015).

Guardian, The (2016) 'China sees "many challenges" in 2016 as trade slumps on weak external demand', 13 January. Available at: www.theguardian.com/business/2016/jan/13/china-sees-many-challenges-in-2016-as-trade-slumps-on-weak-external-demand (accessed 13 January 2016).

Gurr, T.R. (1981) 'Historical trends in violent crime: A critical review of the evidence', *Crime and Justice: An Annual Review of Research*, 3: 295–353.

Hadfield, P. (2006) *Bar Wars: Contesting the Night in Contemporary British Cities*. Oxford: Oxford University Press.

Hadfield, P. (2009) 'Nightlife and crime in international perspective', in P. Hadfield (ed.), *Nightlife and Crime: Social Order and Governance in International Perspective*. Oxford: Oxford University Press. pp. 3–18.

Haines, K.R. and Case, S.P. (2015) *Positive Youth Justice: Children First, Offenders Second*. Bristol: Policy Press.

Hale, B. (2001) 'Equality and the judiciary: Why should we want more women judges?', *Public Law*, 489.

Hale, B. (2005) 'Making a difference? Why we need a more diverse judiciary', *Northern Ireland Legal Q*, 56: 281–92.

Hale, C. (1996) 'Fear of crime: A review of the literature', *International Review of Victimology* 4: 79–150.

Halford, S., Savage, M. and Witz, A. (1997) *Gender, Career and Organisations: Current Developments in Policing, Nursing and Local Government*. London: Macmillan.

Hall, C. (1992) 'Feminism and feminist history', in C. Hall, *White, Male and Middle Class: Explorations in Feminism and History*. Cambridge: Polity Press.

Hall, E. (1993) 'Smiling, deferring, and flirting: Doing gender by giving "good service"', *Work and Occupations*, 20(4): 452–71.

Hall, M. (2012) *Victims of Crime: Policy and Practice in Criminal Justice*. London: Routledge.

Hall, N. (2013) *Hate Crime* (2nd edn). London: Routledge.

Hall, S. (2002) 'Daubing the drudges of fury: Men, violence and the piety of the hegemonic masculinity thesis', *Theoretical Criminology*, 6(1): 35–61.

Hall, S. (2012) *Theorizing Crime and Deviance: A New Perspective*. London: Sage.

Hall, S. and McClean, C. (2009) 'A tale of two capitalisms: A preliminary analysis of homicide rates in Western Europe and Anglo American societies', *Theoretical Criminology*, 13(3): 313–39.

Hall, S. and Winlow, S. (2015) *Revitalizing Criminological Theory: Towards a New Ultra-Realism*. London: Routledge.

Halliday, F. (2007) 'The fates of solidarity and abuse', in D. Downes, P. Rock, C. Chinkin and C. Gearty (eds), *Crime, Social Control and Human Rights: From Moral Panics to States of Denial*. Cullompton: Willan.

Hallsworth, S. (2013) *The Gang and Beyond: Interpreting Violent Street Worlds*. Basingstoke: Palgrave.

Hamilton, C. (2011) *Guidance for Legislative Reform of Juvenile Justice*. New York: The Children's Legal Centre, UNICEF.

Haney, L. (2013) 'Mother as punishment: The case of parenting in prison', *Signs*, 3991: 105–30.

Hanmer, J. and Maynard, M. (eds) (1987) *Women, Violence and Social Control*. London: Macmillan.

Hanmer, J. and Saunders, S. (1990) *Women, Violence and Crime Prevention: A Study of Changes in Police Policy and Practices in West Yorkshire*, Violence, Abuse and Gender Relations Study Unit Research Paper 1. Bradford: Bradford University.

Hannah-Moffat, K. (2001) *Punishment in Disguise: Penal Governance and Canadian Federal Women's Imprisonment*. Toronto, ON: University of Toronto Press.

Hannah-Moffat, K. (2002) 'Creating choices: Reflecting on choices', in P. Carlen (ed.), *Women and Punishment: The Struggle for Justice*. Cullompton: Willan.

Hannah-Moffat, K. (2004) 'Gendering risk at what cost: Negotiations of gender and risk in Canadian women's prisons', *Feminism and Psychology*, 14(2): 243–9.

Hannah-Moffat, K. (2006) 'Pandora's Box: Risk/need and gender-responsive corrections', *Criminology and Public Policy*, 5(1): 1301–11.

Hannah-Moffat, K. (2010) 'Sacrosanct or flawed? Risk, accountability and gender-responsive penal politics', *Current Issues in Criminal Justice*, 22(2): 193–215.

Harper, G. and Chitty, C. (2005) *The Impact of Corrections on Re-offending: A Review of What Works*, Home Office Research Study 291. London: Home Office.

Harper, G., Man, L.-H., Taylor, S. and Niven, S. (2005) 'Factors associated with offending', in G. Harper and C. Chitty, *The Impact of Corrections on Re-offending: A Review of What Works*, Home Office Research Study 291. London: Home Office.

Harris, P. and Salkeld, L. (2009) 'Price of depravity: Parents' fury as nursery paedophile Vanessa George gets just seven years' jail', *Mail Online*, 16 December. Available at: www.dailymail.co.uk/news/article-1235934/Vanessa-George-jailed-seven-yearschilling-abuse-children-care.

Hart, B. (1993) 'Battered women and the criminal justice system', *American Behavioral Science*, 36: 624–38.

Hassell, K. and Brandl, S. (2009) 'An examination of the workplace experiences of police patrol officers: The role of race, sex, and sexual orientation', *Police Quarterly*, 12(4): 408–30.

Hasso, F. (2005) 'Discursive and political deployments by/of the 2002 Palestinian women suicide bombers/martyrs', *Feminist Review*, 81: 23–51.

Hawton, K., Linsell, L., Adeniji, A., Sariaslan, A. and Faizel, S. (2014) 'Self-harm in prisons in England and Wales: An epidemiological study of prevalence, risk factors, clustering, and subsequent suicide', *The Lancet*, 383(9923): 1147–54.

Hay, C. (1999) *The Political Economy of New Labour: Labouring under False Pretences?* Manchester: Manchester University Press.

Hayman, S. (2006) 'The reforming prison: A Canadian tale', in F. Heidensohn (ed.), *Gender and Justice: New Perspectives*. Cullompton: Willan.

Hearn, J. (1998) *The Violences of Men*. London: Sage.

Hearn, J. (2003) '"Just men doing crime" (and criminology)', *Criminal Justice Matters*, 53(Autumn): 12–13.

Hearn, J. (2015) *Men of the World: Genders, Globalisation and Transnational Times*. London: Sage.

Hearn, J. and Parkin, W. (1987) *'Sex' at 'Work': The Power and Paradox of Organization Sexuality*. New York: St Martin's Press.

Hearn, J. and Whitehead, A. (2006) 'Collateral damage: Men's domestic violence to women seen through men's relations with men', *Probation Journal*, 53(1): 38–56.

Hedderman, C. (2010a) 'Government policy on women offenders: Labour's legacy and the Coalition's challenge', *Punishment and Society*, 12(4): 485–500.

Hedderman, C. (2010b) 'Policy development in England and Wales', in R. Sheehan, G. McIvor and C. Trotter (eds), *Working with Women in the Community*. Cullompton, Devon: Willan.

Hedderman, C., Palmer, E. and Hollin, C. (2008) *Implementing Services for Women Offenders and those 'At Risk' of Offending: Action Research with Together Women*, Ministry of Justice Research Series 12/08. London: Ministry of Justice.

Hedderman, C., Gunby, C. and Shelton, N. (2011) 'What women want: The importance of qualitative approaches in evaluating work with women offenders', *Criminology and Criminal Justice*, 11(1): 3–19.

Heidensohn, F. (1968) 'The deviance of women: A critique and an enquiry', *British Journal of Sociology*, 19: 160–75.

Heidensohn, F. (1985) *Women and Crime*. Basingstoke: Palgrave.

Heidensohn, F. (1989) *Crime and Society*. New York: New York University Press.

Heidensohn, F. (1992) *Women in Control: The Role of Women in Law Enforcement*. Oxford: Oxford University Press.

Heidensohn, F. (1994) 'From being to knowing: Some issues in the study of gender in contemporary society', *Women and Criminal Justice*, 6: 13–37.

Heidensohn, F. (1996) *Women and Crime* (2nd edn). London: Macmillan.

Heidensohn, F. (2000) *Sexual Politics and Social Control*. Buckingham: Open University Press.

Heidensohn, F. (2003) 'Gender and policing', in T. Newburn (ed.), *The Handbook of Policing*. Cullompton, Devon: Willan.

Heidensohn, F. (ed.) (2006) *Gender and Justice: New Concepts and Approaches*. Portland, OR: Willan.

Heidensohn, F. (2012) 'The future of feminist criminology', *Crime Media Culture*, 8(2): 123–34.

Heidensohn, F. and Gelsthorpe, L. (2007) 'Gender and crime', in M. Maguire, R. Morgan and R. Reiner (eds), *Oxford Handbook of Criminology* (4th edn). Oxford: Oxford University Press.

Heidensohn, F. and Silvestri, M. (2012) 'Gender and crime', in M. Maguire, R. Morgan and R. Reiner (eds), *Oxford Handbook of Criminology* (5th edn). Oxford: Oxford University Press.

Held, D. (2000) *A Globalizing World? Culture, Economics, Politics*. London: Routledge.

Henderson, T. (1999) *Disorderly Women in Eighteenth Century London: Prostitution and Control in the Metropolis 1730–1830*. London: Longman.

Henne, K. and Troshynski, E. (2013) 'Mapping the margins of intersectionality', *Theoretical Criminology*, 17(4): 455–73.

Herek, G. and Berrill, K.T. (eds) (1992) *Hate Crimes: Confronting Violence against Lesbians and Gay Men*. London: Sage.

Hester, M. (2013) 'Who does what to whom? Gender and domestic violence perpetrators in English police records', *European Journal of Criminology*, 10(5): 623–37.

Hester, M.L., Kelly, L. and Radford, J. (1996) *Women, Violence and Male Power*. Buckingham and Philadelphia: Open University Press

Hewitt, M. (1992) *Welfare, Ideology and Need*. Hemel Hempstead: Harvester Wheatsheaf.

Hickey, N., McCrory, E., Farmer, E. and Vizard, E. (2008) 'Comparing the developmental and behavioural characteristics of female and male juveniles who present with sexually abusive behaviour', *Journal of Sexual Aggression*, 14(3): 241–52.

Hickman, L.J., Aronoff, J. and Jaycox, L.H. (2004) 'Domestic abuse and dating violence among adolescents: Prevalence, gender distribution, and prevention program effectiveness', *Trauma, Violence, and Abuse*, 5(2): 123–42.

Hill, A. and Helmore, E. (2002) 'Mean girls', *The Observer*, 3 March.

Hill, M. (ed.) (1993) *New Agendas in the Study of the Policy Process*. London: Harvester Wheatsheaf.

Hillyar, A. and McDermaid, J. (2000) *Revolutionary Women in Russia 1870–1917*. New York: St Martin's Press.

Hillyard, P., Sim, J., Tombs, S. and Whyte, D. (2004) 'Leaving a stain upon the silence: Contemporary criminology and the politics of dissent', *British Journal of Criminology*, 44(3): 369–90.

Hird, C. (2006) 'Overview of violent crime', in K. Coleman, C. Hird and D. Povey (eds), *Violent Crime Overview: Homicide and Gun Crime in England and Wales 2004/05*, Home Office Statistical Bulletin 02/06. London: HMSO.

Hitchcock, T. (2005) *English Sexualities 1700–1800*. Basingstoke: Macmillan.

HM Chief Inspector of Prisons (HMCIP) (1997) *Women in Prison: A Thematic Review*. London: Home Office.

HM Chief Inspector of Prison (HMCIP) (2005) *Annual Report of Prisons for England & Wales, 2003–4*. London: HMSO.

HM Chief Inspector of Prisons for England and Wales (2015) *Annual Report 2014–15*, HC 242. London: HMSO.

HM Crown Prosecution Inspectorate (HMCPSI) (2007) *Without Consent Home Office*. London: HMIC.

HM Crown Prosecution Inspectorate and HM Inspectorate of Constabulary (HMCPSI and HMCI) (2002) *A Report on the Joint Inspection into the Investigation and Prosecution of Cases involving Allegations of Rape*. London: HMCPSI and HMIC.

HM Government (2009) *Together We Can End Violence Against Women and Girls: A Strategy*. London: Home Office.

HM Government (2013) *Serious and Organised Crime Strategy*. London: HM Government.

HM Inspectorate of Constabulary (HMIC) (1995) *Developing Diversity in the Police Service: Equal Opportunities Thematic Inspection Report*. London: Home Office.

HM Inspectorate of Constabulary (HMIC) (2013) *Stop and Search Powers: Are the Police Using Them Effectively and Fairly?* London: HMIC.

HM Inspectorate of Constabulary (HMIC) (2014a) *State of Policing: The Annual Assessment of Policing in England and Wales 2013/14*. London: HMIC.

HM Inspectorate of Constabulary (HMIC) (2014b) *Everyone's Business: Improving the Police Response to Domestic Abuse*. London: HMIC.

HM Inspectorate of Constabulary and HM Crown Prosecution Inspectorate (HMIC and HMCPSI) (2012) *Forging the Links: Rape Investigation and Prosecution*. London: HMIC and HMCPSI.

HM Inspectorate of Prisons (HMIP) (2004) *Expectations: Criteria for Assessing the Conditions in Prisons and the Treatment of Prisoners*. London: HMSO.

HM Inspectorate of Prisons (HMIP) (2009) *Race Relations in Prisons: Responding to Adult Women from Black and Minority Ethnic Backgrounds*, thematic report by HM Inspectorate of Prisons. London: HM Inspectorate of Prisons.

HM Inspectorate of Probation (2006) *An Independent Review of a Serious Further Offence Case: Damien Hanson and Elliot White*. London: HMIP.

Hobbs, D., Hadfield, P., Lister, S. and Winlow, S. (2003) *Bouncers: Violence and Governance in the Night-time Economy*. Oxford: Oxford University Press.

Hobbs, D., Winlow, S., Hadfield, P. and Lister, S. (2005) 'Violent hypocrisy: Governance and the night-time economy', *European Journal of Criminology*, 2(2): 161–83.

Hobbs, D., O'Brien, K. and Westmarland, L. (2007) 'Connecting the gendered door: Women, violence and doorwork', *British Journal of Sociology*, 58(1): 21–38.

Hodgkinson, J., Marshall, S., Berry, G., Newman, M., Reynolds, P., Burton, E., Dickson, K. and Anderson, J. (2009) *Reducing Gang Related Crime: A Systematic Review of 'Comprehensive' Interventions*. London: EPPI-Centre, Social Science Research Unit, Institute of Education, University of London.

Hogg, R. (2002) 'Criminology beyond the nation state: Global conflicts, human rights and the "new world disorder"', in K. Carrington and R. Hogg (eds), *Critical Criminology: Issues, Debates, Challenges*. Cullompton, Devon: Willan.

Hohl, K. and Stanko, E. (2015) 'Complaints of rape and the criminal justice system: Fresh evidence on the attrition problem in England and Wales', *European Journal of Criminology*, 12(3): 324–41.

Holligan, C. and Deuchar, R. (2015) 'What does it mean to be a man? Psychosocial undercurrents in the voices of incarcerated (violent) Scottish teenage offenders', *Criminology and Criminal Justice*, 15(3): 361–77.

Home Office (1986) *Domestic Violence – Guidance to the Police*, Circular 69/1986. London: HMSO.

Home Office (1990) *Domestic Violence – Guidance to the Police*, Circular 60/90. London: HMSO.

Home Office (1998) *The Crime and Disorder Act: Community Safety and the Reduction and Prevention of Crime – A Conceptual Framework for Training and the Development of a Professional Discipline*. London: Home Office.

Home Office (2000) *Domestic Violence – Guidance to the Police*, Circular 19/2000. London: HMSO.

Home Office (2001) *A Review of the Victim's Charter*. London: HMSO.

Home Office (2004a) *Statistics on Women and the Criminal Justice System 2003: A Home Office Publication under Section 95 of the Criminal Justice System*. London: Home Office.

Home Office (2004b) *Building Communities, Beating Crime: A Better Police Service for the 21st Century*. London: HMSO.

Home Office (2004c) *Paying the Price: A Consultation Paper on Prostitution*. London: The Stationary Office.

Home Office (2004d) *Women's Offending Reduction Programme*. London: Home Office.

Home Office (2005a) *National Policing Plan 2003–2006*. London: Home Office.

Home Office (2005b) *Rebuilding Lives: Supporting Victims of Crime*, Cm 6705. London: Home Office.

Home Office (2006a) *Respect Action Plan*. London: Home Office.

Home Office (2006b) *Respect Academy* 2006. London: Home Office.

Home Office (2006c) *Statistics on Race and the Criminal Justice System: A Home Office Publication of Section 95 of the Criminal Justice Act 1991*. London: HMSO.

Home Office (2006d) *A Coordinated Prostitution Strategy and a Summary of Responses to Paying the Price*. London: Home Office.

Home Office (2006e) *Statistics on Women and the Criminal Justice System 2005/05: A Home Office Publication under Section 95 of the Criminal Justice System*. London: Home Office.

Home Office (2008) *Tackling Demand for Prostitution Review*. Available at: http://webarchive.nationalarchives.gov.uk/20100418065544/http:/homeoffice.gov.uk/documents/tackling-demand2835.pdf?view = Binary.

Home Office (2010) *Anti-Social Behaviour Tools and Powers: Information Pack for Members of Parliament*. London: Home Office.

Home Office (2011a) *Review of Effective Practice in Responding to Prostitution*. London: UK Government.

Home Office (2011b) *Crime in England and Wales 2010/11*, Home Office Statistical Bulletin 10/11, July. London: Home Office.

Home Office (2012a) *Do You Know if Your Teenager is in an Abusive Relationship?* (Leaflet produced by Home Office and NSPCC). Available at: www.gov.uk/government/uploads/system/uploads/attachment_domestic abuseta/file/97768/parents-leaflet.pdf (accessed 6 August 2013).

Home Office (2012b) *A Call to End Violence Against Women and Girls*. London: Home Office.

Home Office (2013a) *A Call to End Violence Against Women and Girls*. London: HMSO.

Home Office (2013b) *Domestic Violence Disclosure Scheme (DVDS) Pilot Scheme*. London: Home Office.

Home Office (2013c) *Police Service Strength*, Home Office Statistical Bulletin: HOSB 1/13. London: Home Office.

Home Office (2013d) *Home Office Circular 003/2013: New Government Domestic Violence and Abuse Definition*. Available at: www.gov.uk/government/publications/new-government-domestic-violence-and-abuse-definition (accessed 26 April 2015).

Home Office (2014a) *Drug Misuse: Findings from the 2013/14 Crime Survey for England and Wales*. London: Home Office.

Home Office (2014b) *Police Powers and Procedures in England and Wales 2012–13*. Available at: www.gov.uk/government/publications/police-powers-and-procedures-england-and-wales-2012-to-2013/police-powers-and-procedures-england-and-wales-2012-to-2013 (accessed 12 March 2015).

Home Office (2014c) *Anti-social Behaviour, Crime and Policing Act 2014: Reform of Anti-social Behaviour Powers, Statutory Guidance for Frontline Professionals*. London: Home Office.

Hood, R. (1992) *Race and Sentencing*. Oxford: Clarendon Press.

Hood-Williams, C. (2001) 'Gender, masculinities and crime: From structures to psyches', *Theoretical Criminology*, 5(1): 37–60.

Hopkins Burke, R. and Morrill, R. (2004) 'Human rights v. community rights: The case of the anti-social behaviour order', in R. Hopkins Burke (ed.), *Hard Cop, Soft Cop: Dilemmas and Debates in Contemporary Policing*. Cullompton: Willan.

Hothi, N. (2005) *Globalisation and Manufacturing Decline: Aspects of British Industry.* Bury St Edmonds: Arena Books.

Hough, M. (2004) 'Modernisation, scientific rationalism and the Crime Reduction Programme', *Criminal Justice*, 4(3): 239–53.

Houlbrook, M. (2013) 'Fashioning an ex-crook self: Citizenship and criminality in the work of Netley Lucas', *Twentieth Century British History*, 24(1): 1–30.

House of Commons Justice Committee (2013) *Women Offenders: After the Corston Report*. Available at: www.parliament.uk/documents/commons-committees/Justice/Women-offenders.pdf.

Howard League for Penal Reform (1997) *Lost Inside: The Imprisonment of Teenage Girls*, Report of the Howard League Inquiry into the use of Prison Custody for Girls Aged Under 18. London: Howard League.

Howard League (2012) *APPG Inquiry on Girls and the Penal System*. Available at: www.howardleague.org/appg-inquiry/.

Howard League (2014) *Commission on Sex in Prison: Coercive Sex in Prison*, Briefing Paper 3. London: Howard League.

Howard League for Penal Reform (2015a) *Report on the Inquiry into Preventing Unnecessary Criminalisation of Women*. London: Howard League.

Howard League (2015b) *Latest Prison Population Figures Week Ending Friday 17th July*. Available at: www.howardleague.org/weekly-prison-watch/ (accessed 20 July 2015).

Hoyle, C. (2012) 'Victims, the criminal process and restorative justice', in M. Maguire, R. Morgan and R. Reiner (eds), *The Oxford Handbook of Criminology* (5th edn). Oxford: Oxford University Press.

Hucklesby, A. (2001) 'Police bail and the use of conditions', *Criminal Justice*, 1(4): 441–63.

Hudson, B. (1987) *Justice Through Punishment: A Critique of the Justice Model of Corrections*. London: Macmillan.

Hudson, B. (2001) 'Human rights, public safety and the probation service', *Howard Journal*, 40(2): 103–13.

Hudson, B. (2003) *Justice in the Risk Society*. London: Sage.

Hughes, D.M. (2002) 'The use of new communications and information technologies for sexual exploitation of women and children', *Hastings Women's Law Journal*, 13(1): 129–48.

Hughes, G. (2007) *The Politics of Crime and Community*. Basingstoke: Palgrave.

Hughes, G. and Muncie, J. (2002) 'Modes of youth governance: Political rationalities, criminalisation and resistance', in J. Muncie, G. Hughes and E. McLaughlin (eds), *Youth Justice: Critical Readings*. Milton Keynes: Open University Press.

Hughes, L. (2005) 'The representation of females in criminological research', *Women and Criminal Justice*, 16(1/2): 1–28.

Human Rights Watch (2006) *World Report: Events of 2005*. New York: Human Rights Watch.

Human Rights Watch (2013) *Saudi Arabia: New Law to Criminalize Domestic Abuse*, 3 September. Available at: www.hrw.org/news/2013/09/03/saudi-arabia-new-law-criminalize-domestic-abuse (accessed 7 July 2015).

Hunter, R. (2015) 'More than just a different face? Judicial diversity and decision-making', *Current Legal Problems*: 1–23.

Hunter, R., McGlynn, C. and Rackley, E. (eds) (2010) *Feminist Judgements: From Theory to Practice*. Oxford: Hart Publishing.

Hurl-Eammon, J. (2005) *Gender and Petty Violence in London, 1680–1720*. Columbus: Ohio State University Press.

Hurrell, K. (2013) *Race Disproportionality in Stops and Searches, 2011–12*, Equality and Human Rights Commission Briefing Paper 7. London: Equality and Human Rights Commission.

Independent Police Commission (IPC) (2013) *Policing for a Better Britain*. Laindon: Anton Group.

Independent Police Complaints Commission (IPCC) (2008) *Independent Investigation – Executive Summary. Contact between Banaz Mahmood and the Metropolitan Police Service and the West Midlands Police 2005–2006*. London: IPCC.

Independent Police Complaints Commission (IPCC) (2010a) *Independent Investigation into the Metropolitan Police Service's Inquiry into Allegations against John Worboys*. London: IPCC.

Independent Police Complaints Commission (IPCC) (2010b) *Independent Investigation into the Metropolitan Police's Inquiry into Allegations against Kirk Reid*. London: IPCC.

Independent Police Complaints Commission (IPCC) (2013) *Southwark Sapphire Unit's Local Practices for the Reporting and Investigation of Sexual Offences*, July 2008–September 2009. London: IPCC.

Innes, M. (2003) *Investigating Murder: Detective Work and the Police Response to Criminal Homicide*. Oxford: Clarendon Press.

INQUEST (2005) *Jury Deliver Critical Verdict into Death of Woman in HMP Styal*. London: INQUEST.

INQUEST (2008) *Verdict in Sarah Campbell Inquest: 18 Year Old Woman Who Died in HMP Styal*. London: INQUEST.

INQUEST (2009) *INQUEST Calls for Urgent Action Following Inspectorate Report into HMP Styal*. London: INQUEST.

INQUEST (2010) *Jury Finds Critical Failings by Prison Staff at HMP Styal Contribute to Death of Lisa Marley, a Vulnerable Prisoner at High Risk of Self-Harm*. London: INQUEST.

International Labour Organization (2012) *Global Estimate of Forced Labour*. Available at: www.ilo.org/wcmsp5/groups/public/---ed_norm/--declaration/documents/publication/wcms_181953.pdf.

Jackson, M. (2009) *Together Women Project: Key Lessons Learned to Date*. London: Ministry of Justice.

Jackson, R., Breen Smyth, M., Gunning, J. and Jarvis, L. (2011) *Terrorism: A Critical Introduction*. Basingstoke: Palgrave Macmillan.

Jamieson, J., McIvor, G. and Murray, C. (1999) *Understanding Offending among Young People*. Edinburgh: HMSO.

Jansson, K. (2007) 'Domestic violence, sexual assault and stalking – the 2005–6 British Crime Survey', in K. Coleman, K. Jansson, P. Kaiza and E. Reed (eds), *Homicides, Firearm Offences and Intimate Violence 2005–2007*, Home Office Statistical Bulletin 02/07. London: Home Office.

Jay, A. (2014) *Independent Inquiry into Child Sexual Exploitation in Rotherham*. Rotherham: Rotherham Metropolitan Borough Council.

Jefferson, T. (1990) *The Case Against Paramilitary Policing Considered*. Milton Keynes: Open University Press.

Jefferson, T. (1996) 'From "little fairy boy" to the "complete destroyer": Subjectivity and transformation in the life of Mike Tyson', in M. Mac an Ghaill (ed.), *Understanding Masculinities: Social Relations and Cultural Arenas*. Buckingham: Open University Press.

Jefferson, T. (1997) 'Masculinities and crimes', in M. Maguire, R. Morgan and R. Reiner (eds), *The Oxford Handbook of Criminology* (2nd edn). Oxford: Oxford University Press.

Jefferson, T. (1998) 'Muscle, "hard men" and "iron" Mike Tyson: Reflections on desire, anxiety and embodiment of masculinity', *Body and Society*, 4(1): 77–98.

Jefferson, T. (2002) 'Subordinating hegemonic masculinity', *Theoretical Criminology* 6(1): 63–88.

Jeffreys, S. (2009) 'Prostitution, trafficking and feminism: An update on the debate', *Women's Studies International Forum*, 32(1).

Jeffreys, S. (2012) 'Beyond 'agency' and 'choice' in theorizing prostitution', in M. Coy (ed.), *Prostitution, Harm and Gender Inequality: Theory, Research and Policy.* Aldershot: Ashgate.

Jenkins, C. (2000) 'Gender just', *Police Review*, 108: 22–3.

Jensen, E.L., Gerber, J. and Moshen, C. (2004) 'Social consequences of the war on drugs: The legacy of failed policy', *Criminal Justice Review*, 15(1): 100–21.

Jessop, B. (2003) *From Thatcherism to New Labour: Neo-Liberalism, Workfarism, and Labour Market Regulation.* Lancaster: Department of Sociology, University of Lancaster.

Jewkes, Y. (2005) 'Men behind bars: "Doing masculinity as an adaptation to imprisonment,' *Men and Masculinities*, 8(1): 44–63.

Jewkes, Y. (2015) *Media and Crime* (3rd edn). London: Sage.

Johnson, P. (1995) 'At the intersections of injustice: Experiences of African-American women in crime and sentencing', *Journal of Gender and the Law*, 4: 2–76.

Joint Committee on Human Rights (2002) *The Case for a Human Rights Commission,* Sixth Report, HL, (2002-03 67), HC (2002-03) 489, para 9.

Joint Committee on Human Rights (2003) *Inquiry into Human Rights and Deaths in Custody,* written evidence from inquest, 15 December.

Jones, H. and Cook, K. (2008) *Rape Crisis: Responding to Sexual Violence.* Lyme Regis: Russell House Publishing.

Jones, K. (2006) *Gender and Petty Crime in Late Medieval England.* Woodbridge: Boydell Press.

Jones, M. (2014) 'A diversity stone left unturned? Exploring the occupational complexities surrounding lesbian, gay and bisexual police officers', in J. Brown (ed.), *The Future of Policing.* London: Routledge.

Jones, S. (2008) 'Partners in crime: Study of the relationship between female offenders and their co-defendants', *Criminology and Criminal Justice*, 8(2): 147–64.

Jones, T. (2012) 'Governing security: Pluralization, privatization, and polarization in crime control and policing', in M. Maguire, R. Morgan and R. Reiner (eds), *The Oxford Handbook of Criminology* (5th edn). Oxford: Oxford University Press.

Jones, T. and Newburn, T. (1998) *Private Security and Public Policing.* Oxford: Clarendon Press.

Joseph, I. and Gunter, A. (2011) *Gangs Revisited: What's a Gang and What's Race Got To Do with It.* London: Runnymede Trust.

Joseph, J. (2006) 'Drug offences, gender, ethnicity and nationality: Women in prison in England and Wales', *The Prison Journal*, 86(1): 140–57.

Junger-Tas, J. (2012) 'Delinquent behaviour in thirty countries', in J. Junger-Tas, I. Marshall, D. Enzmann, M. Killias, M. Steketee and B. Gruszczynska (eds), *The Many Faces of Youth Crime: Contrasting Theoretical Perspectives on Juvenile Delinquency across Countries and Cultures.* New York: Springer.

Kaldor, M. (2003) *Terrorism as Regressive Globalisation,* Open Democracy, 25 September. Available at: www.opendemocracy.net/democracy-americanpower/article_1501.jsp (accessed 3 April 2015).

Kallen, E. (2004) *Social Inequality and Social Injustice: A Human Rights Perspective.* Basingstoke: Palgrave Macmillan.

Karmen, A. (2004) *Crime Victims: An Introduction to Victimology* (5th edn). Wadsworth: Thompson.

Kazemian, L. and Maruna, S. (2009) 'Desistance from crime', in M. Krohn, A.J. Lizotte and G.P. Hall (eds), *Handbook on Crime and Deviance*. New York: Springer.

Kelly, L. (1988) *Surviving Sexual Violence*. Cambridge: Polity Press.

Kelly, L. (2014) 'Revisiting the continuum of sexual violence', Keynote Lecture at North East Feminist Gathering, Newcastle upon Tyne, 11–12 October.

Kelly, L. and Westmarland, N. (2015) *Domestic Violence Perpetrator Programmes: Steps Towards Change*, Project Mirabal Project Final Report. University of Durham/ London Metropolitan University.

Kelly, L., Lovett, J. and Regan, L. (2005) *A Gap or a Chasm? Attrition in Reported Rape Cases*, Home Office Research Study 293. London: Home Office.

Kemshall, H. (2008) *Understanding the Management of High Risk Offenders*. Milton Keynes: Open University Press.

Kendall, K. (2000) 'Psy-ence fiction: Governing female prisons through the psychological sciences', in K. Hannah-Moffat and M. Shaw (eds), *An Ideal Prison? Critical Essays on Women's Imprisonment in Canada*. Halifax: Fernwood Press. pp. 94–102.

Kenney, S. (2008) 'Thinking about gender and judging', *International Journal of the Legal Profession*, 15(1): 87–110.

Kenney, S. (2013) *Gender and Justice: Why Women in the Judiciary Really Matter*. New York: Routledge.

Kilday, A. (2007) *Women and Crime in Enlightenment Scotland*. London: Boydell and Brewer.

Kilday, A. (2013) *A History of Infanticide c.1600 to the Present*. Basingstoke: Palgrave Macmillan.

Killias, M'., Aebi, M.F., Aubusson de Cavarlay, B., Barclay, G., Gruszczynska, B. and Harrendorf, S. (2010) *European Sourcebook of Criminal Justice Statistics – 2010*. The Hague, Netherlands: Ministry of Justice.

King, P. (2006) *Crime and the Law in England 1750–1840: Remaking Justice from the Margins*. Cambridge: Cambridge University Press.

Kitsuse, J.I. and Cicourel, A.V. (1963) 'A note on the official use of statistics', *Social Problems*, 11(2): 131–9.

Klenowski, P.M., Copes, H. and Mullins, C.W. (2011) 'Gender, identity and accounts: How white collar offenders do gender when making sense of their crimes', *Justice Quarterly*, 28(1): 46–69.

Kolinsky, E. (1988) 'Terrorism in Western Germany', in J. Lodge (ed.), *The Threat of Terrorism*. Boulder, CO: Westview Press.

Konopka, G. (1966) *The Adolescent Girl in Conflict*. Englewood Cliffs, NJ: Prentice-Hall.

Laite, J. (2011) *Common Prostitutes and Ordinary Citizens: Commercial Sex in London, 1885–1960*. Basingstoke: Palgrave Macmillan.

Laite, J. (2013) 'Immoral traffic: Sex, mobility, labour and the lorry girl in early twentieth century Britain', *Journal of British Studies*, 52(3): 692–721.

Lander, I., Signe, R. and Jon, N. (eds) (2014) *Masculinities in the Criminological Field: Control, Vulnerability and Risk Taking*. Aldershot: Ashgate.

Landor, R. (2009) 'Double standards? Representation of male vs. female sex offenders in the Australian media', *Griffith Working Papers in Pragmatics and Intercultural Communication*, 2(2): 84–93.

Larkin, J. (1988) *The Reshaping of Everyday Life, 1790–1840*. New York: Harper and Row.

Laverick, W. and Cain, L. (2014) *Policing Reform: Consequences for the Gender Agenda and the Female Workforce*. London: BAWP.

Lea, J. (2002) *Crime and Modernity*. London: Sage.

Lee, M. (2011) *Trafficking and Global Crime Control*. London: Sage.

Lees, S. (1989) *Losing Out: Sexuality and Adolescent Girls*. London: Hutchinson.

Lees, S. (1993) *Sugar and Spice: Sexuality and Adolescent Girls*. London: Penguin.

Lester, A. and Clapinska, L. (2005) 'An equality and human rights commission worthy of the name', in L. Clements and P.A. Thomas (eds), *Human Rights Act: A Success Story?* Oxford: Blackwell Publishing.

Lewis, C.F. and Stanley, C.R. (2000) 'Women accused of sexual offenses', *Behavioral Sciences and the Law*, 18: 73–81.

Libal, K. and Parekh, S. (2009) 'Reframing violence against women as a human rights violation: Evan Stark's coercive control', *Violence Against Women*, 15: 1477–89.

Liebling, A. (1994) 'Suicide amongst women prisoners', *Howard Journal of Criminal Justice*, 33(1): 1–9.

Liebling, A. (1995) 'Vulnerability and prison suicide', *British Journal of Criminology*, 35(2): 173–87.

Liebling, A. (2011) 'Moral performance, inhuman and degrading treatment and prison pain', *Punishment and Society*, 13(5): 530–50.

Liebling, A. and Maruna, S. (eds) (2005) *The Effects of Imprisonment*. London: Routledge.

Litvin, D. (1997) 'The discourse of diversity: From biology to management', *Organization*, 4(2): 187–209.

Loftus, B. (2010) 'Police occupational culture: Classic themes, altered times', *Policing and Society*, 20(1): 1–20.

Lombard, N. and McMillan, L. (eds) (2013) *Violence against Women: Current Theory and Practice in Domestic Abuse, Sexual Violence and Exploitation*. London: Jessica Kingsley.

Lombroso, C. and Ferrero, G. (1895) *The Female Offender*. London: T. Fisher Unwin.

Lonsway, K., Wood, M. and Spillar, K. (2002) 'Officer gender and excessive force', *Law and Order*, 50: 60–6.

Lopez, V., Jurik, N. and Gilliard-Matthews, S. (2009) 'Gender, sexuality, power and drug acquisition strategies among adolescent girls who use meth', *Feminist Criminology*, 4(3): 226–51.

Lowthian, J. (2002) 'Women's prison in England: Barriers to reform,' in P. Carlen, *Women and Punishment: The Struggle for Justice*. Cullompton: Willan.

Lukes, S. (1974) *Power*. London: Macmillan.

Lukes, S. (1986) *Power: Readings in Social and Political Theory*. Oxford: Basil Blackwell.

Lyon, D. (ed.) (2003) *Surveillance as Social Sorting: Privacy, Risk and Automated Discrimination*. London: Routledge.

Lyon, J. (2004) 'High price to pay for jailing women', *The Observer*, 18 July.

McAleer, K. (1994) *Dueling: The Cult of Honor in Fin-de-siecle Germany*. Princeton, NJ: Princeton University Press.

McCall, M. (2008) 'Structuring gender's impact', *American Politics Research*, 36: 264.

McCall, M. and McCall, M. (2007) 'How far does the gender gap extend? Decision making on State Supreme Courts in fourth amendment cases. 1980–2000', *Social Science Journal*, 44: 67.

McCarthy, H., Caslin, S. and Laite, J. (2015) *Prostitution and the Law in Historical Perspective: A Dialogue*. Available at: www.historyandpolicy.org/dialogues/discussions/prostitution-and-the-law-in-historical-perspective-a-dialogue.

McCulloch, J. and Pickering, S.J. (eds) (2012) *Borders and Crime: Pre-Crime, Mobility and Serious Harm in an Age of Globalisation*. Basingstoke: Palgrave Macmillan.

McElvain, J.P. and Kposowa, A.J. (2008) 'Police officer characteristics and the likelihood of using deadly force', *Criminal Justice and Behavior*, 35(4): 505–21.

McFarlane, H. (2013) 'Masculinity and criminology: The social construction of criminal man', *The Howard Journal*, 52(3): 321–35.

McGarry, R., Mythen, G. and Walklate, S. (2012) 'The soldier, human rights and the military covenant: A permissible state of exception?' *International Journal of Human Rights. Special Issue: New Directions in the Sociology of Human Rights*, 16(8): 1183–95.

McGlynn, C. (1998) *The Woman Lawyer: Making the Difference*. London: Butterworth.

Mack, K. and Roach Anleu, S. (2012) 'Entering the Australian judiciary: Gender and court hierarchy', *Law and Policy*, 34(2): 313–47.

McKendrick, N., Brewer, J. and Plumb, J. (1982) *The Birth of a Consumer Society: The Commercialisation of Eighteenth-Century England*. Bloomington: Indiana University Press.

MacPherson, Sir William (1999) *The Stephen Lawrence Inquiry – Report*, Cm 4262-0. London. HMSO.

McRobbie, A. (2004) 'Notes on postfeminism and popular culture: Bridget Jones and the new gender regime', in A. Harris (ed.), *All About the Girl: Culture, Power and Identity*. New York: Routledge. pp. 3–14.

McRobbie, A. (2012) *The Aftermath of Feminism*. London: Sage.

Maggio, E. (2008) *Private Security in the 21st Century: Concepts and Application*. Sudbury: Jones and Bartlett Publishers.

Maher, L. (1997) *Sexed Work*. Oxford: Oxford University Press.

Maher, J.M., Pickering, S.J. and Gerard, A. (2013) *Sex Work: Labour, Mobility and Sexual Services*. Abingdon: Routledge.

Malleson, K. (1999) *The New Judiciary: The Effects of Expansion and Activism*. London: Ashgate.

Malleson, K. (2002) 'Judicial appointments: Another nail in the coffin?', *New Law Journal*, 152(7052).

Malleson, K. (2003) 'Justifying gender equality on the bench: Why difference won't do', *Feminist Legal Studies*, 11: 1–24.

Malleson, K. and Banda, F. (2000) *Factors Affecting the Decision to Apply for Silk and Judicial Office*, Lord Chancellor's Department Research Series 2/00. London: Lord Chancellor's Department.

Malleson, K. and Russell, P. (2006) *Appointing Judges in an Age of Judicial Power: Critical Perspectives from Around the World*. Toronto: University of Toronto Press.

Mallicoat, S. (2011) *Women and Crime: A Text/Reader*. Thousand Oaks, CA: Sage.

Malloch, M. and McIvor, G. (2011) 'Women and community sentences', *Criminology and Criminal Justice*, 11(4): 325–44.

Malloch, M. and McIvor, G. (2013) *Women, Punishment and Social Justice*. Abingdon: Routledge.

Mansvelt, J. (2005) *Geographies of Consumption*. London: Sage.

Marks, M. and Fleming, J. (2004) '"As unremarkable as the air they breathe?" Reforming police management in South Africa', *Current Sociology*, 52(5): 784–808.

Martin, D. (2003) 'The politics of policing: Managerialism, modernization and performance', in R. Matthews and J. Young (eds), *The New Politics of Crime and Punishment*. Cullompton: Willan.

Martin, E. and Pyle, B. (2005) 'State High Courts and divorce: The impact of judicial gender', *University of Toledo Law Review*, 36(4): 923–48.

Martin, G. (2006) *Understanding Terrorism* (2nd edn). London: Sage.

Martin, S. (1980) *Breaking and Entering: Policewomen on Patrol*. Berkeley, CA: University of California Press.

Martin, S.E. and Jurik, N. (2007) *Doing Justice, Doing Gender*. London: Sage.

Martinson, R. (1974) 'What works? Questions and answers about prison reform', *Public Interest*, 55 (Spring): 22–54.

Mason, C. (2012) *Too Good to be True: Private Prisons in America*. Washington, DC: The Sentencing Project.

Mathieson, T. (2000) *Prison on Trial* (2nd edn). Winchester: Waterside Press.

Matravers, A. (1997) 'Women and the sexual abuse of children', *Forensic Update*, 5(1): 9–13.

Matravers, A. (2001) 'Breaking the silence' *The Guardian*, 15 February.

Matravers, A. (2008) 'Understanding women who commit sex offences', in G. Letherby, K. Williams, P. Birch and M. Cain (eds), *Sex as Crime?* Cullompton: Willan.

Matthews, R. (2009) 'Beyond "so what?" criminology: Rediscovering realism', *Theoretical Criminology*, 13(3): 341–62.

Matthews, R. (2014) *Realist Criminology*. Basingstoke: Palgrave Macmillan.

Matthews, R., Easton, H., Young, L. and Bindel, J. (2014) *Exiting Prostitution: A Study in Female Desistance*. Basingstoke: Palgrave Macmillan.

Mawby, R. (2012) *Burglary*. London: Routledge.

Mawby, R. and Walklate, S. (1994) *Critical Victimology, International Perspectives*. London: Sage.

Mayor of London (2010) *The Way Forward: Taking Action to End Violence Against Women and Girls, Final Strategy 2010–2013*. London: Mayor's Office.

Mayor of London (2011) *The Way Forward: Action Plan 2011–2012*. London: Mayor's Office.

Mazo Karras, R. (1996) *Common Women: Prostitution and Sexuality in Medieval England*. Oxford: Oxford University Press.

Measham, F. (2002) '"Doing gender – doing drugs": Conceptualising the gendering of drugs cultures', *Contemporary Drugs Problems*, 29(2): 335–73.

Meetoo, V. and Mirza, H. (2007) 'There is nothing "honourable" about honour killings: Gender, violence and the limits of multiculturalism', *Women's Studies International Forum*, 30: 187–200.

Mendelsohn, B. (1956) 'Une nouvelle branche de la science bio-psycho-sociale: Victimologie', *Revue Internationale De Criminologie et de Police Technique*, 10: 95–109.

Menkel-Meadow, C. (1985) 'Portia in a different voice: Speculations on a women's lawyering process', *Berkeley Women's Law Journal*, 39(1): 39–63.

Menkel-Meadow, C. (1986) 'The comparative sociology of women lawyers: The "feminisation" of the legal profession', *Osgoode Hall Law Journal*, 24: 897–910.

Menkel-Meadow, C. (1987) 'Excluded voices: New voices in the legal profession, making new voices in the law', *University of Miami Law Review*, 42(7): 29–53.

Menkel-Meadow, C. (1988) 'Feminist legal theory, critical legal studies and legal education or the "fem crits" go to law school', *Journal of Legal Education*, 38(1): 61–85.

Messerschmidt, J.W. (1993) *Masculinities and Crime: Critique and Reconceptualization of Theory*. Lanham, MD: Rowman & Littlefield.

Messerschmidt, J.W. (1997) *Crime as Structured Action: Gender, Race, Class, and Crime in the Making*. Thousand Oaks, CA: Sage.

Messerschmidt, J.W. (2000) *Nine Lives: Adolescent Masculinities, the Body, and Violence*. Boulder, CO: Westview Press.

Messerschmidt, J.W. (2004) *Flesh and Blood: Adolescent Gender Diversity and Violence.* Lanham, MD: Rowman & Littlefield.

Messerschmidt, J.W. (2005a) 'Masculinities and crime: Beyond a dualist criminology', in C. Renzetti, L. Goodstein and S. Miller (eds), *Masculinities, Crime and Criminal Justice: Original Feminist Readings.* Los Angeles, CA: Roxbury.

Messerschmidt, J.W. (2005b) 'Men, masculinities and crime', in M. Kimmell, J. Hearn and R. Connell (eds), *Handbook of Studies on Men and Masculinities.* Thousand Oaks, CA: Sage.

Miller, J. (2001) *One of the Guys: Girls, Gangs and Gender.* New York: Oxford University Press.

Miller, J. (2008) *Getting Played: African American Girls, Urban Inequality, and Gendered Violence.* New York: NTU Press.

Miller, J. (2010) 'Commentary on Frances Heidensohn's "The deviance of women"', *British Journal of Sociology,* 61: 133–9.

Miller, J. and Mullins, C. (2006) 'Feminist theories of crime,' in F. Cullen, J. Wright and K. Blevins (eds), *Taking Stock: The Status of Criminological Theory (Advances in Criminological Theory Volume 15).* New Brunswick, NJ, and London: Transaction Publications. pp. 217–50.

Miller, S.L. (1999) *Gender and Community Policing: Walking the Talk.* Boston, MA: Northeastern University Press.

Millie, A. (2009) 'Introduction', in A. Millie (ed.), *Securing Respect: Behavioural Expectations and Anti-Social Behaviour in the UK.* Bristol: Policy Express. pp. 1–21.

Mills, A. and Tancred-Sheriff, P. (1992) *Gendering Organisational Analysis.* London: Sage.

Mills, H., Skodbo, S. and Blyth, P. (2013) *Understanding Organised Crime: Estimating the Scale and the Social and Economic Costs.* London: Home Office.

Ministry of Justice (2008) *National Service Framework: Improving Services to Women Offenders.* London: Ministry of Justice, NOMS.

Ministry of Justice (2010) *Judicial Diversity Taskforce: Improving Judicial Diversity.* London: MoJ.

Ministry of Justice (2011) *Judicial Diversity Taskforce: Improving Judicial Diversity.* London: MoJ.

Ministry of Justice (2012) *Judicial Diversity Taskforce: Improving Judicial Diversity.* London: MoJ.

Ministry of Justice (2013a) *An Overview of Sexual Offending.* London: MoJ, Home Office and the Office for National Statistics.

Ministry of Justice (2013b) *Judicial Diversity Taskforce: Improving Judicial Diversity.* London: MoJ.

Ministry of Justice (2013c) *Improving the Code of Practice for Victims of Crime.* London: Home Office.

Ministry of Justice (2014a) *Statistics on Women and the Criminal Justice System.* London: Home Office.

Ministry of Justice (2014b) *Statistics on Women and the Criminal Justice System: A Ministry of Justice Publication under Section 95 of the Criminal Justice Act 1991.* London: Ministry of Justice.

Ministry of Justice (2014c) *Proven Re-offending Statistics Quarterly Bulletin April 2011 to March 2012,* England and Wales, Ministry of Justice Statistics Bulletin, 30 January. London: Ministry of Justice.

Ministry of Justice (2014d) *Diversity Report 2013/14.* London: Ministry of Justice.

Ministry of Justice (2014e) *National Offender Management Service Workforce Statistics,* Ministry of Justice Statistics Bulletin, 30 June. London: Ministry of Justice.

Ministry of Justice (2014f) *Population and Capacity Briefing.* London: Ministry of Justice. Available at: www.gov.uk/government/.../prison-population-q1-2015.xlsx.

Ministry of Justice (2015a) *Youth Justice Annual Statistics.* Available at: www.gov.uk/ government/statistics/youth-justice-annual-statistics-2013-to-2014.

Ministry of Justice (2015b) *Youth Justice Statistics 2013/14,* England and Wales Youth Justice Board/Ministry of Justice Statistics Bulletin, 29 January. London: Ministry of Justice.

Ministry of Justice, Home Office and the Office for National Statistics (2013) *An Overview of Sexual Offending in England and Wales,* Ministry of Justice, Home Office and the Office for National Statistics Statistics Bulletin, 10 January. London: Ministry of Justice, Home Office and Office for National Statistics.

Mohanty, C. (1986) 'Under western eyes: Feminist scholarship and colonial discourses', *Boundary 2,* 12(3): 333–58.

Mohanty, C. (2003) 'Under western eyes" revisited: Feminist solidarity through anti-capitalist struggles', *Signs,* 28(2): 499–535.

Monaghan, L.F. (2004) 'Doorwork and legal risk: Observations from an embodied ethnography', *Social and Legal Studies,* 13(4): 453–80.

Mooney, J. (1993) *The Hidden Figure: Domestic Violence in North London.* London: Islington Council.

Mooney, J. (2009) 'Frances Heidensohn (1942-)', in K. Hayward, S. Maruna and J. Mooney (eds), *Fifty Key Thinkers in Criminology.* London: Routledge.

Moore, D. (2008) 'Feminist criminology: Gain, loss and backlash', *Sociology Compass,* 2(1): 48–61.

Moore, L. (2011) 'The Convention on the Rights of the Child comes of age: Assessing progress in meeting the rights of child in custody in Northern Ireland', *Northern Ireland Legal Quarterly,* 62(2): 217–34.

Moran, L. (2009) 'What kind of field is "Law, gender and sexuality"? Present concerns and possible futures', *Feminist Legal Studies,* 17(3): 309–13.

Morgan, G. and Rushton, R. (1998) *Rogues, Thieves and the Rule of Law: The Problem of Law Enforcement, 1718–1800.* London: UCL Press.

Morgan, R. (2012) 'Crime and justice in the "Big Society"', *Criminology and Criminal Justice,* 12(5): 463–81.

Morley, R. and Mullender, A. (1994) *Preventing Domestic Violence to Women,* Police Research Group Crime Prevention Series Paper No. 48. London: HMSO.

Mort, F. (2000) *Dangerous Sexualities: Medico-Moral Politics in England since 1830.* London: Routledge.

Muller, B. (2013) 'Borderworld: Biometrics, AVATAR and global criminalisation', in F. Pakes (ed.), *Globalisation and the Challenge to Criminology.* London: Routledge. pp. 129–45.

Mumola, C. (2000) *Incarcerated Parents and Their Children* (No. 182335). Washington, DC: US Department of Justice, Office of Justice Programs.

Muncie, J. (2008) 'The "punitive turn" in juvenile justice: Cultures of control and rights compliance in Western Europe and the USA', *Youth Justice,* 8(2): 107–21.

Muraskin, R. (ed.) (2012) *Women and Justice: It's a Crime.* Upper Saddle River, NJ: Pearson Education/Prentice-Hall.

Murphy, T. and Whitty, N. (2006) 'The question of evil and feminist legal scholarship', *Feminist Legal Studies,* 14(1): 1–26.

Murphy, T. and Whitty, N. (2007) 'Risk and human rights in UK prison governance', *British Journal of Criminology',* 47(5): 798–816.

Murphy, T. and Whitty, N. (2013) 'Making history: Academic criminology and human rights', *British Journal of Criminology*, 53(4): 568–87.

Murray, J. and Murray, L. (2010) 'Parental incarceration, attachment and child psychopathology', *Attachment and Human Development*, 12(4): 289–309.

Murray, J., Farrington, D.P. and Sekol, I. (2012) 'Children's antisocial behavior, mental health, drug use, and educational performance after parental incarceration: A systematic review and meta-analysis', *Psychological Bulletin*, 138(2): 175–210.

Myhill, A. and Allen, J. (2002a) *Rape and Sexual Assault of Women: Findings from the British Crime Survey*, Findings 159. London: Home Office.

Myhill, A. and Allen, J. (2002b) *Rape and Sexual Assault of Women: The Extent and Nature of the Problem. Findings from the British Crime Survey*, Home Office Research Study 237. London: Home Office.

Mythen, G. (2014) *Understanding the Risk Society: Crime, Security and Justice*. New York: Palgrave Macmillan.

NACRO (2005) *Making a Difference: NACRO Annual Review*. London: NACRO.

Naffine, N. (1997) *Feminism and Criminology*. Cambridge: Polity Press.

Narasaiah, M.L. (2005) *Globalisation and Information Technology*. New Delhi: Discovery Publishing House.

Natarajan, M. (2008) *Women Police in a Changing Society*. Aldershot: Ashgate.

National Probation Service (2005) *Human Resources Workforce Profile Report* (Issue 2). London: Home Office.

National Union of Students (2010) *Hidden Marks*. Available at: http://hiddenmarks.org. uk/2010/ (accessed 26 October 2015).

Naughton, M. (2005) 'Redefining miscarriages of justice: A human rights approach to unearth subjugated discourses of wrongful criminal conviction', *British Journal of Criminology*, 45(2): 165–82.

Naylor, B.G. (2013) 'Protecting the human rights of prisoners in Australia', in P. Gerber and M. Castan (eds), *Contemporary Perspectives on Human Rights Law in Australia*. Pyrmont, NSW Australia: Thomson Reuters.

Naylor, B.G. (2014) 'Human rights and respect in prisons: The prisoners' perspective', *Law in Context*, 31: 84–124.

Naylor, B.G. (2015) 'Researching human rights in prison', *International Journal for Crime, Justice and Social Democracy*, 4(1): 79–95.

Nederveen Pieterse, J. (2015) *Globalization and Culture: Global Melange* (3rd edn). Lanham, MD: Rowman & Littlefield.

Nelken, D. (2009) 'Comparative criminal justice: Beyond ethnocentricism and relativism', *European Journal of Criminology*, 6: 291–311.

Nelken, D. (2010) *Comparative Criminal Justice*. London: Sage.

Nelken, D. (2013) 'The challenge of globalisation for comparative criminal justice', in F. Pakes (ed.), *Globalization and the Challenge to Criminology*. London: Routledge. pp. 9–26.

Ness, C. (2007) 'The rise in female violence', *Daedulus*, 136(1): 84–93.

New Law Journal (2006) 'Human Rights Act applies to British troops abroad', 22 June. Available at: www.newlawjournal.co.uk/nlj/content/human-rights-act-applies-british-troops-abroad (accessed 26 October 2015).

Newburn, T. (2002) 'Modernisation, New Labour and criminal justice policy', *Criminal Justice Matters*, 46.

Newburn, T. (2013) *Criminology* (2nd edn). London: Routledge.

Newburn, T. and Stanko, E. (eds) (1994) *Just Boys Doing the Business: Men, Masculinity and Crime*. London: Routledge.

Newman, J. (2000) 'Beyond the new public management? Modernizing public services', in J. Clarke, S. Gerwitz and E. McLaughlin (eds), *New Managerialism, New Welfare*. London: Sage.

Neyroud, P. (2011) *Review of Police Leadership and Training*. Available at: www. homeoffice.gov.uk/publications/consultations/rev-police-leadership-training/ report?view = Binary.

Neyroud, P. and Beckley, A. (2001) *Policing, Ethics and Human Rights*. Cullompton: Willan.

Nickel, J. (1992) *Making Sense of Human Rights: Philosophical Reflections on the Universal Declaration of Human Rights*. Berkeley, CA: University of California Press.

Norrie, A. (2001) 'A criminal justice, judicial interpretation, legal right: On being sceptical about the Human Rights Act 1998', in T. Campbell, K.D. Ewing and A. Tomkins (eds), *Sceptical Essays on Human Rights*. Oxford: Oxford University Press.

Oakley, A. and Cockburn, C. (2013) *The Cost of Masculine Crime*, Open Democracy, 13 March. Available at: www.opendemocracy.net/5050/ann-oakley-cynthia-cockburn/cost-of-masculine-crime (accessed 12 January 2015).

Oberwittler, D. and Kasselt, J. (2014) 'Honor killings', in R. Gartner and B. McCarthy (eds), *The Oxford Handbook of Gender Sex and Crime*. Oxford: Oxford University Press.

O'Brien, E., Carpenter, B. and Hayes, S. (2013) 'Sex trafficking and moral harm: Politicised understandings and depictions of the trafficked experience', *Critical Criminology*, 21: 401–15.

O'Brien, K., Hobbs, D. and Westmarland, L. (2008) 'Negotiating violence and gender: Security and the night time economy in the UK', in S. Body-Gendrot and P. Spierenburg (eds), *Violence in Europe*. New York: Springer. pp. 161–73.

O'Brien, P. (1983) 'The kleptomania diagnosis: Bourgeois women and theft in late nineteenth-century France', *Journal of Social History*, 17: 65–77.

O'Byrne, D. (2012) 'On the sociology of human rights: Theorising the language-structure of rights', *Sociology*, 46(5): 829–43.

Occhipinti, J.D. (2014) 'Transnational criminality', in J. Sperling (ed.), *Handbook of Governance and Security*. Cheltenham: Edward Elgar. pp. 427–51.

O'Connell Davidson, J. (2008) 'Trafficking, modern slavery and the human security agenda', *Human Security Journal*, 6: 8–19.

O'Donnell, I. (2004) 'Prison rape in context', *British Journal of Criminology*, 44: 241–55.

Office for National Statistics (ONS) (2015a) *Crime Statistics, Focus on Violent Crime and Sexual Offences, 2013/14*. London: ONS.

Office for National Statistics (ONS) (2015b) *Crime in England and Wales, Year Ending September 2014*, Statistical Bulletin, 22 January. London: ONS. Available at: www. ons.gov.uk/ons/dcp171778_392380.pdf (accessed 10 March 2015).

Oldridge, D. (2002) *The Witchcraft Reader*. Milton Keynes: Psychology Press.

Oliver, B. (2007) 'Preventing female-perpetrated sexual abuse', *Trauma, Violence and Abuse*, 8(1): 19–32.

Osterberg, E. (1996) 'Gender, class and the courts: Scandinavia', in C. Emsley and L. Knafla (eds), *Crime History and Histories of Crime: Studies in the Historiography of Crime and Criminal Justice in Modern History*. Westport, CT: Greenwood Press.

Owers, A. (2004) 'Prison inspection and the protection of human rights', *European Human Rights Law Review*, 2: 108–17.

Ozbilgin, M.F. and Tatli, A. (2011) 'Mapping out the field of equality and diversity: Rise of individualism and voluntarism', *Human Relations*, 64(9): 1229–53.

Packer, H. (1968) *The Limits of the Criminal Sanction*. Stanford, CA: Stanford University Press.

Padfield, N. and Maruna, S. (2006) 'The revolving door at the prison gate', *Criminology and Criminal Justice*, 6(3): 329–52.

Page, A.D. (2007) 'Behind the Blue Line: Investigating police officers' attitudes toward rape', *Journal of Police and Criminal Psychology*, 22(1): 22–32.

Pakes, F. (2010) *Comparative Criminal Justice* (2nd edn). Cullompton: Willan.

Palk, D. (2006) *Gender, Crime and Judicial Discretion 1780–1830*. Woodbridge: Boydell Press.

Parity (2013) *Men and Women and the Criminal Justice System: Appraisal of Published Statistics*, Parity Briefing Paper. Available at: www.parity-uk.org/Briefing/MenandWomenandtheCJSfComplete.pdf (accessed 15 May 2015).

Parmar, A. (2013) 'Stop and search in London: Counter-terrorist or counterproductive', in L. Weber and B. Bowling (eds), *Stop and Search: Police Power in Global Context*. London: Routledge. pp. 17–30.

Parmar, A. (2014) 'Configuring ethnic identities: Resistance as a response to counterterrorist policy', in C. Phillips and C. Webster (eds), *New Directions in Race, Ethnicity and Crime*. London: Routledge.

Parole Board (2015) *The Parole Board for England and Wales Annual Report and Accounts 2014/15*, HC 211. London: Parole Board.

Patten Report (1999) *A New Beginning: Policing in Northern Ireland*, The Independent Police Commission on Policing in Northern Ireland, Belfast.

Pearson, G. (1983) *Hooligan: A History of Respectable Fears*. Basingstoke: Macmillan.

Pearson, G. (2009) '"A Jekyll in the classroom, A Hyde in the street": Queen Victoria's hooligans', in A. Millie (ed.), *Securing Respect: Behavioural Expectations and Anti-Social Behaviour in the UK*. Bristol: Policy Express. pp. 41–74.

Pease, K. (2015) 'Repeat victimisation: Taking stock', in J. Shapland and M. Hall (eds), *Victimology*. Farnham: Ashgate.

Peltonen, M. (2003) *The Duel in Early Modern England: Civility, Politeness and Honour*. Cambridge: Cambridge University Press.

Peresie, J. (2005) 'Female judges matter: Gender and collegial decision making in the federal courts', *Yale Law Journal*, 114(7): 1759–90.

Peter, T. (2009) 'Exploring taboos: Comparing male and female perpetrated child sexual abuse', *Journal of Interpersonal Violence*, 24(7): 1111–28.

Phillips, A. (2010) *Gender and Culture*. Cambridge: Polity Press.

Phillips, C. and Bowling, B. (2012) 'Ethnicities, racism, crime and criminal justice', in M. Maguire, R. Morgan and R. Reiner (eds), *The Oxford Handbook of Criminology* (5th edn). Oxford: Oxford University Press.

Phipps, A. and Young, I. (2012) *That's What She Said – Women's Students' Experiences of 'Lad Culture' in Higher Education*. London: National Union of Students.

Phoenix, J. (2002) 'Youth prostitution policy reform: New discourse, same old story', in P. Carlen (ed.), *Women and Punishment: The Struggle for Justice*. Cullompton: Willan.

Phoenix, J. (2006) 'Regulating prostitution; controlling women's lives', in F. Heidensohn (ed.), *Gender and Justice: New Concepts and Approaches*. Cullompton, Devon: Willan.

Pickering, S. (2010) *Women, Borders and Violence: Current Issues in Asylum, Forced Migration and Trafficking*. New York: Springer.

Pickering, S. and Lambert, C. (eds) (2004) *Global Issues: Women and Justice*. Sydney Institute of Criminology: Federation Press.

Pickering, S.J. and Weber, L. (eds) (2006) *Borders, Mobility and Technologies of Control*. Dordrecht, The Netherlands: Springer.

Piquero, A.R., Schubert, C.A. and Brame, R. (2014) 'Comparing official and self-report records of offending across gender and race/ethnicity in a longitudinal study of serious youthful offenders', *Journal of Research in Crime and Delinquency*, 1: 31.

Pitts, J. (2012) 'Reluctant criminologists: Criminology, ideology and the violent street gang', *Youth and Policy*, 109: 27–45.

Plotnikoff, J. and Woolfson, R. (1998) *Policing Domestic Violence: Effective Organizational Structures*. London: Home Office.

Pollack, S. (2000) 'Dependency discourse as social control,' in K. Hannah-Moffat and M. Shaw (eds), *An Ideal Prison? Critical Essays on Women's Imprisonment in Canada*. Halifax: Fernwood Press. pp. 94–102.

Pollack, S. (2010) 'Labelling clients "risky": Social work and the neo-liberal welfare state', *British Journal of Social Work*, 40: 1263–78.

Pollack, S. and Kendall, K. (2005) 'Taming the shrew: Mental health policy with women in Canadian federal prisons', *Critical Criminology: An International Journal*, 13(1): 71–87.

Pollack, O. (1950) *The Criminality of Women*. Philadelphia: University of Pennsylvania Press.

Polletta, F. (2009) 'How to tell a new story about battering', *Violence Against Women*, 15: 1490–508.

Porzecanski, A. (1973) *Uruguay's Tupamaros*. New York: Praeger.

Potter, H. (2015) *Intersectionality and Criminology: Disrupting and Revolutionising Studies of Crime*. Abingdon: Routledge.

Povey, D. (ed.) (2004) *Crime in England and Wales 2002/03: Supplementary Volume I: Homicide and Gun Crime*. London: Home Office.

Pratt, J. (2007) *Penal Populism*. London: Routledge.

Pratt, N. (2012) 'The gender logics of resistance to the "war on terror": Constructing sex-gender difference through the erasure of patriarchy in the Middle East', *Third World Quarterly*, 33: 10.

Prentice, E. (2000) 'Dark side of girl power', *The Times*, 22 November.

Prenzler, T. and Sinclair, G. (2013) 'The status of women police officers: An international review', *International Journal of Law, Crime and Justice*, 41(2): 115.

Prins, H. (2010) *Offenders, Deviants or Patients? Explorations in Clinical Criminology*. Hove: Routledge.

Prison Reform Trust (2011) *Reforming Women's Justice: Final Report of the Women's Justice Taskforce*. London: Prison Reform Trust.

Prison Reform Trust (2015) *Bromley Briefings Summer 2015*. London: Prison Reform Trust.

Putallaz, M. and Bierman, K.L. (eds) (2004) *Aggression, Anti-Social Behaviour and Violence among Girls*. New York: Guilford.

Puwar, N. (1997) 'Reflections on interviewing women MPs', *Sociological Research Online*, 29(1).

Quek, K. (2013) 'A civil rather than criminal offence? Forced marriage, harm and the politics of multiculturalism in the UK', *The British Journal of Politics and International Relations*, 15(4): 626–46.

Quinton, P. (2013) 'The formation of suspicions: Police stop and search practices in England and Wales', in L. Weber and B. Bowling (eds), *Stop and Search: Police Power in Global Context*. London: Routledge. pp. 5–16.

Rabe-Hemp, C. (2008) 'Female officers and the ethics of care: Does officer gender impact police behaviours?', *Journal of Criminal Justice*, 36: 426.

Rabe-Hemp, C. (2009) 'POLICEwomen or PoliceWOMEN? Doing gender and police work', *Feminist Criminology*, 4: 114–29.

Rackley, E. (2002) 'Representations of the (woman) judge: Hercules, the Little Mermaid and the Vain and Naked Emperor', *Legal Studies*, 22(4): 602–24.

Rackley, E. (2006) 'Difference in the House of Lords', *Social and Legal Studies*, 15(2): 163–85.

Rackley, E. (2007) 'Judicial diversity, the woman judge and fairy tale endings', *Legal Studies*, 27(1): 74–94.

Radford, J. and Stanko, E. (1996) 'Violence against women and children', in M. Hester, L. Kelly, and J. Radford (eds) *Women, Violence and Male Power*. Buckingham: Open University Press.

Radford, L. and Gill, A. (2006) 'Losing the plot? Researching community safety partnership work against domestic violence', *Howard Journal of Criminal*, 45(4): 369–87.

Radford, L. and Tsutsumi, K. (2004) 'Globalization and violence against women – inequalities in risks, responsibilities and blame in the UK and Japan', *Women's Studies International Forum*, 27: 1–12.

Rafter, N. and Gibson, M. (2004) 'Editors introduction', in C. Lombroso and G. Ferrero, *Criminal Woman, the Prostitute and the Normal Woman* (trans. Nicole Rafter and Mary Gibson). Chapel Hill, NC: Duke University Press.

Rafter, N.H. and Heidensohn, F.M. (eds) (1995) *International Feminist Perspectives in Criminology*. Buckingham: Open University Press.

Raikes, S. (2002) 'A model for community safety and community justice', *British Journal of Community*, 1(1).

Raine, J. (2002) 'Modernisation and criminal justice,' in D. Ward, J. Scott and M. Lacey (eds), *Probation: Working for Justice*. Oxford: Oxford University Press.

Ray, L. (2011) *Violence and Society*. London: Sage.

Reilly, J., Muldoon, O. and Byrne, C. (2004) 'Young men as perpetrators and victims of violence in Northern Ireland: A qualitative analysis', *Journal of Social Issues*, 60(3): 469–84.

Reiner, R. (2007) *Law and Order: An Honest Citizen's Guide to Crime and Control*. Cambridge: Cambridge University Press.

Renzetti, C. (2013) *Feminist Criminology*. London: Routledge.

Renzetti, C., Edleson, J. and Bergen, R. (eds) (2010) *Sourcebook on Violence Against Women*. Thousand Oaks, CA: Sage.

Renzetti, C., Goodstein, L. and Miller, S.L. (eds) (2006) *Rethinking Gender, Crime and Justice: Feminist Readings*. Los Angeles, CA: Roxbury.

Reskin, B.F. and Hartmann, H. (1986) *Women's Work, Men's Work: Sex Segregation on the Job*. Washington, DC: National Academy Press.

Resnick, J. and Curtis, D. (2011) *Representing Justice: Invention, Controversy, and Rights in City-states and Democratic Courtrooms*. New Haven, CT: Yale University Press.

Respect Task Force (2006) *Respect Action Plan*. London: Home Office.

Riechel, P. (2005) *Handbook of Transnational Crime and Justice*. London: Sage.

Rifkin, J. (1984) 'Mediation from a feminist perspective: Promise and problems', *Law and Inequality*, 2: 21–2.

Ringrose, J. (2006) 'A new universal mean girl: Examining the discursive construction and social regulation of a new feminine pathology', *Feminism and Psychology*, 16(4): 405–24.

Ritchie, B. (1995) *Compelled to Crime: The Gender Entrapment of Battered Black Women*. New York: Routledge.

Ritzer, G. (1993) *The McDonaldization of Society*. Thousand Oaks, CA: Pine Forge Press.

Rivera-Garza, C. (2001) 'The criminalisation of the syphilitic body: Prostitutes, health crimes and society on Mexico City, 1867–1930', in R. Salvatore, C. Aguirre and G. Joseph (eds), *Crime and Punishment in Latin America*. Durham, NC: Duke University Press.

Robertson, I.J.M. (1997) 'The role of women in social protest in the Highlands of Scotland, c. 1880–1939', *Journal of Historical Geography*, 23: 187–200.

Rock, P. (1994) 'The social organisation of British criminology', in M. Maguire, R. Morgan and R. Reiner (eds), *The Oxford Handbook of Criminology*. Oxford: Oxford University Press.

Rose, R. (2005) *Learning from Comparative Public Policy: A Practical Guide*. London: Routledge.

Roth, K. (1994) 'Domestic violence as an international human rights issue', in R. Cook (ed.), *Human Rights of Women: National and International Perspectives*. Philadelphia: Pennsylvania Press.

Roth, R. (1987) *The Democratic Dilemma: Religion, Reform and the Social Order of the Connecticut River Valley of Vermont, 1791–1850*. New York: Cambridge University Press.

Roth, R. (2009) *American Homicide*. Cambridge, MA: Belknap Press of Harvard University Press.

Roth, R. (2014) 'Gender, sex and intimate-partner violence in historical perspective', in R. Gartner and B. McCarthy (eds), *The Oxford Handbook of Gender Sex and Crime*. Oxford: Oxford University Press.

Rowe, M. (2013) *Race and Crime: A Critical Engagement*. London: Sage.

Royal Geographical Society (2013) *Consumption Controversies: Alcohol Policies in the UK*. Available at: www.rgs.org/NR/rdonlyres/88DF6837-E68B-4301-9376-B30E0FA72F21/0/RGSPolicyAlcohol5c_AWSingle.pdf (accessed 15 July 2015).

Ruff, J. (2001) *Violence in Early Modern Europe 1500–1800*. New York: Cambridge University Press.

Russell, D. (1975) *The Politics of Rape: The Victim's Perspective*. Lincoln, NE: Stein and Day Publishers.

Ryan, M. (1981) *Cradle of the Middle-Class*. New York: Cambridge University Press.

Sanders, T. (2004) 'The risks of street prostitution: Punters, police and protesters', *Urban Studies*, 41: 1703–17.

Sanders, T. (2005) *Sex Work: A Risky Business*. Portland, OR: Willan.

Sanders, T. and Hardy, K. (2015) 'The political economy of "lap dancing": Contested careers and women's work in the stripping industry', *Work, Employment and Society*, 29(1): 119–36.

Sanders, T., O'Neill, M. and Pitcher, J. (2009) *Prostitution: Sex Work, Policy and Practice*. London: Sage.

Sandler, M. and Coles, D. (2008) *Dying on the Inside: Examining Women's Deaths in Prisons*. London: INQUEST.

Scarry, E. (1985) *The Body in Pain: The Making and Unmaking of the World*. New York: Oxford University Press.

Schrecker, T. and Bambra, C. (2015) *How Politics Makes Us Sick: Neoliberal Epidemics*. Basingstoke: Palgrave.

Schuck, A.M. and Rabe-Hemp, C. (2005) 'Women police: The use of force by and against female officers', *Women and Criminal Justice*, 14(4): 91.

Schuller, R.A. and Stewart, A. (2000) 'Police responses to sexual assault complaints: The role of perpetrator/complainant intoxication', *Law and Human Behavior*, 24: 535–51.

Schulz, D. (1995) *From Social Worker to Crime Fighter: Women in United States Municipal Policing*. Westport, CT: Praeger.

Scott, D.G. (2013) 'The politics of prisoner legal rights', *Howard Journal of Criminal Justice*, 53(3): 233–50.

Scott, K. (2014) 'Violence against children in families', in R. Gartner and B. McCarthy (eds), *The Oxford Handbook of Gender Sex and Crime*. Oxford: Oxford University Press.

Scraton, P. (2002) 'Defining "power" and challenging "knowledge": Critical analysis as resistance in the UK', in K. Carrington and R. Hogg (eds), *Critical Criminology: Issues, Debates, Challenges*. Cullompton, Devon: Willan.

Scraton, P. and McCulloch, J. (2006) 'Deaths in custody and detention', *Social Justice*, 33(4): 1–14.

Scraton, P. and Moore, L. (2004) *The Hurt Inside: The Imprisonment of Women and Girls in Northern Ireland*. Belfast: Northern Ireland Human Rights Commission.

Segal, J. (2000) 'Representative decision making on the federal bench', *Political Research Quarterly*, 53(1): 137–50.

Segrave, K. (1995) *Policewomen: A History*. Jefferson, NC: McFarland.

Segrave, M.T., Pickering, S.J. and Milivojevic, S. (2009) *Sex Trafficking: International Context and Response*. Cullompton, Devon: Willan.

Senior, P. (2002) *Regional Resettlement Framework: Consultative Document for GOYH*, July. SHU Press.

Senior, P. (2005) 'Are you thinking what I am thinking?', *British Journal of Community Justice*, 3(3): 1–3.

Senior, P., Crowther-Dowey, C. and Long, M. (2007) *Understanding Modernisation in Criminal Justice*. Milton Keynes: Open University Press.

Serious Fraud Office (2015) *Serious Fraud Office: Annual Report and Accounts 2014–15*, HC 38. London: SFO.

Shackle, S. (2011) 'Britain attempts to weaken European domestic violence deal', *New Statesman*, 8 March. Available at: www.newstatesman.com/blogs/the-staggers/2011/03/human-rights-women-violence (accessed 26 October 2015).

Sharpe, C. (2009), 'The trouble with girls today: Professional perspectives on young women's offending', *Youth Justice*, 9(3): 254–69.

Sharpe, G. (2011) *Offending Girls: Young Women and Youth Justice*. Abingdon: Routledge.

Sharpe, G. (2015) 'Re-imagining justice for girls: A new agenda for research', *Youth Justice: An International Journal*.

Sharpe, G. and Gelsthorpe, L. (2009) 'Engendering the agenda: Girls, young women and youth justice', *Youth Justice*, 9(3): 195–208.

Sharpe, J. (1999) *Crime in Early Modern England 1550–1750*. London: Longman.

Shaw, M. and Hannah-Moffat, K. (eds) (2000) *An Ideal Prison? Critical Essays on Women's Imprisonment in Canada*. Halifax: Fernwood Publishing.

Shearing, C. and Stenning, P. (1981) 'Modern private security: Its growth and implications', *Crime and Justice*, 3: 193–245.

Sheehan, R., McIver, G. and Trotter, C. (eds) (2011) *Working with Women Offenders in the Community*. Cullompton: Willan.

Shelley, L. (2010) *Human Trafficking: A Global Perspective*. Cambridge: Cambridge University Press.

Shen, J., Chanda, A., D'Netto, B. and Monga, M. (2009) 'Managing diversity through human resource management: An international perspective and conceptual framework', *The International Journal of Human Resource Management*, 20(2): 235–51.

Shoemaker, R. (2001) 'Male honour and the decline of violence in eighteenth-century London', *Social History*, 26: 190–208.

Shore, H. (1994) 'The trouble with boys: Gender and the "invention" of the juvenile offender in early nineteenth-century Britain', in M. Arnot and C. Usborne (eds), *Gender and Crime in Modern Europe*. London: UCL Press. pp. 75–92.

Silvestri, M. (2003) *Women in Charge: Policing, Gender and Leadership*. Cullompton, Devon: Willan.

Silvestri, M. (2006) 'Doing time: Becoming a police leader', *International Journal of Police Science and Management*, 8(4): 266–81.

Silvestri, M. (2007) 'Doing police leadership: Enter the new smart macho', *Policing & Society*, 17(1): 38–58.

Silvestri, M. (2015) 'Gender diversity: A hop, skip and a jump forwards and back', *Policing: A Journal of Policy & Practice* (Special Issue on Police Diversity), 9(1): 56–64.

Silvestri, M. (forthcoming) *Gender and Policing: Narratives of Crisis, Change and Continuity Policing Civil Societies in Times of Economic Constraints*. Bramshill, UK: CEPOL.

Silvestri, M. and Paul, C. (2015) 'Women in police leadership', in J. Fleming (ed.), *Police Leadership: Rising to the Top*. Oxford: Oxford University Press.

Silvestri, M., Tong, S. and Brown, J. (2013) 'Gender and police leadership: Time for a paradigm shift', *International Journal of Police Science and Management*, 15(1): 61–73.

Sim, J. (1990) *Medical Power in Prisons: The Prison Medical Service in England 1774–1989*. Milton Keynes: Open University Press.

Simpson, A. (1988) 'Dandelions on the field of honour: Duelling, the middle classes, and the law in nineteenth century England', *Criminal Justice History*, 9: 99–155.

Simpson, S. and Gibbs, C. (2006) 'Making sense of intersections', in K. Heimer and C. Kruttschnitt (eds), *Gender and Crime: Patterns in Victimization and Offending*. New York: New York UniversityPress.

Sjoberg, L. and Gentry, C.E. (eds) (2011) *Women, Gender and Terrorism*. Athens, GA: University of Georgia Press.

Smart, C. (1977) *Women, Crime and Criminology*. London: Routledge and Kegan Paul.

Smart, C. (1989) *Feminism and the Power of the Law*. London: Routledge.

Smith, G. (2002) 'Reasonable suspicion: Time for a re-evaluation', *International Journal of the Sociology of Law*, 30: 1–16.

Smith, G. (2014) 'Long-term trends in female and male involvement in crime', in R. Gartner and B. McCarthy (eds), *The Oxford Handbook of Gender Sex and Crime*. Oxford: Oxford University Press.

Smith, R. (2007) *Youth Justice: Ideas, Policy and Practice* (2nd edn). Cullompton: Willan.

Snider, L. (2003) 'Constituting the punishable woman: Atavistic man incarcerates postmodern woman', *British Journal of Criminology*, 43(2): 354–78.

Social Exclusion Unit (2002) *Reducing Re-offending by Ex-Prisoners*. London: Cabinet Office.

Songer, D. and Crews-Meyer, K. (2000) 'Does gender matter: Decision making in State Supreme Courts', *Social Science Quarterly*, 81(3): 750–62.

South, N. (1998) 'Late-modern criminology: "Late" as in "dead" or "modern" as in "new"?', in D. Owen (ed.), *After Sociology*. London: Sage.

Spalek, B. (2006) *Crime Victims: Theory, Policy and Practice*. Basingstoke: Palgrave.

Spencer, H. and Broad, R. (2012) 'The "groundhog day" of the human trafficking for sexual exploitation debate: New directions in criminological understanding', *British Journal of Criminology*, 18: 268–81.

Spierenburg, P. (1998) *Men and Violence: Gender, Honour, and Rituals in Modern Europe and America*. Columbus: Ohio State University Press.

Squires, P. (2009) '"You Lookin at Me?": Discourses of respect, disrespect, identity and violence', in A. Millie (ed.), *Securing Respect: Behavioural Expectations and Anti-Social Behaviour in the UK*. Bristol: Policy Express. pp. 239–266.

Squires, P. and Stephen, D. (2005) *Rougher Justice: Anti-Social Behaviour and Young People*. Cullompton: Willan.

Stanislawski, H.B. (2004) 'Transnational "bads" in the globalized world: The case of transnational organized crime', *Public Integrity*, 6(2): 155–70.

Stanko, B. (2002) *Taking Stock: What Do We Know About Interpersonal Violence* (ESRC Violence Research Programme). London: Royal Holloway University of London.

Stanko, E. (1985) *Intimate Intrusions: Women's Experiences of Male Violence*. London: Routledge.

Stanko, E. (1989) 'Missing the mark: Policing battering', in J. Hanmer, J. Radford and E. Stanko (eds), *Women, Policing and Male Violence*. London: Routledge.

Stanko, E. (1990) *Everyday Violence*. London: Virago.

Stanko, E. (1995) 'Women, crime and fear', *Annals of the American Academy of Political and Social Science* (special edition edited by W. Skogan, 539: 46–58.

Stanley, J. (ed.) (1995) *Bold in Her Breeches: Women Pirates across the Ages*. San Francisco, CA: Pandora.

Stark, E. (2007) *Coercive Control: How Men Entrap Women in Personal Life*. New York: Oxford University Press.

Stark, E. (2009) 'Rethinking coercive control violence against women', *Violence Against Women*, 15(12): 1509–25.

Steffensmeier, D. and Herbert, C. (1999) 'Women and men policymakers: Does the judge's gender affect the sentencing of criminal defendants', *Social Forces*, 77: 1163.

Steffensmeier, D.J., Schwartz, J., Zhong, H. and Ackerman, J. (2005) 'An assessment of recent trends in girls' violence using diverse longitudinal sources: Is the gender gap closing?', *Criminology*, 43(2): 355–405.

Steffensmeier, D.J., Schwartz, J. and Rochea, M. (2013) 'Gender and twenty-first-century corporate crime: Female involvement and the gender gap in Enron-era corporate frauds', *American Sociological Review*, 78(3): 448–76.

Stenson, K. (2005) 'Sovereignty, biopolitics the local government of crime in Britain', *Theoretical Criminology*, 9(3): 265–87.

Stern Review (2010) *An Independent Review into How Rape Complaints are Handled by Public Authorities in England and Wales*, a report by Baroness Vivien Stern. London: Home Office.

Stevens, M. (2012) 'London women, the courts and the golden age: A quantitative analysis of female litigants in the fourteenth and fifteenth centuries', *The London Journal*, 37: 67–88.

Stewart, A. and Madden, K. (1997) 'Police officers' judgements of blame in ... the impact of legal and extralegal factors', *Law and Human Behaviour*, 4: 81–99.

Stone, R. (2014) *Civil Liberties and Human Rights* (10th edn). Oxford: Oxford University Press.

Stone, R., Kemp, T. and Weldon, G. (1994) *Part-time Working and Job Sharing in the Police Service*, Police Research Series Paper 7. London: Home Office.

Storrs, E. (2004) 'Our scapegoat: An exploration of media representations of Myra Hindley and Rosemary West', *Theology and Sexuality*, 11(1): 9–28.

Straw, J. and Boateng, P. (1996) *Bringing Rights Home: Labour's Plan to Incorporate the European Convention on Human Rights into UK Law*. London: The Labour Party.

Stretton, T. (1998) *Women Waging Law in Elizabethan England*. Cambridge: Cambridge University Press.

Sudbury, J. (2004) *Global Lockdown: Race, Gender and the Prison–Industrial Complex*. London: Routledge.

Sun, I.Y. (2007) 'Policing domestic violence: Does officer gender matter?', *Journal of Criminal Justice*, 35: 581–95.

Sutton, R. and Farrall, S. (2004) 'Gender, socially desirable responding and the fear of crime', *British Journal of Criminology*, 45: 212–24.

Swann, W.B. Jr., Polzer, J.T., Seyle, C. and Ko, S. (2004) 'Finding value in diversity: Verification of personal and social self-views in diverse groups', *Academy of Management Review*, 29: 9–27.

Taft, J. (2004) 'Girl power politics: Pop-culture barriers and organizational resistance', in A. Harris (ed.), *All About the Girl: Culture, Power and Identity*. New York: Routledge. pp. 69–78.

Themudo, N.S. (2009) 'Gender and the Nonprofit Sector', *Nonprofit and Voluntary Sector Quarterly*, 38(4): 663–83.

Thiara, R.K. and Gill, A.K. (eds) (2010) *Violence against Women in South Asian Communities: Issues for Policy and Practice*. London: Jessica Kingsley Publishers.

Thomas, T. (2005) *Sex Crime: Sex Offending and Society*. Cullompton: Willan.

Thornton, M. (1996) *Dissonance and Distrust: Women in the Legal Profession*. Melbourne: Oxford University Press.

Tierney, J. (1996) *Criminology Theory and Context*. London: Harvester Wheatsheaf.

Tilley, N. (ed.) (2005) *Handbook of Crime Prevention and Community Safety*. Cullompton: Willan.

Tipping, S., Chanfreau, J., Perry, J. and Tait, C. (2012) *Employment Relations Research Series 122*. London: Department for Business, Innovation and Skills.

Todd, J. and Spearing, E. (1993) *Counterfeit Ladies: The Life and Death of Moll Cutpurse and the Case of Mary Carleton*. London: Pickering and Chatto.

Townsend, M. and Syal, R. (2009) *Up to 64,000 Women in the UK are Child Sex Offenders*. Available at: www.guardian.co.uk/society/2009/oct/04/uk-female-child-sexoffenders.

Travers, M. (2007) *The New Bureaucracy: Quality Assurance and its Critics*. Bristol: Policy Press.

Travis, A. (2014) 'Police telling victims to solve crime by themselves', *The Guardian*, 4 September. Available at: www.theguardian.com/uk-news/2014/sep/04/police-telling-victims-solve-crimes-themselves (accessed 15 January 2015).

Travis, A. (2015) 'Knife crime up in England and Wales for first time in four years', *The Guardian*, 16 July. Available at: www.theguardian.com/uk-news/2015/jul/16/knife-in-england-and-wales-up-for-first-time-in-four-years (accessed 16 July 2015).

Treadwell, J. and Garland, J. (2011) 'Masculinity, marginality and violence: A case study of the English Defence League', *British Journal of Criminology*, 51(4): 621–34.

True, J. (2012) *The Political Economy of Violence against Women*. Oxford: Oxford University Press.

Tuffin, R. and Baladi, Y. (2001) *Flexible Working Practices in the Police Service*, Home Office Police Research Paper No. 147. London: Home Office.

Turchik, J.A. and Edwards, K.M. (2012) 'Myths about male rape: A literature review', *Psychology of Men and Masculinity*, 13(2): 211–26.

UN Women (2014) *A Gender Perspective on the Impact of Drug Use, the Drug Trade and Drug Control Regimes*, UN Task Force on Transnational Organized Crime and Drug Trafficking as Threats to Security and Stability – Policy Brief on Gender and Drugs. New York: United Nations.

UNICEF (2014) *AS Statistical Snapshot of Violence against Adolescent Girls*. Available at: www.unicef.org/publications/files/A_Statistical_Snapshot_of_Violence_Against_Adolescent_Girls.pdf (accessed 26 October 2015).

UNICEF (2015) *Ending Violence against Women*. Available at: www.unwomen.org/en/what-we-do/ending-violence-against-women/facts-and-figures.

United Nations (1955) *Standard Minimum Rules for the Treatment of Prisoners*, Office of the High Commissioner for Human Rights. New York: United Nations.

United Nations (1977) *Standard Minimum Rules for the Treatment of Prisoners*, Office of the High Commissioner for Human Rights. New York: United Nations.

United Nations (1995) *Platform for Action*, report of the Fourth World Conference on Women, Beijing, September (UN Publication, E96.IV.13). New York: United Nations.

United Nations (2002) *Optional Protocol to the Convention against Torture and Other Cruel, Inhuman or Degrading Treatment or Punishment*, Office of the United Nations High Commissioner for Human Rights. New York: United Nations.

United Nations (2008) *Convention on the Rights of the Child*. Available at: http://www2.ohchr.org/english/bodies/crc/docs/AdvanceVersions/CRC.C.GBR.CO.4.pdf.

University of Leicester (2014) *The Leicester Hate Crime Project: Gendered Hostility*, Briefing Paper 2. Leicester: University of Leicester.

UNODC (2012) *Global Report on Trafficking in Persons*. Vienna/New York: United Nations.

UNODC (2013a) *Drug Trafficking*. Available at: www.unodc.org/unodc/en/drug-trafficking/index.html (accessed 12 May 2015).

UNODC (2013b) *Gender Mainstreaming in the Work of UNODC: Guidance Note for UNODC Staff*, United Nations Office on Drugs and Crime. Vienna/New York: UNODC.

Urwin, P., Karuk, V., David, A., Dodds, I. and Moss, G. (2011) *The Strategic Economic Impact of Diversity on Business Performance*. Diversity Works for London.

Van Dijk, J., Tseloni, A. and Farrell, G. (eds) (2012) *The International Crime Drop: New Directions in Research*. New York: Palgrave Macmillan.

Van Kesteren, J., van Dijk, J. and Mayhew, P. (2014) 'The international crime surveys: A retrospective', *International Review of Victimology*, 20(1): 49–69.

Vandiver, D.M. and Walker, J.T. (2002) 'Female sex offenders: An overview and analysis of 40 cases', *Criminal Justice Review*, 27: 284–300.

Vigarello, G. (1998) *A History of Rape: Sexual Violence in France from the 16th to the 20th Century*. Cambridge: Polity Press.

Villiers, P. (2003) 'Philosophy, doctrine and leadership: Some core beliefs', in R. Adlam and P. Villiers (eds), *Police Leadership in the Twenty-first Century: Philosophy, Doctrine and Developments*. Winchester: Waterside Press.

Von Hentig, H. (1948) *The Criminal and His Victim*. New Haven, CT: Yale University Press.

Von Hoffer, H. (2011) 'Punishment and crime in Scandinavia, 1750–2008', in M. Tonry and T. Seppala (eds), *Crime and Justice: A Review of Research*. Chicago: University of Chicago.

Von Knop, K. (2007) 'Female Jihad: Al Qaeda's women', *Studies in Conflict Terrorism*, 30(5): 397–414.

Waaland, P. and Keeley, S. (1985) 'Police decision making in wife abuse: The impact of legal and extralegal factors', *Law and Human Behavior*, 9: 355–66.

Wacquant, L. (2009) *Punishing the Poor*. Durham, NC: Duke University Press.

Waddington, P.A.J. (1999) *Policing Citizens*. London: UCL Press.

Wadham, J. and Modi, K. (2004) 'Policing and the Human Rights Act', in R. Hopkins Burke (ed.), *Hard Cop, Soft Cop: Dilemmas and Debates in Contemporary Policing*. Cullompton: Willan.

Wahidin, A. (2016) *Ex Combatants, Gender and Peace in Northern Ireland: Women, Political Protest and the Prison Experience*. Basingstoke: Palgrave.

Waiton, S. (2001) *Scared of the Kids?: Curfews, Crime and the Regulation of Young People*. Sheffield: Sheffield Hallam University.

Walby, S. (2011) *The Future of Feminism*. Cambridge: Polity Press.

Walby, S. and Allen, J. (2004) *Domestic Violence, Sexual Assault and Stalking: Findings from the British Crime Survey*, Home Office Research Study 276. London: Home Office.

Walby, S., Towers, J. and Francis, B. (2014) 'Mainstreaming domestic and gender-based violence into sociology and the criminology of violence', *Sociological Review*, 62(S2): 187–214.

Walker, C. (2003) *Crime, Gender and Social Order in Early Modern England*. Cambridge: Cambridge University Press.

Walker, P. (1997) 'Wife beating, boxing, and broken noses: Skeletal evidence for the cultural patterning of interpersonal violence', in D. Martin and D. Frayer (eds), *Troubled Times: Violence and Warfare in the Past*. Amsterdam: Gordon and Breach.

Walklate, S. (1989) *Victimology: The Victim and the Criminal Justice Process*. London: Unwin Hyman.

Walklate, S. (2004) *Gender, Crime and Criminal Justice* (2nd edn). Cullompton: Willan.

Walklate, S. (2012) 'Response 2: Can the Big Society listen to gendered voices', *Criminology and Criminal Justice*, 12(5): 495–9.

Walkowitz, J.R. (1980) *Prostitution and Victorian Society: Women, Class and the State*. Cambridge: Cambridge University Press.

Wallace, H. (1998) *Victimology: Legal, Social and Psychological Perspectives*. Boston, MA: Allyn and Bacon.

Walters, R. (2003) 'New modes of governance and the commodification of criminological knowledge', *Social and Legal Studies - An International Journal*, 12(1): 5–26.

Watson, J. (2007) *Where are All the Women?* London: Equal Opportunities Commission.

Weber, L. and Pickering, S. (2011) *Globalization and Borders: Death at the Global Frontier*. Basingstoke: Palgrave Macmillan.

Weber, L., Fishwick. E. and Marmo, M. (eds) (2014) *Crime, Justice and Human Rights*. Basingstoke: Palgrave Macmillan.

Weber, M. (1946) 'Bureaucracy', in H. Gerth and C. Wright Mills (eds), *From Max Weber: Essays in Sociology*. New York: Oxford University Press. pp. 196–244.

Webster, C. (2007) *Understanding Race and Crime*. Milton Keynes: Open University Press.

Webster, C. (2014) 'Negotiating identities: Ethnicity, religion and social cohesion in London and Bradford', in C. Phillips and C. Webster (eds), *New Directions in Race, Ethnicity and Crime*. London: Routledge.

Weinburg, L. and Eubank, W. (1987) 'Italian women terrorists', *Terrorism*, 993: 241–61.

Weinburg, L. and Eubank, W. (2011) 'Women's involvement in terrorism', *Gender Issues*, 28: 22–49.

Weitzer, R. (2007) 'The social construction of sex trafficking: Ideology and the institutionalisation of a moral crusade', *Politics and Society*, 35: 447–75.

Weitzer, R. (ed.) (2010) *Sex for Sale: Prostitution, Pornography and the Sex Industry*. London: Routledge.